PROSE POEMS OF THE FRENCH ENLIGHTENMENT

To George

Prose Poems of the French Enlightenment

Delimiting Genre

FABIENNE MOORE
University of Oregon, USA

ASHGATE

Published by
Ashgate Publishing Limited
Wey Court East
Union Road
Farnham
Surrey, GU9 7PT
England

Ashgate Publishing Company
Suite 420
101 Cherry Street
Burlington
VT 05401-4405
USA

www.ashgate.com

British Library Cataloguing in Publication Data
Moore, Fabienne
Prose poems of the French Enlightenment: delimiting genre
  1. Prose poems, French – History and criticism 2. French poetry – 18th century – History and criticism 3. Enlightenment – France
  I. Title
  841.5'09

Library of Congress Cataloging-in-Publication Data
Moore, Fabienne.
  Prose poems of the French Enlightenment: delimiting genre / by Fabienne Moore.
    p. cm.
  Includes bibliographical references and index.
  ISBN 978-0-7546-6318-8 (alk. paper)
    1. Prose poems, French—History and criticism. 2. French poetry—18th century—History and criticism. I. Title.

PQ491.M68 2009
841'.509—dc22

2008042584

ISBN: 978-0-7546-6318-8

Contents

List of Illustrations   *vii*
Acknowledgements   *ix*

Introduction   Off Limits: Prose Poems of the French Enlightenment   1
    Genealogies of the Prose Poem   4
    De-limiting Genre   9
    Genre Trouble   13
    Prose Poems of the French Enlightenment   25

1 Telemacomania   29
    A "*Je-Ne-Sais-Quoi*:" Hybridity   34
    Télémaque, Source of Inspiration for Aragon   37
    "Le délire véhément des lyres"   39
    "Je ne sais où je suis"   42
    Sexual and Baroque Undertow   44
    Minerva as Mentor   48
    Takes from Marivaux and Rousseau   51
    Nostalgia for the Epic   55

2 Prose vs. Poetry   63
    A Provocateur: Houdar de La Motte (1672–1731)   70
    A Bastard Style: The Prose Poem's Impossible Affiliation   76
    The Myth of the French Language: Rivarol's Triumph of Prose 95

3 Birth of the Poem in Prose   101
    A Sentimental Journey: Montesquieu's *Temple de Gnide*   103
    In Praise of Republican Virtues   112
    Pastoral Melancholy   120

4 Translation to the Rescue   125
    Pseudo-Translations   125
    The "Querelle d'Homère"   134
    Gessner and Ossian   137

5 Back to the Bible   145
    Robert Lowth on Ancient Hebrew Poetry   148
    Rousseau's *Le Lévite d'Ephraïm*: "Une manière de petit
      poëme en prose"   157
    Biblical Epics in Prose   169

6 The Reformation   179
    Quietism   180
    Illuminism   186
    Eschatology   206

7   New Rhythms   211
         Évariste Parny: Orality   213
         Chateaubriand's *Atala*   223
         Sébastien Mercier: Visions   237

Conclusion   The Farewell of Telemachus and Eucharis   245

Appendix 1   Abbé Fraguier, *"A Discourse to shew that there can*
                   be no Poems in Prose" (1719)   *249*
Appendix 2   *Bitaubé,* Guillaume de Nassau, or The Foundation of
                   the United Provinces (1775)   *259*
Appendix 3   Collin d'Harleville, *"Dialogue between Prose and*
                   Poetry" (1802)   *267*
Appendix 4   *"Dialogue entre la Prose et la Poésie" (1809)*   *273*
Bibliography   *277*
Index   *295*

List of Illustrations

1 Frontispiece. Le Cousin Jacques, *Marlborough, Poëme comique en prose rimée*. Londres, 1783. Reproduced with permission of the Bibliothèque Nationale de France, Paris.   14

2 Frontispiece. Charles-Georges Coqueley de Chaussepierre, *Le Roué Vertueux. Poëme en prose en quatre chants.·* Lausanne, 1770. Reproduced with permission of the Bibliothèque Nationale de France, Paris.   18

3 "Chant quatre." Charles-Georges Coqueley de Chaussepierre, *Le Roué Vertueux. Poëme en prose en quatre chants.* Lausanne, 1770, 20. Reproduced with permission of the Bibliothèque Nationale de France, Paris.   19

4 "Chant quatre." Charles-Georges Coqueley de Chaussepierre, *Le Roué Vertueux. Poëme en prose en quatre chants.* Lausanne, 1770, 21. Reproduced with permission of the Bibliothèque Nationale de France, Paris.   20

5 "Chant quatre." Charles-Georges Coqueley de Chaussepierre, *Le Roué Vertueux. Poëme en prose en quatre chants.* Lausanne, 1770, 22. Reproduced with permission of the Bibliothèque Nationale de France, Paris.   21

6 "Chant quatre." Charles-Georges Coqueley de Chaussepierre, *Le Roué Vertueux. Poëme en prose en quatre chants.* Lausanne, 1770, 23. Reproduced with permission of the Bibliothèque Nationale de France, Paris.   22

7 "Chant quatre." Charles-Georges Coqueley de Chaussepierre, *Le Roué Vertueux. Poëme en prose en quatre chants.* Lausanne, 1770, 24. Reproduced with permission of the Bibliothèque Nationale de France, Paris.   23

8 "Chant quatre." Charles-Georges Coqueley de Chaussepierre, *Le Roué Vertueux. Poëme en prose en quatre chants.* Lausanne, 1770, 25. Reproduced with permission of the Bibliothèque Nationale de France, Paris.   24

9   Title-page. Louis-Claude de Saint-Martin, *Le Crocodile, ou la guerre du bien et du mal, arrivée sous le règne de Louis XV; Poème épico-magique en 102 chants*. 1799. Reproduced with permission of the Bibliothèque Nationale de France, Paris.   193

10   First page. Louis-Claude de Saint-Martin, *Le Crocodile, ou la guerre du bien et du mal, arrivée sous le règne de Louis XV; Poème épico-magique en 102 chants*. 1799. Reproduced with permission of the Bibliothèque Nationale de France, Paris.   194

11   Jacques-Louis David, *Adieux de Télémaque et d'Eucharis*. 1818. Oil on canvas, 34 $^3/_8$ x 40 $^1/_2$ in. Los Angeles, The J. Paul Getty Museum. Used with permission of the J. Paul Getty Museum, Los Angeles.   246

Acknowledgements

A project of many years, this book is a history of ideas discovered and explored with colleagues and friends in the United States and France. Philippe Roger's unwavering support helped me navigate these two worlds while his own critical forays continue to inspire me. I am grateful to Richard Sieburth for spurring my interest in prose poetry and for his stimulating intellectual direction along the way. Julie Candler Hayes's thoughtful suggestions helped me improve the book and her intellectual support proved essential. I have traveled the road of writing and revising with fellow *dix-huitièmiste* Joanna Stalnaker, whom I thank for her attentiveness and advice. My gratitude goes to my editor, Ann Donahue, for her commitment and patience.

I owe beautiful moments of peace and inspiration to several stays at the Maison de Chateaubriand in the Vallée aux Loups, thanks to its director Bernard Degout. I put finishing touches on the book under the auspices of the Centre d'Étude de la Langue et de la Littérature Françaises des XVIIᵉ et XVIIIᵉ siècles at the Sorbonne headed by Sylvain Menant, whose own work on eighteenth-century French poetry showed me the way to impeccable scholarship.

In the department of Romance Languages at the University of Oregon, I had the good fortune of finding encouraging colleagues who created an environment conducive to being a scholar and a teacher. I am deeply indebted to the members of the Early Modern Group for their close readings of early drafts. I am pleased to acknowledge here the finesse and insights of Nathalie Hester and Leah Middlebrook whose meticulous critique matched their enthusiasm for this topic.

I want to thank deeply Marie-Claire and Eric Segonds for their generous hospitality throughout the years: their kindness and open hearts made my research in Paris the most rewarding experience.

À George, un merci tout simple mais le plus grand de tous.

Introduction
Off Limits:
Prose Poems of the French Enlightenment

In the *Encyclopédie, ou Dictionnaire raisonné des sciences, des arts et des métiers,* the Chevalier de Jaucourt defines "poëme en prose":

> POEME EN PROSE, (*Belles-Lettres*) genre d'ouvrage où l'on retrouve la fiction & le style de la poésie, & qui par-là sont de vrais *poëmes*, à la mesure & à la rime près; c'est une invention fort heureuse. Nous avons obligation à la poésie en prose de quelques ouvrages remplis d'avantures vraisemblables, & merveilleuses à la fois, comme de préceptes sages & praticables en même tems, qui n'auroient peut-être jamais vû le jour, s'il eût fallu que les auteurs eussent assujetti leur génie à la rime & à la mesure. L'estimable auteur de Télémaque ne nous auroit jamais donné cet ouvrage enchanteur, s'il avoit dû l'écrire en vers; il est de beaux *poëmes* sans vers, comme de beaux tableaux sans le plus riche coloris. (*D.J*) [1]

> [PROSE POEM, (*Belles Lettres*): A genre of work wherein one finds the fiction and style of poetry, by which they are true *poems*, except for rhyme and measure. It is a felicitous invention. We owe to poetry in prose works filled with adventures both credible and marvelous as well as precepts both wise and feasible, which might have never seen light if their authors had to subject their genius to rhyme and measure. The esteemed author of Telemachus would have never given us this enchanting work if he had to write it in verse. There are beautiful *poems* without verse, just as we have beautiful paintings without the richest colors.]

This book takes as its point of departure Jaucourt's 1765 definition of prose poetry in lieu of modern ones to historicize our notions of eighteenth-century poetry, and draw the field of eighteenth-century studies into the wider conversation that seeks, through historicizing, to counter the "lock" maintained by Romanticism on our view of what poetry is and means. A significant aim of *Prose Poems of the French Enlightenment: Delimiting Genre* is to return us to an understanding of the nature and the stakes of the "poëme en prose," as they were perceived in the eighteenth century. As a result, this study questions two a-prioris: that prose poems were the creation of nineteenth-century Romanticism, and that Romanticism liberated poetic expression when it favored lyric poetry, whether in verse or prose. This legacy so closely shapes France's literary landscape that the Romantics have long become poetry's undisputed "liberators." I propose a less narrow and predictable interpretation, namely that it is the direct confrontation with the question of poetry's

---

[1]   *Encyclopédie, ou Dictionnaire raisonné des sciences, des arts et des métiers* (Stuttgart, 1967), vol. 12, 836–7. Unless otherwise indicated all translations are my own. I did not modernize the spelling of the sources consulted.

essence that enabled the prose writers' emancipation. As Jaucourt's definition reminds us, the essence of poetry was long believed to reside in noble diction (verse) and elevated fiction. But the classics had left open a second path to define poetry besides the criteria of "nombre" (poetic rhythm), namely inspiration, the poet as "vate" and not just technician.[2] Steve Monte argues that "it is possible to think of the prose poem as emerging in response to a gradual change in aesthetics. Instead of the literary-historical terms 'Romanticism' and 'classicism,' it is perhaps better to speak of an emphasis of affect over form. When the essence of poetry is no longer believed to reside in its external features but rather in the intensity of the response it elicits in the reader, the possibility exists for something like the prose poem."[3] I discuss throughout the book how this possibility rose with the dawn of the Enlightenment only to encounter strong opposition. Although prominent at the time, French eighteenth-century "poëmes en prose" have been neglected as too indeterminate or minor to be relevant. Monte's reminder of the history of the term offers a useful clarification:

> For its eighteenth-century opponents, "poème en prose" was at best a bad figure of speech; for those who supported the idea of poetry in prose, the term was literal and signified removing merely one of the generic features of epic, the necessity of writing in verse. Though united in cause, the proponents of the *poème en prose* were of two very different camps. On the one hand there were those who, like the philosophes, argued for prose in the name of truth; on the other, there were those who saw the issue as primarily one of taste. ... Those who argued in the name of taste influenced profoundly the eighteenth and early-nineteenth-century *poème en prose*. Though their own poems strike the modern reader as almost parodies of poems with their apostrophe-filled and grandiose rhetoric, their general legacy is an aesthetic of unmediated expression.[4]

In addition to our shift in taste, a further obstacle impedes an accurate appreciation of eighteenth-century prose poems and puts them off limits: they do not fit into constructed categories about the Enlightenment, which literary history has magnified as the triumphal age of prose, equally thriving within its traditional, non-fictional domain and its newly conquered territories (drama and fiction). In focusing on prose poems, I wish to challenge the separation of prose from poetry in Enlightenment literary production. I also wish to encourage studies of the European Enlightenment that consider the experimental currents questioning the dominance of novelistic prose to write fiction.

Prose poems are one of the least known "inventions" of the French Enlightenment, to borrow Jaucourt's phrase. Charles Baudelaire is often credited with mastering this new genre when he sought to translate his "spleen" toward

---

[2]   On the debate about the nature of poetry and verse, see Timothy Steele, *Missing Measures. Modern Poetry and the Revolt against Meter* (Fayetteville and London, 1990), chap. 2–3, 69–170.

[3]   Steve Monte, *Invisible Fences: Prose Poetry as a Genre in French and American Literature* (Lincoln, 2000), 16–17.

[4]   Ibid., 17.

nineteenth-century Paris into "petits poèmes en prose." I would like to argue that the "spleen" of some eighteenth-century writers toward the Enlightenment actually prompted this new means of expression. The melancholy rising from modernity is tied to the rise of prose poems as a hybrid and unstable genre. The shock of modernity always brings the anxiety of loss: this study records how disenchanted authors turned toward the past to retrieve sources such as Homer, the epic, the pastoral, the Bible, Ossian, and the primitive, favoring nature and music to construct alternatives to the world of reason. These took the shape of prose poems: Fénelon dreamt of benevolent leadership in *Les Aventures de Télémaque*; Montesquieu painted nymphs and shepherds in love in *Le Temple de Gnide*; Rousseau tried to reconcile the rights of individuals and community in *Le Lévite d'Ephraïm*; Chateaubriand imagined a mythopoetic American wilderness in *Atala*, to name the four most influential authors.

"Comment être poète en prose?" [How to be a poet in prose?], Rousseau wondered.[5] Was Jean-Jacques revolting against meter when he asked this question? There was neither a revolt nor a revolution to dismantle verse; on the contrary, it remained the pinnacle of the Republic of letters throughout the century. By focusing too exclusively on Enlightenment novels, we lost sight of the poetry that occupied the center of literary production and criticism. I suggest a new approach: when we return poetry to historical preeminence, experiments to reform poetry become central to understanding how authors dealt with their readers' taste for more prose, with critics' rules favoring verse, and with the aspiration to advance the status of poet in a modern, increasingly prosaic world. Could authors write prose that would attain the dignity of poetry; in other words, could they give readers the pleasure of "difficulty conquered" that verse offered? Fénelon, Montesquieu, Rousseau, Marmontel, Mercier, and Chateaubriand either did not think it possible or did not have the heart to change prosody to suit their critical worldview. By contrast, they saw a great opportunity to pry open the poetic domain via prose, a prose in which drama and the novel were successfully invested. To do so, they would bring the qualities of verse poetry as well as music into prose fiction: prose would seek diction, images and rhythms on the model of poetry to make prose more like poetry. Enter prose poems—crucial manifestations of the positioning of prose authors as modern poets in their own right.

Taking stock of the crisis of verse poetry and the rise of prose—each fostered by modernity—authors have experimented with conjoining the poetic and prosaic, from the Enlightenment to Baudelaire, all the way to modernists like Mallarmé, Max Jacob, André Breton, and John Ashbery. But the inaugural resistance occurred in the specific context of a European eighteenth century in the throes of momentous scientific, philosophical, and socio-economic changes. The thematic and formal traits of the Enlightenment's prose poems all confess nostalgia. The paradox at the heart of this enterprise is that nostalgia created a new means of expression for the future.

---

[5]   Cited by Suzanne Bernard, *Le Poème en prose de Baudelaire à nos jours* (Paris, 1959), 29.

Initially prose authors remained traditionalists with respect to poetry: they revered verse as sacred and indispensable even though they were aware that its aura had dissolved, replaced by ornamental effects. A few prose authors, however, were groundbreakers and real entrepreneurs when it came to conquering new poetic turf: they experimented and pushed boundaries throughout the century; they investigated the origins of language and music to capture lost and new rhythms, thereby gaining a new understanding of poetic essence. Rather than focusing on harmonious poetic prose as the liberating medium (such as Rousseau's *Rêveries*), I emphasize controversial, some would say archaic, prose poems to reveal a retrospectively constructed literary history that neglected the genre's origins as a conflicted dynamics between past and present, meter and rhythm, poetry and prose. Beyond a clarification of the history and aesthetics of prose poems, my ambition is to demonstrate that Rousseau's urgent question "How to be a poet in prose?" went beyond technique to the core of poetic creation: the philosopher was wondering how to be a poet *and* be modern, how to write poetry in a modern age—hence its relevance for our times. We need to understand this question to appreciate the development of poetry in the modern age following Baudelaire's reply: "Sois toujours poète, même en prose" [Always be a poet, even in prose.][6]

Genealogies of the Prose Poem

A genealogist researches filiations whereas an archeologist researches ancient things. Researching the prose poems of the French Enlightenment involves both archeological and genealogical approaches. From my archeology, a paradox will emerge: my first-hand examination of over sixty works (many of them out of print) establishes that eighteenth-century prose poems defy terminology. First, there is the issue that they differ so radically from each other. Second, they differ from Baudelaire's famous prose poems as well as later examples. However, all match Jaucourt's definition of the "poëme en prose" in the *Encyclopédie* — "genre d'ouvrage où l'on retrouve la fiction & le style de la poésie, & qui par là sont de vrais *poëmes*, à la mesure & à la rime près." These poetic fictions often drew their topics from the Bible, mythology, and history, and told stories replete with adventures "vraisemblables" and/or "merveilleuses" as indicated in Jaucourt's definition. As far as their poetic diction is concerned, parataxis (short, declarative sentences without coordination or clauses) remained a favorite choice, reminiscent of the Old Testament. "Poëmes en prose" were often divided into "cantos," like epic poems, and were usually long, from a few pages to several volumes. Titles, prefaces, and embedded meta-references invariably tried to establish the legitimacy of a poem *without* verse. A more precise definition than Jaucourt's long eluded authors and critics, who often named as a "poëme en prose" a work of fiction that challenged or strived to reconcile the division between prose and poetry. However,

---

[6]   Baudelaire, *Mon cœur mis à nu*, in *Œuvres complètes* (Paris, 1976), vol. 1, 670.

a double signal identifies them for readers: a legitimizing preface in defense of elevated prose; and the conspicuous insertion, within prose, of traditional poetic traits such as allegory, ekphrasis, epithets, inversions, and others, save for rhyming meter. However misguided we might judge these attempts to turn prose into poetry with the help of formal features, they are consistent with contemporary takes on poetry, as exemplified by Jaucourt's definition. My detailed readings concentrate on these authorial strategies to frame prose poems so that readers would interpret them as poetry.

Prose Poems of the French Enlightenment will provide readers of prose poetry new, original sources to understand the genre's beginnings. For scholars of the Enlightenment, a corpus will emerge to challenge the neat division between eighteenth-century poetry perceived as antiquarian and eighteenth-century prose fiction regarded as innovative. Only recently did textbooks devoted to prose poems lift the genre into the French academic curriculum.[7] Yet textbooks as well as anthologies of French prose poetry, beginning with the first compilation by Maurice Chapelan in 1959, only mention the eighteenth century parenthetically as the cradle of poetic prose, not of the "poëme en prose." Suzanne Bernard's seminal *Le Poème en prose de Baudelaire jusqu'à nos jours* (1959) might be partly responsible for the notion that poetic prose was the eighteenth century's sole contribution to the emergence of prose poems.[8] I propose new evidence to complete Bernard's prehistory by emphasizing interpretative strategies behind the controversial label "poëme en prose." Poetry today is more narrowly defined than the all-encompassing field it once was; the term now precludes long, non-lyrical prose texts, regardless of their explicit framing and composition as poems. This segregation, born of post-Romantic definitions and criteria for poetry, fails to account for the existence and role of eighteenth-century prose poems of all stripes in the formation and history of the genre. Jean Roudaut's innovative *Poètes et grammairiens au XVIIIᵉ siècle. Anthologie* (1971) corrected this reductive perspective, but it is the inclusion of excerpts from prose poems in recent anthologies devoted to French eighteenth-century poetry that reflects the growing acceptance and poetic interest of once marginal texts, although the

---

[7]   Michel Sandras, *Lire le poème en prose* (Paris, 1995); Yves Vadé, *Le poème en prose* (Paris, 1996).

[8]   "On peut dire que le XVIIIᵉ siècle fait lentement, à travers de nombreuses tentatives, l'acquisition des principes essentiels au poème en prose (resserrement, brièveté, intensité d'effet, unité organique); ainsi passera-t-on de la prose poétique, qui est encore prose, au poème en prose, qui est avant tout *poème*." [We can say that the XVIIIth century, through numerous attempts, slowly acquires the principles essential to the prose poem (tightening, brevity, intensity of effect, organic unity); we thus move from poetic prose, which is still prose, to the prose poem, which is above all *poetry*.] Bernard, *Le Poème en prose de Baudelaire jusqu'à nos jours*, 19. Bernard's approach is inflected by a post-Romantic aesthetics that grants the Enlightenment advances in prose but not in poetry. In particular, the criterion of brevity as a necessary condition of poeticity is anachronistic when applied to pre-Romantic poetry in prose or verse.

criterion of length proved a limit to the publication of complete texts.[9] Nowadays, length should no longer be an obstacle: I hope to make available online an "open" anthology devoted to prose poems of the French Enlightenment to prompt us to reconsider the issue of brevity as one of the "traditional qualities recognized in the prose poem itself at its best," and to supplement and historicize Mary Ann Caws and Hermine Riffaterre's theoretical frameworks.[10] One wishes for more critical editions of individual works, as has already happened with Rousseau's *Le Lévite d'Ephraïm*. Whether it be Montesquieu's little-known *Temple de Gnide*, Cazotte's fantasist *Ollivier, poëme*, Saint-Martin's allegorical *Le Crocodile,* or Grainville's apocalyptic *Le Dernier homme*, selected scientific editions would provide missing links in the history of genre formation as well as bring aesthetic diversity to a field arbitrarily dominated by novels and theater.

There is only a single, pioneering work in English on eighteenth-century "poëmes en prose." Written in 1936, Vista Clayton's *The Prose Poem in French Literature of the Eighteenth Century* has remained to this day the standard reference and provides a very useful, descriptive overview of a corpus admittedly hard to circumscribe. Christian Leroy, for instance, does not endorse Clayton's term "poëme en prose" as appropriate for a corpus so diverse as to include lyrical hymns such as Reyrac's *Hymne au soleil* and epic ventures like Marmontel's *Les Incas*.[11] My own decision to retain the term "poëme en prose," instead of "poésie en prose" as Leroy advocates, finds its justification in textual evidence that the confusing, oxymoric nature of the term "poëme en prose" served authors, critics, opponents, and proponents in adjudicating the literary experiments under way (see my four appendices). While I am mostly in agreement with Clayton's identification of some sixty prose poems, I propose some adjustments.[12] Volney's *Les Ruines*, though it begins like a "poëme en prose," switches to a long philosophical

---

[9]   Catriona Seth has selected, prefaced, and annotated the section on eighteenth-century poetry in the Pléiade *Anthologie de la poésie française, XVIIIe siècle, XIXe siècle, XXe siècle*, eds Martine Bercot, Michel Collot, and Catriona Seth (Paris, 2000), 1–436. Michel Delon, the editor of *Anthologie de la poésie française du XVIIIe siècle* (Paris, 1997), explained that he had to "réduire à la portion congrue la part du poème en prose dont le domaine est vaste et les limites floues" [reduce to the shortest allowance the share of the prose poem, whose domain is vast and borders vague], 449.

[10]   Mary Ann Caws, Preface, *The Prose Poem in France. Theory and Practice* (New York, 1983), viii. Hermine Riffaterre makes the same argument in favor of brevity in her introduction to the volume (xi).

[11]   See Christian Leroy, *La Poésie en prose française du XVIIe siècle à nos jours. Histoire d'un genre* (Paris, 2001), 7–10. Though I differ on the issue of terminology, I agree with the main thrust of Leroy's literary history of prose poetry and his demonstration that "la poésie en prose ne se limite ni ne commence au poème en prose moderne" [prose poetry is neither limited to, nor begins with, the modern prose poem]. Ibid., 10.

[12]   Let us also mention two corrections. The *Voyage à Paphos*, long attributed to Montesquieu, was a forgery. Denis Vairasse's *Histoire des Sévarambes* (1787) was the abbreviated edition of a utopian novel published in 1677–1679. See Aubrey Rosenberg, ed. *L'Histoire des Sévarambes. Denis Veiras* (Paris, 2001).

meditation that does not really seek poetic elevation. Several interesting texts need to be added to the corpus Clayton initially established, such as Boesnier's *Mexique Conquis* (1752), Coqueley de Chaussepierre's *Le Roué vertueux* (1770), Louis-Sébastien Mercier, *Songes et visions philosophiques* (1788), François Verne's *La Franciade, ou l'Ancienne France. Poëme en seize chants* (1790), Fournier de Tony, *Les Nymphes de Dyctyme ou révolutions de l'empire virginal* (1790), or the anonymous and remarkable *La Pariséide ou les amours d'un jeune patriote et d'une belle aristocrate, poeme héroi-comi-politique, en prose nationale* (1790). I discovered prose poems by women authors absent from Clayton's bibliography, Mme Dufresne's *Idylles et pieces fugitives* (1781) and Marie-Uranie Rose Monneron, *Annamire, poëme en trois chants* (1783). No doubt more are yet to surface, penned by authors with obscure names, but whose contributions to the genre matters in that they confirm the establishment of a trend. One can also cite a special case Clayton did not include, Lucile de Chateaubriand, whose three prose poems first appeared in the *Mémoires d'outre-tombe* of her famous brother. My approach differs significantly from Clayton and from studies on eighteenth-century literature in the importance I give to Fénelon and Chateaubriand in the prehistory of prose poems. Neither writer usually emerges as an Enlightenment figure. But close textual analyses reveal that their thought and writings are germane to understanding the conflicted aesthetics of eighteenth-century France and bring to the fore the dystopia shadowing the Enlightenment movement. Finally, though the eighteenth century under consideration is a long one, from Fénelon to Chateaubriand, I consider the publication of Grainville's *Le Dernier homme* (1805) to be an emblematic turning point, whereas Clayton posited Quinet's *Ahasvérus* (1833) as a closure to her inquiry. The opposition of Grainville (1746–1805) to Enlightenment philosophers, his decision to convey his apocalyptic vision of the end of the human race via a prose poem in ten songs, and his suicide offer an exemplary illustration of an author who channeled what I term the "spleen" of the Enlightenment through a form symbolic of instability.

My purpose is also to complement the genealogies set forth by French scholars, Suzanne Bernard (*Le Poème en prose de Baudelaire à nos jours*, 1959) and Nathalie Vincent-Munnia (*Les Premiers poèmes en prose*, 1996), who did not wholly contend with the European eighteenth century.[13] Even the important recent volume edited by Vincent-Munnia and dedicated to the *Origines du poème en prose français* (2003) arbitrarily begins in 1750.[14] Other attempts have been made to delimit a chronological framework for the "tradition" of prose poems, for instance anchoring prose poetry in the seventeenth century when the system of rhyme came under attack in tragedies (Leroy).[15] My intention in "delimiting"

---

[13] Nathalie Vincent-Munnia, *Les Premiers poèmes en prose: généalogie d'un genre dans la première moitié du dix-neuvième siècle français* (Paris, 1996).

[14] Nathalie Vincent-Munnia, Simone Bernard-Griffiths, Robert Pickering, eds, *Aux origines du poème en prose français (1750–1850)* (Paris, 2003).

[15] Pierre Moreau, *La Tradition française du poème en prose avant Baudelaire* (Paris, 1959); Anna Jechova, François Mouret, and Jacques Voisine, eds, *La Poésie en prose des*

genre is not so much to establish boundaries, always open to challenge, nor merely to find precursors to modern prose poems, though I will propose texts that problematize the genre's genealogy: my first concern is to clarify the meaning of eighteenth-century prose poems, to understand their ideological connotations, and establish their pivotal contribution in the redistribution and reformulation of genres and in the reversal of the classical hierarchy in favor of the lyric, a metamorphosis that was neither unanimous nor carried to term before 1800, but that was nevertheless sufficiently engaged and popular to be crowned with success in the nineteenth century.

The foremost specialists on eighteenth-century French poetry, Michel Delon, Édouard Guitton, and Sylvain Menant have acknowledged in their respective works the vexing question of the intersection between prose and poetry. Menant admitted that "une étude d'ensemble des relations entre prose et poésie à l'âge classique ... reste à faire" [a global study of the relationships between prose and poetry in the classical age remains ... to be done].[16] By recovering here the "project of poetry" in the eighteenth century, I do not intend to displace or diminish its "project of prose," to borrow a phrase that Elizabeth Fowler and Roland Greene applied to early modern Europe.[17] Rather, I seek to examine the concomitance of both projects. In other words, I intend to bear in mind equally the perspective of prose and that of poetry in their respective variety and complexity. Though I have insisted here on poetry as the lesser known domain of Enlightenment letters, the eighteenth century is as replete with "ad hoc prose forms" as the sixteenth and seventeenth centuries Fowler and Greene examined—one of these forms being the newly minted prose poem. While the editors' goal in their volume of essays on the project of prose was "to make the poetics of prose visible in a wide array of literary and nonliterary instances," I illuminate the poetics of prose via the single, albeit multifaceted, prism of prose poetry.[18] In so doing, I follow the chronological adjustments Fowler and Greene proposed with regard to two important critical stances: first, Jeffrey Kittay and Wlad Godzich pinpointing the emergence of prose in the thirteenth century;[19] second, Henri Meschonnic's articulation of the moments when prose and poetry conjoin and then disjoin. For Fowler and Greene, empirical evidence suggests that in fact prose is still 'emerging' in the early modern period and my own study further prolongs the emergence of prose until the mid-eighteenth century. Fowler and Greene then contend with Meschonnic's argument that "the binary distinction between poetry and prose is a fairly recent one, endorsed by the Romantics and developed by formalist and structuralist theorists of the twentieth

---

Lumières au romantisme: 1760–1820 (Paris, 1993); Leroy, *La Poésie en prose française du XVIIe siècle à nos jours.*

[16]   Sylvain Menant, *La Chute d'Icare. La Crise de la poésie française (1700–1750)* (Geneva, 1981), 352.

[17]   Elizabeth Fowler and Roland Greene, *The Project of Prose in Early Modern Europe and the New World* (Cambridge, 1997).

[18]   Fowler and Greene, *The Project of Prose*, 1–6.

[19]   Jeffrey Kittay and Wlad Godzich, *The Emergence of Prose: An Essay in Prosaïcs* (Minneapolis, 1987), 4.

century," later to be "undone" by modernism and post modernism. Fowler and Greene explain that "the modern dichotomy between poetry and prose is often visible in sixteenth- and seventeenth-century texts," and such is the case as well during the Enlightenment. [20] Because it shapes our understanding of literature so completely and uncritically, the duality between prose and poetry is perhaps the most basic and difficult assumption to question. But early experiments in prose poetry prove that this duality had become arbitrary, and that a *formal* definition of poetry had become impossible. This undermining of the Aristotelian separation between prose and poetry is one of the least noted revolutions born of the Enlightenment. To highlight this change, I lean on Meschonnic's groundbreaking work on poetics, which offers a radical new understanding of *rhythm* as a non-formalist notion that escapes the sterile opposition prose/poetry.[21]

De-limiting Genre

Barbara Johnson dismissed genealogical approaches to the prose poem as imprecise and random: "La liste des généalogies revues et corrigées s'étend à l'infini: du *Livre du promeneur* à *Télémaque*, de Chateaubriand à la Bible, les 'origines' du poème en prose se retrouvent toujours plus en amont dans les eaux troubles du fleuve de l'histoire littéraire" [The list of revised and amended genealogies goes on forever: from the *Livre du promeneur* to *Télémaque*, from Chateaubriand to the Bible, one keeps finding the "origins" of prose poems further up stream in literary history's troubled waters.] [22] Although Johnson remained skeptical vis-à-vis a history of the prose poem's sources, she turned toward the past when emphasizing "l'intertextualité conflictuelle" of Baudelaire's prose poems, and when unveiling the layer of clichés that composes them: far from excluding history, she encountered it in the folds of prose poetry.[23] Baudelaire linguistically appropriated other authors to insert his writing within "une histoire intertextuelle qui le dépossède de lui-même" [an intertextual history that dispossesses him]. To penetrate this multi-layered "intertextual history," as I propose to do by investigating the determinant role of the eighteenth century, further confirms the prose poem's slippery nature described by Johnson: "le même procès interminable d'interférence intertextuelle ... aboutit à une même impossibilité de fixer ou de totaliser un ensemble d'éléments qui garantiraient les limites sûres d'une interprétation" [the same endless process of intertextual interferences ... results in the same impossibility to determine or encompass a set of elements that would

---

[20]   Ibid.

[21]   Henri Meschonnic, *Pour la poétique II* (Paris, 1973); *Critique du rythme, anthropologie historique du langage.* (Paris, 1990); *La Rime et la vie* (Paris, 1989). See also Henri Meschonnic and Gérard Dessons, *Traité du rythme. Du vers et des proses* (Paris, 1998).

[22]   Barbara Johnson, *Défigurations du langage poétique: La Seconde révolution baudelairienne* (Paris, 1979), 19.

[23]   Ibid., 156, 142.

guarantee the reliable limits of an interpretation].[24] Therefore, a less anachronistic and more dynamic interpretation emerges as soon as one renounces the dubious impulse for synthesis, and draws out instead the "intertextual interferences" that are so essential to getting closer to understanding the aesthetic riddle of prose poetry. We will see telling examples, such as Louis Aragon's Dadaist recovery of Fénelon's *Les Aventures de Télémaque*, or Rousseau's pastoral rewriting of a chapter from the Old Testament.

As many scholars and readers have experienced, the prose poem is a genre harder to define and delimit than—let's say—novels, short stories, or plays. It does away with versification—including free verse whose typographical inscription still anchors the poem on the page and makes it recognizable as such. Formalist approaches to prose poetry have settled for a dynamics between opposites (Bernard), which Johnson deconstructed as a dysfunction that ends up affecting our capacity to give a critical definition: "Ni antithèse, ni synthèse, le poème en prose est le lieu à partir duquel la polarité—et donc, la symétrie—entre présence et absence, entre prose et poésie, *dysfonctionne*. La description du poème en prose n'est possible qu'à partir du fait que toute tentative de le décrire finit par se subvertir elle-même" [Neither antithesis nor synthesis, the prose poem is the place where polarity—therefore symmetry—between presence and absence, prose and poetry, *dysfunctions*. Describing prose poems is only possible once it is understood that any descriptive attempt ends up subverting itself].[25] To escape this impasse and the limitations of a formalist focus, Michel Beaujour has convincingly argued in favor of an ontological reading of modern prose poems as "short epiphanies":

> The focus on prose poems signals the poet's more or less conscious choice of a poetics derived from the quasi-theological belief that "poetic language" is ontologically—rather than formally—different from ordinary language. This ontological difference (and motivation) gives access, through an experience less esthetic than visionary or epiphanic to a "poetic universe" inhabiting, so to speak, the obverse of language, which can never denote nor connote it.[26]

The pre-Baudelairian prose poems examined here complicate Beaujour's reading as they carry first and foremost an Enlightenment project that is epistemological rather than ontological in nature. Certainly, a new "poetic universe" unfettered by rhymes was accidentally discovered when Fénelon's narrative became public, and awareness of poetry's "ontological" essence slowly rose out of experiments in prose poetry. But as eighteenth-century *prosateurs* gradually discovered "the obverse of language," most translated their discovery into self-reflexive, self-conscious fictions (some parodic), while only a handful transmuted this new knowledge into visions and epiphanies. What we see at play in early prose poems is the Enlightenment breaking rules that it invented, and inventing anew while also

---

[24] Ibid., 144.

[25] Ibid., 37.

[26] Michel Beaujour, "Short Epiphanies: Two Contextual Approaches to the French Prose Poem," in *The Prose Poem in France: Theory and Practice*, eds Mary Ann Caws and Hermine Riffaterre (Paris, 1983), 52.

problematizing these inventions. This is why epistemological and semiological readings better capture the spirit of Enlightenment prose poems than an ontological approach partial to nineteenth-century poetry.

In pondering the meaning of modern prose poetry, Beaujour further speculated that "[i]n the face of 'prose poems' of this type, the cultural split between the petty bourgeoisie of traditional expectations and the modernist aristocracy of consciousness is seen to gape painfully. This discrimination may well be, in the last analysis, the true social and cultural function of those modernist artifacts which deliberately disregard or reject constituents traditionally built into an art form: representation in painting, the stage in theatre, melody in music, narrative in novels, motion in films, metrical language in poetry."[27] Beaujour's association of the bourgeoisie with artistic tradition, and aristocracy with a modern elite "of consciousness" can only apply to post-revolutionary French society. By contrast, under the ancien régime, the aristocracy was leaning toward conservatism whereas a rising bourgeoisie provoked aesthetic revaluations and challenges to poetic status quo. Nevertheless, Beaujour's identification of a cultural clash based on a social gap at the core of anti-conventionalism in art can be traced back to the eighteenth century and reveal a similar phenomenon: a socio-cultural split translated into aesthetic discrimination at the inception of prose poems. This is what Jonathan Monroe has termed the "politics of genre" after mapping out prose poetry as "that place within literature where social antagonism of gender and class achieve *generic* expression, where aesthetic conflicts between and among literary genres manifest themselves concisely and concretely as a displacement, projection and symbolic reenactment of more broadly based social struggles."[28] Monroe left unanswered the intriguing question of the origins of this aesthetic projection of social struggles: could not prose poems be in "that place" precisely because they were born of a revolutionary eighteenth century where class struggles exploded? My hypothesis is that prose poems still carry this initial rebellion against the tyranny of class in the freedom they take with expression and form. Though Enlightenment authors remain for the most part more self-restrained than Baudelaire when he called on his "hypocritical reader," their defiance is unmistakable, as they dared to conceive poems *in prose* in an age where versification ruled poetry.

We are not used to thinking about "the fate of poetry in the philosophical age."[29] Yet poetry is a discourse and an activity, both radically historical and empirical. Like poetic systems, poetry's situation and its contradictions are historically specific: identical elements do not have the same value when used in a different historical context.[30] For the translator and scholar Henri Meschonnic, "[l]e problème de l'œuvre, comme celui de la poétique, n'est pas la *beauté*, mais *l'historicité*" [the issue in an artwork as in poetics is not beauty but

---

[27]   Ibid., 56.

[28]   Jonathan Monroe, *A Poverty of Objects: The Prose Poem and the Politics of Genre* (Ithaca, 1987), 18.

[29]   I borrow the phrase from Michel Paul Guy de Chabanon's poem, *Sur le sort de la poësie en ce siècle philosophe*. 1764 (Geneva: 1970).

[30]   Henri Meschonnic, *Les États de la poétique* (Paris, 1985), 241.

historicity.][31] As he defines it, "l'historicité est une tension des contraires: à la fois ce qui a, comme toute œuvre, sa situation historique et ce qui a pour activité d'en sortir indéfiniment. D'avoir une activité qui continue au-delà de son temps et même de sa culture, en quoi s'accomplit en elle la *modernité* comme présence indéfiniment continuée au présent" [Historicity is a tension of contraries: to have, like any artwork, its historical situation *and* to be actively and indefinitely working to leave it; to continue to be active beyond its time and even its culture, whereby modernity accomplishes itself through it as a presence indefinitely continued in the present].[32] Meschonnic's historicist perspective serves as a more accurate guide to the practice and theory of poetry in the eighteenth century than the considerations of formal beauty that have contributed to discarding most of the Enlightenment poetic production. We need to refocus on the tension between the situation of poetry in the 1700s and a practice of prose poetry that seeks a way out of sclerosis and continues to question traditions and limits. I will therefore ask what are the specifics of poetry's situation in the field of Belles-Lettres during the eighteenth century, and where its modernity resides. Let me briefly sketch here some preliminary answers to both questions.

The period 1700–1750 witnessed a poetry in crisis that Sylvain Menant metaphorically compared to "la chute d'Icare" [Icarus's fall].[33] Notwithstanding novelty acts like descriptive poetry (Jacques Delille) and energetic philosophical poems (e.g. Voltaire's "Tremblement de terre de Lisbonne"), the permanence of a lyrical tradition (Jean-Baptiste Rousseau's religious odes), and felicitous exceptions (André Chenier), poetry for the most part was falling under the combined excesses of metrics and witticism. On the one hand, the exactitude and accuracy of meter led to, paradoxically, convoluted expression: ideas got lost or diluted by strict formal constraints. On the other hand, poetry had become a game, a social skill to shine in public rather than an inspired expression of beauty and enthusiasm. Fugitive, circumstantial, it favored and rewarded wit and lightness, serving the passion of the times for play and games. Perhaps more prevalent and intensive than ever before, poetic activity yielded a flurry of generic mélanges and much inconsequential verses—witness the wares of countless almanacs.

Given this backdrop, the novel, the theater, minor and hybrid fiction genres flourished, suggesting that the Enlightenment was also engaged in the painful but irrevocable process of replacing ideals and overturning boundaries, and in moving away from purity, toward balance, equilibrium and equipoise, not in the sense of symmetry, proportion, or duality (other forms of purity), but in blending, merging, and "métissage." Enlightenment authors appeared fascinated by métissage, as well as revolted. Modernity resides in this vital (con)fusion, the emblem of which we

---

[31]   Meschonnic and Dessons, *Traité du rythme*, 47.

[32]   Ibid., 46.

[33]   Menant, *La Chute d'Icare*. See also Chabanon. *Sur le sort de la poësie en ce siècle philosophe*, 7–16. For a linguistic perspective on the evolution of prose and poetic styles, see Ferdinand Brunot, *Histoire de la langue française des origines à nos jours* (Paris: 1966), vol. 6.

discover in prose poems. Willy-nilly, hybridity became the reality of modernity in the eighteenth century in art as in life. Let us underline this paradox: while most authors hung on to the principles of imitation of a beautiful nature, which meant a pure, unadulterated nature, the Enlightenment was torn on the issue of purity; the intellectual lure of purity was offset by its socio-political rejection. As absolute monarchy by divine right was assailed, a hybrid political system, parliamentary monarchy, was advocated. As the supremacy of blue blood became contested, the mixing of classes and origins appeared. As a single revealed religion abused its authority, philosophers fought for tolerance and coexistence of a plurality of religions. As explorers and travelers charted new territories, Eurocentric homogeneity had to confront global diversity and deal with the consequences of interpenetration. The myth of purity endured, but as nostalgia, a gaze turned back toward a lost paradise. In various degrees and not always consistently, writers of the Enlightenment perceived the danger of advocating purity with its risks of fanaticism, intolerance, and supremacy. In literature, canonization and generic categorization were/are about purification and separation, defended by some, challenged by others.

Genre Trouble

In 1740 Voltaire published a *Recueil de pièces fugitives en prose et en vers*. In 1776, Mme la comtesse de***, aka Fanny de Beauharnais, offered her *Mélanges de poésies fugitives et de prose sans conséquence*. The compilation of verse and prose in one volume was not a new phenomenon, but the characterization of poetry as "fugitive" and prose as "without consequence" exemplified the eighteenth-century vogue for short, unpretentious, circumstantial verse and prose pieces at the outer margins of the system of genres, in defiance of high poetry and eloquent prose.[34] If we continue our promenade along the path of eighteenth-century poetry, we encounter Peyraud de Beaussol's 1768 *Écho à Narcisse, poème en trois chants dans un genre nouveau qui tient de l'héroïde, de l'élégie et de l'idylle*. The long title typifies another liberating gesture: a mixing of genres to neutralize all labels in favor of an undefined "new genre." Irreverence toward established boundaries prevails in the subtitle of Louis Abel Beffroy de Reigny, who, under the pseudonym Le Cousin Jacques, published *Marlborough, poëme comique en prose rimée* in 1783: the coinage "comic poem in rhymed prose" facetiously overturns the Establishment of prose and poetry by proposing an oxymoron (see Figure 1).

Piqued by this generic riddle, I looked for Cousin Jacques' publications and found more teasing: in 1783, *Les Petites-Maisons du Parnasse, ouvrage comico-littéraire d'un genre nouveau, en vers et en prose*, and *Turlututu, ou la Science du bonheur, poème héroi-comique en huit chants et en vers*; in 1791, *Nicodème*

---

[34] In 1776, Claude-Joseph Dorat also published a collection bearing the same title, *Mélanges de poésies fugitives et de prose sans conséquence*. On the literary phenomenon of "fugitive poetry," see Nicole Masson, *La Poésie fugitive au XVIIIᵉ siècle* (Paris, 2002) and Menant, *La Chute d'Icare*, chap. V, 217–72.

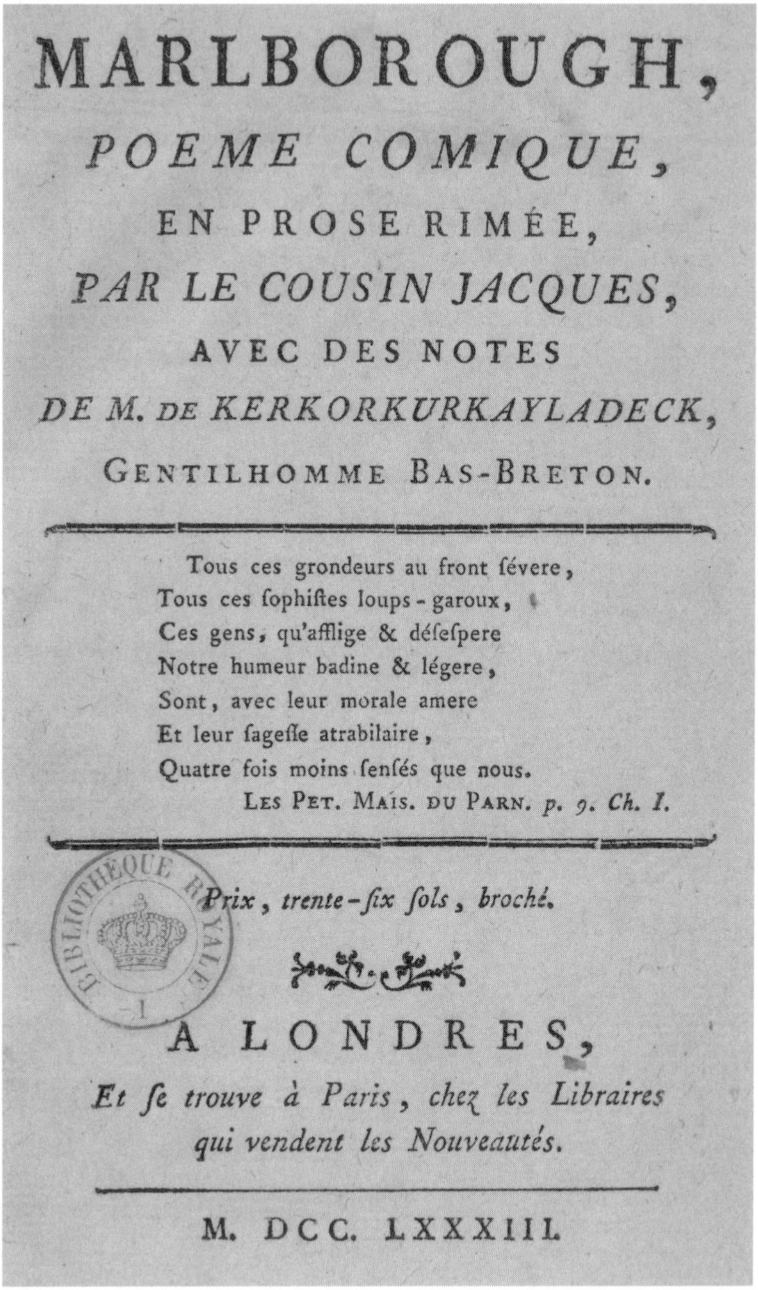

MARLBOROUGH,

POEME COMIQUE,

EN PROSE RIMÉE,

PAR LE COUSIN JACQUES,

AVEC DES NOTES

DE M. DE KERKORKURKAYLADECK,

GENTILHOMME BAS-BRETON.

> Tous ces grondeurs au front févere,
> Tous ces fophiftes loups-garoux,
> Ces gens, qu'afflige & défefpere
> Notre humeur badine & légere,
> Sont, avec leur morale amere
> Et leur fageffe atrabilaire,
> Quatre fois moins fenfés que nous.
> LES PET. MAÍS. DU PARN. *p. 9. Ch. I.*

Prix, trente-fix fols, broché.

A LONDRES,

*Et fe trouve à Paris, chez les Libraires
qui vendent les Nouveautés.*

M. DCC. LXXXIII.

Fig. 1   Frontispiece. Le Cousin Jacques, *Marlborough, Poëme comique en prose rimée.* Londres, 1783.

dans la lune, ou la Révolution pacifique, folie en prose et en trois actes, mélée d'ariettes et de vaudevilles; in 1796, *Turlututu, empereur de l'Isle vertu, folie, bêtise, farce ou parodie comme on voudra, en prose et en trois actes*; and finally, in 1797, *Un Rien, ou l'Habit de Noces, folie épisodique en un acte et en prose, mélée de vaudevilles et d'airs nouveaux*. Eighteenth-century writers took a particular delight in juxtaposing the spheres of prose and verse. Obviously, this idiosyncratic list tells us a much more troubled story than the smoothed over history we have inherited from accounts of eighteenth-century literature, and the objective of this book is to challenge the framework of neat divisions through which we read and interpret literature and poetry. Randomly selected, these examples typify a thornier literary field than is usually represented by histories of eighteenth-century literature. What preliminary hypotheses can we draw from the above sample of titles?

Cousin Jacques' mix-and-match labeling game with long titles signals both the imperative to identify genres and the ultimate impossibility of meeting this imperative in a cross-pollinated literary field.[35] As we will see, the increasingly impossible requirement to frame literature both fostered and hampered the innovation of prose poems. Readers might initially consider prose poems as a subgenre, yet it was also a hybrid subgenre: there is potentially a prose version for every verse genre (idyll, epic, dramatic, and lyric), which renders a definition of the plural prose poem very difficult. The trouble of delimiting a form not yet established is compounded by the fact that the form often superimposes itself onto predominant, established generic categories. Monroe considers this "nexus of generic interactions" key to examining "to what extent the prose poem's power has been due to its historically bound subversive relation to competing, better established genres such as the verse lyric and the novel."[36] Indeed, eighteenth-century prose poems reveal that authors worked on shifting ground: they absorbed, as well as participated in, the displacement of not only the lyric and the novel, but also pastoral, epic, and dramatic genres.

Cousin Jacques' titles remind us more specifically of the importance of theater (and opera) as a genre rich in experimentations, one far more innovative, daring, popular, and successful than any other literary mode in the eighteenth century. Though not always approved, playwrights had been juxtaposing verse and prose for a long time.[37] More and more plays in prose were written and performed in the second half of the century under the combined influence of Diderot, Beaumarchais, and Mercier. The three dramatists buttressed their innovations with critical essays, and translated their ideological convictions about the arbitrary nature of the social ladder into aesthetic choices shunning similarly arbitrary hierarchies among genres.[38] This unique relation between the theater and the social ladder it portrayed

---

[35] The phenomenon also applies to versified poetry, witness Jean-Joseph Vadé's "La pipe cassée, poëme épitragipoissardihéroicomique" (3rd ed., 1755).

[36] Monroe, *A Poverty of Objects*, 18.

[37] On prose tragedies, see Leroy, *La Poésie en prose française*, 32–55.

[38] Denis Diderot, *Entretiens sur le fils naturel* (1757), *Discours sur la poésie dramatique* (1758); Beaumarchais, *Essai sur le genre dramatique sérieux* (1767); Louis-Sébastien Mercier, *Du Théâtre ou Nouvel Essai sur l'art dramatique* (1773). See Michel

facilitated the abolition of generic hierarchies as far as plays were concerned, a victory not yet achieved by eighteenth-century poets. It is essential to bear in mind the development of the theater when investigating poetry, since theater was an integral part of what poetry meant during that period.[39] Comedy, in particular, had been a privileged genre for questioning, disrupting, and mocking conventions, as Cousin Jacques's farcical titles suggest, embracing comedy's antic subversions. Indeed, Diderot's dramatic innovations began with *Le Fils naturel*, a prose comedy. The comic mode migrated to the novel as soon as the new genre emerged in the seventeenth century, precisely to mock its extravagant plots, as did Charles Sorel in 1627 with *Le Berger Extravagant, où parmi les fantaisies amoureuses on void les impertinences des Romans et de la Poësie*. Similarly, as I will show in my first chapter, Marivaux mocked Fénelon's hugely successful *Les Aventures de Télémaque*, the first fiction to be interpreted as a prose poem. Marivaux's novel, *Le Télémaque travesti* (1775) exposed the mannerisms of "telemacomania," parodying the salient components of prose poems, which many authors had reverently tried to imitate. One of the laws of a new genre's formation seems to be that parody accompanies its birth, a parody often adopting the new genre's form. Therefore it is no surprise that a few authors penned self-reflexive prose poems poking fun at the instability and hybridity of this newcomer, the prose poem.[40]

Let us consider briefly a particularly revealing parody and radical example of what I propose to call "para-prose poetry." Similar to meta-poetry, which stages its own self-reflexivity, para-prose poetry is a self-referential parody that mocks the emerging genre. The most unexpected discovery in the course of my excavation of Enlightenment prose poems was certainly *Le Roué vertueux* (see Figure 2). It was published in 1770 by a lawyer and royal censor well known as an "amateur comedian," Charles-Georges Coqueley de Chaussepierre (1711–1791), and reprinted at least once.[41] The author provides an initial framework with an oxymoric title that qualifies as virtuous a man presumed guilty and condemned

---

Delon, Robert Mauzi, and Sylvain Menant eds, *Histoire de la littérature française: De l'Encyclopédie aux Méditations* (Paris, 1997), 195.

[39] There are numerous points of comparison between drama and prose poems, for example on the issue of "le naturel." As the bourgeois drama emerges, "la référence à la nature n'est pas sans ambiguïté. ... La revendication de naturel qui fonde le choix de la prose cache souvent les pires invraisemblances." [the reference to nature is not without ambiguities. ... The claim for the natural which justifies the choice of prose often hides the worst improbabilities]. Delon, Mauzi and Menant eds, *Histoire de la littérature française*, 196.

[40] At least four prose poems exploit a mock-heroic vein: Claude Marie Giraud's *Diabotinus ou l'orvietan de Salins. Poëme héroi-comique. Traduit du languedocien* (1749); Jean-Baptiste Guiard de Servigné's *Le Rhinocéros* (1750); Jacques Cazotte's *Ollivier. Poëme* (1763); and Louis-Claude de Saint-Martin's *Le Crocodile, ou la guerre du bien et du mal, arrivée sous le regne de Louis XV. Poëme épico-magique en 102 chants* (1799).

[41] See Martine de Rougemont, *Paradrames. Parodies du drame 1775–1777* (Saint-Etienne, 1998), and her presentation of *Monsieur Cassandre, ou les effets de l'amour et du vert-de-gris*, a parody of bourgeois drama written by Coqueley de Chaussepierre in 1775 (17–21). My coinage "para-prose poetry" is modeled after Rougemont's "paradrame" referring to parodies of plays.

to death penalty at the wheel. A first subtitle situates the genre as a "prose poem in four cantos," while a second subtitle suggests a possible future for the text, namely a staging: "Propre à faire, en cas de besoin, un Drame à jouer deux fois par semaine" [Apt to become, if needed, a drama to be performed twice a week.] As with numerous eighteenth-century fictions, the elaborate paratext sets up a framework for readers' expectations, which includes the expectation of the unexpected. A curious literary and typographical artifact, the text consists of a few fragmentary phrases and single words separated by blanks and punctuation marks (see Figures 3–8).

A synopsis of each canto precedes the punctuated but *missing* narrative. From the summaries, we learn the gist of the story, built around *quid pro quo*: a cesspit emptier, M. Lafosse, ("vidangeur sans odeur de la rue Saint-Martin") has been hanged by mistake, and his wife and daughter plan to steal his corpse. Saint Leu, an apprentice brick layer and the daughter's fiancé, tries to save the family's belongings from expropriation, but kills his own father by mistake when the latter intervenes, suspecting a robbery. Saint Leu is executed on the wheel for his parricide; the woman who was to have been his bride kills herself, and her mother dies of grief. The traditional page layout (the heading "poëme en prose" on each right-hand page, formal inscription of the beginning and end of each canto) frames fifty-two pages of blanks interspersed with isolated words and punctuation marks. As an extreme and unique parody of "poëme en prose," this publication reveals much about a poetic climate and changing aesthetics in the second half of the eighteenth century. Something drastic had to have happened to the understanding and codification of prose and poetry by 1770 for Coqueley de Chaussepierre to wink knowingly at his readers with such a truncated prose poem. In terms of subject matter, the text gives lower class characters dignity via morality, thus arguing in favor of representations of the underclass as worthy of poetry (echoing Wordsworth's manifesto). At the same time, the text translates the working underclass' disempowerment as well as the artist's resignation. As the writer leaves off filling in his poem, consequently the voice of the people stays fragmentary: only its vehemence and its ineffectual protests remain. Such is the significance of the multiple vocative *oh!* and *ah!*, exclamatory interjections, emphatic negations, and tragic lexicon.[42] The engravings that accompany the text (such as Saint Leu's revolt or the scene of his public execution) even seem to anticipate revolutionary violence. Typographically finished and illustrated, but deliberately incomplete, the poem imparts the urgency of its message versus the lesser importance of narrative closure. Mercier shrugged off the author's literary "arlequinades."[43] But through *Le Roué vertueux*, however jokingly unaware, Coqueley de Chaussepierre executes poetry: he antithetically executes/makes a poem about five violent deaths and executes/cuts it out.

---

[42]   Julie Candler Hayes interprets the text as a "satire of Diderot's 'style haletant,'" Coqueley de Chaussepierre being an "enemy of the serious genre," namely bourgeois drama. *Identity and Ideology: Diderot, Sade, and the Serious Genre* (Amsterdam, Philadelphia: 1991), 86 and 100.

[43]   See Rougemont, *Paradrames*, 18.

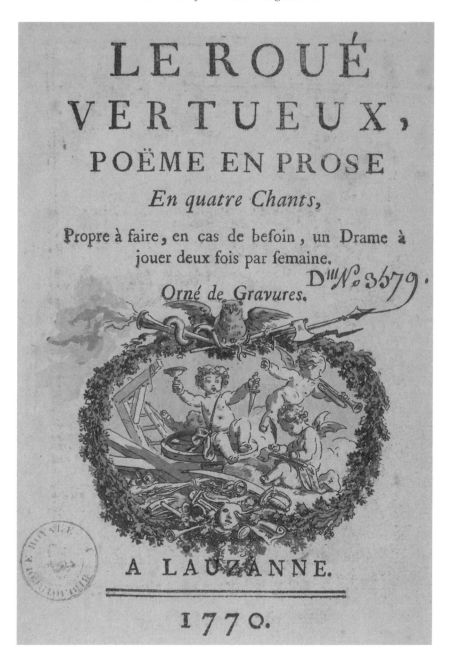

Fig. 2   Frontispiece. Charles-Georges Coqueley de Chaussepierre, *Le Roué Vertueux. Poëme en prose en quatre chants.* Lausanne, 1770.

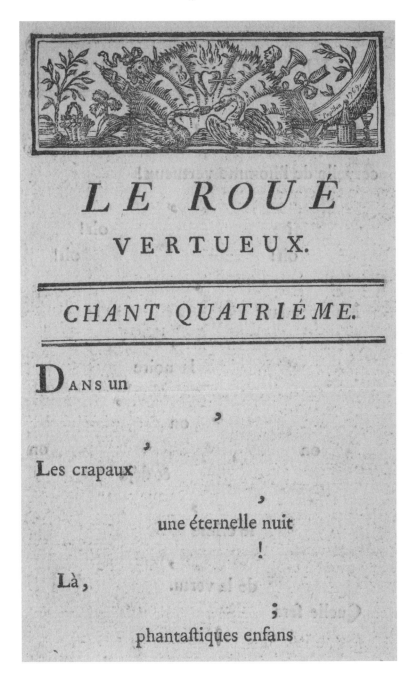

Fig. 3   "Chant quatre." Charles-Georges Coqueley de Chaussepierre, *Le Roué*
Vertueux. Poëme en prose en quatre chants. Lausanne, 1770, 20.

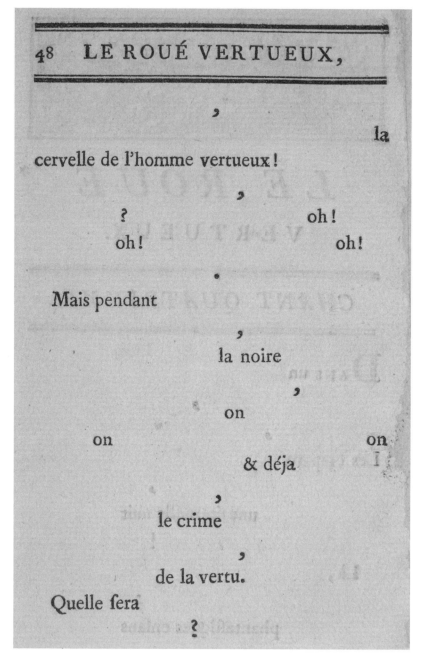

Fig. 4   "Chant quatre." Charles-Georges Coqueley de Chaussepierre, *Le Roué Vertueux. Poëme en prose en quatre chants.* Lausanne, 1770, 21.

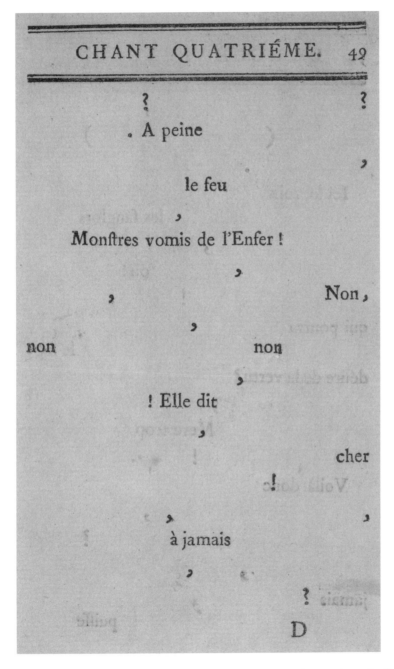

Fig. 5 "Chant quatre." Charles-Georges Coqueley de Chaussepierre, *Le Roué Vertueux. Poëme en prose en quatre chants.* Lausanne, 1770, 22.

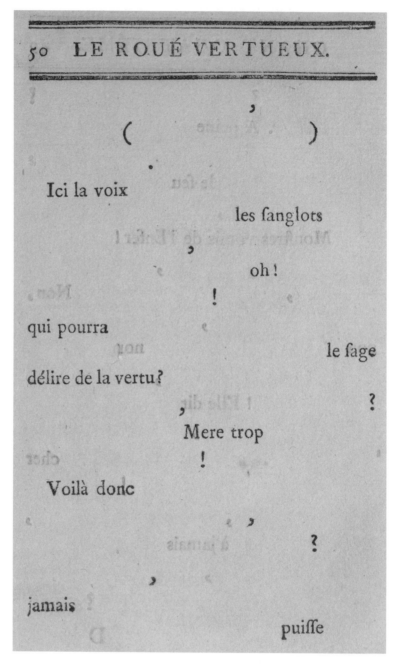

Fig. 6   "Chant quatre." Charles-Georges Coqueley de Chaussepierre, *Le Roué Vertueux. Poëme en prose en quatre chants.* Lausanne, 1770, 23.

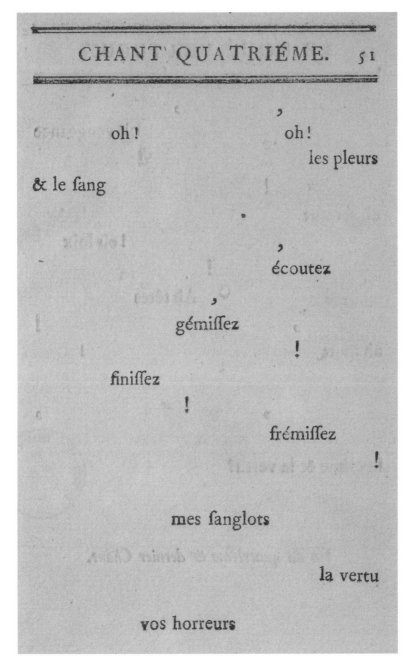

Fig. 7   "Chant quatre." Charles-Georges Coqueley de Chaussepierre, *Le Roué Vertueux. Poëme en prose en quatre chants.* Lausanne, 1770, 24.

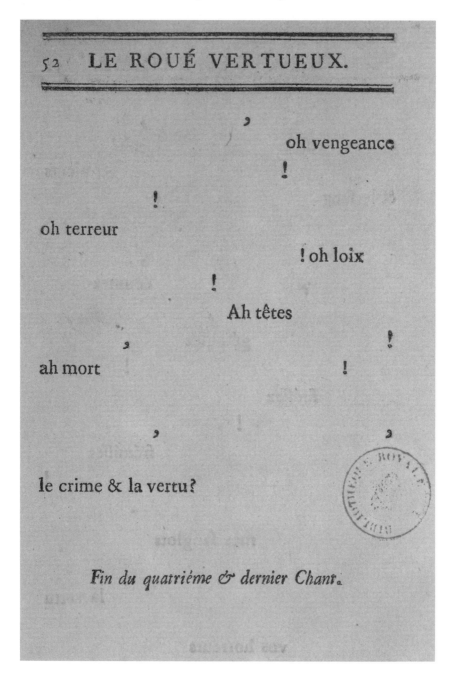

Fig. 8   "Chant quatre." Charles-Georges Coqueley de Chaussepierre, *Le Roué Vertueux. Poëme en prose en quatre chants.* Lausanne, 1770, 25.

Self-consciously, by reflecting the "epistémè" of the Enlightenment and its system of signs, *Le Roué vertueux* challenges us to include epistemological and semiological approaches to enrich Beaujour's ontological interpretation of the prose poem.[44]

Prose Poems of the French Enlightenment

The following chapters focus on finding answers to a complex set of interconnected questions evoked earlier: What are eighteenth-century "poëmes en prose"? Why did authors experiment with this new form and critics disagree on its value? How do these texts affect our understanding of eighteenth-century French literature and our understanding of prose poetry? Throughout, we discover an increasingly overt agenda that allies prose with the principles of freedom and equality defended by the philosophes, while versification remains associated with authority and superiority.

The first chapter revisits the first text to be called "poëme en prose," a work read throughout Europe until the early twentieth century, Fénelon's *Les Aventures de Télémaque* (1699). I argue in favor of a strong link between Fénelon's choice of prose to continue Homer's epic poem and the fin-de-siècle aspiration for better political governance and accessible leadership. Fénelon used prose instead of verse to advocate for less absolute aesthetic and political rules. Prose poems as a new means of expression revealed the discontent with absolutism in politics and poetry. In addition, I argue that Fénelon portrayed passions as another form of the absolute with dangerous consequences. The famous episode wherein Calypso falls in love enchanted Fénelon's contemporaries thanks to its seductive prose, yet the seduction acts as a warning that passions subvert reason and politics. Two centuries later, the twentieth-century surrealist poet Louis Aragon wrote a prose poem that is a shorter, more erotic version of *Télémaque*'s subversive episode, thus building a bridge between seemingly remote eighteenth-century poetry and modern prose poetry. Comparing the two versions exposes the baroque and sexual undertow of Fénelon's text as well as its reformist ideology. Indeed, Aragon also metamorphosed Fénelon's political message into a Dadaist manifesto inserted at the center of the poem, an open revolt against his own times. From the eighteenth-century best-seller to one of the most important pre-surrealist works, from their inception until today, prose poems share three constants: intertextuality, hybridity, and an ambivalent modernity.

Once *Télémaque* triggered the emergence of prose poems, prefaces and commentaries multiplied, debating and theorizing the contentious phenomenon. Chapter 2 captures the long struggle to define prose vs. poetry and develops the argument that this debate also reflects a struggle with modernity. The chapter brings out three movements: provocation, confusion, and attempted resolution. Many, such as the critic La Motte, welcomed the unseating of the "monarchy of

---

[44] Beaujour, "Short Epiphanies," 50.

verse" and encouraged more provocations. Others, like Voltaire, denounced and resisted the unraveling of genres as a bastardization and a devaluation of high poetry. As prose poems questioned the supremacy of verse, they exposed arbitrary aesthetic rules that came to symbolize the excesses of absolutism. Yet authors and critics struggled and disagreed for a long time on granting equality and freedom to prose, causing confusion, which is reflected in the *Encyclopédie*'s articles. Toward the end of the century, authors came to value the creative power of prose, and welcomed prose poems as a destabilizing category that would advance the cause of modernity in favor of equality. I single out Rivarol's alternative strategy to frame the issue in terms of national language to assert the independence of modern French over foreign prose.

Only the anonymous *Temple de Gnide* published in 1725 aroused such delight and enchantment as *Télémaque*. Though it has been considered a minor work, this underestimated and misunderstood pastoral allegory reveals the melancholy of one of the first Enlightenment philosophes. Montesquieu chose to salvage mythology at a time when it was under siege from the philosophical avant-garde, to convey his humanistic and poetic vision of love in contrast to the Regency's decadent morals. Chapter 3 exposes how the deft articulation between form and content in the *Temple de Gnide* communicated a spatial and temporal nostalgia: such nostalgia for a pastoral space and for virtuous times echoed themes Montesquieu developed in his fiction, and foreshadowed the conclusions of his philosophical works. A close reading of Montesquieu's *Temple de Gnide* helps discern the specific stylistic and thematic traits by which it sought a poetic affiliation. Because these stylistic conventions recur systematically throughout the century, the *Temple de Gnide* stands as a paradigm for the most distinctive features of the eighteenth-century prose poem as it developed in the second half of the century.

Why did Montesquieu feign the role of translator to introduce his prose poem? An essential source of rejuvenation and inspiration, prose translations of classical and foreign poetry propelled the dissociation of poetry from versification, hence the gradual awareness that poetry did and could exist without the ornament of verse. Chapter 4, "Translation to the Rescue," examines the role of Anne Dacier's prose *Iliad*, then turns to the second half of the century, which discovered original rhythms in the prose translations of Gessner's poems and Macpherson's *Ossian*. I argue that this moment of recognition, however important (and too often postdated to the Romantic era), did not suffice to invent "modern" prose poems. After this initial breakthrough, writers went through a transitional phase: they envisioned unversified poems as prose translations of virtual poems. I analyze this widespread strategy of "pseudo-translation," in imitation of Montesquieu, to show that it promoted hybridity ("métissage") and no longer purity as vital to poetry.

Whereas the previous chapter revealed how translations deconstructed the myth of purity, Chapter 5, "Back to the Bible," looks at how the eighteenth century constructed a mythology of poetry's origins, which has endured until today. The first part of the chapter highlights a surprising source of inspiration for an Enlightenment normally considered secular. The Bible in the vernacular, mother of all translations and all prose poems in many respects, stood in the eighteenth century as a model of poetic utterance divinely inspired and free of formal rules. This chapter recovers Robert Lowth's groundbreaking analyses of Hebrew sacred poetry (1753) and Charles Batteux's work on poetics (1746–1763), in particular their unprecedented emphasis on lyrical poetry. Lowth sought to demonstrate that a poetic utterance dating back to the divine creation of man was embedded at the core of the Bible. Lyrical expression, therefore, carried with it the memory of its origin. The symbolic return to the origins (of mankind and poetry) through lyricism is a defining trait of biblical epic prose poems penned by Enlightenment authors, including Rousseau and later, Chateaubriand.

When Rousseau asked "How to be a poet in prose?" the Bible, his daily companion, emerged as the model for an authentic poetic language unconstrained by the artifice of verse. This is best revealed in *Le Lévite d'Ephraïm* (written in 1762; published posthumously in 1781), a rewriting in neoclassical style of a violent passage from the book of Judges. Like Montesquieu's *Temple de Gnide,* this minor work from the pen of France's most original philosopher has been shunned as unworthy of his œuvre because of its odd theme and stilted style. Yet like Montesquieu, Rousseau chose to write a prose poem to work out a resolution to troubling issues raised in his fiction and treatises. I expose how the biblical passage is rewritten to reconcile the rights of individuals with those of the community, and further, how prose poems embody the quest for "the origin of languages" theorized in the *Essai sur l'origine des langues.*

As analyses of Hebrew poetry, new interpretations of the Bible, and essays—such as Rousseau's—on the origins of language multiplied, their controversial, unscientific conclusions challenged Enlightenment's rationality. Chapter 6 focuses on this turning point—a spiritual and aesthetic "reformation," countercurrent to the traditional understanding of the eighteenth century. I make the case that spirituality, eclipsed by the dominant ethos of progress and rationality, found a refuge in a form poetic enough to match the spiritual elevation sought by authors, yet modern enough to attract readers more favorably inclined toward prose than verse. Beneath the desire for a reformation of poetry, I read a strategy to integrate men's and women's spiritual longings within the philosophical revolution under way. Indeed, the unorthodox faith of eighteenth-century practitioners of prose poetry suggests a strong connection with their writing. Fénelon's advocacy of universal love, "quiétisme," influenced his choice of humanist prose. Rousseau's "natural religion" and Bernardin de Saint-Pierre's pastoralism belong to a similar spiritual vein, inspiring their lyrical narratives. The Revolution did not interrupt but intensified the poetic and spiritual quest, as evidenced by Saint-Martin's mystical "illuminism"—a movement too hastily dismissed as counter-Enlightenment. This chapter links the well-documented mysticism of nineteenth-century French prose poets with these earlier authors, whom I argue were precursors in sacralizing language, thereby reforming the poet's mission and status.

The seventh and last chapter, "New Rhythms," highlights three emblematic figures at the close of the century. The works of the poet Évariste Parny (1753–

1814), Chateaubriand (1768–1848), and the author/journalist Louis-Sébastien Mercier (1740–1814) expose how poetic systems and their contradictions are always radically historical and specifically situated. I discuss how Parny's poetry took a drastic turn after the Revolution, not only in terms of inspiration (from love to war) but also in terms of genres (from the lyrical to the epic), and in terms of form (from prose poetry to allegorical verse). Before the Revolution, Parny's poetry was a vocal search, the quest for a lyrical voice; after the Revolution, his poetry turned away from orality toward figures, a return to images and representations. Chateaubriand, who often referred to himself as a "sauvage," sought to recreate a sacred, inherently poetic, unmediated language in *Atala*'s Indian songs. But his ideal of primitive "poetics" clashed with the tragic reality of the effects of Christianization upon Native Americans.

Finally, Mercier's reformist views on French language and literature place him at the forefront of his century's movement to modernize the field of Belles-Lettres. Although Mercier also wrote visionary fictions, this most eloquent and perceptive defender of prose was a conflicted practitioner of the "poëme en prose." As Mercier's œuvre is finally being reprinted, its cross-breeding of old and new genres needs to be questioned as closely as the modern accents of his manifestoes.

In dismissing eighteenth-century "poëmes en prose" or misreading their obscure origins, literary history has shaped a positivist narrative of French Enlightenment literature as well as prose poetry. The texts examined in this study evince as much a modern thrust toward an experimental aesthetic as a cautious, conservative adherence to neoclassical dictums. This is the primordial tension at the core of the texts and theories exposed here. When Bernard interrogated the essence of the French prose poem, she found it in its duality: "le poème en prose, non seulement dans sa forme, mais aussi dans son essence est fondé, sur l'union des contraires: prose et poésie, liberté et rigueur, anarchie destructrice et art organisateur ... De là sa contradiction interne, de là ses antinomies profondes, dangereuses et fécondes; de là sa tension perpétuelle et son dynamisme." (33) [the prose poem, not only in its form but also in essence, is founded upon the union of contraries: prose and poetry, freedom and rigor, destructive anarchy and organizing art ... Hence its internal contradiction, hence its profound, dangerous, and fecund antinomies; hence its perpetual tension and dynamism.] These antinomies, intrinsic to post-Baudelairian prose poems Bernard analyzed, also presided over the genre's emergence, as it broke through a hyper-regulated literary field. The current misunderstanding as to the exact nature of eighteenth-century prose poems comes, simply, from the anachronistic projection of a post-Romantic definition of poetry. This definition presents poems as ontological and autotelic, whereas eighteenth-century prose poems still followed the Horatian "delectare" and "prodesse" mantra. In addition to the didactic purpose pursued by authors, this study will highlight a "purposiveness" behind each text, to use Kant's terminology: many writers of prose poems pursued a quest for a socio-political, historical, and spiritual consciousness to set the Enlightenment and later, the turmoil of the Revolution, in perspective.

Chapter 1
Telemacomania

Fénelon fut le premier auteur qui à la cour ait parlé du peuple.
[Fénelon was the first author who spoke of the people to the court.]

Louis-Sébastien Mercier[1]

Reviewing a new edition of Fénelon's *Les Aventures de Télémaque*, a critic
from the French daily *Libération* remarked: "La prose poétique de Fénelon est
kitsch comme un printemps à Eurodisney."[2] [Fénelon's poetic prose is kitsch like
springtime at Eurodisney.] In the twentieth century, Fénelon's style thus compared
to a spring day in European Disneyland, the epitome of kitsch. This perception
of Fénelon's flowery prose as bordering low and popular taste for artificial
wonderlands rejects *Télémaque*'s aesthetic as outmoded while acknowledging its
former popular appeal, a clue perhaps to its phenomenal success. A bestseller in
France and abroad for over a century, *Les Aventures de Télémaque* (1699) enjoyed
a popularity and longevity hard to imagine nowadays when references to the
classics and mythology have faded, when literary taste shuns didacticism, and
when we perceive as precious a style meant to seem natural. None other than
Balzac tolled the knell of all that *Télémaque* represented: the appeal of myths
and allegories, the taste for the marvelous, the longing for classical epic heroes
and deeds, the nostalgia for a golden age in politics and poetics. In his famous
description of the Vauquer's bourgeois boardinghouse at the opening of *Le Père
Goriot* (1834), Balzac embedded a damning commentary on Fénelon's utopia.
When we penetrate into the first-floor "salon," we discover on its walls a colorized
wallpaper depicting scenes from Fénelon's prose poem. Its reproducibility as
wallpaper and its presence in the pension Vauquer doubly confirms its downgrading
as "kitsch"—decorative, mass-produced, and mass-consumed:

> Le surplus des parois [du salon] est tendu d'un papier verni représentant les
> principales scènes de *Télémaque*, et dont les classiques personnages sont coloriés.
> Le panneau d'entre les croisées grillagées offre aux pensionnaires le tableau du
> festin donné au fils d'Ulysse par Calypso. Depuis quarante ans cette peinture
> excite les plaisanteries des jeunes pensionnaires, qui se croient supérieurs à leur
> position en se moquant du dîner auquel la misère les condamne.[3]

---

[1]   Louis-Sébastien Mercier, "Si le poète dramatique doit travailler pour le peuple,"
in *Du Théâtre* (1773), in *Mon Bonnet de nuit suivi de Du Théâtre*, ed. Jean-Claude Bonnet
(Paris, 1999), 1322.

[2]   Eric Loret, "Cahier livres," *Libération*. March 9, 1995.

[3]   Honoré Balzac, *Le Père Goriot* (Paris, 1976), 53.

[The rest of the wall space is covered with varnished paper depicting the principal scenes from *Télémaque*, with the classical characters in color. The panel between the meshed windows presents the borders with a picture of the banquet given by Calypso for Ulysses' son. For forty years this painting has provoked numerous sallies from the younger residents, who try to demonstrate their superiority by making fun of the fare to which their penury condemns them.][4]

The tenants' jokes, comparing Calypso's lavish spread as she greeted Telemachus to their own skimpy meals, made a mockery of Fénelon's *locus amoenus* and its utopian abundance. Balzac continued his realist description with an implicit debunking of Fénelon's best-selling aesthetics as lifeless: the absence of fire in the stone fireplace, the faded artificial flowers "caged" in vases on the mantelpiece, and the tasteless bluish marble clock mock a bygone aesthetics. Most memorable is the insufferable smell of the parlor, "une odeur sans nom dans la langue" [an odor for which there is no name in the language] also a metaphor for time and decay ("[cette pièce] sent le renfermé, le moisi, le rance" [it smells stuffy, mouldy, rancid]), the olfactory negation of the ambrosia so often invoked in *Télémaque*.[5] Before moving on to the dining room, Balzac summarized the parlor's decorative wallpaper as "ces plates horreurs" [dull horrors]. The oxymoron seems to refer to the horrible dullness and staleness of the room, yet could we not speculate that the epithet "plates" conveyed above all Balzac's verdict concerning Fénelon's celebrated descriptions, and therefore should be translated literally? Philostratus' *Les Images ou Tableaux de platte peinture* had long been an enticing model for artistic descriptions, and Fénelon's contemporaries raved about the pictorial quality of scenes from his prose poem.[6] Rendering them as "flat horrors" on wallpaper, Balzac literally flattened the poetic embellishments that generations of readers had enjoyed, the better to discard the "kitsch" of Fénelonian prose in favor of his realistic *Comédie humaine*.

And yet *Les Aventures de Télémaque* is in its own right a remarkable human comedy, if only because, as Mercier reminded us, "Fénelon fut le premier auteur qui à la cour ait parlé du peuple" [Fénelon was the first author who spoke of the people to the court.] *Les Aventures de Télémaque* had a determining influence on European Enlightenment and on generations of authors as it proposed an aesthetic competing both with traditional and modern genres (epic poetry and the novel).[7] The aim of this chapter is to reveal the pivotal role of Fénelon's prose poem in destabilizing the French generic system, and to understand what Thomas Bebee

---

⁴   Honoré Balzac, *Père Goriot*, trans. A.J. Krailsheimer (Oxford, 1999), 4–5. Translation modified.

⁵   Balzac, *Père Goriot*, 53, trans. Krailsheimer, 4–5.

⁶   Blaise de Vigenère translated Philostratus' *Les images ou tableaux de plattes peintures* in 1578, an edition illustrated with engravings starting in 1614. See Philostrate, *La Galerie de Tableaux* (Paris, 1991).

⁷   See Albert Chérel, *Fénelon au XVIIIᵉ siècle en France (1715–1820): Son prestige, son influence* (Geneva, 1970).

refers to as "ideological struggles" behind the generic instability provoked by Fénelon's text:

> [I]f genre is a form of ideology, then the struggle against or the deviations from genre are ideological struggles. Jameson locates literature outside the constraints of genre. I locate it in those texts where the battle is most intense, where the generic classification of a text determines its meaning(s) and exposes its ideology.[8]

Bebee's theoretical approach of "the ideology of genre" can be fruitfully applied to eighteenth-century prose poems, which I read as chief among "those texts where the battle is most intense," beginning with the work that jumpstarted the ideological struggle between prose and poetry, *Les Aventures de Télémaque*. Balzac's choice to situate the realist novel in contradistinction to Fénelon's prose epic perfectly illustrates the "genre's volatility and flux as a cultural system." The trimphant Balzacian novel succeeded in overshadowing an alternative fictional genre, making us forget its covert, subversive nature.

Primarily a book on morals and politics, wrapped in the fiction of Ulysses' wandering son, filled with classical reminiscences and contemporary political allusions, *Les Aventures de Télémaque* was extraordinarily successful at pleasing readers eager to conjoin usefulness and delight ("l'utile et l'agréable"), and who enjoyed entertaining adventures that included wise instructions on life. The exasperated reaction of Fénelon's most virulent critics, Nicolas Gueudeville and the abbé Faydit, testifies to the sweeping success of *Les Aventures de Télémaque*. Faydit's book began with an explanation of its title: "Je l'ai intitulé *Telemaco-manie*, pour marquer l'injustice de la passion, & de la fureur avec laquelle on court à la lecture du Roman de Telemaque, comme à quelque chose de fort beau, au lieu que je prétends qu'il est plein de deffauts, & indigne de l'Auteur."[9] [I have called it *Telemaco-mania* to emphasize the injustice of the passion and furor with which people have been hurrying to read the novel of Telemachus, as if it were something truly beautiful, whereas I claim it is full of flaws and unworthy of its author.] Faydit was contesting the misplaced admiration for a new aesthetics, which to him unacceptably breached traditional codes. However invisible Fénelon's transgression might have become today, his prose epic transformed politics and literature: Fénelon imagined a democratic opening vs. the closure of absolutism, which he conveyed by means of a prose overture toward poetry.

Fénelon's "project of prose" in *Télémaque* has received scant attention, even though the reason for, and the possibility of, the book's existence can only be understood by taking into account Fénelon's choice of prose. Fénelon broke away from the eloquent, rhetorical style of his previous religious treatises and sermons

---

[8]   Thomas Bebee, *The Ideology of Genre* (Pennsylvania Park, 1994), 19.

[9]   Abbé Faydit, *La Télémacomanie, ou la censure et critique du roman intitulé: Les Avantures de Telemaque Fils d'Ulysse, ou suite du quatrieme Livre de l'Odyssée d'Homere* (1700), 5.

to try out a prose fit to continue the Homeric poem and entice his young pupil. This book of adventures was specifically written for the Duke of Burgundy, grandson of Louis XIV, a potential ruler who, it turned out, would never reign. Fénelon overcame the practical challenge to instructing an impetuous young man through what might be called the pedagogy of prose, since verse would prove inadequate to render the pulse of the hero's emotions, and would distort the pace of his journey to match a pre-given rhyme scheme. In addition, prose left Fénelon free to daydream about and idealize benevolent government in the absence of real world pressure, given that Fénelon's pupil was normally not destined to rule.[10] Fénelon chose prose to continue Homer's epic poem as befitting the fin-de-siècle aspiration for accessible leadership, better governance, and an end to socio-political subjection.[11] By using prose instead of verse, he advocated for less absolute aesthetic as well as political rules.

We can see how much of a threat Fénelon's text represented in Gueudeville's critique from 1700 which ties the book's style and its content as equally nonsensical and outright disgusting. First comes the denunciation of *Télémaque*'s distasteful "flowery, sugary" style, downgrading its genre in the category of Scudéry's novels. The critic purposely avoids the nobler terms poem or poetry, referring alternatively to "petit Roman," and to poetic or versified prose. In bad taste, the public's hunger for the book signals the beginning of a decline, which the author fears is not only aesthetic but also "un fâcheux augure pour la durée de la Monarchie" [an unfortunate augur for the lasting of the Monarchy].[12] The remainder of the critique completely subverts Fénelon's idealized portrait of a benevolent king by claiming it as a realistic mirror to the "fair" economic, political, and religious decrees of Louis XIV (on taxes, wars, and the extermination of "Huguenotism.")[13] Morever, Gueudeville's eulogy of Louis the Great's absolutism praises as a positive sign the lack of parliamentary debate and the absence of "Cahiers [de doléances] sédicieux presentez dans une assemblée par les Députez du Peuple" [seditious cahiers presented in an assembly by the People's deputies.][14] It is quite stunning to find a reference to the "cahiers de doléances" in a work from 1700 critical of the first prose poem—such cahiers were only written under Henry IV and would only be written one more time for the 1789 Réunion des états généraux, prelude to the Revolution—a reference which seems indicative of the subversive power of

---

[10]   See Pierre Barbéris, "Télémaque/Modernité, Désir/Roman/Utopie et Langage de la Contre-Réforme," in *Je ne sais quoi de pur et de sublime ... Télémaque*, ed. Alain Lanavère (Orléans, 1994), 30.

[11]   "Gouverner les peuples contre leur volonté, c'est se rendre très misérable, pour avoir le faux honneur de les tenir dans l'esclavage" [To assume the government of a people by force, is to make one's self very miserable, to have the false glory of keeping them in subjection.] Fénelon, *Les Aventures de Télémaque* (Paris, 1995), 157. *The Adventures of Telemachus, the Son of Ulysses*. Translated by Tobias Smollett (Athens and London, 1997), 100. Hereafter cited in text.

[12]   Nicolas Gueudeville, *Critique générale des Aventures de Télémaque* (1700), 62.

[13]   Ibid., 82.

[14]   Ibid., 77–8.

people's prose and the concern that it might infiltrate poetry and politics, with a disastrous outcome. The author remarks that poverty suits French people; therefore it is only fair to maintain them in such state. By the end of the pamphlet, Fénelon's poetics clearly emerge as dangerous politics: "Si un Roi observoit tous ces divins préceptes, il deviendroit la victime de son Peuple, & sa condition seroit pire que celle d'un particulier."[15] [If a King observed all these divine principles, he would become the victim of his people, and his condition would be worse than that of a private person.] The critic seems to fear that Fénelon's *Télémaque* announced what we now know as the French Revolution.

Almost overnight, the prose poem became a new means of expression emblematic of the discontent with absolutism in poetry and politics. *Télémaque* inaugurated this struggle on a symbolic level by substituting the dictatorship of verse for the freedom of prose, and by replacing an absent father figure with the allegorical figure of Minerva. Instead of a chief exercising personal authority, Fénelon presented his pupil and readers with the abstract entity of a Marianne-like Republic, a collegial authority and benign polity. In place of the masculine, autocratic father and monarch, Minerva embodies the humanist ideal of a republic—a republic of prose.

We should note here that Fénelon and his contemporaries were living in a France on the edge, within a changing Europe wherein northern Protestant countries, economically and politically more liberal, were rapidly emerging.[16] How could French people resist this influence? Fénelon was well aware that one of the Protestants' weapons of conquest was, of course, their Bible: the sharp edge of Luther's prose translation had cut through Catholic allegorical interpretations. The penetration of minds was easier, the reading of the world simpler, the conquest of markets faster. If Fénelon's humanist utopia was a Counter-Reformation as Pierre Barbéris argues, it is logical that he chose to voice his project in the same "prosaic" language as the Reformers.[17] Markedly different from his own former style, this more supple prose, able to voice "la solitude, l'angoisse, la mort, l'appel de la mer et de l'ailleurs, l'erreur, la quête" [solitude, anguish, death, error, quest, the call of the sea and of the beyond] also departed radically from Bossuet's.[18] At the time when Fénelon wrote *Télémaque*, Bossuet was a towering rival whose *Discours sur l'histoire universelle* offered an austere religious model of thinking and teaching. To displace this discourse, to tell a spiritual story, and imagine a different history than Bossuet's, there had to be a means as powerful as eloquence but more innovative than neoclassical verse—hence a foray into unorthodox, un-Cartesian prose poetry. I will return to this crucial link between the tradition of "devout humanism" represented by Fénelon and the choice of prose poetry in Chapter 6 to show how it might explain the aesthetic choices of authors like Rousseau.

---

[15] Ibid., 86.

[16] See Barbéris, "Télémaque/Modernité," 30.

[17] Ibid., 41.

[18] Ibid., 31.

A *"Je-Ne-Sais-Quoi"*: Hybridity

Télémaque's utopian Counter-Reformation was political as well as literary: in politics, it remained a dream, taken up by a succession of political thinkers; in literature, it turned into a competition with versified poetry to establish prose. For its commentators, *Télémaque* is a "je ne sais quoi," an unclassifiable text, but has "un je ne sais quoi," a fascinating seductive power embodied in Mentor that Montesquieu, Rousseau, Chateaubriand, and lesser-known eighteenth-century *prosateurs* sought to capture. Why was the genre of *Les Aventures de Télémaque* so constantly revisited? The ideological import of its aesthetics, which I have just suggested, is also rooted in the politics of genre. In a century where strict rules and the theory of *imitatio* dominated the literary field, one should look first for the ways in which Fénelon circumvented dogma and tradition. In a pertinent analysis, Noémi Hepp showed how the book breached the hierarchy of genres and escaped classification both as an epic poem and as a novel.[19] Although it retained key elements of the classical epic poem (for instance an opening *in medias res*, the presence of gods, the importance of war), Hepp argues that the main action is too abstract to fit the tenets of epic poetry. It pushed to the extreme Le Bossu's requirement that the epic poem improve morals via an allegorical story. Telemachus's adventures are not motivated by the necessity of action, as in Homer's *Odyssey* or Virgil's *Aeneid*. The action is mostly an interior one, the hero's moral improvement: "C'est un voyage de l'âme passant du règne de la nature à celui de la grâce."[20] [It is the journey of a soul moving from the reign of nature to the reign of grace.]

Hepp shows how the characterization of the hero is yet another element dissociating Fénelon's work from an epic poem: there is none of the traditional, required *hubris* in Telemachus, only virtue and obedience combined with gratuitous acts of heroism. Testing one's valor at will—and not from necessity—was a staple of seventeenth-century novels, such as Madeleine de Scudéry's famous *Cyrus* and *Clélie*. Telemachus is related to "héros de roman" in the sense that his personality and actions lack verisimilitude given his youth. Lack of verisimilitude is also palpable in many of the plot's episodes, reminiscent of *L'Astrée*'s carefree, idealized environment, wherein the sheep take care of themselves while the characters engage in discursive courtship. Hepp also points to the twisted, convoluted nature of many an adventure recounted by Telemachus as being akin to the complicated episodes commonly found in novels. The narrative contract between the characters, the creation of suspense, and the love triangle at the beginning of the book also partake of the techniques of the novel. This was not lost on Fénelon's contemporary critics. Adversaries of the novel quickly classified *Télémaque* as belonging to the

---

[19] Noémi Hepp, "De l'épopée au roman. L'*Odyssée* et *Télémaque*," in *Je ne sais quoi de pur et de sublime*, ed. Alain Lanavère, 223–35.

[20] Ibid., 227.

reviled genre.[21] For critics such as the abbé Faydit, the "gallant" (i.e., erotic) content of the story left no doubt concerning the generic determination of the work and its forerunners, as his scathing apostrophe to Fénelon reveals:

> Il semble que vous ayez vécu toute vôtre vie avec les anciens Poëtes & M[y]thologistes ... & que vous sçachez vos Scuderis & vos Desjardins par cœur, tant vous parlez bien Roman, & avez bien pris les manieres de ces Auteurs & Autrices Galantes. ... vous êtes tout d'un coup tombé dans la basse region des faiseurs de Romans, des Perraults & des Perroquets. [22]

> [It seems that you have lived all your life with ancient poets and mythologists ... and that you know your Scudérys and your Desjardins by heart, since you speak so well, like a novel, and have taken up the manners of these gallant men and women authors. ... you have suddenly fallen into the low region of novel makers, of Perraults and parrots.]

Despite its connection to both the novel and the epic poem, *Les Aventures de Télémaque* eventually failed to satisfy convincingly the requirements of one or the other. Hepp saw this failure in the prevailing indeterminacy of the book. First, there is an incertitude about "la nature du beau: est-il dans l'art ou dans la nature?"[23] [the nature of the beautiful: is it in art or nature ?] exemplified by the description of Calypso's cave, fraught with baroque tendencies. Further, Fénelon's conception of the gods is a hybrid of polytheism (in keeping with their classical origins) and monotheism (Fénelon's credo), resulting in far-fetched resolutions of conflict. Finally, a moral incertitude weighs on the entire narrative:

---

[21] Faydit found *Télémaque* doubly heretical: it resembled a novel, and its author was a religious leader who should have submitted to the Church's condemnation of such fictions: "la Coupe du Vin empoisonné de la Prostituée de Babylone; car c'est ainsi que les Pères ont nommé tous ces Livres détestables, qui, sous des fictions ingenieuses, & élegamment écrites, ne contiennent que des Histoires de Galanterie & d'amourettes, des descriptions fabuleuses du Temple, & du Palais de Venus, & de l'Isle enchantée de l'Amour, & de l'Empire du petit Cupidon avec ses fléches, comme du plus grand des Dieux" [the poisoned wine cup of Babylon's whore; for this is how the Fathers have called all these detestable books which under ingenious, well-written fictions only contain stories of seduction and love affairs, fabulous descriptions of Venus' temple and palace, of love's enchanted island, and little Cupid's empire, decked with arrows as if the greatest of gods.] Faydit considered that the unfortunate popular success of *Télémaque* had spread the seed of corruption farther than any of Fénelon's questionable theological doctrines: "Mr. De Cambray a plus offensé Dieu, & plus fait de mal en composant *son Telemaque*, qu'en composant *ses Maximes des Saints*, en écrivant un Roman de Galanteries, qu'en écrivant un Livre Heretique, & remply des erreurs du Quietisme" [M. de Cambray has offended God more by composing his *Telemachus* than by composing his *Maxims of the Saints,* more by writing a novel of seduction than by writing a heretical book, filled with the errors of Quietism.] Faydit, *Télémacomanie*, 19 and 29.

[22] Ibid., 42.

[23] Hepp, "De l'épopée au roman," 232.

L'auteur oscille entre pessimisme et optimisme ... On sent le dilemme du
pédagogue qui voudrait à la fois encourager son élève à rechercher le bien en le
convainquant qu'il est accessible, et le préparer à arracher sans fin les mauvaises
herbes de l'existence, en lui en montrant la multiplicité.[24]

[The author hesitates between pessimism and optimism ... One senses the
dilemma of the pedagogue who would like both to encourage his student to
search for the good by convincing him that it is accessible, and to prepare him to
pull out the weeds of existence endlessly, by pointing out their multiplicity.]

Hepp concludes that it was not so much the non-adherence to the principles of the
epic poem or those of the novel that undermined generic classification, but the fact
that Fénelon's pedagogical imperatives led to a crisscrossing of perspectives: "s'il
y a unité d'inspiration au plan éthique, elle ne se traduit pas en unité d'inspiration
au plan esthétique, et c'est pour cela surtout que nous ne pouvons classer l'œuvre
dans aucun genre littéraire."[25] [If there is unity of inspiration ethically, it does not
translate into unity of inspiration aesthetically; therefore we cannot classify this
work in any literary genre.]

Hepp tackled the issue of genre to conclude with an impossible classification.
Barbéris reread *Télémaque* to redefine its modernity for twentieth-century readers,
but reached an impasse on the issue of its genre. While in agreement with the
analyses of both critics, I would argue that their conclusions side-step a crucial
issue: "telemacomania," in other words the amazing publishing phenomenon of
Les Aventures de Télémaque, and the colossal impact it had on literary debates
of all kinds.[26] What generated interest and endless conversations could only be
that which could not be pinpointed, which confounded expectations and remained
elusive: the seduction of the *je-ne-sais-quoi*, the evasion of class(ification). *Les
Aventures de Télémaque* defines itself precisely by the indeterminate, uncertain
rank it occupies on the ladder of literary production. Reflecting on the problematic
genre of Baudelaire's *Petits poèmes en prose*, Barbara Johnson reminded us that
"le 'poétique' *n'est rien d'autre qu'un code*. C'est ce fonctionnement de la poésie
en tant que code qu'interroge Baudelaire dans *L'Invitation au voyage* en prose. Et
si le 'genre' des *Petits poèmes en prose* fait problème, c'est à cause d'une semblable
lutte des codes qui a lieu à la fois entre les poèmes en prose et les poèmes en vers,
et *à l'intérieur* de chaque poème en prose."[27] [What is 'poetical' is nothing but
a code. The way poetry works as a code is what Baudelaire wonders about in
L'Invitation au voyage in prose. The 'genre' of *Small Prose Poems* is problematic
because of a similar *competition of codes* taking place between prose poems and
poems in verse, and *within* each prose poem.] Fénelon's prose epic inaugurated
a similar struggle between a neoclassical poetical code and the modern code of

---

[24]   Ibid., 233.
[25]   Ibid., 234.
[26]   Faydit, *Télémacomanie*, 18.
[27]   Johnson, *Défigurations*, 106.

prose. In addition, the book's mixing and matching of genres horizontalized an established hierarchical structure, thus opening endless speculations about the advisability of reproducing this breakthrough gesture in literature, with concerns that it might spill over into society. Very likely, this critical vista onto new generic combinations was not the real cause for the average reader's enthusiasm. He or she was simply, massively, conquered by the readability, accessibility, and promises of the text—a direct, if magnified, result of Fénelon's pedagogical strategy. *Les Aventures de Télémaque* was not originally intended for publication and only came to print inadvertently. Writing this work for the sole benefit of his pupil, Fénelon had the unparalleled freedom to bend the rules and accommodate the means to his educational goal. The aesthetic indeterminacy noted by Hepp cannot be interpreted as a shortcoming. The space of the "entre-deux" has the advantage of rallying opposites, be it pagan and Christian gods, nature and art, pessimism and optimism, or prose and poetry. As in Calypso's cave, opposites attract, offering readers an imaginary space of possibilities out of the confines of socio-political and aesthetic stratification.

One has to wait until the twentieth century to find an original understanding of *Télémaque*'s complexities and poetical riches: by this I do not mean literary critics, but a poet, Louis Aragon, whose first major publication somewhat surprisingly and humorously relied on the Fénelonian bestseller. Let us fast forward to post-WWI France: a twenty-five-year-old Aragon (1897–1982), who had just met André Breton and Tristan Tzara, founder of the Dadaists, wrote a prose poem titled *Les Aventures de Télémaque*, a "hypertext" or imitation of Fénelon's bestseller.[28] What exactly inspired Aragon and why? His exceptional prose poem *en miroir* draws from those elements in Fénelon's text that are already poetically and erotically charged, from its baroque undercurrent to its distortion of reality and its disregard for verisimilitude. When one reads the two prose poems side by side, the poetic unbinds the didactic and vice versa. Granted, a twentieth-century poet, a surrealist moreover, was bound to be inspired by the more modern aspects of the original text, but this renders the comparison between Fénelon and Aragon all the more illuminating. While neoclassical, Fénelon's prose poem points toward modernity: it already contained for Aragon some of the elements that surrealism would cultivate.

Télémaque, Source of Inspiration for Aragon

Aragon published *Les Aventures de Télémaque* in 1922, the same year as another prose poetic venture to rewrite the *Odyssey*, James Joyce's *Ulysses*. Aragon's short text—an imaginative gloss of Fénelon's *Les Aventures de Télémaque* written two centuries earlier—represents one of the most important pre-surrealist works,

---

[28] Louis Aragon, *Les Aventures de Télémaque* (Paris, 1966). See Gérard Genette, *Palimpsestes. La littérature au second degré* (Paris, 1982), 14. For a comparative analysis of Aragon's and Fénelon's texts, see 505–9.

a creative recapitulation of Aragon's Dadaist experience. Aragon's prose poem condenses the first six books of Fénelon's fiction, a beginning also known as the famous Calypso episode. Aragon's process of "transtylisation" offers surprising insights into the early eighteenth-century text now more or less fossilized in anthologies.[29] Aragon learnt how to read and, as Gérard Genette suggests, also learnt how to write from this very book.[30] *Télémaque,* as well as Chateaubriand's *Atala,* were commonly included in grammar courses as writing models—one of many significant connections between the two "poëmes en prose." Aragon retrieved and rewrote a familiar story, in the lineage of Lautréamont's subversive practice of rewriting the classics.

Leaving out the political passages most often excerpted from *Télémaque* for inclusion in school curricula, Aragon embraced only the controversial and erotic Calypso episode, thereby disrobing the book of its long-standing demagogic garb. He heightened the one episode that enchanted, disturbed, or outraged Fénelon's contemporaries, that elicited the most commentaries and controversies because it stood out as completely *novel.* The ascending pace of the chapters, the constant wavering of the main characters, and chassé-croisé of lovers build a suspense markedly different from pastoral narratives and precious novels such as *L'Astrée* and *Cyrus.* Fénelon's depiction of the havoc wrecked by intense passion was a classical reminiscence of Virgil's Dido, perhaps an echo of Racine, but also anticipated the evolution of the budding genre of the novel, which was moving away from the Princesse de Clèves's restrained emotions toward the passionate intensity of Rousseau's character Julie. As Barbéris underlines:

> l'utopie-projet doit absolument tenir compte du fait passionnel et désirant, intégrer certaines formes de l'intense que la modernité ne saurait ignorer. ... Le "charme" du roman de Fénelon ne serait-il pas venu de là, de cette reconnaissance (aux deux sens de légitimation et d'exploration) du désir et de l'amour comme inévitables composantes de toute modernité?[31]

> [the project/utopia must absolutely take into account passion and desire, and integrate certain forms of intensity that modernity cannot ignore. ... Could not the "charm" of Fénelon's novel come from this fact, from this recognition (both in the sense of legitimation and exploration) of desire and love as unavoidable components of modernity?]

Moving away from ancient tradition of "amour courtois" as well as Racine's representations of passion as tragic, in other words leaving behind medieval courtship as well as Jansenist condemnation, the prelate Fénelon portrayed love with aplomb and suspense, as a thrilling but ambiguous emotion that threatens critical judgment, yet with which reason must contend. Neither idealized as in medieval romances nor chastised as in Catholic sermons, Fénelon's portrayal of love, couched in seductive prose, was risqué and psychologically astute.

---

[29] Genette, *Palimpsestes*, 413.

[30] Ibid., 509.

[31] Barbéris, "Télémaque/Modernité," 35–6.

"Le délire véhément des lyres"

Contrasting the first pages of Aragon and Fénelon exposes the powerful erotic undertones of Telemachus's first trial. Aragon's brilliant condensation goes to the gist of the story, a strip tease that eventually exposes Telemachus, Mentor, Calypso, and Eucharis in the nude. The first sentence of each text launches the same plot with contrasting images.

> Calypso ne pouvait se consoler du départ d'Ulysse. Dans sa douleur, elle se trouvait malheureuse d'être immortelle. Sa grotte ne résonnait plus de son chant; les nymphes qui la servaient n'osaient lui parler. (Fénelon 31)[32]

> Calypso comme un coquillage au bord de la mer répétait inconsolablement le nom d'Ulysse à l'écume qui emporte les navires. Dans sa douleur elle s'oubliait immortelle. Les mouettes qui la servaient s'envolaient à son approche de peur d'être consumées par le feu de ses lamentations. (Aragon 13–14)[33]

The sober style of Fénelon's opening in short, declarative sentences conveys Calypso's pervasive sadness. In contrast, a flourish of stylistic features marks Aragon's rearrangement: the dispersal of the consonant [c] and the vowel [o] from the name Calypso, in the first sentence, conjures both the word "écho" and its echoing effect. The comparison of Calypso to a seashell reinforces this acoustic image with the reverberating sound of endless waves. The dramatically condensed "elle s'oubliait immortelle," the nymph-like seagulls, and the metaphoric burning fire of Calypso's lamentations, all intensify the original poetic opening while preserving its subtle tone.

Closely following Fénelon, Aragon then projects onto an anthropomorphic landscape Calypso's obsession with Ulysses, whose laughter, shouts, and caresses remain suspended in the air. Thus the beginning of both texts draws out the irony of depression when suffered in an eternal springtime:

> Elle se promenait souvent seule sur les gazons fleuris dont un printemps éternel bordait son île: mais ces beaux lieux, loin de modérer sa douleur, ne faisaient que lui rappeler le triste souvenir d'Ulysse, qu'elle y avait vu tant de fois auprès d'elle. (Fénelon 31)[34]

---

[32] "Calypso remained inconsolable for the departure of Ulysses. Thus afflicted, she found herself miserable in being immortal. Her grotto no longer resounded with her songs. Her attendant nymphs were afraid to speak to her." Fénelon, *AT*, trans. Smollett, 3.

[33] "Like a seashell on the beach, Calypso disconsolately repeated the name of Ulysses to the foam that carries ships afar; unmindful in her sorrow of her immortal self. The seagulls in attendance took flight when she approached for fear of being consumed by the fire of her lamentations." Aragon, *AT*, trans. Huberts, 35.

[34] "She often walked solitary upon the flowery turf, which a perpetual spring had diffused around her island. But these charming retreats, far from ass[u]aging her grief, served only to recall the melancholy remembrance of Ulysses, by whom she had been so often accompanied." Fénelon, *AT*, trans. Smollett, 3.

> Le rire des prés, le cri des graviers fins, toutes les caresses du paysage
> rendaient plus cruelle à la déesse l'absence de celui qui les lui avait enseignées.
> (Aragon 14)[35]

When a shipwreck brings Mentor and Telemachus ashore, the goddess understands
immediately that this look-alike Ulysses is his son:

> Cependant Calypso se réjouissait d'un naufrage qui mettait dans son île le fils
> d'Ulysse, si semblable à son père. (Fénelon 32)[36]

> Cependant Calypso retrouvait avec joie son amant fugitif en ce jeune naufragé
> qui s'avançait vers elle. Connaître déjà ce corps qu'elle apercevait pour la
> première fois la troubla plus que ne faisaient ces taches brillantes, les varechs
> collés par l'eau vive aux membres polis de Télémaque. Elle se sentit femme et
> feignit la colère. (Aragon 14)[37]

However short, Fénelon's sentence inscribes between the lines Calypso's actual
phantasm through the phrase "mettre dans son île" and the phonetic proximity of
"île" and "lit," suggesting "un naufrage qui mettait dans son *lit* le fils d'Ulysse."
Aragon chose to spell out the goddess's joy and desire: Telemachus is her "fugitive
lover." The poet follows the goddess's eyes following the contours of the young
man's glistening body, and utters her troubling discovery: "Connaître déjà ce corps
qu'elle apercevait pour la première fois ..." (Aragon 14). The delightful paradox
of knowing yet not knowing, the tantalizing "première fois" juxtaposed with the
gaze of the déjà-vu electrifies this first encounter. Calypso heightens her pleasure
by resisting a powerful attraction, feigning to be displeased by the intrusion.
Suddenly, in each version, the gaze overpowers speech:

> Calypso, étonnée et attendrie de voir dans une si vive jeunesse tant de sagesse et
> d'éloquence, ne pouvait rassasier ses yeux en le regardant; et elle demeurait en
> silence. Enfin elle lui dit: "Télémaque, nous vous apprendrons ce qui est arrivé
> à votre père." (Fénelon 32)[38]

---

[35] "The laughter of the meadows, the cries of the fine gravel, all the caresses of the
landscape made her miss more cruelly the absent lover who had taught her to perceive
them." Aragon, *AT*, trans. Huberts, 35.

[36] "Mean while this goddess rejoiced at the shipwreck which had thrown on her isle
the son of Ulysses so much the image of her father." Fénelon, *AT*, trans. Smollett, 4–5.

[37] "Meanwhile, Calypso joyfully rediscovered her fugitive lover in that young
castaway advancing toward her. Her foreknowledge of this body which she had never
glimpsed before troubled her more than the shining spots of seaweed the surging waters
had pasted on Telemachus's polished limbs. Feeling womanly, she gave a false display of
anger." Aragon, *AT*, trans. Huberts, 36.

[38] "Calypso astonished, and affected by so much wisdom and eloquence in such
early youth, surveyed him in silence, as if her eyes could never be satisfied. At length,
'Telemachus,' said she, 'we will inform you of what has happened to your father.'" Fénelon,
AT, trans. Smollett, 4.

Calypso, mieux attentive aux mouvements de son cœur qu'à ceux de ces discours, n'osait rompre par la parole ou le mouvement le charme qui retenait ses regards sur cette forme trop humaine. Le vertige qui brouilla ses yeux l'engagea par la crainte de soi-même à casser tout à coup le silence.

"Télémaque, votre père ..." (Aragon 15)[39]

Aragon elaborated on what remained implicit in Fénelon's scene, as the latter revolved around the powerful negation of the verb "rassasier," suggesting the intensity of Calypso's appetite. Stories become a means of exchange: Calypso detains the knowledge of Ulysses' fate, and Telemachus the exciting tale of his own adventures. Calypso's contract is implicit in Fénelon, explicit in Aragon. After singing Ulysses' deeds, she offers Telemachus happiness (that is to say her body) and her kingdom: "vous trouvez ici une divinité prête à vous rendre heureux et un royaume, qu'elle vous offre" [you here find a divinity ready to make you happy, with a kingdom in your reach].[40] Aragon's Calypso offers herself forthrightly: "acceptez, Télémaque, ma couche, mon royaume et la divinité" [accept, Telemachus, my bed, my kingdom, and godliness] and Telemachus is ready to succumb: "A ces mots le jeune homme rougit et attacha si bien ses regards au corps de la déesse qu'il n'entendit que distraitement le récit des aventures d'Ulysse" [At these words, the young man blushed and stared so intently at the body of the goddess that he paid but little attention to the tale of Ulysses' adventures].[41] The name of the father is drowned in "le délire véhément des lyres" [the vehement delirium of the lyres], the hero is overwhelmed by "les pavots des paroles" [narcotic words], "les contes du désir" [the tales of desire] against which Mentor vainly warned his protégé.[42] Beseeched—besieged—by the goddess eager to learn the secret of his heart, Aragon's Telemachus begins to tell the story of his adventures, which abruptly ends three pages later with a concluding sentence that lures the reader into anticipating the rest of the young man's journey, whereas Aragon, telescoping time, is anticipating the imminent danger of love assailing young Telemachus.[43] Henceforth departing from Fénelon's pedagogical treatise, the remainder of the poem follows the characters as they relinquish their wills to passion, unto death.

Fénelon developed a lengthier narrative. The longer Calypso holds Telemachus captive under her gaze with entreaties to tell his story in detail, all the while ensuring that interruptions prolong her pleasure, the longer Fénelon holds his

---

[39] "Calypso, more attentive to the motions of her heart than to the movements of his speech, did not dare break, either by word or gesture, the charm that riveted her eyes to this all too human form. The dizziness that blurred her vision forced her, for fear of herself, to shatter all a sudden the silence. 'Telemachus, your father ...'" Aragon, *AT*, trans. Huberts, 37.

[40] Fénelon, *AT*, 36, trans. Smollett 7.

[41] Aragon, *AT*, 19, trans. Huberts, 42.

[42] Fénelon, *AT*, 17–18, trans. Smollet, 40.

[43] Aragon, *AT*, 23.

reader's interest. Therefore Calypso urges Telemachus to hold back (his story/ further pleasure) until the next morning.[44]

The following two books relate the hero's adventures in search of Ulysses. The sixth book recounts his first experience of love and his struggle to resist, which reaches a climactic conclusion. The ravages of passion rang true to the ears of Fénelon's contemporaries. Though introduced by the hackneyed arrows of the cherub Love, allegory quickly gives way to a very realistic portrayal of Calypso's black jealousy, of Telemachus's mad infatuation with Eucharis, and the nymph's disorder. Calypso cannot make herself be loved despite her immortal might, nor stop loving *because* of her immortality. Telemachus wishes to follow Mentor, but is held back by the magnet of Eucharis' yet-to-be-discovered body: the dilemma faced by each character brings chaos and anarchy to the island. The escape vessel is eventually set on fire upon the orders of an infuriated Calypso. Only a push and a shove by Mentor into the "onde amère" [bitter sea] awaken Telemachus back to his (moral) senses. I read Fénelon's take on the passions as another form of the absolute with dangerous consequences. The famous episodes of Calypso falling in love and of Telemachus under Eucharis' spell enchanted Fénelon's contemporaries thanks to a seductive prose, yet the seduction acts as a warning that passions subvert reason and politics.

"Je ne sais où je suis"

Eighteenth-century admirers and detractors alike kept mentioning and commenting on a specific episode: the description of Calypso's abode at the opening of the book. This description holds the key to deciphering the long-standing appeal of the book, and the reason behind the new generic label coined on its behalf, "poëme en prose." Again, Aragon's gloss on *Les Aventures de Télémaque* provides an enlightening clue to the acclaimed page describing Calypso's grotto. Or rather, Aragon's choice *not* to rephrase the first half of the description indicates his satisfaction with the original as it stood. Why would the surrealist poet be content with a paragraph, which, upon a first reading, does not seem to hold any surprises?

> On arriva à la porte de la grotte de Calypso, où Télémaque fut surpris de voir, avec une apparence de simplicité rustique, tout ce qui peut charmer les yeux. On n'y voyait ni or, ni argent, ni marbre, ni colonnes, ni tableaux, ni statues: cette grotte était taillée dans le roc, en voûte pleine de rocailles et de coquilles; elle était tapissée d'une jeune vigne qui étendait ses branches souples également de tous côtés. Les doux zéphyrs conservaient en ce lieu, malgré les ardeurs du soleil, une délicieuse fraîcheur. Des fontaines, coulant avec un doux murmure sur des prés semés d'amarantes et de violettes, formaient en divers lieux des bains aussi purs et aussi clairs que le cristal; mille fleurs naissantes émaillaient

---

[44] "Il est temps, lui dit-elle, que vous alliez goûter la douceur du sommeil après tant de travaux" ["It is time," said she, "that you refresh yourself with a little rest after such immense fatigue."] Fénelon, *AT*, 79, trans. Smollett, 39.

les tapis verts dont la grotte était environnée. Là on trouvait un bois de ces arbres touffus qui portent des pommes d'or, et dont la fleur, qui se renouvelle dans toutes les saisons, répand le plus doux de tous les parfums. Ce bois semblait couronner ces belles prairies et formait une nuit que les rayons du soleil ne pouvaient percer. Là on n'entendait jamais que le chant des oiseaux ou le bruit d'un ruisseau, qui, se précipitant du haut d'un rocher, tombait à gros bouillons pleins d'écume et s'enfuyait au travers de la prairie. (Fénelon 33)

[When they arrived at the entrance of Calypso's grotto, Telemachus was astonished to see such a profusion of all that could delight the view, mingled with the appearance of rural simplicity. True it is, here was neither gold nor silver, neither marble columns, pictures, nor statues: but the grotto was scooped out of the rock in arcades abounding with pebbles and shell-work; and it was lined with a young luxuriant vine, extending its pliant branches equally on every side. The balmy zephyrs here preserved a most delicious coolness, in spite of the sun's heat. Fountains, sweetly murmuring as they ran along the meadows, adorned with amaranths and violets, formed in different parts delightful baths, as pure and transparent as crystal. A thousand springing flowers enameled the green carpet with which the grotto was surrounded. And here was seen a wood of those trees that bear the golden apple, which flower in every season, and diffuse the sweetest of all perfumes. This wood that seemed to crown those charming meads produced a shade which the sun's rays could not penetrate. There nothing was ever heard but the songs of birds, or the sound of a rivulet, which gushing from a rock on high, and boiling and foaming as it fell, escaped across the adjacent meadow.] (Smollett 4–5)

The carefully drawn description could be interpreted as heralding the age of descriptive poetry, the hallmark of eighteenth-century poetics. This description, however, is not at all comparable in nature with Jacques Delille's descriptive poems (aside from the absence of rhymes.)[45] Indeed, what sets it apart, as Aragon immediately perceived, was not the descriptive quality of the passage, but the imaginary nature of the description, the fact that it is non-representational. The description conveys Fénelon's fantasy of so-called "natural beauties," which Calypso reveals to her guest. This paradisiacal space is purely imaginary and metaphoric. The particular delight, or annoyance, of Fénelon's contemporaries derived from the unfamiliar reading experience created by this wonderland. One of Fénelon's most vocal critics, Nicolas Gueudeville, thus dissected the description:

Où ce sublime auteur veut-il donc nous placer? Dans la Grotte? Hors de la Grotte? Tout de bon je ne sçais où je suis ... Quel est cet espèce de Roc dans le sein duquel on trouve un paysage enchanté, & où l'on peut goûter tous les délices de la Zone tempérée? Depuis que le Monde est Monde, s'est-on jamais avisé de dire que le vent servit de parasol au fond d'une grotte?[46]

---

[45] See, for instance, Jacques Delille's *Les Jardins*, in particular the third song on "jets d'eau," in *Anthologie de la poésie française du XVIIIᵉ siècle*, ed. Michel Delon, 360–61.

[46] Gueudeville, *Critique générale des Aventures de Télémaque (1700)*, 69–70.

[Where does this sublime author want to put us? Inside the cave? Outside the cave? Truly, I know not where I am ... What kind of rock is this, wherein one finds an enchanted landscape, and tastes all the delights of a temperate climate? Since the world has existed, has anyone dared say that the wind served as a parasol at the bottom of a cave?]

In his adherence to codes of verisimilitude, which legitimized imaginary, pastoral descriptions as long as they did not wander into uncharted realms, the critic cannot account for such a disturbing, *un*real site. Like his contemporaries, he found himself lost in poetic space. I would conjecture that Aragon's delight with the Fénelonian fantastic space meant he felt no need to change it. The cave is, already, anachronistically, "surrealist," at the antipodes of the representational mode we have come to associate with the genre of the novel. Indeed, antithesis rules this poetic space: the defining rhetorical figure of the passage is both obvious and subtly woven into the description. Antithesis comes in five pairs: 1) simplicity yet richness: the "appearance of rustic simplicity" is transcribed within a semantic field of riches ("voûte," "cristal," "émailler," "tapis," "pommes d'or," "couronner," "parfums," "chant"); 2) inside yet outside: "une jeune vigne" and "des zéphyrs" bring nature *inside* the cave; 3) hot yet cool: "malgré les ardeurs du soleil, une délicieuse fraîcheur;" 4) outside yet inside ("des bains," "les tapis verts" surround the cave); 5) day yet night ("une nuit que les rayons du soleil ne pouvaient percer"). In this world of paradoxes, there is but one season, a perpetual spring, symbolized by the constant blossoming, "dans toutes les saisons," of orange trees, conveyed by the softness of tactile ("branches souples," "doux zéphyrs"), auditory ("doux murmure"), visual ("fleurs naissantes"), and olfactory sensations ("le plus doux de tous les parfums"). In keeping with the tradition of a golden age fantasy of abundance, Fénelon employed the required tropes. However, the construction of a logically impossible space undermines the illusion he attempted to create: therein lay the poetry and mystery of a description whose magic held sway over so many imaginations.

Sexual and Baroque Undertow

The second half of Fénelon's description paints the view outside the cave: comparisons and metaphors invent a universe not so much disorienting as metamorphosed by a poetic gaze.

La grotte de la déesse était sur le penchant d'une colline. De là on découvrait la mer, quelque fois claire et unie comme une glace, quelquefois follement irritée contre les rochers, où elle se brisait en gémissant, et élevant ses vagues comme des montagnes. D'un autre côté, on voyait une rivière où se formaient des îles bordées de tilleux fleuris et de hauts peupliers qui portaient leurs têtes superbes jusque dans les nues. ... On apercevait de loin des collines et des montagnes qui se perdaient dans les nues et dont la figure bizarre formait un horizon à souhait pour le plaisir des yeux. Les montagnes voisines étaient couvertes de pampre vert, qui pendait en festons: le raisin, plus éclatant que la pourpre, ne pouvait se cacher sous les feuilles, et la vigne était accablée sous son fruit. Le figuier, l'olivier, le grenadier et tous les autres arbres couvraient la campagne et en faisait un grand jardin.

Calypso, ayant montré à Télémaque toutes ces beautés naturelles, lui dit ... (Fénelon 34)

[The grotto of the goddess was situated upon the declivity of a little hill, from whence there was a prospect of the sea, sometimes clear and smooth as glass, sometimes as madly raging, dashing itself against the rocks with furious din, and spouting its billows mountain high. On the other side was the view of a river that formed a number of islands, bordered with flowering limes, and tall poplars that raised their lofty heads even to the clouds. The different streams by which the islands were formed, seemed to sport along the field; one rolling its crystal waves with rapidity, a second gliding with a gentle sleepy course; while others in long meanders returned as if they meant to revisit their source, and seemed incapable of leaving those enchanted scenes. At a distance appeared a number of hills and mountains, which seemed to lose themselves among the clouds, and whose fantastic figures formed an agreeable horizon to delight the view. The neighbouring mountains were covered with verdant vines hanging in festoons, and so loaded with fruit, that their leaves could not conceal the ripe clusters, more beautiful than the finest purple. The country was covered with all kind of trees, the fig, the olive, and the pomegranate; so that it looked like one extensive garden.

Calypso, having shewn these natural beauties to Telemachus ...] (Smollett 5)

Aragon transmuted the water imagery of this passage into a pervasive sexual symbolism of foamy glistening rocks, interior seas, and phallic penetration:

La grotte de la déesse s'ouvrait au penchant d'un coteau. Du seuil, on dominait la mer, plus déconcertante que les sautes du temps multicolore entre les rochers taillés à pic, ruisselants d'écume, sonores comme des tôles et, sur le dos des vagues, les grandes claques de l'aile des engoulevents. Du côté de l'île s'étendaient des régions surprenantes: une rivière descendait du ciel et s'accrochait en passant à des arbres fleuris d'oiseaux; des chalets et des temples, des constructions inconnues, échafaudages de métal, tours de briques, palais de carton, bordaient, soutache lourde et tordue, des lacs de miel, des mers intérieures, des voies triomphales; des forêts pénétraient en coin des villes impossibles, tandis que leur chevelure se perdait parmi les nuages; le sol se fendait par-ci par-là au niveau de mines précieuses d'où jaillissait la lumière du paysage; ... Le décor se continuait à l'horizon avec des cartes de géographie et les portants peu d'aplomb d'une chambre Louis-Philippe où dormaient des anges blonds et chastes comme le jour. Lorsqu'elle lui eut montré toutes ces beautés naturelles, Calypso dit à Télémaque. (Aragon 16)

[The Goddess's cave opened on the slope of a hill. Its threshold dominated a sea more disconcerting than shifts of weather; multicolored among precipitous rocks streaming with foam, sonorous as sheet metal, and, on the backs of waves, the great wing slaps of nightjars. The inland regions brought many a surprise: a river descended from the skies and, in its passage, hooked on to trees blooming with birds. Villas and temples, unknown structures, metal scaffoldings, brick towers, cardboard palaces formed a heavy and twisted braid bordering lakes of honey, landlocked seas, triumphal ways; forests wedged into impossible towns while their hair vanished in the clouds; here and there the ground split open to the level of precious mines from which flashed forth the landscape light; ... The setting stretched to the horizon by means of maps and the deviant struts of a Louis-Philippe bedroom where angels slept, blond and chaste as the day.] (Huberts 38)

Decrypting the latent content of the "natural" world in and around the grotto, Aragon's reading unlocked the desire and pleasure embedded in the education treatise, thus subverting its pedagogical intent.

Fénelon extended the puzzling paradoxical inner world of Calypso's grotto into an outer world replete with contrasts: each watery element (sea, waves, river, streams) is linked to an earthy element (rocks, mountains, islands), and earthy elements (poplars, hills and mountains) are linked to the sky (clouds), thereby uniting water, earth and sky. Fénelon also constructed his paragraph around the balance between wild and domesticated nature: the wild sea vs. the streams and their enchanting banks; the intimidating, fantastic shapes of the mountains vs. the alignment of the vines and the fruit trees in the "extensive garden." The island thus reconciles contraries, unlike Calypso's inner world, shaped by unresolved contradictions.

Moreover, the union of contraries takes place in a playful symphony. Parallel constructions underscore this baroque theme of play ("de là ... de l'autre côté;" "quelques fois ... quelques fois;" "les uns ... d'autres ... d'autres"), introducing continuity (between sea and land, streams and islands) and alternation (between calm and wild sea, between one stream's rolling waters, the sleepy course of another, and the meandering path of yet another). The mountains' festive attire, "covered with verdant vines hanging in festoons," and grapes "more beautiful than the finest purple" are also playful. The whole landscape seems to be participating in a merry performance: "les divers canaux ... semblaient se jouer dans la campagne," [the different streams ... seemed to sport along the field]; "la figure bizarre [des montagnes] formait un horizon à souhait pour le plaisir des yeux," [their fantastic figures formed an agreeable horizon to delight the view] and grapes play hide and seek as "le raisin ... ne pouvait se cacher sous les feuilles" [their leaves could not conceal the ripe clusters.] It is important to emphasize here the baroque tendencies of Fénelon's text. As Genette noted in the case of the poet Saint-Amant, "l'âme baroque ... se cherche et se projette dans le fugace et l'insaisissable, dans les jeux de l'eau, de l'air et du feu" [the baroque soul ... feels its way and projects itself into the fugitive and the elusive, into the playing of water, air and fire.] [47] The theme of play, in its wider sense of the world as a stage, and the symbolic importance

---

[47]   Gérard Genette, *Figures I* (Paris, 1966), 9.

of the sea in Télémaque's wanderings are central to this aesthetics.[48] The world of antithesis that lured contemporary readers and later prose poets also reflects a principle of baroque poetry:

> [T]oute différence est une ressemblance par surprise, l'Autre est un état paradoxal du Même, disons plus brutalement, avec la locution familière: l'Autre *revient au Même*. L'univers baroque est ce sophisme pathétique où le tourment de la vision se résout—et s'achève—en bonheur d'expression. [49]

> [Every difference is a resemblance by surprise, the Other is a paradoxical state of The Same; let us say it more bluntly, with the familiar phrase: the Other comes back to The Same. The baroque universe is this pathetic sophism where tormented vision is resolved and ends as a felicitous phrasing.]

With *Illuminations* Arthur Rimbaud broke this baroque mirror of self into the modern split subject—from "l'Autre revient au Même" to "Je est un autre." Rimbaud's *Illuminations*, via its phantasmagoric visions, constitutes a crucial intertext to Aragon's *Les Aventures de Télémaque*. Fénelon's nymph Eucharis appears as the heralder of Spring in *Après le déluge*, the first prose poem of *Illuminations*.[50] Aragon's "villes impossibles" directly invoke Rimbaud's "Villes" poems, in particular his second "Villes," and its association of urban and sea-related vocabulary: "Des chalets de cristal et de bois qui se meuvent sur des rails et des poulies invisibles. ... Des fêtes amoureuses sonnent sur les canaux pendus derrière les chalets. ... Sur les passerelles de l'abîme et les toits des auberges l'ardeur du ciel pavoise les mâts" [Castles of crystal and wood move on rails and invisible pulleys ... Festivals of love sound upon the streams which seem to hang in mid-air, behind the chalets. ... On the footbridges of the abyss, and on the roofs of the inns, the burning sky clings to the masts in little flags of shimmering heat.][51] In turn, Rimbaud's poem echoes the precious—and dangerous—fantastic maritime universe of Fénelon's Calypso: "Au-dessus du niveau des plus hautes crêtes, une mer troublée par la naissance éternelle de Vénus, chargée de flottes orphéoniques et de la rumeur des perles et des conques précieuses, —la mer s'assombrit parfois avec des éclats mortels" [Above the level of the highest crests is a sea troubled by the eternal birth of Venus, and covered with choric fleets and the distant murmurs of pearls and rare sinuous shells. Sometimes the sea grows dark with mortal thunders.][52] Parallelisms in imagery and vocabulary between Fénelon's Calypso episode and Rimbaud and Aragon's prose poems confirm the inaugural quality of the former. Fénelon forever transformed the *locus amoenus* dear to readers of pastorals into a complex vision fusing art and nature, imagination and reality, a

---

[48]   Ibid., 18.

[49]   Ibid., 20.

[50]   Arthur Rimbaud, "Après le déluge," *Illuminations* (Paris, 1984), 155–6.

[51]   Rimbaud, "Villes," *Illuminations*, 172–3; "Towns I," *Prose Poems from Les Illuminations*. Trans. Helen Rootham (London, 1932), 73.

[52]   Ibid.

world of comparisons and metaphors couched in prose that spurred the creation of subsequent prose poems. The sexual promises of Calypso's world and the dream universe it represents inspired two modern prose poets, thus demonstrating that Fénelon's poetic descriptions initiated a radically different use of prose dissociated from rationality and mere eloquence.

Minerva as Mentor

The comparison with Aragon's version has exposed the baroque and sexual undertow of Fénelon's text. But as we will see, Aragon further metamorphosed Fénelon's political message by inserting a Dadaist manifesto at the heart of his poem, in rebellion against his own times. Following his model, Aragon adopted Minerva, disguised as Telemachus's mentor, as the messenger of a reformist aesthetics and ideology.

The mysterious being at Telemachus's side speaks for the first time after the goddess Calypso's departure: Fénelon introduced Mentor as an "homme vénérable" whose identity Calypso cannot guess (she is an inferior goddess and does not know everything). Aragon describes him as "an abstraction" that the goddess cannot decipher (14). In the guise of an old man, Minerva, goddess of knowledge and wisdom, accompanies, guides, and protects Telemachus, unbeknownst to him. This imaginary character is central to Fénelon's pedagogical project, acting as an observer, a listener, and a substitute father figure. In addition, Mentor plays Fénelon's double as a tutor. A proto-*Bildungsroman* written to educate the Dauphin, *Télémaque* fits in the lineage of pedagogical books written for future governing princes to initiate them to leadership by progressively unveiling lessons of life and governance.

Mentor's double character as tutor and Minerva inscribes binarism at the core of the text. The harmony of contrasts surrounding the goddess's dwelling had paved the way for the introduction of Mentor as a paradox incarnate—a dual nature that encapsulates the ambivalence of Fénelon's writing. Immortal goddess and mortal human, woman and man, Mentor's sexual indeterminacy reflects the pervasive indeterminacy of the genre to which the text belongs. Indeed, one finds hermaphrodism embedded in many later prose poems, as in Baudelaire's "Le Tyrse," which embodies the genre's hybrid nature. I do not mean that Fénelon's prose poem foreshadows Baudelaire's per se, but I want to emphasize how *Les Aventures de Télémaque* already questioned in an unexpected manner issues of genre and gender. Implicitly associating poetry with the feminine and prose with the masculine was not an unprecedented gesture, as my next chapter will show. Nor should we mistake Fénelon for a transgressor when it came to gender norms. But though Fénelon's vision of gender did not overcome traditional binary opposition (as numerous examples attest), he proposed an intriguing reconciliation embodied by Minerva/Mentor, namely a "douce force."[53] The quality of "douceur" and the

---

[53] Mentor's sacred nature reveals itself when he plays the lyre and sings, transfixing his audience: "A peine osait-on respirer, de peur de troubler le silence et de perdre quelque

epithet "doux/douce" proliferate around the good masculine characters in striking contrast with a relentless denunciation of "mollesse" associated with the feminine and the effeminate. Fénelon rejected the extremes of masculinity (power) and femininity (softness) in favor of a combination of strength and sweetness. I wish to argue that this triangle maps out the gendered character of prose, poetry, and poetry in prose at the turn of the eighteenth century: in the literary field where *Télémaque* emerged, prose was becoming more powerful, whereas verse (now rarely epic) was softening poetry. Fénelon's denunciation of "mollesse" targeted aesthetics, not just morality and politics. Abhorrent "mollesse" stood as a metaphor for a political field peopled by flattering courtiers and its corollary, a poetic field reduced to seductive versification. In contrast, the "douceur forte" advocated (and embodied) by Minerva/Mentor proposed an alliance that translated politically into Republican virtues alleviating monarchy, and aesthetically into prose adopting poetics.

The very indeterminacy of Mentor's nature is the key to his mysterious power. He rises above the finite and comprehensible. Twice, a key phrase summarizes the impossibility of a definition: "Quand on le regarde de près, on trouve en lui *je ne sais quoi* au-dessus de l'homme" [Upon a nearer view, there appears in him something more than human.][54] When Calypso attempts to force Mentor into revealing his secret, she feels an inexplicable resistance: "Mais elle sentait toujours *je ne sais quoi* qui repoussait tous ses efforts et qui se jouait de ses charmes" [But she always found in him a certain secret energy, that repelled all her efforts, and baffled the force of her charms.][55] The essence of the eloquent Mentor is unnamable. Endowed with the two attributes of sacred poetry—mystery and superiority—Mentor symbolizes the writer's aspiration to invent a compelling mode of writing that is ineffable yet luminous, divine yet secular. Aragon captured this luminescence in a striking image:

> Pendant que Télémaque parlait, Mentor, fatigué du voyage, avait cessé de se surveiller et des rayons lumineux s'échappaient de son front. Calypso le regardait avec un étonnement mêlé de méfiance: le vieillard s'en aperçut, éteignit aussitôt la clarté de son crâne et prit un air modeste. (Aragon 20)

---

chose de ce chant divin ... La voix de Mentor n'avait aucune douceur efféminée. Mais elle était flexible, forte, et elle passionnait jusqu'aux moindres choses. Il chanta d'abord les louanges de Jupiter, père et roi des dieux et des hommes, qui, d'un signe de sa tête, ébranle l'univers. Puis il représenta Minerve qui sort de sa tête, c'est-à-dire la sagesse, que ce dieu forme au-dedans de lui-même et qui sort de lui pour instruire les âmes dociles" Fénelon, 152. [Hardly durst they venture to breathe, for fear of interrupting the silence, and losing some of these divine touches; they were in pain too, lest he should stop too soon. Mentor's voice had nothing of an effeminate softness in it, but was strong, pliant, sweet, and affecting. He first sang the praises of Jupiter, the father and king of gods and men; who, with a nod, shakes the vast universe. His next subject was Minerva, who sprung from Jupiter's head; by which is meant the wisdom that is formed therein, and which from thence descends to illuminate such as are open to instruction.] Fénelon, *AT*, trans. Smollett, 96. I will return in Chapter 6 to Fénelon's "divine" to argue that it also shaped the choice of poetry in prose.

[54] Fénelon, *AT*, 121, trans. Smollett, 69 (emphasis added).
[55] Fénelon, *AT*, 122, trans. Smollett, 72 (emphasis added).

[While Telemachus spoke, Mentor, exhausted by the trip, had ceased to hold himself in check: luminous rays were escaping from his brow. Calypso looked at him with a mixture of astonishment and distrust: noticing this, the old man immediately extinguished the luminosity of his pate and assumed an air of modesty.] (Huberts 43–4)

In showing the beam of light escaping from Mentor's forehead, the gold behind the lying wrinkles (*ment-or* = *or menteur*), Aragon reveals more (and sooner) than Fénelon:

Semblable à un rocher escarpé qui cache son front dans les nues et qui se joue de la rage des vents, Mentor immobile dans ses sages desseins, se laissait presser par Calypso. Quelquefois même, il lui laissait espérer qu'elle l'embarrasserait par ses questions et qu'elle tirerait la vérité du fond de son cœur. Mais, au moment où elle croyait satisfaire sa curiosité, ses espérances s'évanouissaient, tout ce qu'elle s'imaginait tenir lui échappait tout à coup, et une réponse courte de Mentor la replongeait dans ses incertitudes. (Fénelon 122)

[Like a high towering rock, whose summit is hid among the clouds, and which the most furious winds assail in vain, did Mentor remain unshaken in his purposes against all the attempts of the goddess. Sometimes he would make her fancy that she should be able to entangle him by her questions, and extract the secret from the inmost recess of his soul. But the moment she fondly hoped her curiosity would be satisfied, all her hopes vanished. What she thought she had a fast hold of in an instant slipped away: and some concise reply of Mentor reinvolved her in all her doubts and uncertainty.] (Smollett 72)

Mentor resembles a slippery rock whose summit shines in the sun. An old man on the outside, a radiant goddess in the inside, he could symbolize prose enshrining poetry, with the double identity of Mentor/Minerva mirroring the dual identity of the prose poem. Prose veils the bright poetic light at the core of the text, its shiny truth. Mentor's lengthy disquisitions, which have been accused of slowing the narrative, are in fact necessary for Telemachus and the reader to reach truth progressively. This excess of prose, so to speak, is a characteristic of pre-Baudelairian prose poems. Aragon, in the spirit of his model, albeit in a facetious tone, draws attention to the difficulties and excesses of this mode of speech by alluding to the orator Demosthenes: "Le vieillard Mentor gravissait le coteau. Il roulait dans sa bouche un caillou pour se délier la langue, comme chacun sait" [Old Mentor was climbing the slope, rolling in his mouth a pebble to loosen his tongue, as everybody knows.][56] The prosaic rock in the mouth of the poet liberates a flow of words: "Mentor le long de la mer s'exerçait inlassablement à l'éloquence. Il criait tout d'une haleine des phrases difficiles à prononcer" [Along the shore Mentor unflaggingly practiced his eloquence. He shouted all in one breath tongue twisting sentences.][57] At this point, Aragon inserted a five-page "exhortation" transcribed

---

[56]   Aragon, *AT*, 29, trans. Huberts, 56.
[57]   Aragon, *AT*, 30, trans. Huberts, 57.

in italics which corresponds to the Dadaist manifesto he published in *Littérature* under the title *Système Dd. (Introduction à une morale momentanée)* (30–35). This manifesto champions Lautréamont's rhetoric of anti-rhetoric with Dadaist élan. Thus, in the end, even the pedagogical nature of Fénelon's text served Aragon's pursuit of a Dadaist agenda at the antipodes of his predecessor: two hundred years later, "le mentor" could convey still another message.[58]

Poets and novelists are often more creative than academics in interpreting literature. Aragon recognized an inspiring poetics behind a didactic fiction but also played with the process of decoding and encoding that is the hallmark of palimpsest-like narratives such as *Les Aventures de Télémaque*. If we now return to the eighteenth century, we can see more clearly how and why Enlightenment authors prodded *Télémaque*'s poetic layers and imitators capitalized on its success.

Takes from Marivaux and Rousseau

Among the almost unanimously enthusiastic and admiring reactions from Fénelon's contemporaries, I wish to single out Rousseau and Marivaux who re-appropriated Fénelon's text using opposite strategies, each opening new vistas onto the Fénelonian space. In Rousseau's *Émile,* Sophie's sentimental awakening and her passionate longing for a soul mate begins with her infatuation for the character Telemachus: "Sophie aimait Télémaque, et l'aimait avec une passion dont rien ne put la guérir" [Sophie was in love with Telemachus, and loved him with a passion which nothing could cure.][59] Her mother discovers the secret of her languor: "elle voit enfin, avec une surprise facile à concevoir, que sa fille est la rivale d'Eucharis" [she discovered to her great surprise that her daughter was the rival of Eucharis.][60] Sophie explains to her dismayed parents: "je ne veux point un prince, je ne cherche point Télémaque, je sais qu'il n'est qu'une fiction: je cherche quelqu'un qui lui ressemble" [I desire no prince, I seek no Telemachus, I know he is only an imaginary person; I seek someone like him.][61] Predictably, she finds her Telemachus in Émile when he is invited to partake of their supper. Rousseau staged their encounter in a delightful double-entendre scene where Émile alone is unaware of what is truly implied in his identification with Fénelon's hero, suggested by Sophie's father. The repartee of his tutor (whom the narrator called here "his Mentor") identifies Sophie with Eucharis, the nymph invented by Fénelon with whom the hero falls in love:

---

[58]   The name Mentor contains many interesting anagrams and/or echoes: beside the obvious "mentor" and "or" [gold] one finds "tort, mort, tome, mot" [tort, death, volume, word].

[59]   Rousseau, *Émile ou l'éducation* (Paris, 1961), 513. *Émile or Education by Rousseau*, trans. Barbara Foxley (London, 1925), 367.

[60]   Ibid.

[61]   Ibid.

vous êtes arrivés ici, votre gouverneur et vous, las et mouillés, comme Télémaque et Mentor dans l'île de Calypso. Il est vrai, répond Émile, que nous trouvons ici l'hospitalité de Calypso. Son Mentor ajoute: Et les charmes d'Eucharis. Mais Émile connaît l'*Odyssée* et n'a point lu *Télémaque*; il ne sait ce que c'est qu'Eucharis. Pour la jeune personne, je la vois rougir jusqu'aux yeux, les baisser sur son assiette, et n'oser souffler.

["your tutor and you arrived wet and weary like Telemachus and Mentor in the island of Calypso." "Indeed," said Émile, "we have found the hospitality of Calypso." His Mentor added, "And the charms of Eucharis." But Émile knew the *Odyssey* and he had not read *Telemachus*, so he knew nothing of Eucharis. As for the young girl, I saw she blushed up to her eyebrows, fixed her eyes on her plate, and hardly dared to breathe.][62]

Rousseau concludes the scene with the fulfillment of Sophie's secret wish: "son tender cœur palpite de joie, et lui dit que Télémaque est trouvé" [her tender heart is throbbing with joy, and it tells her she has found Telemachus.][63] Eventually Émile's tutor asks Sophie to give up Fénelon's book, which she offers to Émile in exchange for his *Spectator*, a transaction accompanied by the following, gender-specific advice from the tutor: "Etudiez-y les devoirs des honnêtes femmes, et songez que dans deux ans ces devoirs seront les vôtres" [Study the duties of good wives in it, and remember that in two years' time you will undertake those duties.][64] The exchange underscores that, in contrast to *The Spectator,* Fénelon's book was construed as a manual of initiation to leadership and also love, dangerous indeed for its female readers.[65] In the hands of a male reader, Émile, the book turned into a political initiation guide, as he sought to find in the real world Fénelon's happy, utopist society (Salentum) and his good rulers (Idomeneus, Philocles), but became quite disappointed. Émile's tutor was not educating a future king, like Fénelon, but a *citoyen*, hence Rousseau's departure from the imaginary world of *Les Aventures de Télémaque*: "Au reste, Émile n'étant pas roi, ni moi dieu, nous ne tourmentons point de ne pouvoir imiter Télémaque et Mentor dans le bien qu'ils faisaient aux hommes. ... Nous savons que Télémaque et Mentor sont des chimères. Émile ne voyage pas en homme oisif et fait plus de bien que s'il était prince" [Moreover, Émile is not a king, nor am I a god, so that we are not distressed that we cannot imitate Telemachus and Mentor in the good they did ... We know that Telemachus

---

62   Ibid., 525. Rousseau, *Émile*, trans. Foxley, 376–7.

63   Ibid., 528. Rousseau, *Émile*, trans. Foxley, 378.

64   Ibid., 573. Rousseau, *Émile*, trans. Foxley, 413.

65   "Est-il possible que Mr. de Cambray, qui est si éclairé, n'ai pas prévû tant de funestes suites qui proviendront de son Livre? Les jeunes filles les plus modestes, & les Religieuses même les plus austeres s'autoriseront par son exemple, & s'exciteront à lire des Romans" [Is it possible that M. de Cambray, who is so enlightened, has not anticipated the many disastrous consequences that will come of his book? The most modest young women and even the most austere nuns, will feel authorized by his example, and will get excited reading novels.] Faydit, *La Télémacomanie*, 21.

and Mentor are creatures of the imagination. Émile does not travel in idleness and he does more good than if he were a prince.][66] Rousseau's separation of the sentimental and the political in Fénelon's book anticipates Aragon's similar dissociation, and pinpoints sentiments as the origin of readers' *jouissance* in *Les Aventures de Télémaque*. Sophie's powerful reaction to Telemachus's love struggle contrasts with Émile's dissatisfaction with the political treatise. Rousseau later remedied the perceived defects of Fénelon's work by meshing moral lesson and love story in *Julie, ou la nouvelle Héloïse*.

Marivaux's *Le Télémaque travesti* (written in 1714, published and disavowed in 1736) was, according to Frédéric Deloffre's introduction, partly "une œuvre de circonstance, destinée à combattre le parti des Anciens" [a circumstantial work, aimed at combating partisans of the Ancients.][67] When Fénelon animated the ancient Homeric poem and its descriptions (such as Alcinous' gardens), Homer was still popular among readers, but the avant-garde considered him retrograde, outdated and in bad taste, as Moderns such as Perrault and La Motte had argued in their quarrel against the Ancients—a quarrel in which Marivaux participated by subverting Fénelon's *Télémaque*.[68] In September 1775, the *Bibliothèque universelle des romans* published excerpts from Fénelon's work under the category "political and moral novels." The editors then decided to publish the entire first half of Marivaux's parody in the very next volume, in October 1775, under the category "comic novels."[69] The juxtaposition between the venerated text and Marivaux's long parodistic novel (three hundred and twenty pages divided in sixteen books) created a great uproar, a testimonial to the veneration readers still nursed with regard to Fénelon's prose poem seventy-five years after its publication.

Marivaux's story follows the journey of the provincial Brideron, alias Timante, whose uncle (his mentor) forced him to read Fénelon's work. From then on, Timante models from this textual guide his own adventures in search for his father, a captain sent to war in a German regiment. In the tradition of Sorel's *Le Berger Extravagant*, yet another hypertext, Marivaux parodied Fénelon's plot, characters, as well as his style:

> O jeune Brideron! Car le *O*! entroit de moitié dans l'imitation du langage, songez-vous à ce que vous allez faire? ... Cette remontrance n'est pas tout-à-fait aussi noblement exprimée qu'elle devoit l'être, mais ce Mentor de nouvelle fabrique comptoit cinquante années pour le moins d'usage dans un tour d'expression campagnard, & n'étoit métamorphosé en Mentor que depuis quelques heures.[70]

---

[66] Rousseau, Émile, 597.Trans. Foxley, 431.

[67] Frédéric Deloffre, introduction to *Le Télémaque travesti* by Pierre Marivaux (Geneva, 1956), 21.

[68] See Genette, *Palimpsestes*, 210–14.

[69] See Roger Poirier, *La Bibliothèque universelle des Romans. Rédacteurs, textes, public* (Geneva, 1976), 46.

[70] Marivaux, *Le Télémaque travesti* (Geneva, 1956), 54.

[O young Brideron ! for the *O* was half of the way to imitate language, have
you thought of what you are about to do? ... This reproach is not quite as nobly
expressed as it should be, but this Mentor of a new cloth who had at least fifty
years of practice in a rustic turn of phrase metamorphosed into Mentor only a
few hours ago.]

Marivaux attacks the Fénelonian hero's false virtues, born of pride and desire for
admiration.[71] Brideron falls constantly short of matching his model's merits:

[F]ranchement le pauvre garçon sentoit bien que le Télémaque du Livre qu'il
avoit lû, étoit plus courageux que lui, mais il est plus aisé d'être roc dans une
feuille imprimée, d'être tranquille relié en veau, qu'en chair & en os plein de
santé.[72]

[Frankly, the poor boy did feel that Telemachus in the book he had read was far
more courageous than him, but it is easier to be a rock on a printed page, to be
calm when bound in calfskin, than in flesh and blood and full of life.]

The narrator's burlesque prose closely follows Fénelon's text, as is the case with
the episode where Brideron enters the castle of Mélicerte alias Calypso. Fénelon's
famous description is skillfully transposed:

On entra bien-tôt dans le Château. Un Escalier non superbe & hardi, mais simple,
étroit, & rare par ses differens & obscurs détours, conduisoit aux Appartemens.

Les Chambres du Château brilloient d'une beauté naturelle qui ne devoit presque
rien à l'art; l'or, l'argent, & le marbre étoient exilez de ces lieux; mais la fraicheur,
beaucoup de propreté, & le sage arrangement des Meubles, remplaçoient une
inutile magnificence.

Tous les Lits étoient reculez dans un coin sombre, comme pour marquer que le
sommeil & l'obscurité sont amis l'un de l'autre.

... En entrant dans ces Chambres, les yeux, comme dans ces Appartemens
superbes, n'étoient point ébloüis de ce grand jour qui perce à travers ces larges
croisées; ici la lumière & l'obscurité partageoient la place; ils y lutoient tous
deux, le jour s'y trouvoit obscurci, l'obscurité s'y trouvoit éclairée; ils restoient

---

[71]   "dans le fonds le mépris est justement dû à des Heros dont les Vertus ne sont à vrai
dire que des Vices sacrifiés à l'orgueil de n'avoir que des Passions estimables. Admirez-
vous des Hommes qui courent à la Vertu, non par l'envie de la suivre mais pour attraper
l'admiration qui l'accompagne?" [In the end, we ought to despise Heroes whose Virtues are
in fact only Vices sacrificed to the pride of having only respectable Passions. Do you admire
Men who run after Virtue not because they want to pursue it but to catch the admiration that
it entails?] Marivaux, "Avant-Propos de l'Auteur," *Le Télémaque travesti*, 47.

[72]   Ibid., 57–8.

aux prises, & ce combat offroit le spectacle agréable du jour et de la nuit tout ensemble.[73]

[We soon entered the castle. A staircase, not bold and superb, but simple, narrow, and rare on account of its different and obscure turns, led to the apartments.

The rooms of the castle shone from a natural beauty that owed almost nothing to art; gold, silver, and marble were exiled from the place; but coolness, all-around cleanliness, and the wise arrangement of furniture replaced useless munificence.

Every bed was tucked in a somber corner, as if to mark that sleep and obscurity were friends with one another.

... Upon entering these rooms, one's eyes were not blinded by the bright sunlight that shines through the casements as in superb apartments; here, light and darkness divided the space; here, they fought each other, and light was darkened, and darkness was lighted. They remained entwined, and this battle offered the pleasant spectacle of night and day altogether.]

Marivaux constructed a paradoxical space similar to Fénelon, where art and nature, light and day commingled, the better to undermine it with a mock-poetic, mock-heroic tone. This metaphoric exaggeration highlights the ambiguous nature and fragile balance of Fénelon's poem in prose. From a Homeric topos, Fénelon had conjured up a happy vision out of sync with the reality of his time but relished by a nostalgic majority. Marivaux's parody, very briefly sketched here, stirred an indignation symptomatic of the standing of *Les Aventures de Télémaque* by 1775: fondly remembered by most, but no longer sacrosanct.

Nostalgia for the Epic

Les Aventures de Télémaque was the instrument of Fénelon's pastoral mission to educate a virtual ruler. The golden age extolled in the Bétique episode represented an ideal to be reached, not a thing of the past but the picture of a future to be built: "ce n'est plus le regret d'un âge disparu, c'est l'espoir d'un 'âge d'or' à venir, ou dans lequel du moins le rêve peut se reposer à l'aise" [It is no longer the regret of a bygone era, it is the hope of a 'golden age' to come, or where dreams, at least, can rest easily.][74] In his study of *Télémaque*'s reception throughout the eighteenth century, Chérel showed how the initial phase of mystical and theological readings of *Télémaque*'s golden age episodes gave way to a second phase of "laïcisation" [secularization]. Moving beyond the "savante parabole" [learned parable], critics

---

[73]   Ibid., 64.

[74]   Chérel, *Fénelon au XVIIIe*, xvii.

and imitators focused on the literary seduction of the text:[75] in effect, *Télémaque* became the golden horizon of literary hopes and a writing model. "C'est de tous les livres celui que j'aimerois le mieux avoir donné au monde" [Out of all books, this is the one I would have most liked to give to the world], Marmontel confessed in l'*Essai sur les romans.*[76]

As the next chapters will show, paratexts often developed as the result of a strategy to situate problematic literary fictions within a familiar generic framework. But authors also let their readers infer the status of their literary production in a more direct manner, thanks to a palimpsest-like structure—what Genette has coined "hypertextualité" (texts derived from pre-existing texts).[77] A cluster of eighteenth-century epic prose poems can be defined as hypertexts of Fénelon's *Les Aventures de Télémaque*, their common, foundational "hypotext"—itself hypertext to the *Odyssey*. Transformations of *Télémaque* by eighteenth-century prose poets provide additional clues to the genre's early development.

The largest category of authors who sought to emulate *Télémaque* related to it primarily as an epic. In addition to poetic codes (division in cantos, allegories, ekphrasis, time condensation, stock epithets, "style coupé," etc.), authors dutifully adopted the well-known codes particular to the epic: grand scale, lofty tone, long speeches, narration of adventures, Greek or Roman background, to cite the most recurrent. They also imitated traits specific to *Télémaque* but instead of providing an exhaustive list of these appropriations, which concern both form and content, I will focus on their capturing the sentimental aspect of *Télémaque* that undermined its epic status.

I have already noted how *Télémaque* oscillates between epic tradition and the more modern "culture" of the novel. Genette reads this hesitation as clearly leaning toward the "romanesque" or novelistic:

> à travers les erreurs, les tentations surmontées, les épreuves, les bons et mauvais exemples et les leçons opportunes de Mentor, Télémaque subit un véritable apprentissage, évidemment destiné, par procuration, au duc de Bourgogne, et dont le principe (évolution et formation d'un caractère) est tout à fait étranger au fixisme résolu de l'épopée ... et constitue l'un des traits les plus marqués d'une dérive de l'épique au romanesque—fût-il édifiant.[78]

> [Throughout trials and errors, good and bad examples, the temptations he overcame and Mentor's opportune lessons, Telemachus undergoes a genuine apprenticeship, obviously intended, vicariously, for the Duke of Burgundy. Its

---

[75]   Marguerite Haillant, introduction to *Les Aventures de Télémaque, fils d'Ulyssse* by Fénelon (Paris, 1995), 195.

[76]   Cited by Jacqueline Lauret in "Une épopée en prose au XVIIIe siècle," in *Les Incas ou la destruction de l'Empire du Pérou. De l'Encyclopédie à la Contre-Révolution. Jean-François Marmontel (1723–1799)*, ed. Jean Ehrard (Clermont Ferrand, 1970), 203.

[77]   Genette, *Palimpsestes*, 13.

[78]   Ibid., 250–51.

principle (character formation and evolution) is entirely foreign to the epic's definite rigidness ... and represents one of the most outstanding traits of the epic drifting toward the romanesque, albeit edifying.]

Telemachus's emotional and intellectual maturation, at the center of the book, excludes him from the circle of immutable epic characters, and consequently displaces the story into the field of the novel, given that the epic poem's "fixisme psychologique est bien un trait de genre plutôt que de civilisation—on le retrouve d'ailleurs dans l'épopée médiévale" [its fixed psychology is really a characteristic of genre rather than civilization—indeed, it can be found in medieval epics.][79] In light of the hero's character development and Fénelon's pedagogical mission to educate the Dauphin, Genette concludes: "On peut donc définir *Télémaque* comme une greffe sur l'épopée antique d'un (si j'ose ce monstre) *Bildungsroman ad usum delphini*" [Therefore, we can define Telemachus as a graft, onto ancient epic poetry of (if I dare coin such hybrid) a *Bildungsroman* for the dauphin's use.][80] Epic prose poems written in imitation of *Télémaque* followed its lead in the direction of the *Bildungsroman*, like Chancierces's *Les Aventures de Néoptolème, fils d'Achille, Propres à former les Mœurs d'un jeune Prince* (1718, rev. 1756), Puget de Saint-Pierre's *Les Aventures de Periphas, descendant de Cecrops* (1761), Simon Mamin's *Aventures d'Ulysse, dans l'isle d'Aeaea* (1752), Galtier de Saint Symphorien's *Les Céramiques ou Les Aventures de Nicias et d'Antiope* (1760), and Moutonnet-Clairfons's *Les Iles fortunées ou Les Aventures de Bachylle et de Cléobule* (1771). Marmontel's *Bélisaire* (1767) and Jean Pechmeja's *Télèphe* (1784) belong to the same vein of prose poems partly converted into "romans d'apprentissage." In reducing their titles to the hero's name, Pechmeja and Marmontel oriented readers toward the horizon of the novel, a hypothesis confirmed by the division of both works into respectively books ("livres") and chapters rather than cantos ("chants") customary in prose poems.

Within the context of the prose poem's development, this cluster of texts records two interesting phenomena, present in germ in *Télémaque*: first, an intensification of the "drift" toward the novel and second, a divorce between the romanesque and didactic poles of the prose poem as *Bildungsroman*. The first tendency—an irresistible attraction to practices characteristic of novelists, concomitant with an effort to poeticize the text—is particularly noticeable in *Les Iles fortunées* and in *Bélisaire*. *Les Iles fortunées* begins with a reproach against Montesquieu's "miserable ploy" of introducing *Le Temple de Gnide* as a (pseudo) translation (a practice I examine in Chapter 3). Praise for the prose poem's originality follows— a clue to Moutonnet-Clairfons's own poetic ambitions, notwithstanding his de rigueur modesty when referring to his "bagatelle."[81] His foreword indicts the

---

[79] Ibid., 251n1.

[80] Genette, *Palimpsestes*, 251.

[81] Moutonnet-Clairfons, Avertissement to *Les Iles fortunées, ou les aventures de Bathylle et de Cléobule* (1771), in *Voyages imaginaires, romanesques, merveilleux, allégoriques, amusans, comiques et critiques. Suivis des songes, visions, et des romans cabalistiques* (1787), 97.

century's "dominant taste," by which the author has in mind the vogue of romans noirs: "Mon dessein n'a pas été de composer un roman bien noir, bien lugubre, bien horrible, & bien dégoûtant. On ne conversera point ici avec des scélérats abominables" [My goal was not to compose a really dark, gloomy, horrible, and disgusting novel. There will not be conversations with abominable villains.][82] The author contrasts his project ("to interest honest people") with the bad effluence drifting, as it turns out, from across the Channel. The author speaks of himself in the third person:

> [I]l s'amusoit à former la tissure de ce petit roman, dans lequel il tâchoit d'imiter la simplicité grecque, & d'écarter les sombres vapeurs de l'anglomanie, qui causent présentement des vertiges dans toutes les têtes; tandis que le caractère de gaieté nationale s'affoiblit, se dénature & s'anéantit.

> [He enjoyed himself weaving the fabric of this little novel, in which he tried to imitate Greek simplicity, and cast aside the dark vapors of anglomania that are currently provoking vertigo in everyone's head; meanwhile the cheerfulness of our national character is weakening, losing its nature, and dying out.][83]

Moutonnet-Clairfons sets an antithesis characteristic of the anti-novel movement of the last third of the century: not only is the warm Greek genius ostensibly contrasted to somber northern productions, but the author's carefully crafted, clearly and simply laid "tissure" [fabric] is also the aesthetic opposite of the vague and confusing Anglophone "vapors." The argument that anglomania threatens French national character and its celebrated cheerfulness discloses the interconnection between politics and literature in the conflicted relations between France and England.[84] But the author has more scores to settle, as revealing as his offensive against the gothic novel and anglomania. In the sentence immediately after the above citation the author moved without transition to the sentimental vogue, thus connecting this second threat with England as well:

> Malgré toutes les brochures *sentimentales* dont la France est inondée, nous n'en sommes pas devenus plus sensibles & plus heureux. Cette épidémie littéraire

---

[82]   Ibid.

[83]   Ibid., 99.

[84]   In the course of his adventures, the hero disembarks on an island which is clearly England: "Ces Insulaires ont des goûts bien singuliers ... Leurs tragédies monstrueuses, & sans vraisemblance, les occupent agréablement. Les ombres, les spectres, les ossemens, les tombeaux, sont pour eux un spectacle divertissant. Ils outrent toutes les passions. L'amour chez eux est sombre & mélancolique, & les porte aux plus grands excès ... Lorsque ces peuples sont ennuyés de leur existence, & las de vivre, ils se donnent froidement la mort" [These islanders have quite singular tastes ... Their monstrous, improbable tragedies are a pleasant pastime. They find shadows, specters, dead remains, and tombs to be an entertaining spectacle. They exaggerate all passions. Love for them is dark and melancholy and carries them to the greatest excesses. When this people are bored by their existence and weary of living, they coldly kill themselves.] Ibid., 178–9.

est d'autant plus contagieuse, que les femmes, qui donnent actuellement le ton, la fomentent & la propagent. Elles entendent bien peu leur intérêt! Tous ceux qui affichent le titre fastueux de *penseurs*, sont tristes, égoïstes, insociables, pointilleux & arrogans. Quelle fatale révolution! Quel puissant génie pourra nous guérir d'un travers aussi ridicule & aussi dangereux?[85]

[Despite all the *sentimental* brochures that are flooding France, we have not become more sensitive or happier. This literary epidemic is all the more contagious, as women, who at present set the tone, are its instigators and propagators. Little do they understand their self-interest! Those who boast the ostentatious title of *thinkers* are grim, selfish, unsociable, fussy, and arrogant. What a fateful revolution! What powerful genius will cure us from such a ridiculous and dangerous flaw?]

Additional culprits, women and the unnamed Rousseau, are denounced emphatically and violently. References to inundation, epidemic, contagion, and revolution express the devastation of the neoclassical literary field under the eyes of one of its occupants, whose outrage comes from an evident feeling of "expropriation." In *The Sentimental Education of the Novel*, Margaret Cohen explored the permanence and exacerbation of this resistance against the sentimental novel, and against the women who wrote them in early nineteenth-century France, women eventually expropriated by their male competitors—the realist novelists.[86] Moutonnet-Clairfons's chain of association between "roman noir" / anglomania / sentimental novel / women / Rousseau, will carry on well into the next century.

In the end, the author flagrantly ignored his own "avertissement." While the story's incipit balances two contrasting descriptions (a violent storm at sea, followed by the description of a enchanting grotto in imitation of *Télémaque*'s incipit), the narrative yields to the temptation of the gothic novel over the pastoral in two violent episodes, Bachylle's graphic account of the death of mother and child killed by a crocodile in the Nile, and Cléobule's witnessing the atrocious beheading of a sailor caught between two blocks of ice and devoured by a fish.[87] The narrative structure, articulated around two long retrospective accounts, evokes baroque novels: Bachylle narrates the first "récit," takes the reader around Greek islands and multiplies descriptions; the second "récit," told by Cléobule, details a host of misadventures, dissipated youth, reversals of fortune, and travels to exotic foreign lands. In the last two books, the two shepherds resume their pastoral life until the final celebration of Bachylle and Ada's union, blessed by Cléobule, who has become surrogate father. Bachylle's account imitates both *Les Aventures de Télémaque* and *Le Temple de Gnide* as far as it pursues a political and moral agenda with adventures set on Greek islands symbolizing various positive and negative values. Cléobule's story has more "romanesque" traits and proceeds like a *Bildungsroman*.

---

[85] Ibid., 99–100.

[86] Margaret Cohen, *The Sentimental Education of the Novel* (Princeton, 1999).

[87] Moutonnet-Clairfons, *Les Iles fortunées*, 143–5 and 180.

Marmontel's *Bélisaire* offered its readers a subtler paradox than Moutonnet-Clairfons's self-contradictory work. Like *Les Iles fortunées,* Marmontel's fiction exhibits traits akin to the "great baroque novel," a drift toward the romanesque similar to *Télémaque.* [88] Unlike *Les Iles fortunées,* however, this proclivity did not clash with the author's theoretical stance, but with the tradition of a certain poetic language and style. As Robert Granderoute notes in his introduction to *Bélisaire,* Marmontel's prose is laden with poetic figures (images, comparisons, allegories, prosopopoeia, and parallelisms). It evinces a search for poetic style (epic similes, periphrases, choice epithets) and for a more unusual feature, poetic diction, Marmontel's trademark "prose nombreuse" [rhythmical prose]. [89] In addition to blank verse, "[c]'est tout au long du livre qu'alexandrins et octosyllables se mêlent et s'entrelacent—avec une prédilection pour les octosyllables dont se déroulent de véritables strophes" [all along the book, alexandrine and octosyllable verses are mixed and interwoven, with a predilection for octosyllables, deployed in actual stanzas]. [90] The presence of verse within prose, an anathema for eighteenth-century criticism, reminds readers of the text's poetic aspiration toward the music, loftiness and status of epic versification; concurrently, its narrative structure (plot, episodes, and accidents) pulls the text in the direction of hierarchically inferior yet popular novels. If *Bélisaire* is symptomatic of the hybridity of Enlightenment "poëmes en prose," it remains that Marmontel's experimental cadenced prose led to a dead-end: borrowing measure and rhetoric from a moribund neoclassical poetry failed to capture music and images congenial to prose.

Bélisaire's internal contradiction between the poetry of the epic and the prose of the novel is amplified by the tension between "le romanesque" and didacticism. Critics, then and now, have deplored this redoubling of the novelist into a sententious moralist: "La faiblesse romanesque de *Bélisaire* tient au fait que la parole domine le corps central du livre, qu'à partir du chapitre 7 les mots se substituent aux choses et que l'ordre dramatique laisse place à l'ordre discursif et réflexif " [*Bélisaire*'s weakness as a novel comes from the fact that speech dominates the core of the book: from chapter seven on, words are substituted for things, and dramatic order is replaced by discursive and reflexive order.][91] In this respect also, Marmontel aggravated a practice already at work in *Télémaque. Bélisaire* breached the "plaire en instruisant" contract that bound authors to readers. In truth, the very nature of the *Bildungsroman* puts it at risk of a schizophrenic split: the dual components of the "romanesque édifiant"—as Genette called it—that is, love and instruction, could easily part company. Thus, prose poems closely imitating *Télémaque* further dissociated "romanesque" and didactic interests. Readers favored moral and

---

[88]   Robert Granderoute, introduction to *Bélisaire* by Marmontel (Paris, 1994), xxxiii. I am indebted to Granderoute's introduction and notes to *Bélisaire* for my analysis of this prose poem's conflicting features.

[89]   Ibid., xxxviii.

[90]   Ibid., xl.

[91]   Ibid., xxxv.

political edification if and only expertly woven with stories of "apprentissages amoureux" (emulating *Télémaque*'s Calypso episode and *Le Temple de Gnide*)—a preference that finds its parallel in the evolution of the novel itself. The different adaptations that prolonged *Bélisaire*'s success prove the fecund nature of the "poëme en prose" during its earliest stage. *Bélisaire* gave birth to an eclectic progeny, expanding the family tree of prose poems into yet other hybrid species: *Bélisaire ou les Masques tombés, drame histori-philoso-héroï-comique*, "pièce de société de C.-N. Mondolot, composé en 5 actes et en prose" (1768); *Bélisaire, drame en 5 actes et en vers* by Ozicourt (1769); *Bélisaire, comédie héroïque*, "en 5 actes et en prose" (1769) by Mouslier de Moissy; and *Bélisaire*, "tragédie lyrique en quatre actes et en vers libres," by Auguste-Félix Desaugiers (1787).[92] *Bélisaire*'s literary descendants confirm the role of theater and comedy in the implosion of genres. *Bélisaire*'s indeterminacies allowed the genie of literary creation out of its constricting generic bottle, freeing prose as well as poetry.[93] These theatrical productions saw light thanks to "poëmes en prose": in its inception the genre was still in search of itself and contained virtually all others. This multiple generic identity accounted for the complexity and fertility of prose poems, in all respects the bastard children of eighteenth-century literature. From *Les Aventures de Télémaque* to modern creations, prose poems remain in a permanent state of self-destabilization, and carry the threat of their own collapse from the tension between their poetic and prosaic poles.

---

[92] Ibid., lv–lvi.

[93] See Desaugiers's tragedy in free verse, "nouvel écho de la cadence distinctive de la prose de Marmontel" as Granderoute notes (lvii), but also an indication of a poetic experimentation with a more modern versification.

Chapter 2
Prose vs. Poetry

A close reading of *Les Aventures de Télémaque* suggests that contesting the majesty of verse poetry, while an aesthetic battle, was also an expression of dissatisfaction with absolutism and an aspiration to reform; to defend it translated as much a poetic ideal as concern with the loss of order, the leveling of hierarchies, and the prospect of popular insurrection. This chapter argues that the attempt to rationalize, organize, and compartmentalize aesthetics (in continuation of Boileau's 1674 *Art poétique*) proved ultimately impossible, an impossibility that eventually challenged the Enlightenment to rethink poetry and prose according to criteria that transcended classification—imagination, enthusiasm, music, and the sublime—instead of the absolute authority of verse. But disagreements abounded, suggesting the deep, symbolical, socio-political charge of these aesthetic issues in eighteenth-century France. In the course of this chapter, it will become clear that the relationship of verse to poetry was often couched in terms symbolical of the relationship of spectacle to absolute monarchy: just as the ornament of verse became vital to a poetry in decline, so did the extravagance of spectacle compensate for a weakening royal power.[1] Verse might have well become an artifice, but to its defenders verse was essential to maintain the authority of poetry, just as the spectacle of the court and aristocratic performance had become central to absolutism, no matter how onerous. To follow this symbolic thread is to interpret the emergence of poetry in prose not only as an aesthetic breakthrough but also as the socio-political suggestion of a "juste milieu" in rebellion against authoritarian extremes.

As soon as Fénelon's *Les Aventures de Télémaque* appeared, and for over a century afterward, critics and authors reacted to the emergence of the "poëme en prose" with pro and con treatises and reviews that I will now closely examine. Three movements succeeded one another: provocation, led by the critic La Motte on the side of the Moderns; confusion, reflected in the *Encyclopédie*'s articles and resisted by purists like Voltaire; and finally Rivarol's strategy to resolve this struggle, a nationalist discourse on the superiority of the French language.

Before introducing these various positions, I will begin with an overview of how the nature of prose and poetry was perceived over time. Until the seventeenth century, fiction, that is, any imaginative creation, was essentially the domain of *poesy*, and truth the domain of prose. As the Belles Lettres' language of reason (vs. the language of imagination), prose conveyed philosophical systems, historical narratives, scientific and travel discoveries, political and religious views,

---

[1]   See Jean-Marie Apostolidès, *Le Roi-machine. Spectacle et politique au temps de Louis XIV* (Paris, 1981).

and spiritual guidance, thus helping advance critical thinking and knowledge, both sacred and secular. In practice, limiting the domain of prose to non-fictional discourse had long been circumvented by authors of romances on the one hand, and translators on the other. Producing prose fictions did not directly challenge the strict boundaries set by rhetoricians, given that romances were absent from Aristotle's *Poetics*, and later dismissed on the grounds of their extravagance.[2] As far as prose translations of ancient or foreign verse were concerned, they represented in theory a defeat for the French language, not a vindication of prose's potential. In effect, however, the popularity of romances and "belles infidèles" translations compensated for their supposed shortcomings, insuring their continuation. Responding to their readers' enthusiasm, authors and translators pursued their forays, inevitably expanding the limits of prose. By the end of the seventeenth century, enough significant novels had been written to gain legitimacy as fictions in prose: Honoré d'Urfé's *L'Astrée* (1607), Charles Sorel's *Le Berger Extravagant, où parmi les fantaisies amoureuses on void les impertinences des Romans et de la Poësie* (1627), Paul Scarron's *Le Roman comique* (1651), La Calprenède's *Cléopâtre* (1647–1656), Madeleine de Scudéry's *Clélie ou l'Histoire romaine* (1654–1660), Roger de Bussy-Rabutin's *Histoire amoureuse des Gaules* (1665), and Mme de la Fayette's *Princesse de Clèves* (1678), to cite major exemples.[3] The domain of prose fiction expanded and continued to evolve via the theater and the slow transformation of romances into novels.[4] Romanticism further contributed to the expansion of prose and to the restriction of the poetic field by expunging from the latter all non-lyrical genres (drama and the epic), which the classical age, in line with Aristotle, had considered poetry's pinnacle. Simultaneously, Romanticism welcomed and nurtured poetic prose and prose poetry, as verse was no longer of the essence. In short, the Romantics tried to liberate poetic expression, embracing verse, as well as prose, while favoring a definition of poetry based on lyricism. Finally, twentieth-century modernists ushered yet another poetic revolution when adopting free verse in revolt against the persistence of meter.

Where do Enlightenment prose poems fit in this briefly sketched history of the nature of prose and poetry, and the shifting locus of their difference? It is tempting to interpret eighteenth-century prose poems as evidence of a revolt against meter that would foreshadow the modernists' own revolt in the twentieth century. As we will see with La Motte, there was intense, sustained, even increasing dissatisfaction with metrics and versification. The fall from high to low poetic genres distressed many authors and generated frustration and melancholia. Prose poems were born to tell of their disenchantment; they were born as an escape from the fall. However,

---

[2]   Boileau's *Art Poétique* (1674) did not treat novels/romances as an autonomous genre with set rules: Madeleine Scudéry's long novels are only mentioned in passing to note their defects.

[3]   For a complete list, see Ralph W. Baldner, *Bibliography of Seventeenth-Century Prose Fiction* (New York, 1967).

[4]   See Poirier, *La Bibliothèque universelle des romans*.

we need to keep in mind that verse remained prestigious if we are to understand the lasting allure of the alexandrine line and of rhymes—just as aristocratic titles remained coveted and even purchased at great cost throughout the ancien régime. Therefore prose poems of the Enlightenment should be interpreted less as an attack against meter than a conquest of prose. With prose poems, authors tried to transfer the qualities of verse poetry into prose fiction: they sought poetic tropes and rhythm to ennoble prose. Timothy Steele recorded this phenomenon as "prose seeking order on the model of poetry" and contrasted it to its opposite in the twentieth century ("poetry seeking freedom on the model of prose") as modernist poets worked to make poetry more like prose.[5] The Enlightenment's drive to conquer prose, its gesture to elevate prosaics, had subversive humanist and democratic connotations that were only half articulated, as we have seen with Fénelon's *Télémaque*. Drawing from multiple contemporary treatises, this chapter clarifies the nature of poetry and prose in the eighteenth century, and exposes the modernity at stake in the debate between prosaists and versifiers. The lack of consensus that emerged is profoundly characteristic of the Enlightenment.

If we search in more detail for the advent of an autonomous prose, it appears to have occurred in part thanks to the tradition of the "belles infidèles" in the seventeenth century, as Roger Zuber demonstrated. Translators in the vernacular focused their energy not on remaining faithful to originals, but on emulating them in elegant prose.[6] In addition to translators' practice of imitation as key to shaping a versatile and artistic prose, a clear distinction between prose and poetry actually facilitated the establishment of prose. This distinction was best drawn by François de Malherbe (1555–1628), a guardian of poetry's purity, and his disciple Jean-Louis Guez de Balzac (1595–1654), a defender of the "prose d'art" ideal.[7] The independence of prose vis-à-vis poetry was contingent upon the clear differentiation between the two modes of writing. When Malherbe, who, as a poet and critic, established strict rules of clarity governing poetic diction, turned toward translation, "il répudie les ornements, il repousse les figures" [he repudiates ornaments, he rejects figures], thereby refusing the "contamination" of one mode of writing upon the other to avoid some "monstrueux assemblages" [monstrous compositions].[8] Guez de Balzac, too, was "parfaitement conscient des

---

[5]   See Steele, *Missing Measures*, chap. 2, 69–108.

[6]   Roger Zuber, *Les "Belles Infidèles" et la formation du goût classique* (Paris, 1995), chap. 1, 27–32.

[7]   "Malherbe, nourri de la lecture des excellents Poëtes de l'Antiquité, & prenant comme eux la Nature pour modèle, répandit le premier dans notre Poësie une harmonie & des Beautés auparavant inconnues. Balzac, aujourd'hui trop méprisé, donna à notre Prose de la noblesse & du nombre" [Malherbe, nourished on the great poets of Antiquity and like them, taking nature as a model, was the first to bring into our poetry harmony and beauties heretofore unknown. Balzac, overly neglected nowadays, gave our prose nobility and rhythm.] Jean Le Rond d'Alembert, "Discours préliminaire," *Encyclopédie ou Dictionnaire raisonné des sciences, des arts et des métiers*, vol. 1, xxii.

[8]   Zuber, *Les "Belles Infidèles,"* 29, 40.

singularités de la prose par rapport à la poésie" [perfectly aware of the singularity of prose compared with poetry.][9] Whereas a century later Jean-Jacques Rousseau asked himself "how to be a poet in prose?" seventeenth-century prose writers pondered how to avoid writing like a poet.[10] Theirs was a reaction against the fashion of poetic prose, "cette mignardise" [affectation], which flourished (and this is significant) under the *benevolent*, not absolutist, reign of Henry IV and Marguerite de Valois, and which consisted in incorporating poetical figures to emulate the prestige of poetry. On the contrary, Malherbe and Guez de Balzac not only succeeded in maintaining a radical difference between prose and poetry but also in putting on par the two modes of writing, their primary concern being the improvement and modernization of the French language, away from archaism.

The tide turned between 1645 and 1652 when critics began again to compare prose with poetry.[11] In Antoine Furetière's *Nouvelle allégorique ou Histoire des derniers troubles arrivés au Royaume de l'Eloquence* (1658), Rhetoric is a queen and Poetry only a princess. Prince Galimatias is waging a war against the Queen of Rhetoric, but a war also rages within the province of her sister—the princess Poetry—between Rhymes and Reason.[12] Rhymes are defeated and take refuge in religious hymns called "proses."[13] As the allegory continues, poetry remains in second place:

> La Cavalerie postée sur les aîles venoit toute du *Royaume Poëtique*: c'étoit des figures fort bien montées, et qui avoient beaucoup d'élévation par dessus les autres. Ce qui n'étoit pas nouveau; car quelques Anciens nous ont apris, que les vers n'étoient qu'autre chose que de la Prose montée à cheval. Par fois en galopant et en prenant l'essor, elles jétoient de la poudre aux yeux à bien du monde.[14]

> [All Cavalrymen, stationed on the wings, came from *Poetry's Kingdom*. They were handsomely mounted and stood high above the others. This was nothing new, for several ancients have taught us that verses are nothing else but Prose on horseback. Sometimes as they galloped and took flight, they threw dust into many eyes.]

The ingenious allegory subverted the traditional metaphor of dancing poetry vs. pedestrian prose: for Furetière, verse was prose on horseback; in other words versification was a spectacle of cadence and steps that often dazzled, but prose

---

[9] Ibid., 42.

[10] Ibid., 91.

[11] Ibid., 127.

[12] Antoine Furetière, *Nouvelle allégorique ou Histoire des derniers troubles arrivés au Royaume de l'Eloquence* (Toulouse, 2004), 17–18. On the conflict between common sense and rhymes, see Boileau, *L'Art poétique*, I, vol. 27–38, p. 42.

[13] Furetière, *Nouvelle allégorique*, 18. A "prose" is a religious term dating from the Middle Ages designating a rhymed, Latin hymn sung during a solemn mass.

[14] Ibid., 23.

remained the agent of thought. The allegory concludes with the return of peace in the realm of Rhetoric: it remained the richest soil from which authors purchased their wares in a fruitful mercantile exchange.[15] Far from considering this commerce favorable to prose, Zuber sees it as the beginning of its decline.[16] As the ideal of an artistic prose faltered, so did the genre of the "belles infidèles" that had fostered it. A return to the norm followed this brief episode of emancipation as neoclassical poetry returned center stage with prose in the mundane role of servant.[17] This preeminence of poetry was reaffirmed in Fontenelle's allegory, *Description de l'Empire de la Poésie* (1678), which focused on the poetic domain originally described by Furetière.[18] Tellingly, Fontenelle's geographical allegory presented first a very bleak survey of the poetic landscape. The province of "High Poetry" comprising Epic poetry and Tragedy, is unpleasant and tiresome; the province of "Low Poetry," made up of Comedy and Elegy, is built upon marshes. The rivers of Rhyme and Reason cross the Empire of Poetry. Under a thin disguise, the allegory virulently criticized Rhyme as antithetical both to Reason and Common Sense, except in a few instances (not specified) where Rhyme and Reason can be linked, albeit with considerable effort. As it seemingly reestablished the traditional hierarchy favoring poetry over prose, and reinforced poetry's own internal hierarchy (from higher to lower genres), Fontenelle's disparaging assessment, above all, doubted and mistrusted the use of rhyme:

> Ces deux rivières sont assez éloignées l'une de l'autre, et comme elles ont un cours très différent, on ne les saurait communiquer que par des canaux qui demandent un fort grand travail; encore ne peut-on pas tirer ces canaux de communication en tout lieu, parce qu'il n'y a qu'un bout de la rivière de la Rime qui réponde à celle de la Raison; et de là vient que plusieurs villes situées sur la Rime, comme le Virelai, la Ballade et le Chant Royal, ne peuvent avoir aucun commerce avec la Raison, quelque peine qu'on puisse y prendre. De plus, il faut que ces canaux passent par les Déserts du Bon Sens, comme vous le voyez par la carte, et c'est un pays presque inconnu. La Rime est une grande rivière dont le cours est fort tortueux et inégal, et elle fait des sauts très dangereux pour ceux qui se hasardent à y naviguer. Au contraire, le cours de la rivière de la Raison est fort égal et fort droit, mais c'est une rivière qui ne porte pas toute sorte de vaisseaux.[19]

> [These two rivers are rather far apart from each other, and since they run very different courses, they could only be joined with canals that would require a great amount of work. Moreover, one would not be able to build such canals anywhere, because there is only one portion of the river Rhyme that corresponds

---

[15] Ibid., 47–8.

[16] See Zuber, *Les "Belles Infidèles,"* 154.

[17] Ibid., 154–5.

[18] Bernard Le Bovier de Fontenelle, *Description de l'empire de la poésie*, in *Rêveries diverses. Opuscules littéraires et philosophiques* (Paris, 1994), 19–23.

[19] Ibid., 22.

to the river Reason; this is why several towns located on the river Rhyme, such as the Virelay, the Ballad and the Royal Song, cannot have any commerce with Reason, no matter how hard one tries. Further, the canals must go through Deserts of Common Sense, as you can see on the map, and this country is almost unknown. Rhyme is a large river, whose course is tortuous and quite uneven, with very dangerous falls for those who risk navigating its waters. On the contrary, the course of the river Reason is quite even and straight, but this river does not carry all sorts of ships.]

The *Description de l'Empire de la Poésie* contained in germ the more radical positions taken up by Fontenelle and the Moderns later on against the seduction of verse, for verse in their eyes was too often *non*-sense. It is true that Boileau himself, in the opening of his *Art poétique,* had very clearly warned against "monstrous verses" wandering off from straight meaning, but his was a call for more discipline in subjugating rhyme to reason, not grounds for reform.[20]

While Fontenelle still paired prose and poetry as sisters, prose was gradually taking the lead in French letters. We can measure the evolution in favor of prose by comparing two narratives more than a hundred and forty years apart: Jacques de Grille's *Le Mont Parnasse ou de la Préférence entre la Prose et la Poésie* from 1663, and the anonymous "Dialogue entre la Prose et la Poésie" published in 1809 in the *Almanach des prosateurs. Le Mont Parnasse* is a "dialogue des morts," opposing the precious poet Vincent Voiture (1597–1648) and the prose author Claude Favre de Vaugelas (1585–1650) under Apollo's judgment.[21] De Grille's generous notion of poetry, not limited to verse, welcomes prose's artistic accomplishments. Poetry's dominance is enhanced by its patronage of prose and its superiority evident despite its chains. But to "Vaugelas" who praised the freedom of prose, "Voiture" replies: "La Prose est libre comme le sont les gueux; ... la Poësie est esclave comme le sont les Reynes" [Prose is free just as beggars are free; ... Poetry is a slave just as queens are slaves.][22] The striking political symbolism spelled out the equivalence between poetry/royalty and prose/populace, while hinting at the weakness endemic to monarchist power, the fact that supremacy was but a subjection. A hundred and forty years later, the prosaic "tramps" not only beheaded Marie-Antoinette, they toppled the queen of literature, Poetry. The anonymous "Dialogue entre la Prose et la Poésie" staged the last act of this victory.[23] A personified Prose, in turns condescending and mocking, lectures its sickened sister Poetry. Poetry's emphatic greeting gives ammunition to Prose's verdict: poetry suffers from

---

[20]   See Boileau, *Art poétique*, I, vol. 27–30, p. 42; vol. 39–43, p. 43.

[21]   On *Le Mont Parnasse*, see Zuber, *Les "Belles Infidèles,"* 155–6.

[22]   Cited in Zuber, *Les "Belles Infidèles,"* 156n28. See also Moreau, *La Tradition française du poème en prose avant Baudelaire*, 3.

[23]   See Appendix IV, "Dialogue entre la prose et la poésie," in *Almanach des prosateurs* (1809). For a more complete analysis of the dialogue and its context, see Fabienne Moore, "Almanach des Muses vs. Almanach des Prosateurs: The Economics of Poetry and Prose at the Turn of the Nineteenth Century," *Dalhousie French Studies* (Summer, 2004, 67), 17–35.

excessive propriety, affectation, extravagance, lack of common sense, and excess of commonplace—the criticism is without appeal. Poetry's high style is reduced to "drôleries," "enfantillages," and "sottises harmonieuses" [silliness, childishness and harmonious foolishness] whereas Prose has the prerogative of a first-born. Prose's mea culpa—"je sais fort bien être poétique ... mais ce n'est pas ce que je fais de mieux" [I know very well how to be poetical ... but it is not what I do best]—also summarized a century of painstaking efforts, though it confined Prose's poetic ambition to non-fiction (history, mythology, astronomy, mathematics) and ignored that prose authors, via the long legacy of Aristotelian thought, could boast about their poetic achievements in fictional narratives. Poetry agrees to the pact of "cohabitation," acknowledging fatigue in melodramatic accents. The malaise is symptomatic of decadence: regal Poetry wore itself out by not restraining its domain, and overextending itself in subject matters outside its jurisdiction. Its ambition to dominate all was an abuse of power.

The first allegory epitomizes the sovereignty of poetry in the realm of letters and the second its fallen state. Yet there is a noticeable continuity in the search for parity between poetry and prose, as well as hope in overcoming their antagonism. The "artistic prose" De Grille imagined remained the dream of many a critic and writer, from Fénelon to Chateaubriand. In Fontenelle's allegory, the river Reason "ne porte pas toute sorte de vaisseaux" [does not carry all sorts of ships], hinting that prose was still incompatible with certain genres. Twenty years later, the publication of Fénelon's *Les Aventures de Télémaque* shattered this premise. For the first time, prose dealt with a poetic subject matter using poetic diction, thus changing the configuration of the literary map Furetière and Fontenelle had drawn, and creating the new province of prose poetry. Just as important, its hybrid nature was a reaction against the simultaneous rationalizing of prose and poetry. On the one hand, eighteenth-century prose authors adopted either a "clear, algebraic prose" or a "quick, witty prose" as exemplified in Montesquieu's and Voltaire's writings, perhaps because the urgent search for truth eclipsed the pursuit of beauty.[24] On the other hand, poets tightened the rules of versification the better to adhere to a neoclassical ideal of clarity, but poetic enthusiasm faltered. Consequently, whereas Montesquieu, Voltaire, and others sprung up as successors to the prince of eloquence, Guez de Balzac, the eighteenth century did not beget a new Malherbe or Voiture. Unlike the Renaissance and the reign of Louis XIV, during which French prose and poetry were equally admired, successful, and therefore kept separate, eighteenth-century poetry, like the monarchy, struggled for inspiration and survival, pressed by internal and external pressures (such as the invasion of the English novel of manners and competition from prose translation of foreign poetry), while the nostalgia for its prestige kept increasing. This crisis of poetry in the eighteenth century as a mirror to a monarchy in crisis is key to understanding the advent of prose poetry.

---

[24] Gustave Lanson, *L'Art de la prose* (Paris, 1968), chap. IV–XII, 91–210.

A Provocateur: Houdar de La Motte (1672–1731)

Houdar de La Motte's literary experiments rightly belong to a pre-history of the prose poem: although devoid of poetic sentiment, their "geometric" rationality contributed to the dissociation between verse and poetry, and, as importantly, to the breakup of the monopoly of verse over the highest poetic genres—two determining factors in the subsequent development of prose. La Motte is a study in paradox.[25] As a conservative practitioner of poetry, he is representative of its decline in eighteenth-century France. Artless and monotonous versification makes his poems emblematic of "the transformation of classical poetry into artificial poetry," a poetic diction emptied of inspiration and spontaneity.[26] But as a provocative theoretician of poetry and a disciple of Fénelon, La Motte embodies the struggle to modernize and elevate prose by advocating a new freedom against old rules.

In 1713, on the occasion of his *Iliade en douze chants*, an abridged versification of the original, La Motte corresponded with Fénelon, and subsequently published the letters as a contribution to the critical debate generated by the "querelle d'Homère." The correspondence helps explain the evolution of La Motte's theories and his radical turn against versification. Fénelon diplomatically avoided passing judgment on La Motte's "little Iliade," wishing that his correspondent, like "a new Homer" had written instead a "new Poem," an encouragement the Academician followed, as we will see.[27] Fénelon pointed out that his dissatisfaction resided in the inherent weakness of French versification, particularly evident in epic poetry, less so in the ode:

> C'est que les Vers de nos Odes, où les rimes sont entrelacées, ont une variété, une grace & une harmonie que nos Vers Héroïques ne peuvent égaler. Ceux-ci fatiguent l'oreille par leur uniformité. Le Latin a une infinité d'inversions & de cadences. Au contraire le François n'admet presqu'aucune inversion de Phrase; il procede toûjours méthodiquement par un nominatif, par un Verbe, & par son régime. La Rime gêne plus qu'elle n'orne les Vers. Elle les charge d'Epithétes; elle rend souvent la Diction forcée, & pleine d'une vaine parure. En allongeant les discours, elle les affoiblit. Souvent on a recours à un Vers inutile, pour en amener un bon. Il faut avouer que la sévérité de nos règles a rendu notre Versification presqu'impossible. Les grands Vers sont presque toûjours ou languissans ou raboteux ...[28]

---

[25] See Houdar de La Motte, *Textes critiques. Les raisons du sentiment*, eds. Françoise Gevrey and Béatrice Guion (Paris, 2002).

[26] Paul Dupont, *Un Poète-philosophe au commencement du dix-huitième siècle. Houdar de La Motte* (1672–1731) (Geneva, 1971), 19.

[27] [From Fénelon, 9 September 1713], "Echange de lettres de Fénelon et de La Motte," in Houdar de la Motte, *Œuvres complètes* (Geneva, 1970) vol. 1, 282.

[28] Ibid., [From Fénelon, 17 January 1714], 283.

[In our odes, where rhymes are intertwined, verses have a variety, grace and harmony that our heroic verses cannot equal. The uniformity of the latter is tiresome to hear. Latin has an infinite amount of inversions and cadences. To the contrary, French accepts almost no inversion in a sentence. It always proceeds methodically with a nominative, a verb and its complements. Rhyme is an impediment more than an ornament of verses. It burdens them with epithets; it often renders diction stilted and clad in a vain dress. By lengthening lines, it weakens them. Often, one adds an unnecessary verse to bring about a good one. One has to admit that the severity of our rules has made our versification almost impossible. Our great verses are almost always languid or rough ...]

Sanctioned by an authority such as Fénelon, who thought that French versification could not really achieve perfection, and galvanized by the example and success of *Télémaque*, La Motte could launch his crusade against verse. He first systematized the process of "prosification" to demonstrate his argument against the necessity of verse. His complete works present his tragedy in verse *Œdipe* (written in 1726) side by side with the same tragedy in prose.[29] Similarly, a comedy *L'Amante difficile* is given in prose then in verse.[30] He also dared to "translate" into prose the first scene of Racine's tragedy, *Mithridate*, as well as an ode (in verse and about verse) by his friend M. de la Faye. La Motte's *Œuvres Complètes* also feature a section entitled "Proses en vers," which corresponds to religious hymns: the coinage, a wink to his readers, is not surprising given La Motte's subversive agenda. The interest of these exercises is not artistic but theoretical: to engage the reader in a critical comparison between verse and prose to the advantage of the latter. By choosing poetic genres unthinkable without versification (tragedy and the ode), he strove to debunk verse as art to reveal that it was but an artifice.

It should be pointed out that what made possible La Motte's demonstrations is also in some respect what invalidated them: his disregard and lack of understanding for poeticity. Genette underlined that *Mithridate*'s first scene lent itself well to the exercise of prosification because it is a sober, expository scene with a lengthy narrative recapitulating past events, therefore more removed from the poetic density of subsequent scenes.[31] La Faye's ode in verse, also, was easy to de-rhyme: like most contemporary circumstantial poetry, it was more a witty exposition than a harmonious, imaginative poem. The same can be said of La Motte's own mediocre tragedies and comedies.

Nonetheless, the intent behind the gesture was a serious provocation. La Motte did not hesitate to demystify poets' work when it reduced itself to a painstaking search for rhymes—again a statement to be read in the context of the fate of poetry in the first half of the eighteenth century.[32] If versification had become so tiresome

---

[29] La Motte, *Œuvres*, vol. 2, 5–25.

[30] Ibid., vol. 2, 68–111.

[31] Genette, *Palimpsestes*, 306–9.

[32] La Motte, "Comparaison de la première scène de Mithridate avec la même scène réduite en prose," in *Œuvres complètes*, vol. 1, 483.

for poets and readers, why not simply write in prose? La Motte's numerous critical discourses systematically turned toward prose as the finer means of expression. The self-critical La Motte did not pretend that his experiments achieved this goal, but he offered them "to give an idea" of what could be done if better poets set themselves to the task.

Choosing to turn La Faye's *Ode en faveur des vers* into prose was a provocative decision given that its subject matter was a defense of versification. No doubt amused by the irony, La Motte took the stylistic and thematic features of La Faye's ode as the basis of his demonstration. Arguments La Faye put forward in favor of verse, namely, the merit of difficulty, the natural pleasure given by symmetry, and the "force of habit," are refuted. Rhyming is "un travail pénible & frivole ... un exercice mécanique" [a frivolous, painstaking job ... a mechanical exercice], verse is "un mérite accessoire," "un agrément de convention, contre-nature" [a secondary merit, a conventional pleasure against nature], in other words poetry in verse is artificial unlike *Télémaque* which had demonstrated the possibility of poetry without versification.[33] La Faye's comparison of verse with a "jet d'eau" [fountain] is first criticized as inaccurate, then is used as an illustration of verse's artificial character. In contrast to the clever mechanism of fountains, prose is compared to a majestic river:

> Ne puis-je pas comparer à mon tour la libre Eloquence à un fleuve majestueux qui descendant du haut des montagnes, s'œvre un chemin à travers les plaines, & qui se grossissant des torrens & des ruisseaux qu'il trouve sur sa route, fertilise les campagnes qu'il traverse, & devient entre les hommes le lien du commerce & de la société. A qui alors du jet d'eau ou du fleuve donnera-t-on l'avantage? Et qui osera préférer ce badinage, ou, si l'on veut, cette petite merveille de l'art, à la sage magnificence de la nature dont le fleuve donne une si belle idée?[34]

> [In turn, can I not compare free Eloquence to a majestic river, which flows down from the mountains, frays open a path through plains, and, swelling with the torrents and streams that it finds in its way, fertilizes the countryside through which it goes, and becomes between men the link of commerce and society. To which, then, of fountains or rivers, shall we give the advantage? And who shall dare prefer this trifle, or, if you will, this little artistic marvel, to the wise magnificence of nature, of which rivers give such a beautiful idea?]

The comparison illustrates the values of prose: its nobility, strength, fertility, variety, usefulness, and power of communication. Prose is natural, productive, and possesses all the "wise magnificence of nature." However, infringement by verse writers and the tyranny of arbitrary rules have dispossessed prose of its natural rights:

---

[33]   La Motte, "L'Ode de M. de la Faye mise en prose," in *Œuvres complètes*, vol. 1, 162–3.

[34]   Ibid. 166.

[N]e retranchons rien des droits de la prose. Toutes les mesures du discours sans exception, sont, pour ainsi dire, de son domaine qu'elle n'a jamais aliéné; c'est une usurpation des vers de s'en être approprié certaine mesure, & c'est une tirannie de vouloir les interdire à la prose dont elles sont empruntées.

Le jour n'est pas plus pur que le fond de mon cœur,

est originairement de la prose: ce n'est que la continuité de cette mesure qui constitue les vers alexandrins.. [35]

[Let us not take away any rights from prose. Without exception, all the measures of speech belong, so to speak, to its domain, which it never alienated. It is an infringement, on the part of verses, to have appropriated certain measures, and it is a tyranny to want to forbid them to prose from which they have been borrowed. *The day is not purer than the bottom of my heart* is originally prose: it is only the continuation of this measure that constitutes alexandrine lines.]

Insensible and indifferent to the poetic quality of the metaphor he quoted, La Motte espouses a rational aesthetics against the tyranny of versification. A flawed premise, which reduced the nature of poetry to the constraint of verse, led to a conclusion pleading for an extension of the rights of prose: "laissons à la prose *la liberté de tous les genres*, afin de multiplier les bons ouvrages & de contenter tous les goûts" [let us leave to prose the *freedom of all genres*, so as to multiply good works and satisfy all tastes] (emphasis added).[36]

In his response to Voltaire, who suspected that La Motte sought to eliminate versified poetry entirely, the latter dispelled any misunderstanding, while reaffirming that the liberation of prose and "la liberté des stiles" was essential for the progress of literature and taste.[37] La Motte's conclusion makes clear that the crisis of verse was only the symptom of a crisis of genres. While critics such as Raymond Naves have interpreted La Motte's Cartesian attacks against verse as anti-poetry, his objective was to abolish verse as a criterion for *specific* poetic genres. Since verse could not be dissociated from certain genres, it is easy to see why his efforts created a small revolution on Mount Parnassus. Whereas his adversaries feared the demise of poetry, La Motte expressed supreme confidence, as evidenced by his reply to Voltaire: "Ne craignez rien, Monsieur; quand on interdiroit les Vers aux Génies poëtiques, ils trouveroient bien encore l'occasion & les moyens d'être Poëtes en Prose" [Do not fear, Sir, even if verses were forbidden to poetic geniuses, they would still find the occasion and the way to be poets in prose]—a foresight into the revolution that future *prosateurs* were to bring to the Republic of Letters.[38]

---

[35] Ibid., 167.

[36] Ibid.

[37] La Motte, *Suite des Réflexions sur la Tragédie où l'on répond à M. de Voltaire*, in *Œuvres complètes*, vol. 1, 494.

[38] Ibid., 486.

Nothing seems more removed from the subtlety of twentieth-century prose poems than the first self-proclaimed "poëme en prose," *La Libre Eloquence* (1729). La Motte's literary jousts culminated with this banner-like poem celebrating the conquests of prose. Fénelon had broken the taboo of an epic poem in prose; La Motte broke the taboo of an ode in prose, even though he had argued the ode should be the last genre to abandon versification.[39] The dedication of the ode to the cardinal de Fleury, who had exhibited a "particular satisfaction" upon hearing the piece read at the Académie, allows us to trace another influence upon La Motte.[40] The cardinal, a great admirer of ancient Hebrew poetry, had distinguished poetry from versification, ahead of Fénelon, for whom he was a reference.[41] To write an ode in prose, La Motte explains, defies those who confine prose to a low status by excluding it from elevated genres:

> L'Ode suivante a été faite par une espèce de défi, sur ce que des gens prétendoient que la Prose ne pouvoit s'élever aux expressions & aux idées poëtiques. Je pensois au contraire qu'*elle peut prétendre à tous les genres*; & pour le prouver, je traitai la matière même avec tout le faste & toutes les figures de l'Ode. [42]

> [The following ode was written from a sort of challenge, namely that some people pretended that prose could not rise to poetical expressions and ideas. To the contrary, I thought *it could aspire to every genre*; and to prove it, I treated this subject matter with the full rhetorical splendor of the Ode.] (emphasis added)

La Motte's ode proceeds like a demonstration: theoretical and poetical passages alternate, creating an awkward, self-conscious poem from an aesthetic standpoint, and a surprisingly modern, self-reflexive, meta-discursive venture from a critical standpoint. The "poet philosopher" staged his rebellion against the demands of his craft:

---

[39] La Motte, *L'Ode de M. de la Faye, mise en prose*, in *Œuvres complètes*, vol. 1, 163–4. Boileau had distinguished the ode as the only genre that could circumvent methodic order on account of its lyricism. See *Art Poétique*, III, vol. 58–72, pp. 71–2 and his *Discours sur l'ode*, in *Art poétique*, 95.

[40] La Motte, *L'Ode de M. de la Faye*, 157. In 1665, Claude Fleury wrote a manuscript entitled "Remarques sur Homère à M. le Laboureur Bailly de Montmorency," which seems to have circulated before its actual printing in 1728 (without the author's name). Fleury's text was also inserted in 1731 in a supplement to a reprinting of Anne Dacier's translation of Homer, but the editors attributed Fleury's favorable remarks upon Homer's poetry to Pope. For a helpful introduction and Fleury's text, see Noémi Hepp, *Deux Amis d'Homère au XVIIe siècle* (Paris, 1970).

[41] Chérel, preface to *Fénelon au dix-huitième siècle*, xvi.

[42] La Motte, "La Libre Éloquence," in *Œuvres complètes*, 157. Hereafter cited in text.

Rime, aussi bizarre qu'*impérieuse*, mesure *tyrannique*, mes pensées seront-elles toujours vos *esclaves*? Jusques à quand *usurperez*-vous sur elles l'empire de la raison? Dès que le nombre & la cadence l'*ordonnent*, il faut vous *immoler*, comme vos *victimes*, la justesse, la précision, la clarté. (159)

[Bizarre and *imperious* Rhyme, *tyrannical* meter, will my thoughts always be your slave? How long will you *usurp* reason's empire? As soon as rhythm and cadence *demand* it, one must *sacrifice*, as your *victims*, accuracy, precision, and clarity.] (emphasis added)

Throughout the ode, versification is semantically associated with coercion whereas eloquence, as the title celebrates, is synonymous with freedom. As his previous commentaries have already made clear, La Motte espoused the Enlightenment ideal of the conquest of freedom through reason: "C'est à toi seule, Eloquence libre & indépendante, c'est à toi de m'affranchir d'un esclavage si injurieux à la raison" (157). [You alone, free Eloquence, you must free me from a subjugation so injurious to reason.][43] The call for Eloquence to dethrone verse in the realm of letters sounds strikingly similar to the effort to rid the monarchy of absolutism, equally injurious to reason. Eloquence is allegorized as a goddess who appears in response to the poet's exhortation. Its limitless empire extends to the mind, heart, and imagination. No longer bound by the traditional definition of poetry as imitation of beautiful nature, it seeks to be creative and imaginative. Eloquence can therefore emulate poetry, but also extend beyond the traditional field of rhetoric into pure invention, not in the manner of marvelous romances, but with the goal of suspending disbelief, and creating (*poein*) from imagination alone. These prerogatives are taken for granted today, but few had dared to challenge them as readily as La Motte. In view of the rigid partition of poetic and prosaic fields, his questioning of the double boundary—imitation as the field of poetry, non-fiction as the domain of eloquence—made for an avant-garde gesture.

His inspiration liberated, the poet exclaims: "Oui, je puis, sans le secours des vers, m'élever aux plus sublimes fictions" (158). [Yes, I can, without the help of verse, rise to the most sublime fictions.] Taking up Fénelon's cue to be a new Homer, he launches into the description of an epic battle, condensing in a few paragraphs traditional characters (gods, mortals, and a hero) and familiar rhetorical strategies (apostrophes, inversions, allegories, exclamations, comparisons, and superlatives), a purely didactic demonstration less convincing than the preceding argument. La Motte is more successful when not trying to embed examples in his ode but setting the agenda for prose tragedies —"toutes les passions n'auront d'ornement que leur propre vivacité" [all passions shall be adorned solely by their own liveliness]—and prose comedies—"pourquoi se faire un langage forcé, pour

---

[43] La Motte might be countering Boileau's precept (like a slave, rhyme must simply obey) by giving voice to a poet enslaved by rhyme who must subject himself to it, not the reverse. La Motte seemed to suggest that Boileau's rule to submit rhyme to the yoke of reason was a contradiction.

exprimer la naïveté des sentimens et des mœurs?" (158) [why invent a stilted language to express naïve feelings and mores?] The pastoral fragment that follows is a tedious compilation of clichés (the *quid pro quos* of love among shepherds; muses and their pranks, etc.) in almost direct contradiction with the concluding apology of a natural style breathing pastoral freedom and naïveté (159). In the last part of the ode, the poet listens to Polhimnie's complaints, concedes the charm of the muse of verse, but denies her sovereignty. La Motte's hyper-conventional expression has led critics to read him as confining poetry to purely rhetorical devices.[44] I propose that his panegyric in prose, to prose, in fact inaugurates a meta-discourse that will resonate in prose poems to come. Born of a challenge to generic divisions and exclusion from elevated poetic class, the prose poem will retain, as part of its aesthetic, this meta-textuality.

Though his practice never matched his theories (a clue perhaps less of incompetence than ambivalence), La Motte remained a steadfast advocate of prose. Labeled a Modern always on account of his rejection of the classics, he deserves closer scrutiny for the modernity of his programmatic vision regarding the future of prose.[45] Challenging future prose authors to develop old genres into new beginnings constitutes La Motte's lasting legacy to his century.

A Bastard Style: The Prose Poem's Impossible Affiliation

Fraguier denounces a monster

Unwilling to admit the stifling consequences of a hyper-regulated poetic form, some critics took a defensive stance. On August 11, 1719, l'abbé Fraguier presented to the "Académie Royale des Inscriptions et Belles Lettres" a memoir entitled "Qu'il ne peut y avoir de poëmes en prose" [That there can be no Poems in Prose] (see Appendix I).[46] This report to the highest literary body matters greatly: by indicting a trend deemed corrupt, it recorded its actual emergence and the uncertainties and disagreements surrounding its place and its future. Fraguier's memoir marked the entrance of the critic into the space of prose poems, even though it actually negated the legitimacy and existence of such a space. Previous treatises and discourses

---

    [44]   La Motte, *Textes critiques*, 703.

    [45]   See for instance La Motte's contribution to the evolution of theater in France and abroad, in Françoise Gevrey and Béatrice Guion, introduction to La Motte. *Textes critiques*, 29–31.

    [46]   Abbé Fraguier, "Qu'il ne peut y avoir de poëmes en prose [in the margin: "11 d'août 1719"], in *Memoires de litterature tirez des registres de l'academie royale des inscriptions et belles lettres* (1719), 265. "A Discourse to shew that there can be no Poems in Prose. By Mr. L'Abbé Fraguier. Read to the French Academy of Belles Lettres, August 2nd, 1739," in *Select discourses read to the Academy of Belles Lettres and Inscriptions at Paris. Translated from the memoirs of the Academy*, 80–95 (London, 1741). Original and translation hereafter cited in text.

had focused on the specificity of prose and poetry but Fraguier expressed a new
sense of urgency, warning his learned audience that a trespassing had occurred and
might recur. Before examining the "foundation of such an invention" (the tone is
incredulous and disparaging), Fraguier began by criticizing the inconsequence of
writers who failed to respect the boundaries between poetic and prosaic fields:

> Si les personnes d'esprit qui dans les Poëmes mettent la Prose à la place des
> Vers, eussent bien considéré la nature & les conséquences de leur entreprise; ils
> se seroient contentez d'exceller dans les Vers & dans la Prose, sans remuer la
> borne éternelle qui les séparent essentiellement. (265)

> [If certain Wits, who confound Poetry with Prose, had well considered the Nature
> and Consequences of their Enterprize, they would have contented themselves
> with excelling in either, without removing the unalterable Boundaries by which
> they are essentially separated.] (81)

The phenomenon of embellishing prose with poetic ornaments was not new, but
an author like Houdar de La Motte (implicitly accused here) also claimed the
title of "poem" for his endeavors, a displacement of the "unalterable boundaries"
separating prose and poetry tantamount to eradicating poetry (271). Intimating
that the very survival of poetry was at stake in La Motte's sleight of hand,
Fraguier's memoir opened a new stage in the critical discourse on the relationship
between prose and poetry while struggling with an internal contradiction: the wish
to demonstrate the impossibility of the prose poem's existence clashed with the
concern that it already existed. Fraguier's demonstration sought to reestablish
firmly the "eternal milestone" between the two domains ("patrimoines") and set
clear landmarks: cast as a negative, prose is defined by default whereas verse is
deemed essential to poetry. Eighteenth-century poets do not have a choice of tools:
they must use verse (265). Fraguier countered the objection that a poem translated
into prose remained a poem, with the frequently used parallel between the etching
of a painting and the painting itself. The music of verse remained as central to
the art of poetry as color to the art of painting. Fraguier invoked the myth of
Orpheus to account for the origin and magical power of verse (267), and turned to
literary history as a reminder that no ancient writer dare call himself a poet unless
he first produced verses: citing the examples of Apuleius, Lucian, and Cicero,
Fraguier argued that their style was "assez vicieux pour mériter le nouveau nom
de prose poétique" [florid enough to merit the new Name of Poetical-Prose] (94).
Even though the beauty and sublime character of Scipio's dream reached to the
heights of poetry, Ciceronian prose, by virtue of its being prose—no matter how
poetic—had no claim to poetic laurels (275). Verses embedded in a prose narrative
did not suffice to define it as a poem: *L'Astrée*, like all novels and works in prose,
has no right to the title of poem (276). The case of *Télémaque* obviously posed a
challenge, which Fraguier circumvented by second-guessing Fénelon's intentions:
"Je suis persuadé que l'illustre Auteur du *Télémaque* n'a jamais prétendu faire un
Poëme; il connaissoit trop bien chaque partie des Lettres humaines pour ne pas
respecter les bornes qui séparent leur patrimoine" (276). [I am persuaded that the

illustrious Author of *Telemachus* never intended to make it a Poem: He knew too well every part of the *Belles Lettres*, not to pay due Regard to the Limits which divide that Territory into different Provinces] (94). This intentional fallacy—the assumption of Fénelon's intended adherence to the rules— compensated for the impossibility of a generic determination made on the basis of the writing alone.

A series of consequences follows from the indispensable presence of verse. Because of the difficulty of writing good lines in French, prestige, admiration, and glory were due to the poets who successfully surpassed this obstacle. The "difficulté vaincue" signaled a "rare talent," which in turn could only be fueled by the "fire" of "divine inspiration." Fraguier moved away from the Platonic idea of the poet as the gods' interpreter, to poetry as the very language of the gods, which enabled him to set in opposition prose as the language of men. Moreover, poets had distanced themselves from common mortals by forging a separate language when they attributed figurative meaning to common nouns or reverted to ancient words. Fraguier's memoir encapsulated the dichotomies between poetry (i.e. verse) and prose, which we have already encountered in *Télémaque*. The constraint of verse contrasted with the freedom of prose, making the latter less prestigious; the elitism of an ideal poetry that only a few could write and understand contrasted with the egalitarian common language prose offered; and the divine power bestowed upon poets contrasted with the prose writer's human, all too human pen. Prose's accessibility clearly threatened poetry's hegemony in the Belles Lettres field: *prosateurs* might usurp the poet's laurels and his sacred title. Exasperated by this underground revolution, the critic exclaimed: "Car enfin, si l'on est Poëte pour écrire en Prose, tout le Monde voudra être Poëte" (276). [In fine, if one could merit the Name of Poet by writing in Prose, every one would aspire at the Character] (95). In a democratized literary field, all people could have all pretensions—a popularization unacceptable to the critic. As Fraguier's next sentence made clear (albeit offhandedly), the true motive behind his prediction had less to do with infringement of poetic boundaries than with the phenomenon of poetry's popularization: "d'ailleurs les idées qu'on nomme poëtiques, étant *des idées rebattees, & à la portée de tout le monde*, ce sera tous les jours quelque nouveau *monstre* soi-disant Poëme" (276, emphasis added). [And besides, *the Ideas called Poetical being trite, and within the Reach of every one*, every new Day would bring forth some new Monster call'd a Poem] (95). Therein rested the reason for the necessity of verse: it constituted the only element left for eighteenth-century poets to distance themselves from the crowd, since hackneyed diction and subject matter had become accessible to all. Fraguier indirectly admitted here what Menant termed "Icarus's fall"—a metaphor for the fall of the winged poet in the first half of the eighteenth century.[47] The evidence of poetic clichés could have been the occasion to call for rejuvenation; instead, Fraguier accused the "monstrous" prose poem, while defending verse as an ornament now turned essential and essentially elitist.

---

[47]　See Menant, *La Chute d'Icare*.

When prose donned poetic ornaments, there resulted an unsuitable match, "une mascarade bizarre," "comme une vieille Comédienne de campagne, qui plus elle est parée, plus elle est ridicule" (271) [a ridiculous Mascarade, compare it to an old Country Comedian, who, the more she is dressed out, the more ridiculous she is] (88). In opposition to the ethereal poetic muse, a decrepit female actor symbolized the prose poem, anchored in prosaism by the quadrupled weight of provincialism, old age, comedy, and superfluous adornment—a grotesque spectacle since the new and monstrous match of prose and poetry ran counter to nature, as Malherbe had argued in his time. Gueudeville had also criticized Fénelon's prose with a gendered metaphor—"une Courtisane déguisée."[48]

Fraguier asked whether the proximity of prose and poetry in the French language justified blurring their distinction, "l'effacer [la Poësie] et la détruire entierement, & passant la charrue sur la borne, donner à la Prose ce qui a toujours appartenu à la Poësie, & de deux héritages très séparez ne faire plus qu'un seul et même champ?" (271) [utterly effacing and destroying it ... passing the Plow over the dividing Land-marks, and giving to Prose what hath always belonged to Poetry; and thus making, of two distinct Heritages, one and the same common Field?] (87). Plowed fields might remind readers of one possible etymology for verse: *versa*, or furrows—parallel lines breaking off and starting up again, mimicking the effect of verses on a page. If the plowman goes past his field's landmark, the line never returns, and *versa* can go *ad infinitum*, losing its defining character. The two consequences of this unstoppable plowing force are proportionally reverse: on the one hand the debasement of poetry, and on the other, the elevation of prose (269). If elsewhere in the essay Fraguier played down the results of prose poetry as "*disjecti membra Poëtae*," signs of concern outnumbered this one dismissal (272). The lowering of poetry and the rise of prose seemed unacceptable for the critic, who not only spoke of a result completely "vicieux" [flawed/harmful] but also "pernicieux," likely to spread as a contagion. Fraguier used this last adjective in conjunction with *Télémaque*, which confirmed the role of Fénelon's prose epic in shattering the symbolic milestone (271). Fraguier speculated that Fénelon would have been sorry had he realized where the example of *Télémaque* was leading, all the way to the Orient:

> Il [Fénelon] eût été bien fâché de donner un exemple pernicieux, dont l'effet pourroit enfin nous réduire à la pauvreté de quelques Nations de l'Orient, qui n'ont jamais eu de vrais Poëmes. Toute leur Poësie n'est que de la prose cadencée au hazard, & sans nulle mesure certaine de Vers: c'est un assemblage énorme de métaphores outrées, d'hyperboles excessives, & d'épithetes énigmatiques; en un mot leur Poësie est comme leur Musique, qui ne consiste qu'en un assemblage confus & barbaresque de voix & de sons, qui n'ayant entre eux nulle proportion, ne peuvent se réduire aux règles d'une harmonie précise & démontrée arithmétiquement. (276)

---

[48]   Gueudeville, *Critique générale des Aventures de Télémaque*, 59.

[He would have been sorry to have given a pernicious Example, that might, by its Effects, at last have reduced us to the Poverty of some Eastern Nations, which never produced true Poems. All their Poetry is nothing but high-sounding Prose [without any exact measure of verse], and an enormous Assemblage of extravagant Metaphors, monstrous Hyperboles, and affected enigmatical Epithets. In one Word, their Poetry is like their Musick, which consists in a confused barbarous Arrangement of Words and Sounds, which having no Proportion, no Concord, cannot be reduced to the Rules and Measures of Harmony capable of arithmetical Demonstration.] (94–5)

The passage exemplifies the socio-literary construction of the Orient in the eighteenth century as the site of irrationality vs. the "geometric" sensibilities of French thinkers. Lacking a sense of proportion and measure, lacking rules, the Orient incarnated aesthetic vice. Oriental style, which Fraguier characterized as overly hyperbolic and cryptic, stood opposite the much admired neoclassical harmony: it seemed barbarian, namely uncivilized, therefore anathema to the European polite nations, as they were then called. But if Fraguier criticized the Orient as primitive, Fénelon, and many authors in his wake, used it as a way to explore modern themes and ideas, perhaps one might even argue, as a site for "défiguration du langage poétique" [disfiguring poetical language]: on many levels the Orient symbolized the disfiguring of rhetorical tropes, hence the attraction/ repulsion it exerted in a century fascinated by the monstrous.[49]

To conclude, Fraguier's arguments to demonstrate "that there can be no Poems in Prose" rested on Plato's conception of the poet's supremacy, and followed Malherbe and Boileau's strictures about the clear separation of prose and poetry. The new factor in this ancient debate was the weakness of eighteenth-century poetry and its political equivalent, the French monarchy's decline, making it prone to a takeover by prose, the symbolic equivalent of a popular uprising—hence Fraguier's defense of verse as the essential defining criteria. Awareness that poetry had become an empty shell, so to speak, accompanied the fear of the Orient as the dark realm of excess, enormity, and disfiguration.

Several denials countered Fraguier's demonstration on the impossibility of prose poems, but their claims must be examined with circumspection, so entangled and confused the terminology became. More specifically, the emergence of the novel clouded the battleground where prose and poetry carried on their dispute, further muddying generic waters. If Fraguier refused to call a novel a "poëme en prose," others did not deny the appellation: Boileau wrote in 1700 of "ces Poëmes en prose que nous appelons *Romans*" [these prose poems we called *Novels*];[50] abbé Dubos cited *La Princesse de Clèves* and *Télémaque* as "Poëmes en prose,"

---

[49]   See "Les émules de Fénelon," in Marie-Louise Dufresnoy, *L'Orient romanesque en France* (Montreal, 1946), chap. XV, 253–64.

[50]   Cited in Mouret and Voisine eds, *La Poésie en prose des Lumières au Romantisme*, 33. Also in Raymond Naves, *Le Goût de Voltaire* (Paris, 1938), 74; and in Moreau, *La Tradition française du poème en prose avant Baudelaire*, 3n1.

and Fontenelle made the equation: "nos romans, qui sont des poèmes en prose" [our novels, which are prose poems] in the *Digression sur les Anciens et Modernes* (1688).[51] La Motte agreed: "nos Romans, quoiqu'en prose, ne sont-ils pas des Poëmes Epiques?" [although in prose, are not our novels epic poems?][52] In his seminal *De l'Usage des Romans* (1734), Lenglet-Dufresnoy followed the historical approach of Huet's famous *Traité de l'origine des romans* (1670), but whereas Huet hesitated to equate the modern novel with a poem, Lenglet-Dufresnoy was at ease when labeling the new category of the "poëme en prose" in 1734: "Nos premiers Romans étoient aussi en vers, & nous regardons les Romans modernes comme autant de Poëmes en prose; il ne manque à ces derniers que la mesure du vers pour en faire des Poëmes heroïques" [Our first novels were also in verse, and we consider modern novels as so many prose poems; the latter only lack the measure of verse to become heroic poems.][53] For Huet and Lenglet-Dufresnoy, novels in prose had taken the place of novels once written in verse.[54] But if Huet willingly granted the title of poet to the novelist, he never equated novels with poems.[55] Half a century later, Lenglet-Dufresnoy drew the equation but could not venture to assert that poems could be written in prose. In other words, he did not anticipate unversified poetry, but simply recorded the increasingly established genre of the novel, legitimized through the link to ancient practices (novels in verse) and epic poetry. Under the *Maximes à observer dans les Romans*, he carefully stated the *sine qua non* condition underlying his equation between novel and poem: "Je mets pour *première observation* de ne choisir que des sujets nobles, & qui puissent mériter l'attention des honnêtes gens. Je l'ai déjà dit, un Roman est un Poëme

---

51   Jean-Baptiste Dubos, *Réflexions critiques sur la poésie et sur la peinture* (Geneva, 1967), 134. Fontenelle, *Digression sur les Anciens et les Modernes*. In *Rêveries diverses. Opuscules littéraires et philosophiques*, 40.

52   La Motte, *Réflexions sur la critique*. Deuxième partie, in *Œuvres complètes*, vol. 1, 295.

53   Nicolas Lenglet-Dufresnoy, *De l'usage des romans* (Geneva, 1970), 19–20.

54   My focus on the French context fits within the broader trend recorded by Steele of "the shift from fiction in meter to fiction in prose." Steele emphasizes the importance of Philip Sydney's *Apologie for Poetrie* (1583) and Henry Fielding's preface to *Joseph Andrews* in defense of prose fictions. *Missing Measures*, 81–95.

55   "Je ne parle donc point ici des Romans en vers, et moins encore des poëmes épiques, qui, outre qu'ils sont en vers, ont encore des différences essentielles qui les distinguent des Romans: quoiqu'ils aient d'ailleurs un très-grand rapport, et que suivant la maxime d'Aristote, qui enseigne que le poëte est plus poëte par les fictions qu'il invente, que par les vers qu'il compose, on puisse mettre les faiseurs de Romans au nombre des poëtes" [I do not speak here of novels in verse, and even less of epic poems, which aside from being written in verse, have essential differences that distinguish them from novels; however, they also have great similarities, and according to Aristotle's maxim, which teaches that a poet is more a poet thanks to the fictions he invents than to the verse he composes, we can place authors of novels among poets.] Pierre-Daniel Huet, *Traité de l'origine des romans*, 5–6.

heroïque en Prose" [My first observation shall be to choose only noble topics that deserve the attention of honest people. I have already said that a novel is a heroic poem in prose.] [56] Prose advocates, following a tradition dating back to the Renaissance, believed that prose could espouse subject matters as noble as that of poetry. [57] The nobler the subject matter, the more poetic the novel would be.

Although eighteenth-century and twentieth-century criticism have dismissed the confusing labeling of novels as "poëmes en prose," this critical coinage is suggestive of prose authors' new ambitious hope: that prose become the medium of expression not simply of serious eloquence, histories, or extravagant romances, but also of epic and dramatic narratives, long the prerogative of poetry. [58] If, following theater, celebrated English and French novels of the eighteenth century, often epistolary, marked the triumph of prose in the *dramatic* genre, the lesser known and less successful "poëmes en prose" testified to the difficulty of French prose authors to transmute the epic from an acclaimed poetic genre into a successful prose genre. Diverging from Montesquieu's *Lettres persanes*, Prevost's *Manon Lescaut*, Rousseau's *Julie*, or Laclos' *Liaisons dangereuses*, several eighteenth-century prose poems specifically sought to conserve an epic nature, thus nuancing Georg Lukács's emphasis on the novel as the obvious successor to great epic literature. The epic represented a territory to be conquered that eventually legitimized not only novels but also a new way of writing poetry.

Rémond de Saint-Mard on equality

Rémond de Saint-Mard's *Examen philosophique de la poésie en général* (1729) is a discourse on poetic equality, a position reflective of the ambition to let prose rise to its potential. [59] The treatise began with an analysis of the power of images to move the heart, exemplified by the description of Calypso's cave in *Les Aventures de Télémaque*, and by one of Moses's songs in the Bible—two revealing, controversial examples of prose for a treatise on poetry. The author analyzed the object of poetry solely in terms of the heart's affections (23) and deplored the attention that poets, too preoccupied by verse, devoted to "poetry's mechanical beauties" as opposed to its "true and solid beauties" (26). He broke new ground by erasing almost all differences between poetry and prose—"si vous exceptez la petite différence que met entr'elles la rime, la mesure & un usage frequent de la

---

[56]   Lenglet-Dufresnoy, *De l'usage des romans*, 58.

[57]   See Steele, *Missing measures*, 85.

[58]   Steele makes the same point with regard to England, arguing that the emergence of works such as John Lyly's *Euphues,* Philip Sydney's *Arcadia* and Fielding's *Joseph Andrews* "affects poetry profoundly. An increasingly distinctive and popular form of non-metrical fiction, the novel of manners ... gradually absorbs much of the material and audience formerly devoted to poetry," *Missing Measures*, 88.

[59]   Toussaint Rémond de Saint-Mard, *Examen philosophique de la poésie en général* (1729). Hereafter noted in text.

Fable" [if one excepts the small difference that rhyme, measure, and a frequent use of the fabulous, put between them] (59). In effect, Saint-Mard's radical theory recaptured the essence of poetry in depth of feeling, imagination and harmony, and simultaneously equated it with the power of prose:

> [C]ar enfin si l'on nous prend dans la Poësie par le cœur, si l'on y étourdit notre imagination, si l'on nous y gagne par une certaine harmonie, qui est le ton naturel de ce qu'on a à dire, tout cela ne se fait-il pas également dans la Prose? Ne nous subjugue-t'on pas dans l'une & dans l'autre avec les mêmes armes? (32–3)

> [Finally, if the poet moves our heart, bewilders our imagination, wins us over with a certain harmony, which reflects the natural way we speak, does this not all happen equally in Prose? Do not poetry and prose subjugate us with the same weapons?]

Saint-Mard compellingly argued for comparing not form or content but writers' creative impulse, fire and enthusiasm, essentially identical in verse and prose:

> Cet Orateur qui vous agite & qui vous remuë; ce Philosophe qui vous subjugue, qui vous enleve; avec quoi pensez-vous qu'il fasse tout cela? croyez-vous que ce soit simplement avec de la Prose? Hé quoi cette Prose n'est-elle pas de la Poësie, ne voyez-vous pas son feu, ne reconnoissez-vous pas son enthousiasme, & n'est-ce pas comme Poëte qu'on vous assujetit? (61–2)

> [The orator who stirs and moves you, the philosopher who captivates, who enraptures you, how do you think he manages to achieve this? Do you believe it is simply with prose? Come, is prose not poetry and do you not see its fire nor recognize its enthusiasms? is it not a Poet who subjugates you?]

In the perspective of a "*philosophical* examination of poetry" announced in his title, Saint-Mard presented poetry and prose as absolute equals, striving for the same goal. Considering the examples of Malebranche, philosopher but poet too, and Corneille, poet but also philosopher, the author passionately and emphatically declared equality:

> [N]on la rime qui les distingue, ne me les déguise pas. Je les vois tous les deux les mêmes ... je les vois tous les deux grands Poëtes, grands Orateurs, grands Philosophes parce qu'il est de l'essence des grands génies d'être tous les trois ensemble; parce qu'il faut à l'Eloquence, disons plus, parce qu'il faut à la Prose même qu'on veut rendre vive, animée, interessante, autant d'éclat, autant de douceur qu'à la Poësie, parce que toutes les qualitez de l'esprit sont obligées de se réünir, de se confondre, & de s'aller perdre dans la Poësie comme dans la Prose; & qu'en un mot ce n'est que par le bel accord, par l'heureux mélange de toutes ces qualitez, qu'elles acquerent l'une & l'autre, ce beau feu & cette sagesse qui nous enchante. (64–7)

> [No, rhyme, which distinguishes them, does not disguise them for me. I see them as the same. I see them both as great poets, great orators, great philosophers, because the essence of great geniuses is to cohere all three, because eloquence

needs, nay, prose needs, if one wants to make it lively, animated, and interesting, as much luster and sweetness as poetry, because all the qualities of the mind have to join, merge, and lose themselves in poetry as in prose. In a word, it is only thanks to the beautiful agreement and felicitous blending of all these qualities that each acquires the great fire and wisdom that enchant us.]

By focusing on notions of genius, fire, and creative merit, Saint-Mard's analysis eliminated the strict boundary between the fields of prose and poetry and an inequality born of supposedly different aesthetic classes, thus anticipating by many years William Wordsworth's own conclusion: "Is there then, it will be asked, no essential difference between the language of prose and metrical composition? I answer that there neither is nor can be any essential difference."[60] In light of the socio-political context of Louis XV's rule under which Saint-Mard wrote his treatise, this newly proclaimed equality between prose and poetry appears revolutionary—a development of the Enlightenment, before this progress became Romantic.

To contemporary readers, Fénelon's *Télémaque* proved that prose could and should emulate poetry—a conclusion also reached by La Motte's theories and Saint-Mard's philosophical examination. However, a number of authors and critics persisted in maintaining, if not increasing, the divide between prose and poetry, supporting verse without quite admitting the reasons for its decline. Critics viewed themselves as guardians of a tradition—poetry as the supreme art. Verse writers held on to the prestige of their title, while most prose writers from the beginning of the century seemed more interested in an intellectual, objective, and clear prose than a poetic one. Such was the position of Voltaire, whose work in verse and prose exemplified the rigorous, classical division of genres.

Voltaire against the crime of lèse-poésie

Although Voltaire's writings in prose are more appreciated today than his poetry, our modern preference is the mirror opposite of the value Voltaire and contemporaries placed on his versification. To establish his reputation, Voltaire wrote in verse in the major noble genres (epic and tragic), and about philosophical issues: the *Encyclopédie* considered *La Henriade* to be the first French epic poem.[61] He reserved prose for historical writings, critical essays or correspondence, and published a tale in prose, *Zadig*, only after becoming famous, as Menant noted.[62] What position did Voltaire take in the debate of prose vs. poetry? Gwenaëlle Boucher focused on key stylistic issues, like Voltaire's *mélanges* (texts in prose with embedded verses), or "exchanges" (for instance the relationship between poems

---

[60] William Wordsworth and Samuel Coleridge, preface to *Lyrical Ballads* (Oxford, 1969), 163.

[61] Article "Poème," *Encyclopédie*, vol. 12, 822.

[62] Sylvain Menant, introduction to *Voltaire, Contes en vers et en prose* (Paris, 1992), viii. See also Sylvain Menant, *L'Esthétique de Voltaire* (Paris, 1995), 24–5.

and theirs footnotes in prose).[63] In addition to this complex aesthetic, Voltaire's prolific production illustrates in a compelling manner what I propose to call the economics of prose and poetry. Given the competition between prose and poetry, could we not speculate that Voltaire varied the distribution of his investments? His verse production brought high dividends in terms of contemporary readership and notoriety, but over time the interest generated by his prose became the most substantial. The preeminence of Voltaire, who understood quickly how to position himself in this literary marketplace, shifts the familiar opposition of classical vs. modern onto a plane other than aesthetic. His purist attachment to the separation of prose and poetry, and his dismissal of prose poems derive from his classical taste, but also, I suggest, from two related sources: socio-economic—the market value of verse—and socio-political—the maintenance of class privilege. To simplify, the attachment to verse might be both capitalist and elitist. In this dual perspective, Voltaire's famous speculative flair (in finance and publishing) was undeniably modern while his attachment to poetic *cum* social privileges was conservative.

Better than any of his contemporaries, Voltaire mastered the prodigious difficulty of French versification, an acrobatic exercise. We still admire today what Menant regards as his "grande facilité poétique: écrire des vers est pour lui un plaisir, ce qui confère à sa poésie un inimitable cachet de naturel (malgré le respect de toutes les conventions) auquel ses contemporains étaient particulièrement sensibles" [great poetic facility: writing in verse is for him a pleasure, conferring a unique, natural character to his poetry (despite respecting all conventions), which his contemporaries particularly appreciated.][64] To conserve versification meant first of all to gain legitimate admission to the "class" of poets, as well as valorize a rare talent and competence that were getting lost, of which a young and ambitious Voltaire wanted to be the representative above the crowd of mediocre versifiers. Thus in reaction to La Motte's *Œdipe*, published in verse and prose in 1726, the thirty-six-year-old Voltaire reprinted his own *Œdipe* play in 1730 accompanied by a new preface where he clarified the status of prose and poetry, clearly inspired by Fraguier whose reminder that no writer ever took the name of a poet when he did not compose in verse engraved itself in Voltaire's mind for the rest of his career. His conception of the poetic ideal differs much from the notions we have inherited following the Romantic revolution, but it agrees perfectly with the prevalent classical aesthetics of the early part of the century vs. the avant-garde offensive represented by La Motte. According to Voltaire's preface to *Œdipe*, "no one can read" La Motte's prose rendering of the first scene of *Mithridate,* that is to say, the poetry of Racine's drama can no longer be seen or heard.[65] At the same time, and quite paradoxically, La Motte's exercise proved to Voltaire that

---

[63]   Gwenaëlle Boucher, *La Poésie philosophique de Voltaire* (Oxford, 2003), 1–286.

[64]   Sylvain Menant, Article "Poésie," in *Dictionnaire Voltaire*, eds Raymond Trousson, Jeroom Vercruysse, and Jacques Lemaire (Paris, 1994), 168.

[65]   Voltaire, ""Préface d'Œdipe de l'édition de 1730, in *Œuvres Complètes*, vol. 1A (Oxford: 2001), 270.

Racine's poetry was of the highest quality, for the best verses were and had to be as clear as prose.[66] The value of prose and verse consisted in clarity and precision, but "vanquished difficulty" added surplus value to verse. Changing verses into prose revealed whether or not sentences had a clear and natural meaning, instead of being "fillers" imposed by rhymes.[67] Once the test of clarity had been passed, rhymes were essential to establish poetry:

> Le génie de notre langue est la clarté et l'élégance; nous ne permettons nulle licence à notre poésie, qui doit marcher comme notre prose dans l'ordre précis de nos idées; nous avons donc un besoin essentiel du retour des mêmes sons pour que notre poésie ne soit pas confondue avec la prose. [68]

> [The genius of our language is clarity and elegance; we do not allow any license to our poetry, which must proceed, as our prose, in the precise order of our ideas. Therefore we absolutely need the return of the same sounds so that our poetry not be confused with prose.]

It is striking to note how poetic innovators like Wordsworth, Ezra Pound, and T.S. Eliot would return to the argument that "the language of poetry should have what T.S. Eliot called 'the virtues of prose.'"[69] Although sharing the same ideal of clear, energetic poetry as La Motte and later Wordsworth and T.S. Eliot, Voltaire drew opposite conclusions: a systematic defense of verse. The merit of "difficulté vaincue" was the primary source of pleasure in versification, though Voltaire echoed Boileau when admitting that its worth was not intrinsic and consisted only in the pursuit of beauty: "Quiconque se borne à vaincre une difficulté pour le mérite seul de la vaincre, est un fou; mais celui qui tire du fond de ces obstacles mêmes des beautés qui plaisent à tout le monde, est un homme très sage

---

[66] "Il [La Motte] ne songe pas que le grand mérite des vers est qu'ils soient aussi corrects que la prose; c'est cette extrême difficulté surmontée qui charme les connaisseurs: réduisez les vers en prose, il n'y a plus ni mérite ni plaisir" [He does not realize that the great merit of verse is to be as correct as prose; conquering this great difficulty is what charms connoisseurs: if one reduces verses to prose, there no longer is merit nor pleasure.] Ibid., 279n300–301.

[67] When Batteux repeated La Motte's experiment to prosify verses, he reached the same conclusion as Voltaire. See Batteux, "Traité de construction oratoire," in *Principes de la littérature*, 494–5.

[68] Voltaire, "Preface d'Œdipe de l'édition de 1730," in *Œuvres complètes*, vol. 1A, 280.

[69] Steele, *Missing Measures*, 54. Steele cites a crucial moment in Wordsworth's preface when the poet compares prose with poetry: "not only the language of a large portion of every good poem, even of the most elevated character, must necessarily, except with reference to the metre, in no respect differ from that of good prose, but likewise that some interesting parts of the best poems will be found to be strictly the language of prose when prose is well written." Although this argument mirrors Voltaire's, Wordsworth's conclusion is more radical and provocative: "We will go further. It may be safely affirmed, that there neither is, nor can be, any *essential* difference between the language of prose and metrical composition." Steele, *Missing Measures*, 54.

et presque unique." [70] [Whoever is content to vanquish difficulty for its own sake is a fool; but him who retrieves from these very obstacles beauties that please everyone is a truly wise and almost unique man.] Voltaire seemed to forget that the fashionable "bouts-rimés" (short rhyming games) of which he was a master, had no other attraction than the prize of difficulty. According to the above maxim, such witty poetic past-times—in contrast to high poetry—should have been considered as nothing less than folly. As a matter of fact, rhyming games played an important role in the devaluation of verse, but Voltaire ignored the issue, presumably because these *jeux de salon*, although literary, did not belong to literature. [71]

Stepping into aesthetics (the unspecified "beauties"), Voltaire enunciates what La Motte's "geometric" sense never perceived: *harmony* was the source of the diffuse pleasure occasioned by verse. La Faye's "harmonious verse, full of imagination" represented the best evidence against La Motte, as Voltaire ironically concluded: "M. de la Motte nie l'harmonie des vers: M. de la Faye lui envoie des vers harmonieux. Cela seul doit m'avertir de finir ma prose" [Mr. de la Motte denies the harmony of verse; Mr. de la Faye sends him harmonious verses: this alone shall be a warning to end my prose.] [72]

One could respond to Voltaire's "the proof is in the verse" demonstration by offering *Télémaque* as evidence of poetry in prose as harmonious and rhythmic as verse. But harmonious prose did not really fit in anywhere in Voltaire's system: if verse must borrow precision from prose, prose should stay away from the harmony of verse. Loathing the contamination of prose as much as the inappropriate usage of verse (in scientific discourse for instance) and the "mélange des styles," Voltaire made mostly negative comments about *Télémaque* and prose poetry, in the same vein as Fraguier's memoir, which he approved because of the clarity of its distinctions. [73] Although Fénelon has a place inside the sanctuary of the *Temple du goût,* he is busy, Voltaire tells us, correcting the mistakes of his excellent works:

L'aimable auteur du Télémaque, retranchait des détails et des répétitions dans son roman moral, et rayait le titre de poème épique, que quelques zélés lui donnent; car il avouait sincèrement, qu'il n'y a point de poème en prose. [74]

[The author of Telemachus was removing details and repetitions from his moral novel, and was crossing out the title of epic poem given by some zealous readers: for he admitted sincerely that there was no such thing as a prose poem.]

In his *Discours aux Welches,* Voltaire credited the eloquence of Pascal, Bossuet and Fénelon for having turned the ignorant Welches into French citizens with

---

[70] Voltaire, *Préface d'Œdipe de l'édition de 1730,* 281.

[71] See also Boileau's condemnation of epigrams which have "inundated" the fields of prose and poetry. Just as Boileau blamed the unbridled license to rhyme on a popular, provincial contagion, so did he attribute the decadent proliferation of witty epigrams to "le vulgaire," the common public. *Art Poétique,* II vol. 103–38.

[72] Voltaire, *Préface d'Œdipe de l'édition de 1730,* in *Œuvres complètes,* vol. 1A, 283.

[73] Voltaire, *Le Temple du goût,* in *Œuvres complètes,* vol. 9, 174, n (a) and 245n166.

[74] Ibid., 174.

good taste, presumably by their refinement of French prose. Yet again, Fénelon's *Télémaque* drew Voltaire's criticism as being inferior thematically and stylistically to its Homeric and Virgilian sources. A typically Voltairian aphorism summed up and seemingly settled the issue of prose poetry once and for all: "Et oserez-vous dire que la prose de cet ouvrage soit comparable à la poésie d'Homère et de Virgile? O mes Welches! *Qu'est-ce qu'un poème en prose, sinon un aveu de son impuissance?*" [And will you dare say that the prose of this work is comparable to Homer and Virgil's poetry? Oh my dear Welches! *What is a prose poem if not an admission of its impotence?*] (emphasis added). [75] Impotent/powerless prose poems cannot perform the tour de force of versification—the potency/power of the poet being, again, his capacity to overcome such obstacles. For Voltaire, prose had less value than verse because prose was simply too easy.[76] His article "Epopée" in *Questions sur l'Encyclopédie* reiterates his rejection:

> Pour les poëmes en prose, je ne sais ce que c'est que ce monstre. Je n'y vois que l'impuissance de faire des vers. J'aimerais autant qu'on me proposât un concert sans instrumens. Le *Cassandre* de *La Calprenede* sera, si l'on veut, un poëme en prose; j'y consens; mais dix vers du *Tasse* valent mieux. [77]

> [As for poems in prose, I do not know what monster that is. I only see inability to perform and compose for composing verses. I would rather hear a concert without instruments. La Calprenede's *Cassandre* shall be, if you will, a poem in prose; I allow it; but ten verses from *Le Tasse* have better value.

Voltaire also criticized writers' impotence in two instances where he considered verse weakened: when authors preferred blank verse to rhymes (Milton) and when translators translated poems into prose (Anne Dacier).[78] Voltaire conceived poetic

---

[75] Voltaire, "Discours aux Welches," in *Mélanges* (Paris, 1951), 695. In his poem "Le Mondain," Voltaire addressed "monsieur du Télémaque" to mock the severity of utopian Salente, offering mitigated praise for Fénelon's writing: "J'admire fort votre style flatteur, / Et votre prose, encor qu'un peu traînante."[I admire greatly your flattering style/And your prose, though somewhat droning], in *Anthologie de la poésie française du XVIIIᵉ siècle*, 71.

[76] "Ignorez-vous qu'il est plus aisé de faire dix tomes de prose passable que dix bons vers dans notre langue, dans cette langue embarrassée d'articles, dépourvue d'inversions, pauvre en termes poétiques, stérile en tours hardis, asservie à l'éternelle monotonie de la rime, et manquant pourtant de rime dans les sujets nobles?" [Do you not know that it is easier to write ten volumes of passable prose than ten good lines of verse in our language, in this language hampered with articles, devoid of inversions, poor poetic diction, sterile with respect to bold phrases, enslaved to eternally monotonous rhymes and yet lacking rhymes for noble subject-matters?] Voltaire, *Discours aux Welches*, 695.

[77] Voltaire, article "Epopée," in *Questions sur l'Encyclopédie, distribuées en forme de dictionnaire* (1771–1772), vol. 5, 224. See also article "Style," vol. 7, 65–71.

[78] "Je me souviendrai toujours que je demandai au célèbre *Pope*, pourquoi *Milton* n'avait pas rimé son *Paradis perdu*; & qu'il me répondit, *Because he could not*, parce qu'il ne le pouvait pas" [I will always remember that when I asked the famous Pope why Milton had not rhymed his *Paradise Lost*, he answered, *Because he could not.*] Ibid., 223.

creation as a thought process sharpened by verse and rhyme, and not as lyric and metaphoric enthusiasm:

> Je suis persuadé que la rime irritant, pour ainsi dire, à tout moment le génie, lui donne autant d'élancemens que d'entraves; qu'en le forçant de tourner sa pensée en mille manieres, elle oblige aussi de penser avec plus de justesse, & de s'exprimer avec plus de correction. Souvent l'artiste en s'abandonnant à la facilité des vers blancs, & sentant intérieurement le peu d'harmonie que ces vers produisent, croit y suppléer par des images gigantesques qui ne sont point dans la nature. Enfin, il lui manque le mérite de la difficulté surmontée.[79]

> [I am convinced that rhyme, by constantly irritating, so to speak, the mind of the genius, gives to it as much élan as obstacles; by forcing it to turn his thought a thousand ways, it also forces it to think more accurately, and to express itself more correctly. Often when the artist abandons himself to the ease of blank verse, and feels inside him harmony lacking from such verses, he thinks he can make up for it by exaggerated images that are not in nature. Finally, he lacks the merit of vanquished difficulty.]

Rhymes sharpened poetic expression whereas blank verse forced the poet to compensate the absence of musical rhyme with metaphoric exaggeration. Voltaire's leitmotiv is the merit of vanquished difficulty, namely the necessity to overcome the obstacle of versification to prove one's poetic talent.

Despite his obvious frustration with the limited poetic potential of the French language, Voltaire persisted in his defense of versification, arguing that difficulty increased its value, that the genius of each nation dictates its linguistic freedom.[80] He refused to consider as poetic a mode of writing devoid of verse: "On confond toutes les idées, on transpose les limites des arts quand on donne le nom de poème à la prose" [We confuse all ideas, we transpose the limits of the arts when we give the name of poem to prose.][81] Voltaire classified *Télémaque* as a novel, a genre he did not respect much for its lack of seriousness, depth, and difficulty. Had it been a translated poem, *Télémaque*'s style would have been suitable. Only the translation of poetry could have provided the excuse for a poem in prose just as the translation of a play could justify using prose and blank verse—as Voltaire experimented when translating *Julius Caesar*'s first three acts and an oriental poem by Sadi.[82] His warning that tragedy would be forever lost if poets started to write in blank verse, "no more difficult to write than a letter," equally applied to epic poetry, which risked disappearing if no longer governed by difficulty.[83]

---

[79] Ibid., 223–4.

[80] Voltaire, article "Hémistiche," in *Œuvres alphabétiques*, ed. Jeroom Vercruysse, in Voltaire, *Œuvres Complètes*, vol. 33, 152.

[81] Voltaire, *Essai sur la poésie épique*, in *Œuvres complètes*, vol. 3B, 493–4.

[82] Cited in the *Encyclopédie*, vol. 12, article "Poësie orientale moderne," 840.

[83] "[L]es vers blancs ne coûtent que la peine de les dicter. Cela n'est *pas plus difficile à faire qu'une lettre*. Si on s'avise de faire des tragédies en vers blancs, et de les jouer sur notre théâtre, la tragédie est perdue. *Dès que vous ôtez la difficulté, vous ôtez le mérite*" [blank

Just as Fénelon's languid prose irritated Voltaire because he feared the spread of its seduction (hence his insistence on the unique and irreproducible character of Fénelon's prose poem), the success of Montesquieu's fiction annoyed him. La Harpe suggested that Voltaire's irritation came from Montesquieu's condemnation of poets in the famous episode of the library's visit in the *Lettres persanes*: "Ce sont ici les poëtes, c'est-à-dire ces auteurs dont le métier est de mettre des entraves au bon sens, et d'accabler la raison sous les agreements" [Here are poets, namely those authors whose work is to fetter common sense and weigh down reason with embellishments.][84] Voltaire was sensitive to the fact that Montesquieu united in his proscription versifiers and true poets, but also reduced poetry to an unflattering subjection. La Harpe continued: "quand on lui reprochait les traits qu'il lançait contre Montesquieu, [Voltaire] se contentait de répondre, *Il est coupable de lèse-poésie*: et l'on avouera que c'était un crime que Voltaire ne pouvait guère pardonner" [When people reproached him for criticizing Montesquieu, Voltaire would simply reply, "He is guilty of lèse-poetry;" and we have to admit that Voltaire could not readily forgive such a crime.][85] Like all metaphors relating to prose poems (bastard, monster, impotence, shackles), which must be deciphered beyond their rhetorical power, the modern crime of lèse-poésie has strong socio-political connotations: by elevating poetry to majesty, it ranks prose with the people. And Voltaire, like Fraguier, shared Horace's *Odi profanum vulgus & arceo* [I hate the profanely vulgar and reject it].[86]

Voltaire's rigorous adherence to the classical canon of taste applied to his own writings in verse and prose. He excelled in all traditional genres, sought to preserve them—his own status in the Belles Lettres field depended on it—and saw no need to push artistic boundaries, a unique, almost isolated, position in the face of rapidly expanding new literary forms to which so many of his contemporaries contributed. Although he explored philosophical poems as a new poetic genre, I would argue that this invention partook of the rationalization of poetry. In its diverse incarnations (letters, philosophical tales, dictionary articles, historical memoirs), Voltaire's prose remained clear, incisive, intellectual, and humorous when needed; his poetry (epic, philosophical or circumstantial) strictly abided by rules. Yet for all their classical perfection, neither proved adequate for a growing number of writers searching for a new poetics to express a more lyrical self.

---

verses only cost the trouble of dictating them. They are *no more difficult to write than a letter*. If someone decides to write tragedies in blank verse and stage them in our theaters, tragedy is lost. *As soon as you remove difficulty, you remove merit*.] Voltaire, "Avertissement du traducteur," in *Jules César. Tragédie de Shakespeare*, in *Œuvres complètes*, vol. 2, 1095 (emphasis added).

[84] Cited by François de la Harpe, *Cours de Littérature ancienne et moderne* (Paris, 1847), vol. 3, 262.

[85] Ibid.

[86] Horace, *Odes*, Livre III, vol. 1. Cited by Fraguier, *Qu'il ne peut y avoir de poëme en prose*, 268.

The Encyclopédie: Ambiguities

As experimentations in prose poetry multiplied in the second half of the eighteenth century, theoretical discourses struggled to find a definition that would account for the phenomenon, but no consensus emerged. Contradictions between several articles of the *Encyclopédie, ou Dictionnaire raisonné des arts, des sciences et des métiers* (1751–1765) reflected the impossibility of categorizing prose poems. Immediately after the article "POEME," the Chevalier de Jaucourt wrote the entry for "Poëme en prose" with which I opened my introduction:

> POEME EN PROSE, (*Belles-Lettres*) genre d'ouvrage où l'on retrouve la fiction & le style de la poésie, & qui par-là sont de vrais *poëmes*, à la mesure & à la rime près; c'est une invention fort heureuse. Nous avons obligation à la poésie en prose de quelques ouvrages remplis d'avantures vraisemblables, & merveilleuses à la fois, comme de préceptes sages & praticables en même tems, qui n'auroient peut-être jamais vû le jour, s'il eût fallu que les auteurs eussent assujetti leur génie à la rime & à la mesure. L'estimable auteur de Télémaque ne nous auroit jamais donné cet ouvrage enchanteur, s'il avoit dû l'écrire en vers; il est de beaux *poëmes* sans vers, comme de beaux tableaux sans le plus riche coloris. (*D.J.*)

> [PROSE POEM, (*Belles Lettres*): A genre of work wherein one finds the fiction and style of poetry, by which they are true *poems*, except for rhyme and measure. It is a felicitous invention. We owe to poetry in prose works filled with adventures both credible and marvelous as well as precepts both wise and feasible, which might have never seen light if their authors had to subject their genius to rhyme and measure. The esteemed author of Telemachus would have never given us this enchanting work if he had had to write it in verse. There are beautiful *poems* without verse, just as we have beautiful paintings without the richest colors.] [87]

The article almost directly paraphrased Dubos's comments in the section entitled "Des Estampes et des Poëmes en prose," with the difference that Dubos cited *La Princesse de Clèves* (1678) in addition to *Télémaque*.[88] Significantly, Jaucourt kept only the most epic of the two works, removing La Fayette's text from the category of prose poems. However, in his next encyclopedic article, "Poésie," Jaucourt no longer considered prose poems "a felicitous invention" but instead "caprices faits pour être hors de la regle, & dont l'exception est absolument sans conséquence pour les principes" [caprices meant to be outside rules, and whose exception is absolutely without consequence as far as principles are concerned.][89] This time, Jaucourt took up word for word Charles Batteux' argument (from 1746) that prose and poetry were "langues voisins" [neighboring languages],

---

[87]   *Encyclopédie*, vol. 12, 836–7.

[88]   Jean-Baptiste Dubos, "Des Estampes & des Poëmes en prose," in *Réflexions critiques sur la poésie et la peinture* (Geneva, 1967), 134.

[89]   Article "Poésie," *Encyclopédie*, vol. 12, 837.

which could borrow form and/or substance from each other "desorte que tout paroît travesti" [so that all seems disguised.][90] Due to their hybrid character, texts mixing the two modes of writing could not be accounted for in the general definition.[91] Like Batteux, Jaucourt eventually but cautiously accounted for the genre as an exception to the principles of poetry.

We hear a different argument from the author of the unsigned entry on "Prose," who refutes La Motte's arguments in favor of the new prose poem as an "ill-founded paradox," a critique in the same logical vein as Voltaire's separation of genres.[92] The entry unequivocally excluded non-versified texts from the poetic domain:[93]

> La fable de Psyché auroit été appellée *poëme*, s'il y avoit des poëmes en *prose*. Le songe de Scipion, quoique fiction très-noble, écrite en style poétique, ne fera jamais mettre le nom de Ciceron parmi ceux des poëtes latins, de même que parmi ceux de nos poëtes françois nous ne mettons point celui de Fénelon.

> [The fable of Psyche would have been called a poem, if there had been prose poems. Scipio's dream, although a very noble fiction, written in a poetic style, will never put Cicero's name among Latin poets; similarly, we do not put Fénelon among our French poets.][94]

---

[90] Ibid. See Batteux, *Les Beaux Arts réduits à un même principe*, in *Principes de la littérature* (Geneva, 1967), 25–6. The fifth edition of the *Principes de la littérature* contains 1) *Les Beaux-Arts réduits à un même principe,* originally published in 1746; 2) the *Cours de Belles Lettres* (1747 & 1748), and 3) *Construction oratoire* (1763). See "Avertissement," 7.

[91] "Il y a des fictions poétiques qui se montrent avec l'habit simple de la prose; tels sont les romans & tout ce qui est dans leur genre. Il y a même des matieres vraies, qui paroissent revêtues & parées de tous les charmes de l'harmonie poëtique; tels sont les poëmes didactiques & historiques. Mais ces fictions en prose, & ces histoires en vers, ne sont ni pure prose, ni *poésie* pure; c'est un mélange des deux natures, auquel la définition ne doit point avoir égard" [There are poetical fictions that don prose's simple dress: such are novels and everything related to this genre. We even have genuine subject matters, dressed and adorned with all the charms of poetic harmony: such are didactic and historical poems. But these prose fictions and verse histories are neither pure prose nor pure poetry; they are a mixture of both, which the definition should disregard.] Article "Poésie," *Encyclopédie*, vol. 12, 837. The passage is taken from Batteux, *Les Beaux-Arts réduits à un même principe*, 26.

[92] Article "Prose," *Encyclopédie*, vol. 13, 494.

[93] This exclusion is in direct contradiction with the definition of poetry in the *Encyclopédie*'s preface. In the commentary upon the "encyclopedic tree" classifying the arts and sciences, the author explained: "Nous n'entendons ici par *Poësie* que ce qui est fiction. Comme il peut y avoir Versification sans Poësie & Poësie sans Versification, nous avons crû devoir regarder la *Versification* comme une qualité du style, & la renvoyer à l'Art Oratoire" [By poetry, we mean here only fiction. Just as there can be verse without poetry, and poetry without verse, we believe we should consider versification as an attribute of style and consider it a part of Eloquence.] *Encyclopédie*, vol. 1, 1.

[94] Article "Prose," *Encyclopédie*, vol. 13, 494.

Despite the poetic variety evidenced by the texts mentioned, the entry somewhat paradoxically asserted that prose, on account of its uniform pace, could not offer accents as diversified as poetry. The article reinforced the common comparison between pedestrian prose vs. the dance of poetry with another well-known analogy, prose as a drawing ("estampe") vs. poetry as a painting. In keeping with prevailing opinions, the author of the article considered that prose lacked music, movement (verse), and color (images)—quintessential poetic attributes. The author did not explore the logical implications of the analogy, namely did not infer from the existence of superb drawings that artistic prose could similarly rise to superior poetic heights, which Dubos and Jaucourt had acknowledged as a fact: "il est de beaux poëmes sans vers, comme de beaux tableaux sans le plus riche coloris" [There are beautiful poems without verse, just as we have beautiful paintings without the richest colors.][95] But unlike fine pictorial examples, which could be found in great numbers, the eighteenth century lacked evidence of beautiful, unversified poems apart from *Télémaque*. Perhaps this is why the *Encyclopédie* admitted the existence of the "poëme en prose" under the aegis of "POEME," then denied its currency under the definition of "PROSE." Fénelon was acclaimed as the poet of a happy invention, then denied the title. I read these contradictions as emblematic of half a century of disagreements roused by *Télémaque*, but also as symptoms of the Encyclopedists' difficulty in extricating themselves from conventional definitions that an evolving literature had outgrown.

There is no entry for "prose" in the *Supplément* of the *Encyclopédie*, but under "Poeme," one finds a fresh view on the issue. The new entry had been excerpted and translated from Johann Georg Sulzer, the Swiss German philosopher and aesthetician, the author of *Allgemeine Theorie der schonen Kunste und Wissenschaften* (1771–1774), translated as *Théorie générale des beaux-arts*. Trying to determine "les limites exactes qui séparent les perfections de l'éloquence de celles de la poésie" [the exact limits that separate the perfections of eloquence from those of poetry], the article begins with a candid admission that the question has remained unresolved since Aristotle.[96] Sulzer unearthed a long suppressed truth: indecision about the actual difference between prose and poetry stood indeed at the center of the problematic—an indecision proper to the eighteenth century and which would have been inconceivable in Malherbe and Guez de Balzac's time. For Sulzer, this indecision originated from the misunderstood fact that the difference between prose and poetry was one of *degree*, not essence. This difference in degree explained first the difficulty of drawing strict boundaries and second, the existence of works "sur lesquels on est embarrassé de dire s'ils

---

[95] Article "Poëme en prose," *Encyclopédie*, vol. 12, 437. Dubos had written: "Il est de beaux Poëmes sans vers, comme il est de beaux vers sans poësie, & de beaux tableaux sans un riche coloris" [There are beautiful poems without verse, just as there are beautiful verses without poetry and beautiful paintings without rich colors.] Dubos, *Réflexions critiques*, 134.

[96] Article "Poème," *Supplément à l'Encyclopédie*, vol. 21, 423.

appartiennent à l'éloquence ou à la poésie" [about which one is embarrassed to say whether they belong to eloquence or poetry.][97] Sulzer also broke away from the traditional definition of poetry by substituting enthusiasm for imitation as the origin of poetry, a major shift away from Aristotle.[98] The *Supplément*'s article, via Sulzer, criticized imitation and the pursuit and display of faked enthusiasm, further disguised by versification, resulting in "une écorce poétique" [poetic crust] instead of genuine, "natural" poetry.[99] The key Aristotelian principle of poetry, imitation, at the core of Batteux's theory and the *Encyclopédie*'s article "Poème," was hereby downgraded as a servile and sterile attitude.

In his analysis of the "natural characteristics of poems" Sulzer considered that versification had originally a natural affinity with poetry, perfected over time.[100] Yet, though versification represented one of poetry's "distinctive characters" and poets ought to employ it, Sulzer admitted that all discourses inspired by poetic enthusiasm presented some form of "arrangement périodique" [periodic order]: "Ainsi la prose poétique a toujours des tours & des tons par lesquels elle se distingue" [Thus poetic prose has always turns of phrase and tones to distinguish itself.][101] Therefore works that exhibited all the characters of poetry except for versification should not be removed from "the class of poetic works." Sulzer carefully avoided the term "poëme en prose," but indirectly acknowledged its existence: the next paragraph put on equal footing versified and unversified poetry in stating that the form of the poem, whether in verse or poetic prose, did not matter as long as the tone conveyed the particular nuances of the poet's feelings.[102]

In addition to an appropriate tone, a poem should be written in an appropriate language, consisting of figures and images, themselves "un effet très naturel de la verve poétique" [a very natural effect of poetic vigor]. Sulzer quoted Dubos, with whom he stood in agreement: "Ce langage poétique, dit cet habile critique [Dubos], est ce qui fait proprement le poëte, & non la mesure & la rime. On peut, suivant l'idée d'Horace, être un poëte en prose, & n'être qu'un orateur en vers" [Poetic language, claims a fine critic [Dubos], is what truly makes a poet, not meter or rhyme. According to Horace's idea, one can be a poet in prose, and a mere orator in verse.][103] Turning away from tradition and rules to explain the true character of poetry, Sulzer innovated by solely focusing on the poet's inner state and the way in which he translated it into poetic form. Authorities had become irrelevant to help understand this process. Variations in poetic forms too, had little interest for Sulzer, who did not lengthen his article with a detailed classification of poetic genres, found in Jaucourt's definition and Batteux's work. Sulzer's theories

---

[97]   Ibid.
[98]   Ibid.
[99]   Ibid., 425.
[100]   Ibid., 423.
[101]   Ibid., 424.
[102]   Ibid.
[103]   Ibid.

signaled a new understanding of poetic genius, the freedom of its expression, and a change in orientation from traditional French criticism.

In the different articles he authored for the *Encyclopédie* and its *Supplément*, Jean-François Marmontel, also stood on the side of novelty, particularly in his understanding of prose. Marmontel viewed prose as a mode of writing equal, if not superior, to verse, as evidenced by a series of statements: translations of poetry in prose were justified; *Télémaque* represented, with Voltaire's *Henriade*, a model of epic poetry; the "harmony" of heroic verses was "constrained" as opposed to the free harmony of prose.[104]

This brief survey of the *Encyclopédie* confirms the extent to which norms were fluctuating.[105] In this respect, it mirrored the inconsistencies, variations, and reshaping of the categories of prose and poetry under the pressure of evolving genres. As Sulzer keenly observed, the century that prided itself on clarity confronted the paradox that it did not truly know the difference between prose and poetry—in part because it falsely believed that versification constituted the essential discriminating factor.

The Myth of the French Language: Rivarol's Triumph of Prose

The scope of Antoine de Rivarol's *L'Universalité de la langue française* (1785) contrasts with the closely focused perspective of contemporary literary critics. In this famous panegyric to the French language, Rivarol situated the debate about French letters on the international, not national level: he was not concerned about the hierarchy of genres, but the hierarchy of languages. As in Sulzer's analysis, when critics ignored genres to shift their focus to the French language per se, the result emphasized the unique strength of French prose. Clarity and order, its best qualities, also belonged to the best poetry. Rivarol considers poetry as very similar to prose since it primarily solicits a rational mind: "Il faut ... que le poète français plaise par la pensée" [The French poet ... must please through thought.] Rivarol finds "reason within verse" most admirable. Because of this proximity, rhyme remained indispensable to distinguish poetry from prose, as Voltaire also argued.[106] Unlike Voltaire however, Rivarol readily admitted that the charm of French verse, by virtue of its continuity, became tedious. He equated verses with "les débris de la prose qui les a précédés" [the debris of prose that preceded them], thus reversing the "disjecti membra" trope in favor of prose (78). Prose, by virtue

---

[104] Jean-François Marmontel, article "Traduction," *Supplément de l'Encyclopédie*, vol. 21, 953–4; article "Poésie," *Supplément*, vol. 21, 438; article "Epopée," *Encyclopédie*, vol. 5, 830.

[105] See also abbé Reyrac's hesitant terminology ("prose poétique," "petits Poëmes," "morceaux de prose poétique"), "Avant propos" and "Discours Préliminaire," in Reyrac, *Hymne au soleil, Suivi de plusieurs morceaux du même genre* (1782), 7–66.

[106] Antoine de Rivarol, *L'Universalité de la langue française* (Paris, 1991), 79. Hereafter noted in text.

of its anteriority, no longer resembled the scattered limbs of poetry; now poetry appeared as the scattered limbs of prose. The lengthy reign of "verses and gods" in Greece before the reign of "prose and kings" explained the more natural, and at the same time more evolved state of Greek poetry in opposition to a French language "à jamais dénué de prosodie" [forever devoid of prosody] (78).

Rivarol's discussion of verse and prose contrasts interestingly with Voltaire's. When Rivarol claims that anything in verse can be said as accurately in prose, one is reminded of Voltaire's opposite contention, that verse can express more and better ideas than prose.[107] Whereas Voltaire discounted the easiness of prose, Rivarol believed that difficulty hid under prose's "extreme easiness."[108] He argued that prose was the agent of truth, and verse but a disguise, seemingly considering prose in its traditional form of eloquence, not fiction, as well as ignoring the increased sophistication of eighteenth-century novels which belied his claim of transparency. By contrast, the poetic production of the eighteenth century, including Voltaire's, well justified Rivarol's conception of a poetry that was sensible, not sensitive, and universal, not individual. Rivarol attributed the intellectual character of poetry to the qualities of the French language: its "marche ... si leste et si dégagée," [its pace ... so quick and free] (69), "the order and construction of the sentence" (72), and its "admirable clarity" (73). These same qualities explained why "la langue française a été moins propre à la musique et aux vers qu'aucune langue ancienne ou moderne" [The French language was less appropriate to music and verse than any ancient or modern languages] (73). "[C]e n'est point ... parce que les mots français ne sont pas sonores que la musique les repousse: c'est parce qu'ils offrent l'ordre et la suite quand le chant demande le désordre et l'abandon" [It is not ... because French words are not sonorous that music rejects them, it is because they offer order and succession whereas songs require disorder and abandon] (74). Instead of expressing frustration with the inflexibility of French, Rivarol contrasted the "traps and surprises" of languages that allow inversions, to the elegant clarity of French: "La prose française se développe en marchant et se déroule avec grâce et noblesse" [French prose proceeds on foot and unfolds with grace and nobility] (77).

---

[107] "On ne dit rien en vers qu'on ne puisse très souvent exprimer aussi bien dans notre prose, et cela n'est pas toujours réciproque. Le prosateur tient plus étroitement sa pensée et la conduit par le plus court chemin, tandis que le versificateur laisse flotter les rênes et va là où la rime le pousse" [Most often, nothing expressed in verse cannot be expressed as well in prose, which is not always reciprocal. The prose writer holds his thoughts tighter and leads them through the shortest path, whereas the writer in verse loosens the reins and goes wherever rhymes lead him.] Ibid., 77.

[108] "Le versificateur enfle sa voix, s'arme de la rime et de la mesure, et tire une pensée commune du sentier vulgaire; mais aussi que de faiblesses ne cache pas l'art des vers! La prose accuse le nu de la pensée; il n'est pas permis d'être faible avec elle" [The verse writer swells his voice, arms himself with rhymes and measures, and extracts a common thought from the vulgar path. But how many weaknesses hide behind the art of versification? Prose reveals naked thought, it does not allow weakness.] Ibid., 78.

Rivarol's treatise is replete with controversial insights, such as the absence of "prosody" in French prose and the anteriority of prose over poetry, to cite two examples. Perhaps the greatest provocation, worthy of a treatise of its own, lay in the following affirmation: "c'est la prose qui donne l'empire à une langue, parce qu'elle est toute usuelle; la poésie n'est qu'un objet de luxe" [prose gives power to a language, because of its everyday use; poetry is but an object of luxury] (42). Rivarol's critique had strong ideological implications. Cast as an "objet de luxe," poetry is rare, expensive (in terms of labor cost), and reserved for an educated elite; therefore poetry is a dispensable luxury. By contrast, prose is the everyday medium of democratic exchange open to all, like Molière's Monsieur Jourdain requesting his slippers. But the evolution of French literature contradicted Rivarol's generalization about poetry as luxury, as some poetry became a more common and accessible means of expression, while a certain kind of prose was elevated beyond ordinary, common usage.

To return to Rivarol's phraseology, the "empire" of the French language in the eighteenth century was indeed vast, stretching from Paris to St. Petersburg and beyond, but Rivarol's assumption that prose seemed the sole instrument propagating French language is debatable: poetry (drama in particular) was as admired and influential as the prose exchanged in myriad of letters and books circulating on the continent. Prose did have the advantage of being spoken as well as written. The French art of conversation celebrated in the salons spread exponentially. The question of what gives a language power remains salient to this day: is it written literature or spoken language which spreads cultural influence?

The entry on the prose poem in the encyclopedic corpus, despite contradictions in other articles, records a *fait accompli*. If Fraguier's denial was no longer *de rigueur*, critics of eighteenth-century prose poems nonetheless continued to be divided on an already flourishing genre.[109] This was echoed in two later commentaries: in 1805, an anonymous critique of Boiste's *L'Univers, poëme en prose* in the *Spectateur Français* and in 1811, François-Louis Escherny's commentary on poetry and verse. Published at the onset of the nineteenth-century, they indicated the continued struggle to weigh the literary merits of contemporary prose poems.

A "dangerous innovation," a regrettable example set by Fénelon, a "bastard genre" unknown by the Ancients: the commentator of *L'Univers* condemned the aberration of prose poems, based on very strict adherence to classical rules.[110] By contrast, Escherny's more modern criticism began by deploring versification as a substitute for poetry, complained of "ces entraves gothiques du vers français"

---

[109] See Fournier de Tony, "Dissertation sur Télémaque et sur son style," in *Les Nymphes de Dyctyme ou révolutions de l'empire virginal* (1790), i–xxix.

[110] Anon., "Sur la prose poétique, sur la prose rythmique et sur les poëmes en prose, à l'occasion d'un ouvrage de ce genre intitulé l'Univers, poëme en prose," in *Le Spectateur français au XIXe siècle* (1805–1812) (Geneva, 1970), 606–11.

[the gothic fetters of French verse], and described his adverse reaction as a reader of poetry: [111]

> Lorsque je lis une belle page de prose, je me sens à mon aise, rien ne me gêne, ne m'embarrasse, ne me distrait du plaisir que je goûte; je jouis. Lorsque je lis des vers, c'est précisément tout le contraire; ... Cette chûte périodique des sons qui reparoissent à intervalles égaux, me distrait du sens, et me cause la même inquiétude que l'eau qui s'échappe goutte à goutte d'une fontaine mal fermée. [112]

> [When I read a beautiful page of prose, I feel at ease, nothing bothers me, constrains me, distracts me from the pleasure that I taste; I enjoy it. When I read verses, it is exactly the opposite; ... The periodic sounds that drop at regular intervals distract me from their meaning, and cause the same anxiety as water dripping from a fountain that has not been completely turned off.]

Amusingly depicted here, the torture of verse also threatened Fénelon's *Télémaque*, Young, and Ossian, which, time and again, many "métromanes" [metermaniacs] attempted to versify.[113] .

To build his case, Escherny contrasted the dry, cold poetry of Racine, Boileau, Voltaire, and Jean-Baptiste Rousseau with the "mélodie enchanteresse" [enchanting melody] of Buffon, Jean-Jacques Rousseau, Montesquieu, and occasionally Marmontel's prose. He offered the works of these four authors as examples of "ce style nombreux, animé et plein de poésie" [this rhythmical style, animated and poetic] which he advocated (like Mercier and Staël before him).[114] He warned that this "prose nombreuse et mesurée" [rhythmical, measured prose] should not be mistaken with the type of prose "qu'on a jusqu'à présent appelé *prose poétique*, très-mauvais genre, à commencer par *l'Hymne au soleil, Joseph, L'Univers*, et plusieurs ouvrages qui leur ont succédé, et qu'on a décoré du nom pompeux de *poëmes en prose*. On ne trouve dans toutes ces productions, d'ailleurs vides de choses, de pensées et foiblement écrites; on n'y trouve, dis-je, ni nombre, ni mesure, et si le délire poétique se laisse apercevoir dans ces prétendus poëmes, c'est un délire glacial" [a prose that has been called *poetic prose* until now, a really bad genre, starting with *l'Hymne au soleil, Joseph, L'Univers,* and several other works that followed, decorated with the pompous name of *prose poems*. In all these productions, empty of things, thoughts and poorly written, one finds neither rhythm nor measure, and if a poetic enthusiasm can be glimpsed in these so-called poems, it is a glacial enthusiasm.][115] Escherny measured the painful gap between the ambition of poets in prose and their accomplishments, but he himself failed to

---

[111] François-Louis D'Escherny, "De la poésie et des vers," in *Mélange de littérature, d'histoire, de morale et de philosophie* (Paris, 1811), vol. 2, 225.

[112] Ibid., 222–3.

[113] Ibid., 235–6.

[114] Ibid., 270 and 243–4.

[115] Ibid., 269–70.

illustrate his theory of rhythmical prose when offering his readers a stilted, lengthy example.[116] One more time, practice was unable to realize the critical vision of a genre-breaking poetic mode. This is why, in the end, the Enlightenment quarrel of poetry vs. prose saw a victory of Voltaire's views. The immense weight of Voltaire's authority as years passed meant that an author like Boiste, though an articulate defender of "poëmes en prose" eventually yielded to critical pressure by reluctantly changing the title of his work for its second edition—from *L'Univers, poëme en prose en douze chants* (1801) to *L'Univers, narration épique* (1804).[117]

---

[116] Ibid., "Exemple de prose nombreuse et mesurée," chap. XII, 274–307.

[117] Pierre-Claude-Victor Boiste, *L'Univers, narration épique; suivie de notes et d'observations sur le système de Newton et la théorie physique de la Terre* (1804). For Boiste's position in the debate about prose poems, see "Sur le titre *Narration épique*," vol. 2, 467–76.

Chapter 3
Birth of the Poem in Prose

Le Temple de Gnide étant une espece de poëme en prose, c'est à nos écrivains
les plus célebres en ce genre à fixer le rang qu'il doit occuper.

[The Temple of Gnidus being a kind of prose poem, our most famous writers
must determine the rank it shall occupy.]

Jean Le Rond d'Alembert[1]

Les Aventures de Télémaque ruled uncontested for twenty-five years.[2] Imitations
appeared in either verse or prose but none achieved its distinctive style.[3] Only
the anonymous *Temple de Gnide* published in 1725 caused a surprise and an
enchantment similar to *Télémaque*. The slim volume of the *Temple de Gnide*
emulated the poetic vein of its precursor as well as the choice of prose over
verse, but within the pastoral framework of an idyll, instead of an epic, in turn
inspiring many pastoral narratives of various lengths until the Revolution.[4] As
late as 1787, Montesquieu's text was regarded as a benchmark for future prose
poets, earning the praise of one editor as "le Temple de Gnide, espèce de poëme
en prose, digne de servir de modèle à ceux qui voudroient tenter cette carrière
nouvelle" [the Temple of Gnidus, a sort of prose poem worthy to serve as model

---

[1] Jean Le Rond d'Alembert, *Eloge de Monsieur de Montesquieu*, in *Encyclopédie*,
vol. 5, xvii.

[2] In the first half of the eighteenth century, only Jean Roussy pursued the vein of the
prose epic in *Aurélia ou Orléans délivrée* (1738). Epic poems in prose (such as François
Vernes, *La Franciade, ou l'Ancienne France. Poëme en seize chants* [1789]) suddenly
flourished in the years preceding the Revolution. The appearance of two mock epic prose
poems (Giraud's *Diabotinus* in 1749 and Guiard de Servigné's *Le Rhinocéros* in 1750)
constitutes another significant element in the prose poem's emergence during this early
phase.

[3] The most important imitation was Ramsay's allegorical *Les Voyages de Cyrus*
(1727). On Ramsay's role within Fénelon's legacy and his Masonic interpretation of
Télémaque, see Chérel's *Fénelon au XVIIIᵉ*, chap. VI.

[4] For exemple Mise de Marcillac, *Le Temple du destin, ou l'hommage des cœurs
françois, à Madame la Dauphine. Poëme, en cinq chants, en prose* (1770). For a complete
bibliography of editions, translations and adaptations, see Cecil P. Courtney and Carole
Dornier's edition of *Le Temple de Gnide. 1725*, in *Œuvres et écrits divers. Œuvres complètes
de Montesquieu* (Oxford, 2003), vol. 8, 323–427. For an important contemporary analysis,
see Madeleine-Angélique Poisson de Gomez, *Lettre critique sur le livre intitulé, Le Temple
de Gnide. Avec des reflexions sur l'utilité de la véritable Critique, & sur les Poëmes en
Prose* (1725).

for those who would be tempted by this new career.]⁵ But as with *Télémaque*,
we moderns no longer relish instructional fictions via mythology. According to
Jean Starobinski, this "poetic painting of voluptuousness" is Montesquieu's
worst work: "[Montesquieu] a écrit, lui aussi, son œuvre inutile, le Temple de
Gnide—'peinture poétique de la volupté'—mais c'est sa plus mauvaise œuvre,
celle où les défauts de l'époque s'accumulent et prévalent, celle qui, ayant
prétendu appartenir à un monde de formes éternellement jeunes, a vieilli le plus
rapidement" [(Montesquieu) too wrote a useless work, the Temple of Gnidus—
"a poetic painting of voluptuousness"—but it is his worst work, wherein all the
defects of the time multiply and prevail, a work which, pretending to belong to
a world of eternally youthful forms, aged the fastest.]⁶ This chapter revisits this
so-called antique artifact to understand its place within Montesquieu's work and,
more broadly, its role in the formation of the emerging genre of prose poems.
My argument is that the moral philosophy of the *Temple de Gnide* complemented
that of the *Lettres persanes*, and even foreshadowed the conclusions presented in
L'Esprit des lois. However, the problematic status of its genre raises intriguing
questions: What is the significance of a quest for poetic affiliation in a prose author
like Montesquieu? How and why did Montesquieu choose to salvage mythology
at the time when it was under siege by the philosophic avant-garde? Is his prose
poem an example of the Enlightenment's passion for seduction, wherein desire is
hypocritically hidden beneath an archaic form?⁷ After some preliminary remarks
about the text's genesis, I will examine the *Temple de Gnide*, first as a poetico-
sentimental journey, then as a Republican catechism to show that Montesquieu's
approach to mythology and poetry allowed for a realistic portrayal of the passions,
a reflection on gender roles, and idealization of love that should be interpreted as a
direct response to, and an indictment of, the Regency's ethos of pleasure. My final
section is devoted to understanding the pastoral as the Enlightenment's refuge
from modernity.

After the success of the *Lettres persanes* in 1721, Montesquieu spent several
months each year in Paris, leading a worldly life, becoming close to Louis XV's
prime minister, the Duc de Bourbon, in the court of Chantilly, and his mistress,
Mme de Prie, who resided in the castle of Bélesbat near Fontainebleau. In 1725
Bélesbat was the stage of a burlesque and mythological "fête" of the kind the
aristocracy prized during the Regency. A comedy in verse featured the Duc de
Bourbon's sister, the notorious Mlle de Clermont to whose charms Montesquieu
was not indifferent.⁸ The occasion gave rise to a curious courting and writing joust

---

⁵   See "Avertissement de l'éditeur des Voyages imaginaires," preceding Moutonnet-
Clairfons's prose poem, *Les Iles fortunées*, in *Voyages imaginaires*, xii.

⁶   Jean Starobinski. *Montesquieu par lui-même* (Paris, 1971), 18. For a more nuanced
reading, see Catherine Volpihac-Auger, *Montesquieu. Mémoire de la critique* (Paris, 2003),
17–18.

⁷   See Pierre Saint Amand, *Séduire ou la Passion des Lumières* (Paris, 1987).

⁸   For a portrait of the unconventional Mlle de Clairmont, see O. Uzanne, preface to
Le Temple de Gnide (Paris, 1881), vii.

between a cynical Voltaire and an idealistic Montesquieu.[9] Voltaire satirized the spectacle, unmasked its characters and drew out obscenities in the tradition of eighteenth-century satire and comedy, which, Starobinski reminds us, sought to refer to sexuality more literally, whereas mythology had elevated it into figurative paraphrase—"ramener à la littéralité tout ce que le code mythologique aura précédemment transporté dans une dimension métaphorique. Face aux *tableaux* où le désir s'exalte et se divinise, la satire redescend dans le monde quotidien et nous ramène à la réalité de l'instinct à l'état brut" [returning to literalness all that mythological codes previously transported onto a metaphorical plane. In contrast to tableaux wherein desire is exalted and deified, satire descends to the quotidian world and returns us to the reality of raw instincts.][10] Voltaire offered Mlle de Clairmont a dedicated copy of his manuscript, and according to O. Uzanne, who prefaced a reprint of the *Temple de Gnide* in 1881, "Montesquieu, indigné, n'édifia le *Temple de Gnide* que pour mettre en parallèle avec le cynisme de Voltaire l'art fin et voilé des indécences licites" [An indignant Montesquieu only built the *Temple of Gnidus* to parallel Voltaire's cynicism with the veiled, fine art of permissible indecencies.][11] We do not know which suitor's tale Mlle de Clairmont favored, and literary criticism has long forgotten this aesthetic contest between explicitness and *Je-ne-sais-quoi*. Yet there is much to be found in this cameo of antiquity. Montesquieu chose an allegorical interpretation of mythology for epistemological reasons. An instrument of propaganda for Voltaire, a means of communication for Montesquieu, allegory represented first of all a *language*: "la fonction de ce langage est signe social de reconnaissance, entre individus qui savent déchiffrer de la même manière, l'univers des fictions mythiques" [this language functions as a social sign of recognition between individuals who know how to decipher in the same manner the universe of mythological fictions.][12] Analyzing the semantic codes from which the new genre of prose idyll is constructed proves that Montesquieu's *Temple de Gnide* was certainly not "his useless œuvre."

A Sentimental Journey: Montesquieu's *Temple de Gnide*

As mythology has fallen from favor and education no longer centers on mastery of the classics, the *Temple de Gnide* seems at first an outdated, vapid love story compared with the modern questioning of ethnocentrism in the *Lettres persanes* epistolary fiction, and the political weight of the straightforward, energetic prose of *L'Esprit des Lois*. The story's poetic diction, remarkably consistent with neoclassical aesthetic, has not only contributed to the text's illegibility where it was

---

[9] See Voltaire, *La Fête de Bélesbat*, in Voltaire, *Œuvres complètes*, eds Roger J.V. Cotte and Paul Gibbard, vol. 3A, 141–86.

[10] Jean Starobinski, *Le Remède dans le mal. Critique et légitimation de l'artifice à l'âge des Lumières* (Paris, 1989), 243.

[11] Uzanne, preface to *Le Temple de Gnide*, ix.

[12] Starobinski, *Le Remède dans le mal*, 235.

once transparent, but also obscured its innovations. Beneath poetic ornaments, to which I will return, lay the prose canvas of a *Bildungsroman*. Indeed, Montesquieu seemed to have used the vehicle of the idyll to craft a pastoral narrative halfway between Honoré d'Urfé's *L'Astrée* and the sentimental novel later developed by Rousseau—an avid reader of *L'Astrée*—and by women authors of the early nineteenth century. In the year 1725, a highly unusual feature emerges from the *Temple de Gnide*: it is a first person narrative. The descriptive first canto ends with the unexpected revelation that the narrator's voice belongs to one of the characters—never named, henceforth Thémire's lover: "J'ai vû tout ce que je décris. J'ai été à Gnide; j'y ai vû Themire, & je l'ai aimée: je l'ai vûe encore, & je l'ai aimée davantage. Je resterai toute ma vie à Gnide avec elle" [I have been a witness of everything I now describe. I went to Gnidus; there I saw Themira, and I loved her; I saw her again, and I loved her still more. I will remain at Gnidus all my life with her].[13] Epistolary fiction like the *Lettres persanes* had offered an alternative to authors weary of omniscient narrators, but interested in bringing fictional characters closer to the reader. Montesquieu's innovative move in the *Temple de Gnide* was to present the narrative as an eyewitness account by one central character ("j'ai vu" and "je vis" are constantly repeated), who then revealed his own past (canto IV), reported his friend's love-story (canto V), described his personal agony in the throes of jealousy (canto VI), and finally his attempt to seduce Thémire (canto VII). It is the sole case of a first person prose poem I have found—until the meditative and lyrical prose poems at the century's close. The prose poem provided Montesquieu with a framework similar to epistolary fiction to explore the world of sentiment through a first person narrative. Thereby, Montesquieu found himself years ahead of the upcoming sentimental vogue.

Montesquieu gave a helpful descriptive analysis of his prose poem's structure, then removed it when he revised his preface in 1742. The pseudo-translator explains that cantos two and three are linked to the first canto because they continue to explore aspects of Venus's cult: in the second canto, the goddess delivers a succession of oracles to four different characters (a coquette from the island of Crete, a courtesan from Nocrétis, a rich man, and Aristhée); the third canto describes Gnide's sacred games and a beauty contest wherein no fewer than fourteen types of women pass before the reader's eyes. The pseudo-translator noted: "Les Episodes du second & du troisième chant naissent aussi du sujet; & le Poëte s'est conduit avec tant d'art, que les ornemens de son Poëme en sont aussi des parties necessaires" (390) [The episodes of the second and third cantos likewise arise from the subject; and the poet has conducted himself with so much art, that the ornaments of his poem are also necessary parts of it] (iii)— a justification to exonerate the gratuity of ornamental description. Then the prose

---

[13] Montesquieu, *Le Temple de Gnide*, eds Cecil Courtney and Carole Dornier, in *Œuvres et écrits divers. Œuvres complètes de Montesquieu* (Oxford, 2003), vol. 8, 399. Subsequent page references will be from this edition (which reproduces the first 1725 edition) and are hereafter cited in text. Anonymous translation, *The Temple of Gnidus, and Arsaces and Ismenia* (1797), 29. Hereafter cited in text.

poem switches from descriptive to narrative mode. In the fourth canto, Thémire's lover meets Aristhée and relates the story of his adventures before his arrival to Gnidus: how, leaving his native Sybaris in search of virtue, he moved from island to island (Crete, Lesbos, Lemnos, Delos), encountering in the process various (unsatisfactory) types of love (obsessive, homosexual, and so on) until a vision led him to Gnidus where he found Thémire. In turn, in the fifth canto Aristhée recounts his love story with Camille. The pseudo-translator singles out the narrative's twin qualities of variety and innovation:

> Il n'y a pas moins d'art dans le quatrieme & le cinquieme chant. Le Poëte, qui devoit faire réciter à Aristhée l'histoire de ses amours avec Camille, ne fait raconter au fils d'Antiloque ses aventures, que jusques au moment qu'il a vû Thémire; afin de mettre de la variété dans les récits.

> L'histoire d'Aristhée et de Camille est singuliere, en ce qu'elle est uniquement une histoire de sentimens. (390)

> [No less art appears in the fourth and fifth Cantos. The poet who was to make Aristaeus relate the history of his amour with Camilla, does not make the son of Antilochus relate his adventures, till he had seen Themira, in order that these narrations might possess greater variety.

> The history of Aristaeus and Camilla is remarkable, in that it is a history only of sentiments.] (iii)

As he begins his story, Aristhée warns his listener that his life was a purely sentimental and not an epic journey: "Dans tout ce récit, ... vous ne trouverez rien que de très-simple: mes aventures ne sont que les sentimens d'un cœur tendre, que mes plaisirs, que mes peines; & comme mon amour pour Camille fait le bonheur, il fait aussi toute l'histoire de ma vie" (410) [In all my recital, said he, you will find nothing but simple occurrences; my adventures are only the sentiments of a tender heart; nothing but my pleasures and my pains: and as my love for Camilla makes all the happiness, it makes too all the history of my life] (65–6). Unlike the previous canto's forward movement, propelled by the succession of locales and experiences, the sentimental story told in the fifth canto is static, much more so than a pastoral narrative like *L'Astrée*, also centered on love affairs, but which proceeded forward with episodes and "rebondissements" as the characters mixed and matched. Nothing happens in Aristhée's story other than his lyrical praise of Camille's charms and spirit, his pining for her love, his longing for her presence, and his outpouring of sentiment. A rhythmic, lyrical passage like the following eerily anticipates Évariste Parny's 1787 lyrical and melancholy songs, as will be seen in the last chapter:

> Quelquefois elle me dit en m'embrassant, Tu es triste; Il est vrai, lui dis-je, mais la tristesse des amans est délicieuse; je sens couler mes larmes, & je ne sçai pourquoi, car tu m'aimes; je n'ai point de sujet de me plaindre, & je me plains. Ne me retire point de la langueur où je suis, laisse-moi soupirer en même-tems mes peines & mes plaisirs. (411)

[Sometimes, throwing her arms around me, "you are melancholy," she will say. "It is true, I reply, but the melancholy of lovers is luxurious; I feel my tears flow, and I know not why, for thou lovest me; I have no cause of complaint, and yet I complain. Ah! Do not seek to disturb this soft languor; allow me to sigh at once my pleasures and my pains."] (71)

Rather than speculating on Montesquieu's "pre-Romantic" impulse, I suggest that the prose poem provided a means to experiment with different modes of expression (descriptive, narrative, sentimental, and lyrical) free from stifling versification. But the decision not to choose between one or the other reveals both the prose poem's floating generic status and the tension between narration (as in the sentimental novel, which progresses, however slowly) and description (which lyrically drives the fifth canto in its exploration of the lover's heart).

After the fifth canto's lyrical pause, the sentimental story continues. In the sixth canto, Furor and Jealousy seize the two friends until they escape and witness Bacchus and Ariane's "égarements" [frolickings]. Still the prey of misgivings and concern toward Thémire and Camille, "ces objets puissans de notre amour & de notre jalousie" [those powerful objects of our love and of our jealousy] (416), they reminisce about past suspicious incidents and finally meet their beloveds. Thémire protests her love, who lures her into a solitary wood to seduce her. She resists, forbids, and then forgives the unsuccessful perpetrator. The prose poem ends with an exclamation from her seducer: "Elle m'embrassa; je reçus ma grâce, hélas! sans espérance de devenir coupable" (418) [She embraced me, I received my pardon, alas, without the hope of becoming guilty] (98). In the preface, the pseudo-translator drew attention to the poet's craft, referring to the "noeud," the "denoûment," and emphasizing variety (390–91). Montesquieu carefully structured his prose poem as a narration with a subtle progression that no doubt eludes most readers today, but which must have delighted contemporaries attuned to the slightest variations in the classical themes and codes they knew by heart.[14]

The *Temple de Gnide* also leads us on a sentimental journey through the conventions of poetry and its topoi. Montesquieu respected both the difficulty of verse and prose's nobility, so evident in his *Pensées*, where he metaphorized their distinction with traditional water imagery: "La belle prose est comme un fleuve majestueux qui roule ses eaux, et les beaux vers, comme un jet d'eau qui jaillit par force: il sort de l'embarras des vers quelque chose qui plaît" [Beautiful prose is like a majestic river rolling its waters, and beautiful verses, like the water of a fountain that is forced out: something pleasing arises from the constraint of verse.][15] With such a commonly held view, Montesquieu seemed an unlikely candidate to make waves by experimenting with a new poetic genre combining prose's expressive accuracy and verse's elevated diction. Yet the *Temple de Gnide* became the first experiment to systematize what developed into an almost unanimous response to the challenge of poeticizing prose to compensate for the

---

[14] See Carole Dornier, introduction to *Le Temple de Gnide*, in Montesquieu, *Œuvres et écrits divers*, 325–42.

[15] Montesquieu, *Mes Pensées*, in *Œuvres complètes*, vol. 1, 1219.

lost acoustic and intellectual pleasure of rhyme and meter. After Fénelon and Montesquieu, practitioners of prose poems repeated standard poetic conventions in their prose to assure readers of the text's poetic stature. Though not exempt from baroque tendencies, the *Temple de Gnide* features many of the most common neoclassical poetic codes that recurred as stylistic strategies to ennoble prose and showcase Enlightenment authors' poetic ambitions.

The *Temple de Gnide* is divided into seven cantos ("chants") but Montesquieu only introduced this division when he revised the text for its 1742 reprint. In its original form, the narrative was unbroken to match the Greek manuscript, or so the first preface tells us (391). The twenty years separating the text from its revision account for a crucial change in strategy: whereas the original preface sought to reinforce the verisimilitude of the (pseudo) translation, the second preface, whose author was by then famous, surrendered to what had become a standard practice ever since *Télémaque*. Cantos, harking back to the ancients, conveyed a universally shared code, a simple yet immediate visual clue of the text's poetic affiliation.

The essential theme and character of the story, love, allegorized by Venus, emerge from an opening description that is heavily coded. As in *Télémaque,* the first canto describes her Greek island's countryside, the goddess's gardens, and her palace. Aware that pure descriptions broke classical rules, a reproach made by foes of Fénelon's Calypso episode, the pseudo-translator took pains to expose the link between the opening description and the story in the following defense:

> La description de Gnide, qui est dans le premier Chant, est d'autant plus heureuse, qu'elle fait pour ainsi dire naître le Poëme; qu'elle est non pas un ornement du sujet, mais une partie du sujet même: bien différente de ces descriptions que les anciens ont tant blamées, qui sont étrangeres & recherchées. (390)

> [The description of Gnidus in the first Canto, is peculiarly happy, as it in some measure gives rise to the Poem; and as it is not only an ornament to the subject, but a part of the subject itself: a description very different from those which were so much blamed by the ancients, and which are foreign and far fetched.] (ii–iii)

Montesquieu deleted this explanatory segment in his revised preface, perhaps because description had become such a widespread feature that he felt no longer concerned by the need to justify his own. The descriptive paragraph on the island's natural bounties and harmonies closes with an atmosphere of sensuality—"l'air ne s'y respire qu'avec la volupté" (393) [pleasure is inhaled with every breeze]— anticipating the gods and mortals' amorous discourses and behavior. The rich palace and "enchanted" gardens are but a reflection of Venus's beauty and a tribute to the worship of her cult on the Gnidus island she favors among all.

> La ville est au milieu d'une contrée, sur laquelle les Dieux ont versé leurs bienfaits à pleines mains; on y jouit d'un printemps éternel; la terre, heureusement fertile, y prévient tous les souhaits; les troupeaux y paissent sans nombre; les vents semblent n'y régner que pour répandre par tout l'esprit des fleurs; les oiseaux y chantent sans cesse; vous diriez que les bois sont harmonieux; les ruisseaux murmurent dans les plaines; une chaleur douce fait tout éclore; (393)

> [The city stands in the midst of a country on which Heaven has poured forth its choicest blessings with a liberal hand: here reign the glories of eternal Spring; the bountiful earth anticipates every wish; innumerable flocks feed on the plains; the winds breathe only to convey the perfume of the flowers; the birds sing with unceasing melody; you would think that the woods were vocal; the rivulets murmur through the valleys; a genial warmth makes every thing teem with every breeze.] (10)

The description exemplifies an "ideal landscape of poetry," to use Ernst Curtius' phrase, rooted in Homer's amiable, fertile nature, and developed by Theocritus in his pastoral poems; Virgil transposed it to "romantically far away Arcadia, which he himself had never visited," a country described in the *Aeneid* with a favorite epithet, *"amoenus,"* henceforth lending its name to the rhetorical figure that sought to emulate similar descriptions of nature, *"locus amoenus."*[16] Tracing the roots of this trope from Antiquity to the Middle Ages, Curtius underlined that *locus amoenus* eventually possessed "an independent rhetorico-poetical existence": from mere "backgrounds" in the poetry of Theocritus and Virgil, "[such scenes] were soon detached from any larger context and became subjects of bravura rhetorical description. Horace already disapproved of this tendency."[17] The *locus amoenus*, "historically ... a clearly defined topos of landscape description" as Curtius demonstrates, signaled to Fénelon and Montesquieu's readers that they had entered the realm of poetry.[18] Moreover, the following description of Venus's "enchanted gardens" would have reminded readers of Armide's celebrated garden in Tasso's *Jerusalem Delivered*:

> Les Jardins en sont enchantez: Flore & Pomone en ont pris soin; leurs Nimphes les cultivent, les fruits y renaissent sous la main qui les cuëille; les Fleurs succèdent aux fruits. Quand Vénus s'y promène, entourée de ses Gnidiennes, vous diriez que, dans leurs jeux folâtres, elles vont détruire ces jardins délicieux: mais, par une vertu secrète, tout se répare en un instant. (394)

> [The gardens seem the work of enchantment: Flora and Pomona have made them their peculiar care, and they are cultivated by the nymphs of these goddesses: the fruits grow under the hand that gathers them, and flowers succeed the fruits. When Venus walks in these enchanted gardens, surrounded by her fair votaries, the young Gnidian women, you would think that, in their wanton sports, the delicate beauties of that delightful place would be entirely demolished; but, by some secret power, every injury is repaired in a moment.] (11–12)

In stark contrast with the sublime, awe-inspiring, mountainous landscape the Romantic generation sought at the end of the century, pastoral nature remained

---

[16]　Ernst Robert Curtius, *European Literature and the Latin Middle Ages* (Princeton, 1973), 190. On the origins and variations of the "ideal landscape," see chap. 10, 183–202.

[17]　Ibid., 195.

[18]　Ibid., 198.

"riante" because death, decay, ruin, and destruction held no sway over an enchanted (magical) world of spontaneous generation and eternal springtime.

Another of poetry's descriptive topoi, ekphrasis, appears in the first canto in a long development on the decorative paintings inside the temple illustrating Mars and Venus's love affair. Ekphrasis anchored the prose poem in antiquity; Achilles' legendary shield had long been the model for such exercises in visual representation. A repeat performance of this long-established convention inspired even the philosopher d'Alembert: "Nous croyons ... que les peintures de cet ouvrage soûtiendroient avec succès une des principales épreuves des descriptions poétiques, celle de les représenter sur la toile" [We believe ... that the scenes of this work would successfully pass one of the major tests of poetical descriptions, namely to be represented on a canvas.][19] Not only did ekphrasis represent the ultimate expression of the *ut pictura poesis* principle, but its very nature, a "narrative response to pictorial stasis," can be interpreted as an emblem of the conflict between narration and description at the core of incipient prose poems.[20] "Because it verbally represents visual art, ekphrasis stages a contest between rival modes of representation: between the driving force of the narrating word and the stubborn resistance of the fixed image."[21] As modern prose poets discovered as well, ekphrasis represents a *mise en abyme* of the prose poem's conflicting impulses.[22]

The fabric of the text reveals other important poetic indicators. Parataxis, the coordination of clauses without conjunctions, a notable feature in *Télémaque*, is here reinforced by a frequent indenting visually suggestive of verses, for instance in the seventh canto, when the jealous lovers pine after their beloved (416). Parataxis, a frequent style in Latin, compresses prose into a more succinct expression reminiscent of verse. So prevalent did parataxis become in the development of the eighteenth-century prose poem that even Chateaubriand adopted it against the grain of his more ample style as we will see in the last chapter. Though particularly studied, parataxis was meant to convey the characters' simple and naïve language, a paradox that endured even in Chateaubriand's *Atala*. For instance, superlatives, hyperboles, repetitions, parallelisms, and emphatic negations abound ("jamais," "point," "rien," "tout") to elevate prose while stressing simple elocution.

Epithets mark an author's personal style, and Montesquieu was particularly sensitive to their evocative powers: "Je suis porté à croire que les épithètes doivent être fréquentes dans la poésie. Elles ajoutent toujours. Ce sont les couleurs,

---

[19]   D'Alembert, *Eloge de Monsieur de Montesquieu*, xvii.

[20]   James Heffernan, *Museum of Words. The Poetics of Ekphrasis from Homer to Ashbery* (Chicago, 1993), 4–5.

[21]   Ibid., 6.

[22]   See for instance Aloysius Bertand's "Harlem" (*Gaspard de la Nuit*, 1842), Karl Joris Huysmans' "La Kermesse de Rubens," "Claudine" and "Le Hareng saur" (*Le Drageoir aux épices*, 1874); and Paul Valéry's "Zurbaran. Sainte Alexandrine" (*Pièces sur l'art*, 1891). On prose poems and description, see Sandras, *Lire le poème en prose*, 114–25.

les images des objets. Le style de *Télémaque* est enchanteur, quoique chargé d'autant d'épithètes que celui d'Homère" [I tend to believe that epithets must appear frequently in poetry. They add something. They are the colors and images of things. *Télémaque*'s style is enchanting, though as laden with epithets as Homer's.][23] Debates had flared on this question alone, especially since the "querelle d'Homère." Montesquieu's reservation ("quoique") and d'Alembert's warning against "épithètes oisives" [gratuitous epithets] suggest a delicate boundary between felicitous use and uncreative overuse.[24] For its part, and contrary to what one might have hoped from Montesquieu's perceptive comment, *Le Temple de Gnide* does not offer any groundbreaking innovations, rather a fine sense of choice generic epithets to qualify physical and moral traits,[25] sentiments,[26] and situations.[27] The frequent anteposition of generic epithets also draws attention to the text's poetic ambition: "la charmante Thémire," "sa divine épouse," "affreuse mélancolie," "affreuse divinité," "fatal séjour," "mes éternelles amours," "la sombre tristesse," "la cruelle jalousie," "la noire jalousie," "la flatteuse espérance," etc. [charming Thémire; his divine spouse; awful melancholy; awful divinity; fatal stay; my eternal love; somber sadness; cruel jealousy; dark jealousy; flattering hopefulness.] The *Temple de Gnide* displays a few stock periphrases—"plaine liquide" [liquid plain] for the sea (394, 403), "doux pavots" [sweet poppies] for sleep (414)—but Montesquieu mostly shied from these worn out clichés. Notably absent from his descriptions are epic similes (often introduced by "tel ... tel"), which punctuated most prose poems, but given the pastoral generic affiliation of the text, such similes would have been out of place.

Allegories offered the surest means to confer a poeticity in conformity with neoclassical aesthetic. Montesquieu personified natural elements (cf. the river Céphée as a lover courting the nymphs who come close to its banks) and juxtaposed traditional allegories (Flore, Pomone, l'Amour) with more "modern" ones, particularly in the sixth song wherein the two male protagonists, hidden in an obscure cave, confront love's dark side. Allegorical, anthropomorphic creatures help visualize a mental and sentimental state of great agitation:

---

[23]   Montesquieu, *Mes Pensées*, in *Œuvres complètes*, vol. 1, 1023.

[24]   D'Alembert, *Eloge de Monsieur de Montesquieu*, xviii.

[25]   "[Camille] a une taille *charmante*; un air *noble*, mais *modeste*; des yeux *vifs* & tout prêts à être *tendres*" (410) [Her stature is elegant and majestic; she has a noble air, but modest; lively eyes, that seem formed for the expression of tenderness] (66).

[26]   "Mais jamais dans ces lieux *fortunez* elles n'ont rougi d'une passion *sincere*, d'un sentiment *naïf*, d'un aveu *tendre*" (398) [But never in these happy shades did any one blush for a sincere passion, for a pure sentiment, a tender confession] (26).

[27]   "nous fûmes conduits par un chemin de fleurs au pied d'un rocher *affreux*; nous vîmes un antre *obscur*, nous y entrâmes, croyant que c'étoit la demeure de quelque Mortel. O Dieux! qui auroit pensé que ce lieu eût été si *funeste* !" (413) [we were conducted by a path of flowers to the foot of a frightful rock: we saw a dark cavern; we entered it, thinking it the habitation of some mortal. O gods! Who would have thought that such a place had been so fatal!] (76).

[J]'y vis la Jalousie; son aspect étoit plus sombre que terrible; la pâleur, la tristesse, le silence l'entouroient, & les ennuis voloient autour d'elle. Elle souffla sur nous; elle nous mit la main sur le cœur; elle nous frappa sur la tête; & nous ne vîmes, nous n'imaginâmes plus que des monstres ... Nous vîmes une affreuse Divinité à la lueur des langues enflâmées *des serpens qui sifloient sur sa tête*: c'étoit la Fureur. Elle détacha un de ses serpens, & le jeta sur moi: je voulus le prendre; déjà sans que je l'eusse senti, il s'étoit glissé dans mon cœur. ... j'étois si agité qu'il me sembloit que je tournois sous le foüet des furies. Enfin je m'abandonnai, nous fîmes cent fois le tour de cet antre épouvantable: nous allions de la jalousie à la fureur, & de la fureur à la jalousie: nous crions, Thémire; nous crions, Camille; (413)

[I saw the fiend of Jealousy; her aspect was more sullen than terrible; paleness, and sorrow, and silence surrounded her; her languor and lethargy hovered about. She breathed upon us, she put her hand on our hearts, she struck us on the head, and we saw nothing; our imaginations presented nothing to us but monsters. ... We saw a frightful deity by the light of the flames that issued from the mouths of a hundred serpents which hissed upon her head. This was Frenzy. She unloosed one of the serpents, and threw him on me: I would have caught him; but, before I perceived it, he had slid into my heart. ... So violent were the emotions with which my body was agitated: I thought myself abandoned to the scourge of the furies. At last I gave myself up to despair: we went round and round this horrible cavern a hundred times: we passed from Jealousy to Frenzy, and from Frenzy to Jealousy: we cried, Themira! we cried Camilla!] (77–8)

This citation exemplifies numerous stylistic traits shared by scores of other prose poems, while also revealing Montesquieu's personal view of passion—to which I will return later. To that end, figurative expressions are used literally to envision the effects of passion. The accumulation and repetition of the vowel "i" and the sibilant "s" convey the shrill intensity and madness of the scene; and the famously expressive Racinian line (which I italicized) validates the poetic and metaphoric character of what occurs. Further, the adverbial expressions "already" (déjà) and "meanwhile" (cependant), which recur in every prose poem of the period, clearly dissociate this emerging genre from the novel: indeed, in contrast to the novel's "realistic" temporality, poetic time can be compressed or extended. Because the adverbs "cependant" and "déjà" preclude the need for transition between two moments, they accelerate time and condense narration. Such combined poetic strategies—allegorization, assonance, embedded citations, and temporal condensation—testify to the author's effort to ennoble his prose.[28]

Greek gods and goddesses play central roles and mythological references abound throughout the story of *Le Temple de Gnide*. Unlike philosophical allegories embraced by moderns like Voltaire as a legitimate way to rejuvenate poetry, classical mythology greatly divided Enlightenment thinkers and writers.

---

[28] See Carole Dornier's stylistic analysis in her introduction to *Le Temple de Gnide*, in *Œuvres complètes de Montesquieu*, 340–42. For an imitation of *Le Temple de Gnide* using similar poetic strategies, see, Marie-Uranie-Rose Monneron, *Annamire, poëme en trois chants* (1783).

Far from discarding mythology, Montesquieu placed allegorical interpretation at the service of his moral philosophy. In so far as knowledge of myths was widespread among his intended aristocratic audience, Montesquieu used them to communicate, as a pedagogical tool, just like Fénelon's *Télémaque*. In so doing, Montesquieu seemed to be swimming against the tide of the philosophical avant-garde and confirming the skepticism of some that the persistent attraction of myths in a supposedly enlightened eighteenth century belied professed advances in thought and rationality. Many worried that mythology was surviving too well and might triumph over an only temporarily victorious reason and progress. Frank Manuel demonstrated how this lack of confidence was rooted in the still unresolved dichotomy between reason and imagination.

> The imagination was conceived of as a virtually separate compartment of the soul, relatively inaccessible to reason. Often ideas which had been disapproved by the rational faculties took refuge and remained embedded in the imagination: witness the longevity of Greek myths; for even though Christian Europeans no longer believed in them rationally, as the pagans did, the same myths still delighted them in painting and poetry.[29]

If the encyclopedic tree of knowledge later compartmentalized reason and imagination for the sake of classifying human productions such as philosophy and poetry, the Horacian principle of pleasing while instructing in effect called for an artistic blurring of the rational and the poetic: this is what Montesquieu perfectly understood. He pleased by capitalizing on a collective understanding of mythology and rhetorical conventions—which conferred poetic cachet to his prose—*and* reasoned with his readers via a philosophical lesson conveyed through the pastoral, to which I will now turn.

In Praise of Republican Virtues

Rousseau's mitigated appreciation of Montesquieu's "petit roman" made him hesitant to decide as to its usefulness.[30] In the *Rêveries*'s fourth promenade, Rousseau referred to *Le Temple de Gnide* to illustrate his remarks on ...

---

[29] Frank Manuel, *The Eighteenth Century Confronts the Gods* (Cambridge, 1959), 52. Manuel investigates the eighteenth-century struggle to make sense of mythology under science's new strictures. Montesquieu's *Temple de Gnide* must be situated within the context of this century-long debate. By turns allegorizing, debunking, and reevaluating the gods, Enlightenment theorists pondered the issue of mythology, with caution and deference at first, with openness and enthusiasm at the end of the century, under new political circumstances. Manuel underlines the skepticism of rationality exercising its newfound power and prerogatives—a skepticism whose overcoming took a century, until Turgot's and Condorcet's unmitigated affirmation of progress vs. mythopoetics.

[30] See Diderot's similar critical reaction to a 1760 imitation of Montesquieu's prose poem, allegedly translated from the Greek. Diderot, "Carite et Polydore de Barthélemy," in *Œuvres complètes*, vol. XIII. *Arts et Lettres*, ed. Jean Varloot (Paris 1980), 148–60.

lies in literature! Rousseau distinguished between stories with a moral purpose (e.g., apologues and fables) and gratuitous, entertaining fictions without instructional value (the majority of tales and novels).[31] Rousseau went on to condemn Montesquieu's prose poem:

> S'il y a par exemple quelque objet moral dans le *Temple de Gnide,* cet objet est bien offusqué et gâté par les détails voluptueux et par les images lascives. Qu'a fait l'auteur pour couvrir cela d'un vernis de modestie? Il a feint que son ouvrage étoit la traduction d'un manuscrit Grec, et il a fait l'histoire de la découverte de ce manuscrit de la façon la plus propre à persuader ses lecteurs de la vérité de son récit. Si ce n'est pas là un mensonge bien positif, qu'on me dise donc ce que c'est que mentir? Cependant qui est-ce qui s'est avisé de faire à l'auteur un crime de ce mensonge et de le traiter pour cela d'imposteur? (1029–1030)

> [If, for example, there is any moral purpose in the *Temple of Gnidus* it is thoroughly obfuscated and spoiled by voluptuous details and lascivious images. What has the author done to cover it with a gloss of modesty? He has pretended that this work was the translation of a Greek manuscript and has fashioned the story about the discovery of this manuscript in the manner most likely to persuade his readers of the truth of his tale. If that is not a very positive lie, then let someone tell me what lying is. But who has taken into his head to accuse the author of a crime for this lie or call him a deceiver for it?] (32).

Had *Le Temple de Gnide* a moral, Rousseau told his readers, it was "spoiled" by the erotic imagery, veiled under the guise of a pseudo-translation. But Rousseau had to oppose the public's indulgence, which he rebuked for endorsing a dangerous practice and perhaps a corrupted tale:

> On dira vainement que ce n'est là qu'une plaisanterie, ... et que le public n'a pas douté un moment qu'il ne fût lui-même l'auteur de l'ouvrage prétendu Grec dont il se donnoit pour le traducteur. Je répondrai qu'une pareille plaisanterie sans aucun objet n'eut été qu'un bien sot enfantillage, ... qu'il faut détacher du public instruit des multitudes de lecteurs simples et crédules à qui l'histoire du manuscrit narrée par un auteur grave avec un air de bonne foi en a réellement imposé, et qui ont bu sans crainte dans une coupe de forme antique le poison dont ils se seroient au moins défiés s'il leur eut été présenté dans un vase moderne. (1030)

> [In vain will it be said that it is only a joke; ... that the public did not doubt for a moment that he was really the author of the supposedly Greek work of which he passed himself off as the translator. I will reply that if it had no purpose, such a joke was only a very silly and childish prank, ... that it is necessary to

---

31 Jean-Jacques Rousseau, "IV promenade." *Rêveries du promeneur solitaire*, in *Œuvres complètes* (Paris, 1964), vol. 1, 1029. *Reveries of the Solitary Walker*, ed. by Christopher Kelly, trans. by Charles E. Butterworth, Alexandra Cook, and Terence E. Marshall, in *The Collected Writings of Rousseau* (Hanover and London, 2000), vol. 8. Original and translation hereafter cited in text.

differentiate between the learned public and the hordes of simple, credulous readers whom the story of the manuscript, narrated by a serious author with the appearance of good faith, really deceived and who fearlessly drank from a goblet of ancient form the poison of which they would at least have been suspicious had it been presented to them in a modern vessel.] (33)

The indignation of Rousseau, who could not conceive that a serious author would purposely deceive gullible readers (women?) into reading a "poisonous" story, points at the "terreur séductrice" [seductive terror] that Pierre Saint-Amand reads in eighteenth-century novels.[32] Rousseau's severe indictment of the antique-looking goblet of pseudo-translation ends with an ambiguous statement as to the story's actual moral purpose: "Si le Temple de Gnide est un ouvrage utile l'histoire du manuscrit Grec n'est qu'une fiction très innocente; elle est un mensonge très punissable si l'ouvrage est dangereux" (1032) [If the *Temple of Gnidus* is a useful work, the story about the Greek manuscript is only a very innocent fiction; it is a lie very worthy of punishment, if the work is dangerous] (34). At the time when Rousseau was reading the *Temple de Gnide,* the prose poem's design was so obscured by the dusty veil of allegories, and so ill-served by the authorial trick of pseudo-translation, which had become a hackneyed practice, that readers could no longer decipher its original intention. We could speculate on Montesquieu's disappointment had he known that, in the end, his prose poem seemed as licentious a tale as Voltaire's—all the more dangerous for its allegorical veil.

But Montesquieu had clearly explained the motivation behind the *Temple de Gnide* in the 1725 preface, before he eliminated his statement in 1742: "Le dessein du Poëme est de faire voir, que nous sommes heureux par les sentimens du cœur, & non par les plaisirs des sens; mais que notre bonheur n'est jamais si pur qu'il ne soit troublé par les accidents" (391) [The design of the poem is to show that we are made happy by the sentiments of the heart, and not by the pleasure of the senses; but that our happiness is never so pure as to be unruffled by accidents] (iv–v). Unlike Rousseau's ambiguous judgment, d'Alembert left a commentary which acknowledged the story's double-entendre and its author's serious purpose: "Mais ce qu'on doit sur-tout remarquer dans le Temple de Gnide, c'est qu'Anacréon même y est toûjours observateur & philosophe" [But in the *Temple of Gnidus*, one must notice in particular the fact that Anacreon himself is always an eyewitness and a philosopher.][33] As in the *Lettres persanes*, the pleasant fiction of the *Temple de Gnide* tried to instill a useful moral lesson. Intended for young aristocrats, presumably as dissipated as Mlle de Clermont, the prose poem taught the distinction between love and desire to gain an understanding of the nature of love and passion, a goal similar to *Télémaque*'s Calypso episode, in which the hero's attraction for Eucharis contrasts with the virtuous love felt later for Antiope. But as with Fénelon, the episode of seduction proved so fascinating it seemed to obliterate the lesson of virtuous love.

---

[32]   Saint Amand, *Séduire ou la Passion des Lumières.*

[33]   D'Alembert, *Eloge de Monsieur de Montesquieu,* xviii.

Maxims on love constitute the story's most transparent didactic device. Their witty concision and misleading simplicity, their parallelisms and antitheses, echoed the celebrated maxims of the genre's masters, Bussy-Rabutin and La Rochefoucault: "La jalousie est une passion qu'on peut avoir, mais qu'on doit taire" (398) [Jealousy is a passion which may invade the lover, but which he ought never to show] (24); "l'amour qu'on irrite, peut avoir tous les effets de la haine" (416) [Love when it is outraged may produce all the effects of hatred] (91); "Le cœur fixe toujours lui-même le moment, auquel il doit se rendre: mais c'est une profanation de se rendre sans aimer" (398) [The heart itself always fixes the moment for yielding; but it is profanation to yield, without having loved] (26). When spoken by characters using a first or second person pronoun, maxims brought truth still closer to home: "ta beauté fait voir qu'il y a des plaisirs; mais elle ne les donne pas," [thy beauty shows that there are pleasures, but it does not bestow them] (33),Venus says to the courtesan, and to the rich man: "tu achetes des beautez, pour les aimer; mais tu ne les aime[s] pas, parce que tu les achettes" (400) [You buy your mistresses that you may love them; and you do not love them, because you buy them] (34). The maxim can also espouse the lover's circular reasoning: "je t'aime comme je t'aimois; car je ne puis comparer l'amour que j'ai pour toi, qu'à celui que j'ai eu pour toi-même" (412) [I love thee now as I have loved thee before; for I cannot compare the love I now feel but to that I have formerly felt] (72). Subject to the same principle of condensation and economy as verse, and hinging on the "pointe" so beloved in neoclassical poetry, maxims can be interpreted as yet another stylistic strategy to tighten prose and bring it closer to a poem.[34]

D'Alembert singled out the fourth canto, which begins with the birthplace of Thémire's lover, Sybaris, and where Montesquieu the moral philosopher clearly held the poet's quill when describing Sybarites' mores.[35] The long description is a transparent allegory of the increasingly decadent court society Montesquieu observed during the Regency, and an echo of Fénelon's forewarning at the turn of the century: confusion of values—"On ne met point, dans cette Ville, de difference entre les voluptez & les besoins" (406) [In that city, no difference is made between pleasures and necessities] (51)—; decadence of principles—"Les faveurs des Dieux ... ne servent qu'à encourager le luxe, et à flatter la mollesse" (406) [the favours of the gods bestowed on Sybaris, serve only to encourage luxury and to foster sloth] (52)—and above all confusion of genders:

Les hommes sont si efféminez, leur parure est si semblable à celle des femmes, ils composent si bien leur teint, ils se frisent avec tant d'art, ils employent tant de tems à se corriger à leur miroir, qu'il semble qu'il n'y ait qu'un sexe dans toute la Ville. (406)

---

[34] My interpretation of maxims as contributing to the narrative's poetic density is only applicable within the specific context of neoclassical poetry. Romantic poets later rejected witticism and didactics as the epitome of artificiality.

[35] D'Alembert, *Eloge de Monsieur de Montesquieu*, xviii.

[The men are so effeminate; their appearance is so like that of the women; they take so much care of their complexion; they dress their hair with so much art; they waste so much time at their toilet, that you would think there was only one sex in the city.] (52)

The dissolution of masculinity, resulting in "mollesse" and abject physical weakness thematized by Fénelon and ferociously satirized by Montesquieu, makes for passive citizens and jeopardizes the nation's ability to fend off wars and invasions:[36] "Incapables de porter le poids des armes, timides devant leurs Concitoyens, lâches devant les Etrangers, ils sont des Esclaves tous prêts pour le premier maître" (407) [They are incapable of bearing the weight of arms; they are timid before their fellow citizens, dastardly before strangers, and accordingly they are destined to be the slaves of the first master who shall come to invade them] (55–6). Sybarite women have traded virtue for licentiousness: "Les femmes se livrent au lieu de se rendre; ... on ne sçait ce que c'est que d'aimer & d'être aimé, on n'est occupé que de ce qu'on appelle si faussement joüir" (406) [Women cannot be said to yield, for they make no resistance ... the pleasure of loving and being loved is unknown; and what is so falsely called enjoyment, is the only occupation] (52). Unlike the gods' tolerated debaucheries, which are signs of vitality and power, mortals lose their identity, if not their mind, when succumbing to the pleasure of the senses. A striking line evokes the absurd degree of sensitivity to which a life of pleasures can lead: "un Citoyen fut fatigué toute une nuit d'une rose qui s'étoit repliée dans son lit" (407) [a citizen was once discomposed the whole night by a rose that had been folded under him in his bed] (54). Buried in the prose poem these two rhyming verses ("fatigué/repliée," "nuit/lit") evoke a cameo at once humorous and bizarre, as the line's exquisite character mirrors the citizen's extreme delicacy. Sybarites turned their search for pleasure into a moral and economic principle: the pursuit of maximum satisfaction with minimum effort. Disgusted by the city's corrupted air, the narrator leaves pleasures to search for virtue and ethical life. Only virtue and the stoic subordination of pleasure can establish a civic society. Montesquieu, in the wake of Fénelon, pursued a moral and civic purpose in guiding his readers beyond the aesthetic pleasures of mythological allegories.

The sixth canto engages the problem of love from a different perspective, no longer focusing on its mistaken equation with pleasure, but on its no less nefarious exaltation in passion. The depiction of Eros's dark side, experienced in Jealousy and Fury's cave, emphasizes the release of violent impulses and a destructive, anarchical energy, translated into bellicose terms:

---

[36] "Ils passent leur vie sur des sièges renversez, sur lesquels ils sont obligez de se reposer tout le jour, sans s'être fatiguez; ils sont brisez, quand ils vont languir ailleurs" (407) [They pass their lives on the softest couches, on which they are obliged to repose themselves the whole day long, without the excuse of fatigue; for they are bruised and hurt when they languish on any harder place] (55).

allons exterminer les troupeaux qui paissent dans cette prairie; poursuivons ces Bergers, dont les amours sont si paisibles. ... [le temple de l'Amour]: allons détruire, allons briser sa statuë, & lui rendre nos fureurs redoutables. Nous courûmes, & il sembloit que l'ardeur de commettre un crime, nous donnât des forces nouvelles. (414)

["Let us go and exterminate the flocks which feed in this meadow; let us pursue these shepherds whose loves are so peaceful. ... Let us go and raze it [the temple of Love] to the foundation; let us break his statue, and make our fury dreadful to him." We ran, and you would have thought that our eagerness to commit a crime had given us double strength.] (80–81)

The chase seems to echo Virgil's vision of the dangers of sex in Book Three of the *Georgics*, but Montesquieu concerned himself less with the nature of sexuality per se than with love's lost nobility when reduced to sex. Seducing Thémire is her lover's explicit goal just as Vulcan seduces Venus on the murals of the temple. According to Starobinski, "La mythologie de la passion se lasse déjà de représenter les grands sentiments: elle n'est plus qu'une mythologie du plaisir. Ainsi l'exige une société qui ne cache plus son parti pris de jouissance facile" [The mythology of passion already dispenses with representing high sentiments: it is only a mythology of pleasure. This is demanded by a society no longer hiding its bias toward easy enjoyment.][37] Montesquieu turned to mythology precisely to denounce the hedonism of aristocrats and dramatize the exacerbation of passion: the former led to selfish isolation, the latter to jealous exclusivity, as both were inimical to individual wellbeing and social harmony.

Montesquieu's personal view of love and his perspective on masculinity and femininity rises from the *Temple de Gnide*.[38] Throughout the narrative, the male characters' love is depicted as unsteady, driven by physical desire, egocentric and narcissistic, whereas Thémire and Camille's love is calm, constant, chaste, and full of solicitude, as is illustrated by their composure upon their furious lovers' return and Thémire's eventual triumph over her lover's attempt to seduce her. Whereas the narrative uniformly portrays man as a seducer, it dwells on an astonishing number of feminine types, both physical and moral, to emphasize the superiority of the goddess Venus and the shepherdess Thémire. Each woman's struggle to overcome her lover's advances is expressed in words but also pictures: two of the engravings included to illustrate the text depict the respective seduction attempts by Vulcan and Thémire's lover. The first engraving—a black Vulcan carrying off a struggling, half-disrobed Venus—visually translates the ekphrasis, the textual description of the paintings representing Venus' story. Ekphrasis, which I have defined as the confluence between description and narration, between the silence of a visual image and the voice of events, takes on another pivotal role as it gives voice to the violence done to women. Here, the *Temple de Gnide* confirms Heffernan's analysis:

---

37   Starobinski, *Montesquieu par lui-même*, 42–3.
38   See Jeannette Geffriaud Rosso, *Montesquieu et la féminité* (Pise, 1977), chap. VII.

[T]his struggle for mastery between word and image is repeatedly gendered. ... We do well to remember the root meaning of ekphrasis: "speaking out" or telling in full." To recall this root meaning is to recognize that besides representational friction and the turning of fixed forms into narrative, ekphrasis entails prosopopœia or the rhetorical technique of envoicing a silent object. Ekphrasis speaks not only *about* works of art but also *to* and *for* them.[39]

On the walls of the temple, Venus displayed noticeable ambivalence toward her union with Vulcan, and seemed desperate to escape the god's arms and bed (397). But ekphrasis keeps the bed curtains open: "In talking back to and looking back at the male viewer, the images envoiced by ekphrasis challenge at once the controlling authority of the male gaze and the power of the male word."[40] Rather than a nod to the libertine tradition, Montesquieu staged an ideal of strength and resistance that was not a masculine, conquering desire, but resided on the side of women, in perceived feminine fortitude and constancy.

Montesquieu's views were by no means radical; he explicitly rejected two controversial configurations of gender in the *Temple de Gnide*: lesbian love and matriarchal societies. But the positive values incarnated by Venus (beauty and justice) and Thémire (virtue and moderation) contrast with masculine violence and emasculation (virtual for Sybarites, real for eunuchs) and signal Montesquieu's interest in finding a better alternative to male paradigms. *Le Temple de Gnide* offers perhaps the best example of Montesquieu's wish for the political victory of a feminine ethos of conciliation, respect, moderation, also at the core of d'Urfé's pastoral. A chapter entitled "De l'administration des femmes" in *L'Esprit des lois* confirms Montesquieu's wish that women be accepted in the public sphere, though it reminds us as well of his traditionalism when agreeing to their subjugation in the private sphere with a reference to Egyptian society, the same counter example used in the *Temple de Gnide*:

> Il est contre la raison et contre la nature que les femmes soient maîtresses dans la maison, comme cela étoit établi chez les Égyptiens; mais il ne l'est pas qu'elles gouvernent un empire. Dans le premier cas, l'état de foiblesse où elles sont ne leur permet pas la prééminence: dans le second, leur foiblesse même leur donne plus de douceur et de modération; ce qui peut faire un bon gouvernement, plutôt que les vertus dures et féroces.[41]

> [It is against reason and against nature that women be masters at home, as it was established by the Egyptians; but it is not when they govern an empire. In the first case, their state of weakness does not allow preeminence; in the second case, their very weakness gives them more benevolence and moderation, which can lead to a good government, instead of harsh and ferocious virtues.]

---

[39]　Heffernan, *Museum of Words*, 6–7.

[40]　Ibid., 7.

[41]　Montesquieu, *L'Esprit des lois,* livre VIII, ch. 2, ch. XVII, in *Œuvres complètes*, vol. 2, 348.

Pastoral idyll constituted the only genre able to accommodate the ideal of civic virtue and balanced pleasure Montesquieu advocated. Staging a golden age ruled by "Peace, Abundance and Justice," Montesquieu projected on antiquity his idealized vision of a civilized but uncorrupted humanity, offsetting the contemporary decadence he was witnessing. [42] Nostalgia and regret for this state of peace and civility permeate *Le Temple de Gnide*, and surface in the *Pensées*:

> Ce qui me charme dans les premiers temps, c'est une certaine simplicité de mœurs, une naïveté de la nature, que je ne trouve que là, et qui n'est plus à présent dans le Monde (au moins que je sache) chez aucun peuple policé.

> J'aime à voir dans l'Homme lui-même des vertus qu'une certaine éducation ou religion n'ont point inspirées; des vices que la mollesse et le luxe n'ont point faits.

> J'aime à voir l'innocence rester encore dans les coutumes, lorsque la grandeur du courage, la fierté, la colère, l'ont chassée des cœurs mêmes.

> J'aime à voir les Rois plus forts, plus courageux que les autres hommes, distingués de leurs sujets dans les combats, dans les conseils; hors de là, confondus avec eux.[43]

> [What charms me in early times is a certain simplicity of mores, a natural naïveté that I find only then and that is no longer present in any civilized people in the world (as far as I know). I enjoy seeing in man himself virtues not inspired by a certain education or religion, vices not created by idleness and luxury. I enjoy seeing that innocence remains a custom, while great courage, pride and anger have chased it from the heart. I enjoy seeing kings stronger and more courageous than other men, distinguished from their subjects during fights and councils, otherwise impossible to tell apart.]

Far from a "useless fiction" as Starobinski wrote, *Le Temple de Gnide* carried Montesquieu's moral philosophy thanks to a genre the most apt to get his target audience's attention.[44] As in *L'Astrée*, *Le Temple de Gnide* presents a double distanciation in time and space: far from the capital (Athens/Paris), in a refined countryside, and far back in time, to the Roman Empire, back, that is, to the sources of the Republic and its virtuous values. Montesquieu's choice of Roman instead of Greek names for the prose poem's divinities offers a striking evidence of his Republican catechism. Montesquieu's prose poem translated his concern and *désarroi* in the face of corrupted power and moral decadence, a characteristic of the Golden Age myth which consistently resurges in times of crisis.[45]

---

[42] On the triad "Peace, Abundance, and Justice" at the core of the Golden Age myth, see Pierre Bunuel ed., *Dictionnaire des mythes littéraires*, 406.

[43] Montesquieu, *Mes Pensées*, in *Œuvres complètes*, vol. I, 1081.

[44] See Georges Benrekassa, *Montesquieu, la liberté et l'histoire* (Paris, 1987), 64–7.

[45] Bunuel ed., *Dictionnaire des mythes littéraires*, 603.

It is no coincidence that the project succeeding the *Temple de Gnide* became his *Considérations sur les causes de la grandeur des Romains et de leur décadence* (1734). The fall of Rome represents for the modern Occident the paradigm of decadence. The message of hope relayed by the Golden Age myth as allegorized by Montesquieu (an ethical community within a Republic) carried political and ideological significance. Men and women must return to their (Republican) origins or social chaos will ensue. Readers like Rousseau, weary of an ancient mythology so often trivialized by allegorization, perceived but a faint echo of the dogmatic message. Eventually, allegory gave way to history, and *Le Temple de Gnide*'s catechism receded behind Montesquieu's next undertaking, his *Considérations sur les causes de la grandeur des Romains et de leur décadence* and *De l'esprit des lois* (1748).

Pastoral Melancholy

Menant's study of poetry's crisis in the years 1700 to 1750, in particular the chapter devoted to pastorals, sets Montesquieu's prose poem in perspective.[46] A minor but prolific subgenre in the first half of the century for poets like Bernis, Deforges Maillard, Jean-Baptiste Rousseau, Piron, Hénault, and Mme Deshoulières, pastoral poetry leads Menant into a larger investigation of the genre and the theoretical debates that framed its evolution. Conflicted in its goals and form, pastoral poetry was in crisis, and thus contributed to the general crisis of poetry. A relatively minor genre, pastorals nevertheless drew considerable critical attention, propelling essays by Fontenelle, La Motte, Fraguier, Rémond de Saint-Mard, Florian, and analyses by Dubos and Voltaire among others. Leaning on Menant's precisely documented analyses, I will now interrogate how prose was construed within the problematic of the pastoral.[47]

   Le Temple de Gnide verifies Menant's conclusions on "la permanence et la profondeur de l'inspiration pastorale" (151), on the power of myth, of a "rêve tenace, celui du bonheur dans la simplicité" [a tenacious dream of happiness within simplicity] (152), important even, or especially, to a sophisticated philosopher like Montesquieu. *Le Temple de Gnide* enjoyed the same popularity as pastorals in verse, combining two age-old favorite traditions, the Bible's lost edenic paradise and the libertine tradition (113). Like pastoral versified poems, it represented a reaction to social and historical changes: "temptation of irreligion," "incertitude

---

[46]   Menant, *La Chute d'Icare*, 111–53. Hereafter cited in text.

[47]   Pastoral narratives in prose, at the crossroads between poetry and the novel include: Jean-Jacques Barthelemy, *Les Amours de Carite et Polydore* (1760); Mlle Dionis, *Origines des graces* (1777); Robert Martin Le Suire, *Les Noces patriarchales, poëme en prose en cinq chants* (1777); Mme Dufresne, *Idylles et pièces fugitives trouvées dans un hermitage au pied du mont Ste. Odile* (1781); Joséphine Beaufort d'Hautpoul. *Zilia, roman pastoral* (1789); Fournier de Tony, *Les Nymphes de Dyctyme ou révolutions de l'empire virginal* (1790).

under the Regency," "the heart's vagaries," and "society's dispersion" (121). Menant makes a particularly striking argument about contemporary changes in agricultural practices that modified the landscape, especially around urban centers, from one of pastures to predominately tilled fields (125)—thus fueling nostalgic memories for a shepherds' world lost to the industrious "laboureurs" [plowmen]. Poets and writers of provincial origins thus tended to celebrate their (idealized) countryside.[48]

Le Temple de Gnide internalized a double tension inherent to the genre. First, the age-old hesitation between two ancient models of inspiration, Theocritus and Virgil, embodied two worlds, one contemporaneous, the other intemporal—as Menant wrote, "celui de la lutte avec l'histoire [vs]. celui de l'épanouissement au sein d'une nature intemporelle, qui est le monde pastoral, monde antérieur de 'la vie prénatale'" [a world clashing with history (vs.) a world thriving within an intemporal nature, namely the pastoral world, anterior to prenatal life] (151). The two temporalities are similarly interconnected in *Le Temple de Gnide*. Moreover, Montesquieu's poem illustrates the unresolved tension between landscape depiction and the protagonists' dialogues or narrated stories. In tracing the genre's evolution until 1750, Menant sees the eventual victory of the descriptive idyll, such as Mme Deshoulières's, favored over more narrative pastoral genres (the eclogue and dramatic pastoral): "la description prend le pas sur la dramatisation" [description takes over dramatization] (140). By evolving from a fixed to a freer form, the "épître champêtre," pastoral poetry fulfilled simultaneously the rationalists' "realist" demands in favor of a more authentic nature (see Colardeau's and Saint-Lambert's poetry), and the lyrical undercurrent in abeyance. Indeed, this evolution is confirmed in the second half of the century by the remarkable success of Gessner's *Idylles* and their wave of imitations, which I examine in the next chapter.

Menant comments: "Changer de genre plutôt que changer les genres, voilà qui est bien dans l'esprit de ce XVIIIᵉ commençant" [To change a genre instead of changing genres, this is very much in the spirit of the early XVIIIth century] (140). True in the case of verse poets, the statement is contradicted by prose writer's efforts, whose purpose was precisely to change the genre from within, by abandoning what they considered to be major impediments, rhyme and meter.

---

[48]   See Jean-Pierre Claris de Florian, a native of Languedoc, who wrote two popular "romans pastorals," *Galatée, Roman pastoral; imité de Cervantes* (1783), a free imitation of Cervantes interspersed with verse; and *Estelle et Némorin* (1788), an innovative narrative with a distinctive local, i.e., provincial, color: invocation to a new muse, Occitania (34); explanation of the origins of "jeux floraux"—a poetic contest— in Toulouse (233); integration of local historical/legendary types, Clémence Isaure and Lautrec, whose unhappy love is recounted in a verse romance (183–6); authentic touches such as a song given in its original patois in a note (106–7). Florian also innovated with elegiac, moving narratives and melancholy overtones in lamenting his exile from his native countryside (212). Bernardin de Saint-Pierre and Évariste Parny offered yet another variation on the pastoral theme by picturing an exotic locale under the tropics.

I have just shown how Montesquieu found poetic substitutes to compensate for this loss; now remains the larger question of the articulation of prose and poetry vis-à-vis the pastoral. Quite strikingly, the two texts to which Menant refers in support of the pastoral as an unmistakable literary current are Fénelon's *Télémaque* and Montesquieu's twelfth letter on the Troglodyte myth in *Lettres persanes* (118). Another prose narrative, Honoré d'Urfé's *L'Astrée*, played a pivotal role as a model omnipresent in authors' and readers' imagination. The compatibility, if not affinity, between prose and pastoral is so obvious as to be forgotten, however a similar closeness did not bind prose and the epic, which laboriously and unsuccessfully adapted to prose. The evident but concealed affinity between prose and pastoral discloses a buried dialectic, which finds its resolution in the prose poem. The conjunction Menant establishes between poetry and pastoral justly underlines this intriguing but illuminating dialectic moment of the "[r]encontre toute naturelle entre la poésie et le monde pastoral: elle est le langage primitif qui convient à ce monde primitif" [the natural encounter between poetry and the pastoral world: poetry is the primitive language that suits this primitive world] (117). This was persuasively argued by Vico who envisioned antiquity as the age of poetry. Pastoral poems therefore, represented a uniquely felicitous combination of form and theme. For Menant, "[une poésie pastorale] correspond assez bien à l'idée qu'on se fait de la poésie, langage moins moderne que la prose" [Pastoral poetry corresponds quite well to our idea of poetry as a language less modern than prose] (118). For Menant, poetry being less modern than prose conveyed the original and natural voice of the pastoral. However, contemporary debates and pastoral poems composed during the Enlightenment testify to the opposite: far from shepherds' original and simple language, eighteenth-century pastorals in verse represented a hyper-regulated, highly artificial form. Poets and critics were painfully aware of this divide between their ideal—representation of simple times and simple souls—and the reality of neoclassical verse—an artificial and therefore inauthentic discourse for shepherds. Voltaire, uniquely consistent in a century of self-contradictions, refused to keep the pastoral illusion going through such blatantly faked simplicity. If originally verse poetry and pastoral were allies, it was no longer the case in the eighteenth century, notwithstanding the poets' prolific production.

Prose poems emerged as a resolution to this contradiction—a resolution enabled by prose's evolution, from a mode of controlled eloquence to a freer and more direct mode of literary expression. Scholars like La Motte advocated the unconstrained, natural qualities of prose while Montesquieu praised its free-flowing character. Therefore, though prose was not the original voice of the pastoral, it took on this voice after developing into an unaffected, direct mode of expression. The prosaic nature of prose could provide the authenticity, the realism that authors of pastorals desperately sought. Prose poems resolved as well the contradiction of a prose too "modern," in other words, anachronistic, to be a mode of expression for the pastoral: by reappropriating poetic conventions, prose conferred upon itself an antique patina, which veiled its modernist character—all the while authenticating poetic conventions that had grown artificial in verse.

The pastoral "poëme en prose" overcame a double set of contradictions, within poetry on the one hand and within prose on the other. In keeping with the Hegelian dynamics of *Aufhebung* (transcendence with preservation), these contradictions were put aside, both "abolished" and "preserved"—synthesized into prose poetry, as Montesquieu's *Temple de Gnide* demonstrated. The crisis of the pastoral Menant analyzed should be limited to versified poetry: transposed into prose, the pastoral thrived, even if this meant exploring its newly contradictory impulses—foremost the contradiction of prose poetry. Pastoral prose poems offered the advantage of breaking poetry's circularity, of opening the closed world of the poem, and paradoxically, of engaging in an open dialogue with modernity.[49] Menant's own conclusion confirms the transference of the pastoral spirit into modern prose. Explaining why Rousseau's discourses on the sciences and the arts and on inequality were enthusiastically received, Menant writes: "par un renversement inattendu, mais souhaité, ils apportaient au mythe la légitimation critique. Cette humanité estimable et heureuse dont Rousseau affirmait l'existence dans un lointain passé, ses lecteurs la connaissaient bien, sans trop oser croire à sa réalité: elle ressemblait, par beaucoup de côtés, à celle des bergeries" [with an unexpected but hoped for reversal, they brought critical legitimacy to myths. Readers knew quite well the worthy and happy humanity whom Rousseau claimed existed in a distant past: in many ways, it resembled that of pastorals] (152). Consequently, "[l]a crise de la poésie pastorale trouve son dénouement immédiat en dehors de la poésie: non pas dans une réforme des règles du genre (ou des genres), mais dans l'insertion du mythe pastoral dans l'idéologie des Lumières" [the crisis of pastoral poetry finds its immediate resolution outside poetry: not by reforming the rules of the genre (or genres), but by inserting the pastoral myth within Enlightenment ideology] (153). Indeed, ahead of Rousseau, Montesquieu put the poetry of the pastoral at the service of critical thought.

---

[49] For example, Pierre-Victor Malouet's *Les quatre parties du jour à la mer* (1783) contrasts pastoral lands of diligent plowmen, tireless wine growers and happy shepherds, with perilous open seas sailed by captains and mariners to discover new worlds and fetch back luxuries for a wealthy, idle class. The short prose poem describes the ambivalent gains of navigation, "Art sublime, utile autant que funeste, produit de tous les Arts & de la cupidité!" [Sublime art, useful as well as disastrous, the product of all arts, and greed!] (2).

Chapter 4
Translation to the Rescue

In some respects, the emergence of prose poems in the eighteenth century and the surrounding controversy tell the story of the instrumentalization of poetry to promote a certain vision of the Enlightenment, accessible to all people. Likewise and perhaps more obviously, translation became instrumentalized to import a poetic aesthetic that carried a similar vision of openness. Many have underlined the important mediation of translations for introducing new themes, inspiring experimentations in genres, and slowly transforming French national literature, but I wish to return to a more precise understanding of the practices and source texts that framed and often determined the poetic horizon of prose authors: first, pseudo-translation as a ploy to circumvent rules and invent a virtual poetry in prose; second, Homer revisited as a modern poet by Anne Dacier's translation; and finally Gessner and Ossian to the rescue of an Enlightenment short on poetic lyricism.

Pseudo-Translations

Authors experimenting with the new form of prose poems shared with authors of epistolary novels a common strategy to authenticate their text: pseudo-edition and/ or pseudo-translation. Beginning with Montesquieu's *Temple de Gnide,* many prose poems verify Jan Herman's hypothesis, based on Prévost's case, that a pseudo-translation can be recognized by its alleged status as an unpublished manuscript in the original tongue.[1] The "supercherie littéraire" [literary hoax] helped legitimize nascent forms while somewhat protecting their authors. Montesquieu's anonymous preface to the *Lettres persanes*, a famous example of pseudo-edition, is better known than his other anonymous and equally clever forgery, *Le Temple de Gnide*. Its "translator" relates how a Greek manuscript "fell" into his hands when a French ambassador brought it back from the Orient, after discovering it among the books of a Greek bishop. The translator stresses the rarity of his find, given that very few Greek texts survived ruined libraries and negligent owners.[2] The origin of the Greek manuscript remains shrouded in mystery, though the translator/editor claims to have found a chronological clue from internal textual evidence, namely a reference to Sappho. In a paragraph eliminated for the 1743 edition, the translator

---

[1]   Jan Herman, "Le procès Prévost traducteur: traduction et pseudo-traduction au dix-huitième siècle en France." *Arcadia: Zeitschrift fur Vergleichende Literatur Wissenschaft* 25:1 (1990), 1–9.

[2]   Montesquieu, *Le Temple de Gnide*, in *Œuvres et Ecrits Divers. Œuvres complètes*, vol. 8, 389. Hereafter cited in text.

speculates further that the text preceded Terence, since Terence "imitated" a passage at the end of the second canto (391). Anti-dating and cross-referencing situates the alleged Greek manuscript within classical literature, while playing with issues of imitation and plagiarism. The translator spins his illusionist tale in a way strangely anticipatory of Macpherson's claims regarding Ossian's poems: "J'avois d'abord eu dessein de mettre l'Original à côté de la Traduction: mais on m'a conseillé d'en faire une édition à part, & d'attendre les sçavantes Notes qu'un homme d'érudition y prépare, & qui seront bien tôt en état de voir le jour" [I first intended to place the original next to the translation; but I was advised to do a separate edition and wait for the scholarly notes that a man of erudition is preparing and will soon publish] (392). The alleged physical evidence of the original manuscript (like the Persians' original letters "communicated" to their host/editor) preempted the questioning of sources. Once his authorship was discovered, Montesquieu eliminated the above sentence (in the 1743 edition), yet still endorsed his role as pseudo-translator in the tradition of the "belles infidèles" school: "Quant à ma Traduction, elle est fidelle; j'ai crû que les beautez qui n'étoient point dans mon Auteur, n'étoient point des beautez; & j'ai pris l'expression qui n'étoit pas la meilleure, lorsqu'elle m'a paru mieux rendre sa pensée" [My translation is faithful. I believed that beauties not present in my author were not beauties, and I chose not the best phrase when I thought it would better convey his thought] (392). The hoax worked because readers were familiar with such formulations/deceptions, because they occurred and came to be expected in every preface of classics translated à la d'Ablancourt.

Having established his text's authenticity, the pseudo-translator then focused on its nature and genre. Marking the transition between the two parts of the preface, between the establishment of a reading pact via translation, and comments pertaining to the author's newly minted genre, Montesquieu made a reference to Tasso and his successful French translator, the latter being the model that *Le Temple de Gnide*'s translator emulated (392). In 1724, a year before the publication of *Le Temple de Gnide*, Jean-Baptiste de Mirabaud had translated into prose Tasso's *Jerusalem Delivered* with considerable success (twenty-eight editions until 1866). The double aegis of a prose translation and Tasso's Christian epic poem gives a crucial entry into Montesquieu's poetics as a mirror to the double nature of Tasso's poem: for Françoise Graziani, "le Tasse est paradoxalement classique par ses principes poétiques et sa rigueur morale, et maniériste par son style fleuri, l'audace de ses *concetti* et ses alliances de mots" [Tasso is paradoxically classical in his poetic principles and moral rigor, and mannerist in his flowery style, audacious *concetti,* and word alliances.][3] The *Temple de Gnide* and most subsequent prose poems similarly conjugated a classical aesthetic and "baroque" predilections in an unstable combination. Further, Tasso's poem achieved the feat of conjoining a "double postulation épique et romanesque" [a double stance, epic and novel-like.][4] Graziani defines Tasso's ideal, developed in his *Discours de l'art poétique,*

---

    3   Françoise Graziani, introduction to *La Jérusalem délivrée* (Paris, 1997), 29.
    4   Ibid.

as a "forme poétique mixte, capable de combiner et d'équilibrer les charmes de la chanson lyrique à la gravité sublime de l'épopée" [a mixed poetic form, capable of combining and balancing the charms of lyrical song with the sublime gravity of epic poetry.][5] The success of Tasso's poem and its prose translation spurred the vogue for more modern, hybrid poetry—lyrical as well as epic—later in the eighteenth century.

Montesquieu, though he did not emulate the epic aspect of his model, nonetheless proposed a definition (in his 1743 revised preface) similarly split between two genres: "Ce petit Roman est une espèce de Tableau où, l'on a peint avec choix les objets les plus agréables" [This little novel is a kind of picture where the most pleasant objects have been painted] (392).[6] *Narration*—the dominant feature of epic poems—was central to the genre of the novel. Therefore, Montesquieu's definition of a narration as a kind of *description* ("espèce de tableau") created an oxymoron defying synthesis, but which became an ideal for the century's prose poets up to and including Chateaubriand. This impossible dream was already inscribed in *Les Aventures de Télémaque* wherein descriptions (most notably within the Calypso episode) interrupted the hero's "romanesque" and epic adventures. The project of combining narration and description was an experiment in the making within most eighteenth-century prose poems. Simultaneously cause and consequence, the displacement of narrative and descriptive categories coincided with the redefinition of prose and poetry.

Montesquieu's definition of the "petit roman" as "une espèce de tableau" conjures up the "petit tableau" which etymologically defines the idyll. In light of Rousseau's later "petit poème en prose" (*Le Lévite d'Ephraïm*) and Baudelaire's *Petits poëmes en prose (Spleen de Paris)*, Montesquieu's epithet "petit" sounds prescient: etymologically justified by the short genre of the idyll, it conveyed a poetics of the miniature, of artistic condensation in contrast to epic breadth, clearly signaling divergent modes of compositions. In keeping with the conventions of the idyll, "[l]e Public y a trouvé des idées riantes, une certaine magnificence dans les descriptions, & de la naïveté dans les sentimens" [the public found pleasing ideas, a certain magnificence in descriptions, and naïveté in feelings] (392). The ubiquitous epithet "riant" and the expected naïveté were hallmarks of the nature-centered idyll. Clearly, Montesquieu carefully scripted each element of his generic definition to refer to the codes of the genre. His paradoxical statement on the public's reaction—searching for the model that inspired such originality—leads to a veiled justification for breaching the rule of required versification: "Quelques Sçavants n'y ont point reconnu ce qu'ils appellent l'Art. Il n'est point, disent-ils, selon les regles. Mais si l'ouvrage a plû, vous verrez que le cœur ne leur a pas dit toutes les règles" [A few scholars did not recognize what they called art.

---

[5]   Ibid., 30.

[6]   The ubiquitous qualifier "espèce de" suggests indetermination, a hesitation to name and define eighteenth-century emerging genres: Montesquieu characterized the *Lettre persanes* as "une espèce de roman." See "Quelques reflexions sur les *Lettres persanes*," *Lettres persanes*, 33.

They say this work does not obey the rules. But if it has pleased, you will know that the heart has not told them all the rules] (392). Montesquieu's succinct and indirect allusion to the absence of versification elegantly circumvented the issue, favoring taste over rules. In his eulogy of Montesquieu, d'Alembert specifically addressed style by invoking a famous precedent, *Télémaque*: he proposed a new definition of "style poëtique" which no longer hinged on verse but on "chaleur" and "images," animation and figures, suggesting that poeticity resided in inspired images rather than in rhyme or meter, yet cautioning against the adoption of worn-out "ornaments," the cliché allegories of classical culture:

> Emporté par son sujet, il [Montesquieu] a répandu dans sa prose ce style animé, figuré, & poëtique, dont le roman de Télémaque a fourni parmi nous le premier modèle. Nous ignorons pourquoi quelques censeurs du temple de Gnide ont dit, à cette occasion, qu'il auroit eu besoin d'être en vers. Le style poëtique, si on entend, comme on le doit, par ce mot, un style plein de chaleur & d'images, n'a pas besoin, pour être agréable, de la marche uniforme & cadencée de la versification; mais si on ne fait consister ce style que dans une diction chargée d'épithetes oisives, dans les peintures froides & triviales des aîles & du carquois de l'amour, & de semblables objets, la versification n'ajoûtera presqu'aucun mérite à ces ornements usés: on y cherchera toûjours en vain l'ame & la vie.[7]

> [Carried away by his topic, he applied to his prose this animated, figurative, and poetic style, of which the novel *Télémaque* gave us the first model. We do not know why some censors of *Le Temple de Gnide* said on this occasion that it should have been in verse. Poetic style, if we understand by this word, as one should, a genial and colorful style, does not need the uniform, cadenced pace of versification in order to please. But if this style merely consists in diction laden with gratuitous epithets, cold and trivial representations of love's wings and arrows, and similar objects, then versification will add almost no merit to these used ornaments: we will always look in vain for life and spirit.]

Montesquieu's success did not last in a post-neoclassical era, underscoring the difficulty of the poetics d'Alembert and his contemporaries envisioned as they tried to redefine the tenets of neoclassical poetry without abandoning allegorical figures even dearer to them than verse.

Bypassing pretentious critics apt to condemn the frivolous nature of the story, the translator addressed his audience directly, providing a precious testimony as to his intended readership. Young aristocrats—"jeunes gens," "têtes bien frisées & bien poudrées" [young people; well curled and powdered wigs] (392)—and more particularly women, constituted Montesquieu's intended public:

> A l'égard du beau Sexe, à qui je dois le peu de momens heureux, que je puis compter dans ma vie, je souhaite de tout mon cœur que cet Ouvrage puisse lui plaire. Je l'adore encore; & s'il n'est plus l'objet de mes occupations, il l'est de mes regrets. (392)

---

[7]   D'Alembert, *Eloge de Monsieur de Montesquieu*, xvii–xviii.

[With regard to the fair sex, to whom I owe the few happy moments of my life, I wish with all my heart that this work shall please. I still adore it; and if it is no longer the object of my occupations, it remains the object of my regrets]

The remark exposes the philosopher's gallant side and his courtship of Mlle de Clairmont, but also emphasizes the central role of women in pursuing happiness, a point underscored by the feminine ethos championed in the story.

The recourse to pseudo-translation, exemplified by *Le Temple de Gnide*, represents an intriguing component of paratextual discourses. Montesquieu's breach of the rule of verse had been acceptable given the secondary status of pastorals. A similar rebellion within the higher epic genre ran greater risks of upsetting traditionalists, but authors of epic prose poems trusted that similar strategies would validate their choice of prose as well. If one examines epic narratives in prose, they offer examples of discursive strategies to legitimate their genre: Reyrac gave his *Hymne au soleil* to the public as a translation of a manuscript found on a Greek island a few months before the discovery of Homer's tomb; Chérade de Montbron supposedly translated *Les Scandinaves* from "sweo-gothic;" Jean Roussy, in his "Avis du traducteur," introduced *Aurelia ou Orléans délivrée, poème latin traduit en françois* (1738) as the tale of a venerable old man of letters who composed a Latin poem for his personal enjoyment. This private consumption justified the author breaking rules.[8] The translator/editor posed as an eyewitness to the author's existence, then appended footnotes to the story referencing a few verses in the alleged original Latin.[9] The censor's seal of approbation validated the book.[10] By mid-century, some authors still adopted the same hackneyed device to spin a fantastic, convoluted tale for their readers' greater pleasure. Morelly, author of *Naufrage des isles flottantes, ou, Basiliade du célèbre Pilpai. Poëme héroïque traduit de l'Indien* (1753), took the guise of pseudo-translator *cum* discoverer *cum* detective to introduce his epic poem. It begins with a dedication to a sultana written in a pompous, inflated style customary to eighteenth-century dedications to the king, but interspersed with capitalized apostrophes in the second person singular, "TA HAUTESSE" [your highness], a mixture of familiarity and respect to convey oriental style. Supposedly written at the request of the queen, the translation is introduced by a long letter "Sur la vie & les Ouvrages de Pilpai, avec les Avantures du Traducteur" [On the life and works of Pilpai, with the translator's adventures.]

---

[8]   Jean Roussy, "Avis du traducteur," *Aurélia, ou Orléans délivré, Poeme latin traduit en françois* (1738), n.p.

[9]   Ibid., 127, 243.

[10]   "L'Editeur de cet Ouvrage le donne comme une Traduction d'un Poëme Epique Latin qui n'a point été au jour, j'y ai trouvé une imagination vive, des images & des expressions nobles, & si ce n'est qu'une Copie elle peut faire désirer voir l'Original, je crois qu'elle merite d'être imprimée. Fait à Paris ce 2 janvier 1738. DANCHET" [The editor of this work gives it as the translation of an epic poem in Latin previously unknown; I have found a vivid imagination, noble images and turn of phrases; if it is only a copy, which I think deserves to be printed, it makes one wish for the original. Done in Paris, 2 January 1738.] Ibid., n.p.

The letter reconstructs the circumstances of the manuscript discovery in a long narrative full of the suspense and intrigue of a treasure chase. We learn that Indian tablets engraved in gold letters were retrieved from a box adorned with precious stones. The frontispiece reveals the author's name but ends with a mysterious warning: "Ouvrage merveilleux de l'incomparable Pilpai, la perle des Philosophes de l'Indostan & de toute la terre. Plus bas étoit écrit: Ce livre contient des vérités qui ne sont pas bonnes à dire à tout le monde; que les sages ne prodiguent pas aux stupides; que les rois estiment, mais qu'ils n'écoutent pas volontiers: il n'y a qu'une ame intrépide qui se fasse gloire de les tirer de l'obscurité" [A marvelous work from the inimitable Pilpai, the pearl of all philosophers from Indostan and the whole world. Below was written: This book contains truths that are not good to tell everyone, that wise men do not deliver to stupid minds, that kings esteem but do not listen to easily: only an intrepid soul takes glory in bringing them out from obscurity.][11] The narrator believes he chanced upon the original text of Pilpai's famous fables, but a gloss on the title revealed that it is a more serious and enlightened work from Pilpai, "philosophe de la Lumière de l'Inde."[12] A suspicious narrator questions the text's authorship, wondering if this might be a case of forged identity, thereby mocking authorial strategies and readers' prejudice.[13] After this metatextual gesture, the translator relates his adventures, again a tale bristling with exoticism and danger, beginning with the accidental emasculation by a shark of his newly bought slave. One is left to speculate as to the purpose of this opening: it may serve to introduce the obligatory figure of the eunuch in a supposedly oriental poem while mocking this convention by depicting the eunuch as an accident of nature. A dozen pages later, the narrator draws his adventures to an end, and concludes with another metatextual proposition: "Si cette Histoire peut amuser

---

[11]　Etienne Gabriel Morelly, *Naufrage des isles flottantes, ou Basiliade du célèbre Pilpai*. Poëme traduit de l'Indien (1753), vj.

[12]　"Le Naufrage des Isles flottantes est le véritable Homaioun-Nameh, ou Livre auguste, autrement Giavadan-Khird, c'est-à-dire, la Sapience de tous les tems: c'est le regne, le triomphe de la vérité, toujours une, toujours constante, toujours lumineuse malgré les efforts de l'erreur & des préjugés pour l'obscurcir. ... Ici Pilpai ne fait point parler de vils animaux, mais la vérité & la nature elles-mêmes: il personifie, par une ingénieuse allégorie, ces fidèles interprètes de la Divinité; il les fait présider au bonheur d'un vaste Empire; par elles il dirige les mœurs & les actions des Peuples qui l'habitent, & du Héro qui les gouverne; il leur oppose, sous diverses emblêmes, les vices conjurés contre elles, mais artisans de leur propre destruction" [The Shipwreck of Floating Islands is the genuine Homaioun-Nameh, or August Book, in other words Giavadan-Khird, namely The Wisdom of all times: it is the rule, the triumph of truth, always one, constant, and enlightening despite the efforts of error and prejudice to obscure it. ... Here Pilpai does not make vile animals speak, but truth and nature themselves: with an ingenious allegory he personifies the Divinity's faithful interpreters; he has them preside to the happiness of a vast empire; through them he directs the morals and actions of the people living there and the hero who governs them, opposed under various emblems by vices conspiring against them, but artisans of their own destruction.] Ibid., viii–ix.

[13]　Ibid., ix.

TA HAUTESSE, toute véritable qu'elle est, quelque Poëte, ou quelque Faiseur de Romans, ne manqueront pas d'en tirer parti: c'est un canevas tout préparé; il n'y manque que la broderie" [If this story can amuse your Highness, as true as it is, some poet, some novel writer, will not fail to take advantage of it. The pattern is all ready, with only embroidery missing.][14] Morelly's facetious preamble mocked and challenged the literary conventions and practices of his time: it denounced a literature rife with endless variations drawn from a few models, subverted literary clichés, and defied the reader's complacency.

The most emblematic paratextual discourse on the epic prose poem can be found in Bitaubé's *Guillaume de Nassau, ou la Fondation des Provinces-Unies* from 1775 titled "Dialogue entre l'Auteur et un Journaliste" (see Appendix II).[15] It elaborates at length on all the issues and controversies surrounding prose poems, summoning in its favor "orators" (Demosthene, Cicero, Bossuet), novelists (Fielding and Richardson), theoreticians (La Motte), and acclaimed prose poems (David's Psalms, the book of Job, the *Temple de Gnide*, Gessner's poems, and *Joseph*—Bitaubé's own well-received biblical prose poem). The exchange unfolds in the manner of a modern Socratic dialogue whereby the journalist plays the devil's advocate—the devil being the critic—allowing the author to refute objections against the new genre and then propose a definition. The dialogue is born from the journalist's insistence to classify *Guillaume*. The exchange reveals the constraints imposed upon authors to provide readers with guiding titles to establish a framework on how best to approach the text. The protocol of generic identification, however conventional, was deemed essential to the reading experience, or rather to critical appraisal.

Le Journaliste. Ne vous êtes-vous proposé aucun but? N'avez-vous point suivi de modèle? Est-ce une histoire que vous avez faite? Est-ce un roman? Ou votre livre est-il d'un genre nouveau? ...

Le J. Je voudrois savoir dans quelle classe il doit être rangé. Serez-vous content qu'il ait une existence amphibie? On n'en parlera point, faute de savoir comment il se désigne ...

Le J. ... Avouez que vous avez voulu faire un poëme en prose.

L'Auteur. Je vous assure que je ne me suis rien proposé, & que j'ai laissé suivre à mon esprit telle pente qui lui plaisoit.

Le J. Vous avez été inspiré. Mais en littérature on ne se contente pas de cette défaite; on veut donner un titre à un ouvrage, & c'est la première chose qui frappe le lecteur. Malgré vous, on dira que votre livre est un poëme en prose. (i–ii)

---

[14]   Ibid., xxxviii.

[15]   Paul-Jérémie Bitaubé, *Guillaume de Nassau, ou la Fondation des Provinces-Unies. Nouvelle Edition [i.e., seconde] considérablement augmentée & corrigée* (1775), i–xvii. Hereafter cited in text.

[*The Journalist*. Did you not give yourself a goal? Did you not follow a model? Have you written a story? Is it a novel? Or is your work a new genre? ...

J. I would like to know in which class to place it. Will you be happy if it has an amphibious existence? No one will talk about it for want of knowing how it calls itself ... .

J. ... Admit that you wanted to write a prose poem.

The Author. I assure you that I planned nothing, and that I let my mind follow the incline it pleased.

J. You were well inspired. But in literature, one is not satisfied by such a defeat; we want to give a title to a work, and it is the first thing that strikes a reader. Despite yourself, they will say your work is a poem in prose.]

To borrow Genette's terminology, the journalist demanded that the "architext" be explicit and disclose the true nature of the text: "La perception générique, on le sait, oriente et détermine dans une large mesure l' 'horizon d'attente' du lecteur, et donc la réception de l'œuvre" [Generic perception orients and determines in large measure the horizon of a reader's expectations, and therefore the reception of the work.][16] From the author's perspective, this (encyclopedic?) impulse for classification was an obstacle to creativity and experimentation, and possibly a trap set by critics. Therefore, the author persisted in eschewing the classification "poëme en prose" for his own work but was willing to discuss "this kind of writing" generally. Let me emphasize that as Bitaubé's dialogue unfolds, this double standard reflects a terminological slippage from the (objectionable) category "poëme en prose" to the (favored) style of "prose poétique." Whereas the former caused critical discomfort by encroaching into the field of poetry, the latter enriched the less sacred field of prose. Like the "Dialogue entre la Prose et la Poésie" published in the *Almanach des prosateurs* (see Chapter 2 and Appendix IV), Bitaubé's preface indicted the foibles of contemporary poems, without quite yet envisioning a new poetry. Thus the author naturally chose prose as the only remedy to poetry's sclerosis, bracketing the antinomies poetry/prose (and poem/novel).

In the course of Bitaubé's self-reflexive dialogue, the character of the journalist raised common objections against the indeterminate substance of the "poëme en prose." He feared that it might contaminate poetry in the future, encourage the proliferation of prose tragedies, and, further, "disfigure history," pollute poetry with "a muddy torrent" of prose poems, and prove detrimental to the art of verse (xi, xii, xv). The author's counter-arguments rested on the obsolescence of traditional generic categories in light of the advances of contemporary literature: citing the Bible, Fénelon, and the "Prothean" novel, the author argued in favor of prose's potential and its liberation from generic classification. The author implied that if France was to maintain its stature in the realm of letters, poetic prose should perform the same role as blank verse did in the literature of modern nations so that

---

[16]   Genette, *Palimpsestes*, 12.

French writers might thus compensate their disadvantage (x). Finally, after pulling the journalist onto the terrain of prose, the author faced the request to define poetic prose:

> *L'A.* Il y a, je crois, quelque différence entre la prose d'une simple lettre, & celle dont on se sert pour traduire les Poëtes. La prose poétique est aussi noble, & quelquefois plus hardie que la prose oratoire: ses inversions peuvent être plus fréquentes, & plus audacieuses; ses épithètes plus nombreuses & plus pittoresques. Elle n'a pas besoin, autant que le stile oratoire, de cacher l'art: cependant il ne lui conviendroit pas de revêtir tous les ornemens de la poésie; elle sortiroit de son genre & deviendroit ampoulée. On pourroit la placer entre la poésie & le genre oratoire, puisqu'elle emprunte quelque chose de l'une & de l'autre. Malgré le sentiment de ceux qui veulent que l'on traduise les poëtes en vers, on lit avec plaisir les bonnes traductions en prose. Il ne seroit pas impossible d'écrire un ouvrage original, dans le stile que d'habiles Ecrivains ont employé avec succès pour traduire les Poëtes. (v-vj)

> [*Author.* There is, I believe, some difference between the prose of a simple letter, and the one used to translate poets. Poetic prose is as noble, and sometimes bolder than oratorical prose: its inversions can be more frequent and audacious; its epithets more numerous and striking. Unlike oratorical style, it does not need to hide art as much: however, it would not suit it to wear all of poetry's ornaments; it would step out of its genre and become affected. We could place it between poetry and oratorical genre, since it borrows something from each. Despite the opinion of those who want poets translated in verse, we read good prose translations with pleasure. It would not be impossible to write an original work in the style that gifted authors have used to translate poets.]

Bitaubé's definition placed poetic prose along two semantic axes: to employ Roman Jakobson's terminology, metonymically, it lay between poetry and eloquence in a relationship of contiguity; metaphorically, it was akin to translated poetry in a relationship of similarity. The first position required giving more or less weight to poetic ornament to reach a middle ground—the perilous balancing act of Fénelon's successors. The second position consisted in metaphorizing prose poetry as a translation, thus constructing a conceptual and symbolic framework for readers. Imagining a translated poem as the ideal horizon of prose poetry inspired greater stylistic freedom and a fruitful poetic emulation. Indirectly, Bitaubé's definition further legitimized the practice of pseudo-translation as a way to introduce prose poems. "Tout se passe comme si le poème était inséparable par principe de l'existence d'un autre texte; comme si, dans le poème en prose, *l'inédit*, c'est précisément le *réédité*." [It is as if the poem was inseparable by principle from the existence of another text, as if, in the prose poem, novelty was precisely the re-edited.][17] Barbara Johnson's comment on the link uniting the double versions

---

[17] Cited by Nichola Anne Haxell in "The Name of the Prose: A Semiotic Study of Titling in the Pre-Baudelerian Prose-poem," *French Studies: A Quarterly Review* 44, 14 (April, 1990), 161.

(in verse, then prose) of some Baudelaire's poems, aptly characterizes a feature present at the genre's inception: the delimitation of prose poetry's symbolic horizon by a pre-existing poem, ideal or accomplished.

Reviewing Bitaubé's *Guillaume* in *L'Année littéraire* upon its publication in 1775, the critic Élie Fréron targeted Bitaubé's defense of prose poems as useless:

> Dans le *Dialogue, l'Auteur & le Journaliste* dissertent assez longuement & assez inutilement, selon moi, sur l'ancienne & frivole question des Poëmes en prose: & qui doute qu'avec le langage de la Prose on ne puisse produire de grands effets sur l'ame, l'élever et l'attendrir? L'essentiel est d'intéresser, soit en vers, soit en prose.[18]

> [In the dialogue, the author and the journalist speak at length and rather uselessly, in my opinion, about the ancient and frivolous question of prose poems: who doubts that with the language of prose one can produce great effects upon the soul, elevate and move it? The essential point is to stir interest, be it in verse or prose.]

This weary comment helps measure a critical evolution for prose poems since Fraguier represented them as a threat to poetry. Fréron considered the old debate sterile, as authors never managed to articulate a convincing poetics for the new genre, and instead repeated one another *ad nauseam*. Fréron's resolute stance in favor of prose, and his effacement of the issue of genre, however, did not put an end to authorial self-defensive paratexts. In 1809 Chateaubriand, no less weary of the issue, nevertheless yielded to the pressure of his critics' expectations and took pains to justify his epic poem in prose, *Les Martyrs*.

The "Querelle d'Homère"

I believe that the pressing issue of how to revive the epic explains the prolific number of paratexts around prose poems that attempted to recapture the noblest of genres, oftentimes via translations. This enduring effort by Enlightenment authors to write epics testified to nostalgia for action and acts of heroism in an age of reflection. Homer's epic poetry spoke of an active age at the antipodes of the idle comfort of the French educated elite. Perhaps the moderns became so detached from action that they could no longer understand ancient epic poetry. No common ground remained between their refined leisure and the robust earthiness of Homeric Greece. To many authors, "the relevance and validity of the epic poem in the modern world seemed increasingly questionable."[19] But epic poems and drama continued to dominate the literary horizon for most of the eighteenth century. Though France had in Corneille and Racine outstanding dramatists

---

[18]   Élie Fréron, *L'Année littéraire*, vol. XXII (1775), 607.

[19]   See Timothy J. Chamberlain's introduction to *Eighteenth-Century German Criticism*, (New York, 1992), xviii. Ambivalent attitudes regarding epic poetry concerning German writers can be extended to the French context.

whose poetics migrated throughout Europe, she lacked a national epic poet to rival Milton, Dante, or Tasso, and kept pursuing the dream of an epic poem worthy of the Ancients and indicative of the nation's grandeur and artistic superiority. At last, Voltaire published his *Henriade* (1728), received with great critical acclaim within and outside France's borders. Readers admired Voltaire's choice of an era of national history as well as his faithful application of the epic genre's formal rules. Today *La Henriade* stands as the visible crown of the epic iceberg. Voltaire's poem represented a nation's literary ambition, yet his achievement did not reflect the more unorthodox approach of many a contemporary epic poet. In retrospect, as mentioned in Chapter 2, Voltaire's application of the rules—including the separation of the genres of prose and poetry—appears exceptional in light of the experimentations that his contemporaries and predecessors conducted.

After Fénelon inaugurated an epic poem in prose, the translator Anne Le Fèvre Dacier turned out to be the second author to use prose in a narrative previously expected to be written in verse. In 1711, the year Boileau died, the daughter of the famous Greek scholar Tanneguy Le Fèvre published a translation in prose of Homer's *Iliad*, preceded by a long preface wherein she confided her ambition to finally reveal to French readers the true essence of Homer's epic poem, which had been obscured by faulty translations and misconstrued in bad imitations.[20] Instead, the result was a fiery revival of the quarrel between ancients and moderns: as she provided them with the means to read the *Iliad* at long last, the moderns could examine it more closely and could prolong their offensive with renewed vigor. I consider that her approach to translation marked a tremendous step in the history of translation, as well as in the interface of prose and poetry in eighteenth-century France.[21] By succeeding in conveying Homer's poetry through prose, her translation challenged fiction writers into questioning the boundaries of prose and poetry and exploring their intersection, to help renew the faded poetic spirit of the age and to expand and vivify the field of prose. Three years later, in 1714, La Motte published a rebuttal to Dacier, the highly critical "Discours sur Homère," which stirred up a new scandal.[22] The critic censored Homer for excess, boredom, bizarre gods, "le merveilleux," and the hero's self-praise. His recipe for change called for

---

[20] Anne Lefèvre Dacier, *L'Iliade d'Homère, traduite en françois, avec des remarques, par Madame Dacier. Seconde édition, revue et augmentée, avec quelques reflexions sur la préface angloise* (Paris, 1719). References will be to this second edition and hereafter noted in text.

[21] For a detailed inquiry into Dacier's original contribution to the field of translation studies, see Julie Candler Hayes, "Of Meaning and Modernity: Anne Dacier and the Homer debate," *EMF: Studies in Early Modern France* 8 (2002). For a background and analysis of Dacier's theory of translation developed in her preface, see Fabienne Moore, "Homer revisited. Anne Le Fèvre Dacier's Preface to her Prose Translation of the *Iliad* in Early Eighteenth-Century France," *Studies in the Literary Imagination* 33, 2 (Fall, 2000).

[22] La Motte, "Discours sur Homère" in *Œuvres Complètes*, vol. 1, 182–216; Dacier, *Des Causes de la corruption du goust* (1714; Geneva, 1970); La Motte, "Réflexions sur la Critique," in *Œuvres complètes*, vol. 1, 270–340.

accepting his century's finer taste, and transposing rhythm into French language. The result was an abridged *L'Iliade en douze chants*. The two translations, one in prose, one in verse; the abundance and complexity of the critical discourse surrounding them; and the pugnacity of both translators render this literary strife particularly interesting in the wake of the "querelle des Anciens et des Modernes." It sparked an intense debate on the difference between verse and prose, freedom and fidelity, and prompted the question of whether one should modernize the Ancients and if so, how?

I will turn to a brief discussion of La Motte's "Discours sur Homère" before engaging Dacier's translation. In his discourse, La Motte considered whether poets ought to be translated in prose or verse ("S'il faut traduire les Poëtes en prose ou en vers").[23] His three statements in favor of prose translation were in keeping with Dacier's own arguments: "la prose seule est capable des traductions littérales" [only prose is able to translate literally]; "la prose peut imiter les hardiesses de la poësie" [prose can imitate poetry's audacity]; and "la prose fatigue moins que les vers" [prose is less tiresome than verse.][24] Dacier believed that "les Poëtes cessent d'être Poëtes quand ils sont traduits en vers" [Poets cease to be poets when translated in verse] (xl) because verse translators always add to the original. La Motte, and many others, disagreed on that point, judging that Homer is sometimes so defective that the translator, even in prose, is obliged to correct the original. Therefore, a less literal verse translation is acceptable and even recommended as an exercise to improve upon the original. La Motte's argument here should be understood less as an endorsement of versification than an offensive against veneration of the classics. In another essay, "Réflexions sur la critique," La Motte reiterated the same point by proving that the *Iliad*'s many flaws made it a bad poem, which justified his personal effort to correct it.[25] The drawback of versification—the distancing from the source—was turned into an advantage: it allowed La Motte to adapt freely and no longer translate.

In her preface to her prose translation of the *Iliad*, Dacier drew to her side Aristotle and Plato. From Aristotle she retained the idea that verse and prose could coexist in epic poetry; from Plato, she mentioned a prose translation of the *Iliad*'s beginning in the third book of *The Republic*, although she wished he had not used the indirect style of the historian but a direct style (xlj). Then, turning toward the Bible as a literary source, she focused on a concrete example, the only one to be followed, the prose of the Hebrews: "[Ils] ont fait de leur prose une sorte de poësie par un langage plus orné, plus vif & plus figuré" [They turned their prose into a sort of poetry thanks to a language more ornate, lively, and figurative] (xlii). The "golden" language of Hebrew prose, revealed primarily in the Songs, the Psalms, and the Prophets, is evocative of the Golden Age. "[U]ne prose soustenuë & composée avec art" [an elevated, artistic prose] defined for Dacier the kind of

23   La Motte, "Discours sur Homere," 211–12.
24   Ibid., 211.
25   La Motte, "Reflexions sur la critique," 318.

prose closest to poetry (xlii). Unlike d'Ablancourt's refined "prose d'art," thought to improve with time and literary progress, Dacier's own "prose d'art" looked toward the past to recover the lost eloquence of primitive times.

Interestingly, Dacier avoided the phrase "prose mesurée" used then to account for Fénelon's style in *Les Aventures de Télémaque*. Dacier steered clear from this slippery expression conflating prose with poetry. She did not wish to introduce meter in prose; she promoted condensation and artistic composition. French prose was vindicated as a superior mode of translation: "Mais je ne me contente pas de dire que la prose peut approcher de la poësie, je vais plus loin, & je dis qu'en fait de traduction ... il y a souvent dans la prose une precision, une beauté & une force, dont la poësie ne peut approcher" [But I am not simply saying that prose can come close to poetry, I go further and say that, as far as translation is concerned ... prose often has a precision, beauty and strength to which poetry cannot come close] (xlii). Dacier developed her conception of prose translation not as "servile" but as "generous and noble," that is generously open to a galaxy of words across a wider semantic field, and noble in its independence, creativity, and freedom to seek metaphors "without counting words" (xliii)—the petty task of the verse translator.

Undermining the Moderns' efforts to bypass the classics, Dacier countered their proselytizing in favor of progress, clarity, and modernity in the arts. She argued that a faithful translation would reveal time-defying beauties, long buried, and distorted by multiple adaptations. By undoing the layered tapestry of literary history, Dacier revealed a spectacularly fresh canvas and used her provocative scholarship to reclaim Homer as a modern poet. A lover of antiquity and a *femme des Lumières* nonetheless, Dacier pioneered prose translations inspired by a newly recovered poetic enthusiasm to recapture the ancient beauty of poetry, the first step toward re-attaining, if not a golden, at least a better age.

Gessner and Ossian

Inspired by Amyot's translation of Longus' mildly erotic Greek idyll, *Daphnis et Chloé*, the Swiss German Salomon Gessner published *Daphnis* in 1754, a short pastoral divided into three books, innovative in its use of rhythmic prose instead of verse. In 1756 a collection of twenty-nine *Idylles* appeared; in 1758 a biblical narrative, *La Mort d'Abel*; and in 1772 a series of twenty-two *Nouvelles Idylles*. The three works were written in rhythmic prose cultivating euphonic effects, shunning hiatus, and inclined to incorporate, here and there, various meters.[26] Turgot translated *La Mort d'Abel* in 1761 under his German teacher's name ([Michael] Huber) and the *Idylles* in 1762. Henri Meister translated the *Nouvelles Idylles* a

---

[26] See remarks from the translator Henri Meister, in *Œuvres complètes de Gessner*, vol. 1, xxi–xxii. See also Paul Van Tieghem, "Les idylles de Gessner et le rêve pastoral," in *Le Préromantisme. Etudes d'histoire littéraire européenne* (Geneva, 1973), 222.

year after their publication in 1773.[27] Gessner's phenomenal success in Europe (particularly France and Italy) spanned the entire second half of the eighteenth century and beyond until the 1840s: Paul Van Tieghem's census counted eighty-one translations or reprints published in Europe between 1762 and 1846.[28]

Modern critics have considered Gessner's works a watershed in the pre-history of the French prose poem. But contrary to what is often claimed, its success did not rest solely in its original rhythmic prose style. In Germany, versification of Gessner's idylls suggests that his poetic prose was yet not quite legitimate.[29] In France, the peculiarity of Gessner's rhythmic prose was lost when translated by Huber, Turgot, and Meister. The novelty resided primarily, I suggest, in the passage into prose of a genre, the idyll, so far exclusively versified. Prose idylls were, therefore, prose poems. Readers knew of the original form through the translator's preface, which might have further ingratiated them into welcoming this variation on a beloved ancient genre. It has not been emphasized enough that the novelty of Gessner's works for French readers was tied to the transference into prose of poetic codes belonging to the idyll, and not related to the rhythmic quality of an "enchanted" prose to be developed later by, for instance, Chateaubriand. The comparison with the contemporaneous success of Ossian's equally rhythmic prose reveals a similar phenomenon: translation diluted the idiosyncratic measured prose of the original, and therefore the novelty of the reading experience rested in the passage of a traditional versified genre into prose. Again, awareness of the original prose style no doubt played a role in readers' appreciation, yet it was not experienced firsthand, except by readers of the original English, though they too were reading (supposedly) a translation from Gaelic.

Whereas Rousseau's delight in Gessner and for pastorals in general, complemented his philosophy and his view of nature, Diderot's appreciation of the genre seems more surprising: by his express wish, two of his moral tales, *Deux amis de Bourbonne* and *Entretien d'un père avec ses enfants*, were originally bound with Meister's translation of the *Nouvelles Idylles* in 1773: "On fut fort étonné de ce bizarre assemblage, que rien ne justifiait" [People were surprised by this bizarre combination which nothing justified.][30] In fact, a brief examination of Gessner's major innovations might help explain the puzzling juxtaposition with

---

[27]   For the publication and translation history of Gessner's works in Europe, see Van Tieghem, ibid., esp. 217–21 and 233–48.

[28]   Ibid., 248.

[29]   Gessner wonders that "notre plus grand versificateur, Monsieur Ramler, se soit astreint au travail de versifier à nouveau mes Idylles, que j'avais moi-même écrites en *Versen* [c'est-à-dire en strophes ou versets], bien qu'extérieurement sous la forme de la prose" [our greatest author in verse, M. Raimler, committed himself to the work of putting again my idylls in verse which I had myself written in [stanzas], though on the exterior they had the form of prose]. Quoted in Jechova, Mouret, and Voisine, *La Poésie en prose des Lumières au romantisme*, 73.

[30]   Van Tieghem, *Le Préromantisme*, 236.

the French philosopher's tales, and highlight in the process Gessner's contribution to the development of eighteenth-century prose poems.

Gessner's *Nouvelles idylles* differed from the first collection in their staging other characters besides young lovers—fathers, mothers, children, and siblings—the very "secret" of the poet's art according to Diderot.[31] The pastoral circle widened to include blood relations, treated as ideal, in other words, virtuous, types.[32] Even if Diderot's sad tales (as well as his drama) complicated the idyllic picture by exposing humanity's foibles and misery, Gessner's idealized archetypes represented the pendant to Diderot's own realistic archetypes.

Gessner also innovated by transforming the traditional courtly bent of pastorals into lessons of moral wisdom and integrity. A notable evolution from Montesquieu's prose poem, the displacement of allegorical and mythological figures to the periphery implied casting away the gods' notorious immorality the better to place mankind's fundamentally moral character at the center. Though idealized and one-sided (they are always virtuous), characters and situations in Gessner's idylls compared *in essence* to Jean-Baptiste Greuze's depiction of ordinary (and often rural) types trapped in various moral dilemmas. Diderot deemed morality necessary in painting as well as in literature:

> La peinture a cela de commun avec la poésie, et il me semble qu'on ne s'en soit pas encore avisé, que toutes deux elles doivent être *bene moratae*; il faut qu'elle ait des mœurs. Boucher ne s'en doute pas; il est toujours vicieux et n'attache jamais. Greuze est toujours honnête; et la foule se presse autour de ses tableaux.[33]

> [It seems to me no one has yet noticed that painting has in common with poetry the fact that they must be *bene moratae*, they must have good morals. Boucher does not suspect it, he is always flawed and never moves the viewer. Greuze is always honest and the crowd flocks to his paintings.]

---

[31] "Un poète disait d'un autre poète: *Il n'ira pas loin, il n'a pas le secret.* Quel secret? Celui de présenter des objets d'un grand intérêt, des pères, des mères, des femmes, des enfants" [A poet told another poet: *He will not go far, he does not have the secret.* What secret? That of presenting objects of the highest interest, fathers, mothers, women and children.] Denis Diderot, *Essais sur la peinture* (Paris, 1984), 77.

[32] See Jauffret's best-selling *Les Charmes de l'enfance, et les plaisirs de l'amour maternel* (1796), and the acknowledgment of Gessner's direct influence in an "Essai sur l'idylle et le conte pastoral." The collection of thirty-eight prose idylls dwells exclusively on the sentimentally charged mother/child relationship, presented as an exemplary combination of virtue and innocence. In the preface, Jauffret gave historical reasons for his enterprise, correlating the need for and interest in idylls with the Revolution: "Les peintures d'un bonheur simple touchent d'avantage, quand on a vu autour de soi les passions se déchaîner dans toute leur violence" [Pictures of simple happiness are more touching when one has seen passions unleashed in all their violence.] 9–10.

[33] Diderot, *Essais sur la peinture*, 59.

Like Greuze's, Gessner's honest portraits attracted a considerable following, including Rousseau and Diderot. The contrast between François Boucher's grand, lascivious mythological paintings (many commissioned by the marquise de Pompadour, mistress to Louis XV), and Greuze's simple scenes aptly represents the pictorial counterpart to the contrasting prose poems of Montesquieu and Gessner. Montesquieu believed in the *bene moratae*'s principle, perhaps even more than Diderot, but the allegorical world portrayed by Boucher remained a compelling pictorial and literary vehicle for an aristocratic society compulsively identifying with allegorical figures. By mid-century, readers and spectators of various social classes grew more fond of observing themselves and each other in mirrors less ornate but more reflective of social virtues. However idealized the reflection might have been (e.g., Gessner), the verisimilitude of the characters' inwardness won over readers who could perceive idylls as believable thanks to prose: prose enabled directness and simplicity in descriptions, dialogues, and interior monologues; prose served innocence, virtue's corollary in Gessner's idylls; prose became "le langage de la nature."[34] Neoclassical verse would have lessened Gessner's impact, introducing a distancing artfulness antithetical not only to the shepherds' outpouring of emotions, but also to their innocence. Gessner's prose poems fulfilled Diderot's triad "le vrai, le bon et le beau" in an unsuspected yet notable manner, and with a composition in prose—also Diderot's mode of predilection.[35] By placing his moral tales under the tutelage of Gessner's prose poems, Diderot probably hoped to benefit from their success, but more profoundly, he found them more congenial to philosophical and ethical meditation than mythological tales.

I end this chapter on "Translation to the rescue" with translations of Ossian into French: although they shaped many a prose writer's style, they have not been the object of much critical consideration since Van Tieghem's literary history. I focus on Chateaubriand's interpretation of Ossian as exemplary of the powerful Ossianic influence sweeping Europe in the last quarter of the century, and will also highlight the personal manner in which Chateaubriand appropriated Ossianic poetic themes and diction to serve his own vision. The importance I give to Chateaubriand's work in my pre-history of prose poems may seem like a double provocation: he is hardly known as a poet or an Enlightenment figure. But his writings say otherwise when analyzed closely, and I intend through the course of the next chapters to revisit Chateaubriand's early work (*Atala* and *Les Martyrs*) to show how they epitomized a divided subjectivity, the representation of which reframes current views on the poetics of prose.

In his *Mémoires* Chateaubriand confided that he wrote his first work the *Essai sur les révolutions* at night, and devoted his days to translations. Although he undertook each endeavor from economic necessity, Chateaubriand probably hoped that translations would procure him quicker revenues. The production of prose in original or translated texts was financially more rewarding than the production of poetry. Chateaubriand tried his hand at translating excerpts from British authors,

---

[34]   See Meister, Preface, *Œuvres complètes de Gessner*, vol. 1, xxj.

[35]   Diderot, *Essai sur la peinture*, 76.

choosing presumably both what interested him and what might interest a French readership: he selected John Smith, a skillful imitator of Macpherson's *Ossian* (the latter already and successfully translated by Le Tourneur); Milton (translated in prose by Dupré de Saint-Maur, Racine fils, and in verse by Jacques Delille); and James Beattie, unknown in France.

Chateaubriand's decision to choose his translation of three "Ossianic" poems by John Smith (*Dargo, Duthona,* and *Gaul*), among his thousand pages of youthful poetry, for publication in his *Œuvres Complètes* in 1828, indicates the importance that an aging Chateaubriand attributed to Ossian in the formation of his style.[36] Opting for Smith over Ossian offered the advantage of not repeating Le Tourneur's authoritative translation, but Chateaubriand cites finer artistry as the reason for his preference: Smith's talent had "quelque chose de plus élégant et de plus tendre" than Macpherson's.[37] The poems, however, are not exempt from repetitions and obscurities, but Chateaubriand defends his corrections of content and form by invoking Boileau's principle of clarity.[38] The reference to Boileau and the expressed disdain for "le vague et le ténébreux" confirm Chateaubriand's classical taste in poetry from the beginning of his career.[39] At the same time as Chateaubriand was drawn by the somber, elusive Ossianic landscape, characters, and story lines, he favored a direct, clear writing style. Though he mentions only inversions and the complex stories-within-stories structure as his major difficulties, he also confronted the challenge of conveying the intangible and allusive in an exactitude-loving French prose. Chateaubriand's translation, therefore, offers an interesting perspective on how he bridged the divide between what would soon be named "le vague des passions," and a French prose famed for its precision. Van Tieghem has shown that Chateaubriand, as a translator, sacrificed distinctive aspects of the original poems: "Le texte est ... arrangé et perd en précision et en sobriété. ... une traduction agréable, mais peu exacte, souvent décolorée et comme banalisée, et fort abrégée" [The text is ... arranged and loses precision and sobriety ... a pleasant translation, but hardly exact, often discolored, almost common place,

---

[36] Chateaubriand, "Dargo, poëme, traduit du gallique en anglais, par John Smith;" "Duthona, poëme;" "Gaul, poëme," in *Œuvres complètes* (Paris, 1928), vol. 22, 13–76. On the success of John Smith's *Gallic Antiquities* (1780), see Paul Van Tieghem, *Ossian en France* (Geneva, 1967), vol. I, 40. For a synopsis of Smith's fourteen poems, see ibid., 41–4. In the *Essai sur la littérature angloise*, Chateaubriand prefers to quote and translate a passage from John Smith rather than Ossian, arguing that he is less known.

[37] Chateaubriand, preface to *Œuvres complètes* (Paris, 1828), vol. 22, iii.

[38] "J'ai fait disparoître les redites et les obscurités du texte anglois: ces chants qui sortent les uns des autres, ces histoires qui se placent comme des parenthèses dans des histoires. ... nous voulons en France des *choses qui se conçoivent bien et qui s'énoncent clairement*" [I removed repetitions and obscurities from the English text: songs generated out of one another; stories that seem in parentheses within stories. ... In France, we want *things well conceived and clearly enunciated.*] Ibid., iv.

[39] "Quand à moi, je l'avoue, le vague et le ténébreux me sont antipathiques" [As for me, I admit I dislike what is vague and somber.] Ibid.

and seriously shortened.][40] In fact, Chateaubriand's prose sacrificed faithfulness of expression to draw out the musicality of the original English text. Indeed, there is a striking contrast in the preface between Chateaubriand's criticism of obscurities in the original and his concluding remarks on the enduring auditory pleasure he derived from the text, a musical delight undiminished by knowledge of the poems' inauthenticity: "j'écoute cependant encore la harpe du Barde, comme on écouteroit une voix, monotone il est vrai, mais douce et plaintive. Macpherson a ajouté aux chants des Muses une note jusqu'à lui inconnue; c'est assez pour le faire vivre" [I still listen to the bard's harp, as one would listen to a voice, monotonous indeed, but plaintive and sweet. Macpherson added to the Muses' songs a note until then unknown; this alone keeps him alive.] [41] Ossian is prized for his melancholy music, and the reader constantly reminded that the poems are a musical performance ("barde," "voix," and "chant/chanter" recur repeatedly in the three poems). Paradoxically, Chateaubriand's infidelity to the text succeeded in inventing new notes: he condensed the original, removed epithets or replaced them with generic ones, cut some comparisons, added repetitions as well as exclamations for emphasis, and, for instance, replaced the name "Crimora" by the invented, more harmonious "Evella." The result, as Van Tieghem argued, did take liberties with the original, but captured the rhythmic tempo of Ossianic style more closely than accurate, literal translations. To be more precise, the characteristics of Smith's poems in Chateaubriand's version include periphrases and substantives with a high "volume sonore," exclamations (thirty-eight "ô"), repetition of first names in lieu of pronouns; frequent feminine endings; and the echoing vowel "a" in the future and past tenses, and in the characters' first names. [42] The sentence's structural condensation reinforces these acoustic elements: there are very few sentence lengtheners such as polysyllabic words, epithets, and conjunctions of subordination or coordination; the syntax of each sentence is overly simple; and the majority of sentences have an uncomplicated binary rhythm with frequent parallelisms or oppositions. Overall, short, simple sentences give the impression of similar "style coupé" than the paratactic prose poems written after Fénelon. It strives to be natural, fresh, modern, yet its model is primitive poetry. In brief: "extérieurement une prose d'art, et qui se souvient du vers" [from the outside, an artistic prose, which remembers verse.][43] As in Le Tourneur's translation, the novelty resides in the combination of artistic prose—with which authors have been experimenting for a century—with the powerful, dark tone colors of graveyard poetry.

---

[40] Van Tieghem, *Ossian en France*, vol. II, 621. For a comparison between Chateaubriand's and Hill's translations, see ibid., 623.

[41] Chateaubriand, preface to *Œuvres complètes* (Paris, 1828), vol. 22, v.

[42] See Jean Mourot's analyses on the sonority and volume of Chateaubriand's style in *Le Génie d'un style. Chateaubriand. Rythme et sonorité dans les Mémoires d'outre-tombe* (Paris, 1960), 180–225.

[43] Ibid., 88.

If the range of rhetorical tropes in *Dargo, Duthona,* and *Gaul* remains very limited as seen above, description is also deliberately restricted to a few key words, such as the landscape sketched over again with the same terms: "rocher," "bruyère," "torrent," "océan," "forêt," "lune," "étoiles," "brouillard," etc. [rock, heather, torrent, ocean, forest, moon, stars, fog]. This minimalism induces repetition, which results in an incantatory, "rhapsodic" prose style. Because the semantic field gravitates solely around sadness, loss, and death, this "rhapsodic" style, based on condensation, simplification, and repetition, heightens the pathos of the poems. The number of occurrences below gives a sense of the overwhelmingly melancholy atmosphere of the three poems:[44]

45	ombre(s) [shadow(s)]
41	nuit [night]
40	tombe/tombeau/tomber [tomb, tombstone, to tumble]
18	mort/mourir/mortelle [death, to die, mortal]
18	triste/esse/ement [sad, sadness, sadly]
18	soupirer/soupir(s) [to sigh, sigh(s)]
18	larme(s) [tear(s)]
15	passer/passé [to pass, past]
11	solitaire(s) [solitary]
10	silence [silence]
10	fantôme(s) [ghost(s)]
9	pleurer/pleur(s): [to weep, weeping]
9	désert(e)(s) [desert(s)]
8	sombre(s) [sombre]
8	oublier/oublié [to forget, forgotten]
7	ténèbre(s)/ténébreux [darkness, dark]
4	ruines [ruin(s)]

Moreover, the emphatic negation "point" is repeated a startling forty-two times and the strong negative "plus" thirty-nine times. The cumulative effect of the predominantly negative vocabulary and the incessant echo throughout the three poems of similar sounds, words, structures, and stories reproduce the distinct poetic atmosphere of Ossian (and its variations, "ossianides") better than Hill's more accurate literal translation.

Chateaubriand's translation reveals the decisive impact of Ossian (via Macpherson, Smith and other imitators) on his own writing. I will argue that in his subsequent works, Chateaubriand dissociated the style and content of Ossianic poetry and re-appropriated them in two different writing styles. He adopted the archaic music of the "rhapsodic" *style coupé* to poeticize certain prose passages

---

[44] This word search was facilitated by the CD-Rom of Chateaubriand's complete works: *François-René de Chateaubriand, Les Itinéraires du romantisme.* The word search covered the 53 pages of the three translated texts: *Dargo* (16 pages); *Duthona* (17 pages); *Gaul* (20 pages).

in his fiction and ennoble them (as discussed in Chapter 7 with the example of *Atala*). This self-conscious poetic parataxis, neither new nor terribly successful, was not "natural" to Chateaubriand. But when he integrated the new Ossianic themes and vocabulary within his classical, periodicized style, he experienced a breakthrough. The secret of Chateaubriand's enchanted prose, the reputed "accent Chateaubriand," lies in the importation of modern Ossianic themes into a classically structured sentence. Jean Mourot has demonstrated Chateaubriand's constant adhesion to Aristotelian rhetoric instilled by his education and furthered by his natural inclination, principles he instinctively integrated with his personal poetics, his own "poésie des tombeaux." Mourot gives the key to understanding the inner working of Chateaubriand's prose: the contradiction between a classically trained ear and a romantically inclined mind.

> [I]l amène ses mots favoris aux points de la ligne orale où ils comblent le plus naturellement l'attente; où ils se correspondent selon un rythme simple et sensible; là où la vieille rhétorique enseigne qu'ils ne sauraient manquer leur effet. Dans une lettre à Amédée Pichot, à propos de versification, il notait la contradiction de son oreille "demeurée classique" avec son "esprit romantique"; la remarque vaudrait pour sa prose; on l'y reconnaît à la fois à ses mots "romantiques" et à la place "classique" qu'il leur assigne; sa marque propre est dans ce contraste.[45]

> [He brings his favorite words to parts of the oral line where they most naturally fulfill expectations, where they correspond with one another according to a simple and perceptible rhythm; where old rhetoric teaches that they shall not miss their effect. In a letter to Amédée Pichot, on the subject of versification, he noted the contradiction between his ear "which remained classical," and his "Romantic mind." The remark applies to his prose: we can recognize him thanks both to his "Romantic" words and the "classical" place that he assigns them. His trademark resides in this contrast.]

Although Mourot explains the reasons for Chateaubriand's "oreille classique," he does not trace to Ossian the source of the favorite words that inspired this "esprit romantique."[46] To overlook the importance of the Nordic bard for Chateaubriand's sense of poetry is to miss the resonance of his haunting theme of the Fall and the essence of his self-representation as a new (yet ancient) bard.

---

[45]   Mourot, *Le Génie d'un style*, 250.

[46]   Mourot does not mention Ossian or refer to Chateaubriand's translation in his otherwise enlightening study of *Le Génie d'un style*.

Chapter 5
Back to the Bible

La Bible, ce divin monument lyrique.

Victor Hugo[1]

This chapter explores the paradox of a return to the Bible precisely during the so-called secular Enlightenment: at the same time as Encyclopedists and philosophers fought against the Church, scholars in France and England turned the Bible into the focus of inquiries about language and poetry that reached a wider audience than in the previous century.[2] Authors leaned on a poetic reading of the Bible to escape formalism and versification, and developed lyrical narratives in prose with biblical subject matters. The circulation of Longinus' *Traité du sublime*, translated by Boileau (in 1674) and annotated by André Dacier (in 1683) facilitated this evolution, as well as Anne Dacier's innovative defense of poetry and enthusiasm in her translations. Alongside Boileau and her husband André, she belonged to a classicism that initiated the tradition of the sublime on each side of the Channel, which is too often overlooked.[3] Boileau had developed Longinus' biblical examples, notably Genesis "Fiat Lux," to illustrate the sublime and its requirement of stylistic simplicity.[4] The religious nature of examples of the sublime gave rise to misunderstanding with Pierre-Daniel Huet—Anne Dacier's mentor—who denounced the equation of the sublime with rhetoric.[5] While Boileau's new preface of 1701 refined his definition by adding secular examples like Corneille's drama, Anne Dacier worked at reconciling both Boileau and Huet, conceiving her translation as evidence of the *Iliad*'s sublime, similar in essence to the sublime of sacred texts.[6]

---

[1]   Victor Hugo, Preface, *Cromwell* (Paris, 1968), 77.

[2]   See Roger Mercier, "La question du langage poétique au début du XVIIIᵉ siècle. La Bible et la critique."

[3]   See Litman, *Le Sublime en France*, 67. Litman remarks on the paradox that the new aesthetic conception of the sublime undermined Boileau's own *Art poétique* and would eventually bring down classicism itself.

[4]   See Roger Mercier, "La question du langage poétique," 277–81; and Nicolas Cronk, *The Classical Sublime: French Neoclassicism and the Language of Literature* (Charlottesville, 2002), chap. 4, 77–117.

[5]   See Gilles Declercq, "Boileau-Huet: la querelle du Fiat lux," in *Pierre-Daniel Huet (1630–1721): actes du colloque de Caen* (12–13 November 1993), ed. Suzanne Guellouz (Paris and Seattle, 1994), 237–62.

[6]   See Fabienne Moore. "1711: The Advent of Homer in French Prose. An Anatomy of Madame Dacier's Ground-Breaking Translation," *SVEC* 06 (2008): 193–213.

As this aspect of Enlightenment research has not received much attention, I will first highlight the theoretical contributions of Robert Lowth (1710–1787) and the abbé Charles Batteux (1713–1780) in the revival of lyricism, linked to biblical poetry, then examine a literary application, Jean-Jacques Rousseau's biblical prose poem, *Le Lévite d'Éphraïm*. Historians and readers of literature have privileged Rousseau's harmonious poetic prose as the liberating medium that let Rousseau bypass versification as well as apply his musical sensibility. Rousseau has long been celebrated as a "poet in prose" on account of the lyrical poetic prose of many passages in his novel *Julie,* the *Confessions,* and the famous "Fifth Promenade" in the *Rêveries,* justly considered crucial in the genealogy of prose poetry. My thesis is that the aesthetic achievement of these texts, while undeniable, has legitimized a reading of Rousseau that seems too narrow, predictable, and somewhat divorced from the literary history of his time. Like Montesquieu's *Temple de Gnide,* the neoclassical venture of *Le Lévite d'Éphraïm* reveals that the imperfect new genre was expressively chosen to convey the philosophical and moral message of a self-reflective, conflicted subject caught between tradition and modernity. I will add to my examination of the Enlightenment's return to the Bible a few more examples, most notably Chateaubriand's *Les Martyrs,* which also garnered mixed reviews, including its author's self-critique. In the wake of the Revolution, Chateaubriand further christianized the melancholy experience of earlier prose poets by turning it into an experience of the Fall. With *Les Martyrs,* the problematic of prose vs. poetry shifted to the opposition Romantic vs. classical.

In 1758 when Gessner published his biblical poem in prose *La Mort d'Abel* (translated in French in 1761), he hoped to placate censors who had harshly judged his first pastoral poem *Daphnis,* a story of adolescent love imitated from Longus' sensuous romance, *Daphnis et Chloé.*[7] In his preface Gessner justified his choice of a biblical instead of mythological episode as worthy of a new, more serious poetry: "Elle présente l'histoire sainte par ses endroits les plus saillans, met à profit, pour en augmenter la crédibilité, les circonstances les plus convaincantes et les réflexions les plus instructives." [It presents sacred history through its most striking moments, and takes advantage of the most convincing circumstances and the most instructive reflections to increase verisimilitude.][8] According to Gessner, poetry did not degrade or desecrate the Scriptures; on the contrary, it represented religion's natural interpreter: "elle est faite pour être, et a toujours été l'interprete de la religion; ... elle lui a rendu de grands services, et ... il n'est pas de langage plus propre pour élever l'ame à des sentiments d'honneur et de piété" [it is written, and was always written to be religion's interpreter; ... it has rendered it great services, and ... no language is most apt to elevate the soul to feelings of honor and piety.][9] Gessner argued that Catholic and Protestant religion had long allowed biblical

---

[7]　　See Van Tieghem, *Le Préromantisme,* 219.

[8]　　Gessner, "Préface de l'Auteur," *La Mort d'Abel,* in *Œuvres complètes* (n.d.), vol. 1, viii.

[9]　　Ibid., vii.

topics to be staged in the theater. Still, Gessner's translator insisted on the novelty of the poem's structure, form, and tone, before making conflicting claims as to the source of the poem's originality.[10] Novelty derived from the subject matter, "the most remarkable event of sacred history, after the fall of our parents," Abel's death (xvii). Nevertheless the poet's graceful portrayal of sentiments—"tableaux de sentimens"—represented its main attraction (xvii).[11] Before determining the poem's value, the translator oscillated between the genres of the epic and the idyll, and conceded that although the poem did not adhere to rules governing epic poetry, Gessner's naïve and lifelike descriptions put him on par with Milton. Taking stock of the genres' commingling, Chateaubriand judged that the poem's main flaw resided in the displacement of the epic in favor of the idyll and the resulting lack of verisimilitude when Oriental pastoral kings become innocent Arcadian shepherds.[12] The divergent opinions of Gessner's translator and Chateaubriand illumine the poem's most original feature: the lyrical treatment in prose of a biblical story. The Bible had inspired tragedies, epic poems, and odes (most notably from Jean-Baptiste Rousseau and Lefranc de Pompignan), but this time, a work of fiction embraced a biblical story exclusively for its *bathos*, even softening Cain's cruelty to stir readers' compassion. Gessner's predilection for pastorals probably helped him tune in to the Bible's lyrical voice, and so did Friedrich Gottlieb Klopstock's poetry and critical essays. Author of (among other works) a religious epic, *The Messiah* (1742), Klopstock invoked a sublime, higher poetry that would "move the entire soul," and considered "the main design of religion" as the goal to be imitated by poetry: "great wondrous events that have occurred, still more wondrous that shall occur! Truths of the same kind! The decorum of religion! The loftiness! The simplicity! The gravity! The sweetness! The beauty!"[13] Gessner shared Klopstock's vision of the Bible and his "new emphasis on *movere*, in contrast to the Enlightenment preference for *prodesse* and *delectare*, poetry that instructs and delights."[14] Emphasis on emotions meant that the lyrical mode was progressively upstaging the epic, an evolution most notable in England and Germany, but much slower, or rather more subterranean in France, as Chateaubriand's attachment to the epic confirmed well into the nineteenth century. In his essay on sacred poetry introducing the *Messiah*, Klopstock urged the emulation of the *spirit* and

---

[10] Ibid., "Préface du Traducteur," xvi.

[11] Ibid., xvii.

[12] Chateaubriand, *Génie du christianisme* (Paris, 1978), 641.

[13] Friedrich Gottlieb Klopstock, *On Sacred Poetry*, in *Eighteenth-Century German Criticism*, ed. Timothy J. Chamberlain, 77. Klopstock composed his poem over thirty-five years, hence partial translations. The first two songs of *The Messiah* were translated into French in 1750 by Tscharner. D'Autelmy and al. published a translation of songs 1 to 10 in 1769. Finally a complete translation by Pierre Petit, *La Messiade,* appeared in 1795. See Philippe Van Tieghem, *Les Influences étrangères sur la littérature française* (Paris, 1967), 253–5.

[14] Chamberlain, introduction to *Eighteenth-Century German Criticism*, xx.

"main design" of religion, but clarified twice that this injunction did not concern the "style" or "expression" of biblical poetry.[15] Inspired by Arthur Young, Klopstock read the Bible as a work of genius and originality which could provide a source of poetic inspiration for original odes or plays (Klopstock was the celebrated author of both), but not a source for poetic diction. This disjunction between the form and spirit of the Scriptures corresponded to a new stage in the eighteenth-century rediscovery of the Bible as a poetical text. In the first half of the century, the sacred poetry of Jean-Baptiste Rousseau and Lefranc de Pompignan had sought to deliver a religious message above all: "Ils n'emploient pas explicitement son contenu [l'Ancien Testament] comme un ensemble de figures applicable au temps présent: la grandeur de cette poésie est dans un aspect, si l'on veut, 'symboliste,' son terrible secret étant laissé à découvrir au lecteur" [They do not use explicitly (the Old Testament's) content as a wealth of figures applicable to the present time: the greatness of their poetry is in its "symbolist" aspect, if you will. Its terrible secret is left for the reader to discover.][16] The militantism and righteousness of early eighteenth-century French sacred poetry, always versified, and its emphasis on God's wrath, differed greatly from the second wave of poems inspired by the Bible:[17] Gessner's *La Mort d'Abel* was meant to touch readers' hearts, to encourage sympathy by picturing human struggles, to stir sentiments with an effusive display of tears—in other words, by embracing the Bible's lyricism. In the second phase of the prose poem's emergence, under the influence of new critical readings of the Bible as poetry, a newfound respect for lyricism competed with attachment to the still superior epic mode, resulting in hybrid narratives often incorporating both poetic codes, such as Rousseau's *Lévite d'Éphraïm*. Before proceeding with Rousseau, however, I wish to underscore the determining role played by Lowth, who analyzed the Bible as ancient Hebraic poetry, leading the way for a critical understanding of the nature of the sublime in poetry and its relevance for prose.

Robert Lowth on Ancient Hebrew Poetry

Neither Klopstock's ideal of "sacred poetry" nor Gessner's lyricism would have been possible without the aesthetic revolution and revelation brought by Robert Lowth's 1753 *De Sacra Poesi Hebraeorum* (*Lectures on the Sacred Poetry of the Hebrews*). Lowth's groundbreaking analyses of the Bible as a literary text paved the way for Gessner's poem, its enthusiastic reception in France, and subsequent imitations and variations. Lowth's collection of thirty-four lectures constituted a turning point, in mid-century, for authors and critics searching for sources of inspiration and new models to end poetry's crisis. Lowth scrutinized the Old

---

[15]   Klopstock, *On Sacred Poetry*, 77.

[16]   Menant, *La Chute d'Icare*, 332.

[17]   See for instance Reyrac's hymn in prose in three cantos, "La Création" in *Hymne au soleil, Suivi de plusieurs morceaux du même genre qui n'ont point encore paru.* 6th edition (1782).

Testament, not as a theologian but as a literary critic, claiming for the first time that "poetry which proceeds from divine inspiration is not beyond the province of criticism."[18] Lowth projected onto the Scriptures traditional rhetorical categories (genres, figures, and poetic diction), while trying to maintain the Bible's autonomy vis-à-vis Greek and Latin rhetorical principles.[19] The paradoxical result presented ancient Hebrew poetry as an extraordinary repository of examples illustrating ancient rhetoric, *and* as a superior masterpiece against which classical and modern texts were measured. Lowth's endeavor went a step beyond his predecessors (in France, Louis Thomassin, Etienne Fourmont, Claude Fleury, Bossuet, and Fénelon) in offering a methodical literary analysis of the Old Testament read as ancient Hebraic sacred poetry.[20] Lowth also innovated in considering the Bible's various contributors as singular artists, poetic geniuses divinely inspired but retaining individual styles.[21]

Lowth's methodical criticism innovated by its object, the Bible, but even more original was his subtle yet unmistakable reversal of the hierarchy of traditional genres in favor of the lyric and the dramatic. Indeed, the critic's seemingly objective

---

[18] Robert Lowth, Table of Contents, *Lectures on the Sacred Poetry of the Hebrews* (Boston, 1815), xiii. Hereafter cited in text.

[19] The third part of Lowth's treatise projects the traditional division of genres onto the Old Testament and classifies its sacred poetry under traditional categories (prophetic, elegiac, lyric, didactic, etc.). Lowth prefaced it with an interesting caveat: "What remains at present, is to distribute into its different classes the whole of the Hebrew poetry, and to mark whatever is worthy of observation in each species. In forming this arrangement it will be hardly expected that I should uniformly proceed according to the testimony of the Hebrews, or on all occasions confirm the propriety of my classification by their authority; since it is plain that they were but little versed in these nice and artificial distinctions. ... it will be sufficient for the accurate explanation of the different characters of the Hebrew poetry, if I demonstrate that these characters are stamped by the hand of nature." Ibid., 240.

[20] On French theorists, see Menant, *La Chute d'Icare*, 315–16, and Roger Mercier, "La question du language poétique," 260–72. Lowth's treatise adopts a systematic approach to define the particular "genius" of Hebrew poetry, and to encompass all its aspects. The subdivisions of his three main parts, "the nature of verse, the style, and the arrangement," deal respectively with 1) Hebrew meter, 2) sententious, figurative, and sublime styles of Hebrew poetry, and 3) different genres of Hebrew poetry (prophetic, elegiac, didactic, lyric, idyllic, dramatic).

[21] "I shall endeavour to detract nothing from the dignity of that inspiration, which proceeds from higher causes, while I allow to the genius of each writer his own peculiar excellence and accomplishments. I am indeed of opinion, that the Divine Spirit by no means takes such an entire possession of the mind of the prophet, as to subdue or extinguish the character and genius of the man: the natural powers of the mind are in general elevated and refined, they are neither eradicated nor totally obscured" (213–14). The question of whether divine inspiration was distinct from or confounded with poetical enthusiasm remained controversial in the first half of the century (see Menant, 316 and Roger Mercier, 259–60 and 266). Here, Lowth clearly separates them, in conformity with his view on the prophets' individual genius.

approach was in fact predetermined by his aesthetic evaluation of the Bible's most sublime moments, e.g., the Psalms, the Song of Solomon, the odes of David and Moses, the Lamentations of Jeremiah, the book of Job, to name but the most frequently praised. Consequently, the treatise devoted many pages to figurative and sublime styles, and to lyrical and dramatic modes, in keeping with Lowth's hierarchy of preferences. [22] Professing his highest regard for numerous passages in the course of his work, Lowth singled out three narratives that he considered the most sublime: "the thanksgiving ode of Moses" after crossing the Red Sea (within lyrical poetry), the Song of Solomon (within dramatic poetry), and towering above all, "single and unparalleled," unclassifiable but "in the highest rank of Hebrew poetry," the book of Job, to which he exclusively devoted his last three lectures.

Thus a superficial examination of the table of contents already indicates the profound originality of Lowth's 1753 treatise: exhibiting a keen awareness of the power and sublimity of lyric poetry, Lowth's work must be read alongside the contemporary authors whom literary historians usually credit with unleashing the lyrical mode in their "poésie des tombeaux": Arthur Young (*Night Thoughts* 1742–1745), James Hervey (*Meditations Among the Tombs* 1748), and Thomas Gray (*Elegy Written in a Country Church-Yard* 1751). Further, Lowth's treatise, by stressing the poetical expressivity of the Bible, might have inspired Gessner (the *Mort d'Abel* dates from 1758) as well as Macpherson, whose *Poems of Ossian* (1760–1763) betrayed similarities with certain biblical expressions. The poetics Lowth elaborated in his treatise, matched in importance Arthur Young's celebrated *Thoughts on Original Composition* (1759). His critical examination of the Bible contributed to the reevaluation of poetry that took place in mid-century throughout Europe by offering alternative examples to those dissatisfied with, or weary of, Greek and Latin models, who sought to escape graciously from the hierarchically superior but increasingly wanting epic and tragic genres. The widespread success of Lowth's treatise insured the diffusion of his bold, enthusiastic endorsement of the Bible as a literary text. Unlike efforts by earlier poets to reappropriate a sacred voice to convey their own message, who thus made themselves the target of accusation of profanation, Lowth's strictly critical approach "objectified" the sacred text, calling attention to its craft. Though the treatise is nowhere programmatic (or only in so far as learning Hebrew is concerned), it brimmed with potential applications, inspiring a new poetics favoring lyricism, the assertion of the sublime style, and the "mixing" of traditional genres.

The French reception of Lowth's work on the Bible seemed to have been prepared by Batteux's *Principes de la littérature,* though I have not been able to establish whether Lowth and Batteux were aware of each other's work. The *Principes* regrouped three books previously published independently of each other.

---

[22]   Whereas only one lecture is devoted to the "sententious style," nine lectures are dedicated to the "figurative style," and four lectures to the "sublime style." In the third part, whereas one lecture each treats of "didactic poetry," and the "idyllium," four lectures focus on "prophetic poetry," three on "lyric poetry" and five on "dramatic poetry." In addition, two lectures are devoted to "elegiac poetry."

Batteux had originally exposed his theory of imitation as the governing principle of all art in *Les Beaux arts réduits à un même principe*, which appeared in 1746. Urged by critics to provide young readers with concrete applications of his theory, he then wrote nine treatises under the title *Cours de Belles-Lettres, distribué par exercices*, published in 1747 and 1748: they consisted of *De l'Apologue, De l'Églogue, De l'Épopée, Du Poëme Dramatique, De la Poësie Lyrique, De la Poësie Didactique, De l'Épigramme & De l'Inscription.* "Ces huits Traités contiennent toute la Poëtique" [These eight treatises contain the whole poetics], explained Batteux in the "Avertissement."[23] *Des Genres en Prose* constituted the ninth treatise. Lastly, in 1763, Batteux published a third volume, *De la Construction Oratoire des mots*, a stylistic examination of eloquence in prose. Like Lowth's treatise, Batteux gave unprecedented importance to lyrical poetry, placed on an equal footing with epic and dramatic poetry. The first and last genres (apologues and epigrams) were minor, the second and the antepenultimate were subgenres (eclogues and didactic poetry). There appeared a new triad: epic, dramatic, lyric. By almost exclusively focusing on Batteux's principle of imitation, admittedly traditional, eighteenth-century scholarship has neglected this newfound equality among the three genres. But Gérard Genette turned to Batteux when interrogating the origins of the tripartition epic/lyric/dramatic, a tripartition not substantiated in Aristotle or Plato as had been frequently assumed, but instead an early modern hijacking of genres ("détournement générique").[24] Genette construed Batteux's justification of the inclusion of lyrical poetry as a clever maneuver thanks to which lyrical poetry became integrated within an Aristotelian and Platonic system that had rejected it. Batteux's "Traité de la poésie lyrique" tackled first the prickly issue of generic definition, subtitling its first chapter "What lyric poetry is," thus confirming Genette's claim that this was by no means an established category like the epic and dramatic. Genette viewed Batteux's mission impossible as a "dernier effort de la poétique classique pour survivre en s'ouvrant à ce qu'elle n'avait pu ni ignorer ni accueillir" [a last effort by classical poetry to survive by opening itself onto what it could neither ignore nor welcome.][25] Accustomed to the marginalization of lyric poetry during the Enlightenment (a phenomenon less theorized today than the evolution of epic and dramatic genres in the same period), followed by its triumphant return in Romantic and post-Romantic thought and writing, we have overlooked how Batteux's prescient definition synthesized a new order of rules:

> Le genre lyrique veut être grand, riche, sublime, hardi: il demande des tours singuliers, des elans, des traits de feu, des ecarts. Il ne veut point d'ordre sensible: il évite les détails trop analysés, les généralités scientifiques, les subtilités: il lui faut des objets qu'on voie, qu'on touche, qui remuent. Voilà les règles. (290)

---

[23] Charles Batteux, Avertissement, *Principes de la littérature*, 7. Hereafter cited in text.

[24] Gérard Genette, "Introduction à l'architexte," in *Théorie des genres*, eds. Gérard Genette and Tzetan Todorov (Paris, 1986), 116. See also 93–7 and 113–18.

[25] Ibid., 113–14.

[The lyrical genre will be noble, rich, sublime, and bold: it requires striking turns, élans, flashes of fire, and exceptions to the rules. It does not want a rational order. It shuns descriptive details, scientific generalities and subtleties: it must have objects that can be seen, touched, and can rouse the heart. These are its rules.]

Lowth similarly emphasized "the amazing power of lyric poetry" (15). Written in mid-century, Batteux and Lowth's pronouncements opened striking new venues for their contemporaries, not the least Jean-Jacques Rousseau.

Citing examples given by Batteux in *Des Beaux Arts* (David, Pindar, and Horace), Genette argued that traditional poetics could neither "ignore nor welcome" these authors. But his demonstration only concerned itself with the evolution of generic categories per se, so Genette did not analyze the specific nature of the lyric poetry under consideration.[26] This is what a comparison between Batteux's exposition on lyrical poetry and Lowth's study of the Bible allows us to do. Their concordant theories expose the components which, it will turn out, are directly related to, and likely initiated, new directions in the poetic quest by the second half of the century. Though their approach to criticism differed (literary in the case of Batteux and more historically oriented for Lowth), the similarities between the conclusions reached by the two contemporaries are striking, though I shall emphasize again that further research is needed to establish a direct influence. Nevertheless, Batteux and Lowth provide an essential context to foreground a new analysis of Jean-Jacques Rousseau's *Le Lévite d'Ephraïm*, and ultimately help situate the sources and horizon of eighteenth-century lyrical prose poems.

Lowth's critical assessment of the Bible stood apart from earlier praise of biblical style due to his knowledge of the Hebrew language. Just as Dacier's mastery of Greek helped her capture the spirit and letter of Homeric poetry, Lowth's understanding of Hebrew provided his readers with a unique entry into the *texture* of the biblical text. His linguistic comments on the singularities of the Hebrew language revealed a mode of expression operating in stunningly different ways than not only contemporary European idioms, but also ancient Greek and Latin tongues. With expert pedagogical acumen, Lowth shuttled back and forth between comments on the idiosyncrasy of the original language and how biblical scripters used it to their advantage to produce specific effects. He shone light on a patchwork of genres, styles, figures, tones, and even tenses, hitherto considerably homogenized or blurred by translation's veil.

A first revelation concerned the "Hebrew metre." As much as Lowth hoped to demonstrate a clear rule governing Hebrew metrics, its nature proved particularly baffling and elusive, the opposite of the "copious, flowing, and harmonious" Greek verse:[27]

---

26   Ibid., 114.

27   "Since it appears essential to every species of poetry, that it be confined to numbers, and consist of some kind of verse (for indeed wanting this, it would not only want its most agreeable attributes, but would scarcely deserve the name of poetry) in treating of the poetry of the Hebrews, it appears absolutely necessary to demonstrate, that those parts at least of the Hebrew writings which we term poetic, are in a metrical form, and to inquire whether

Its form is simple above every other; the radical words are uniform, and resemble each other almost exactly; nor are the inflexions numerous, or materially different: whence we may readily understand, that its metres are neither complex, nor capable of much variety; but rather simple, grave, temperate; less adapted to fluency than dignity and force: so that possibly they found it necessary to distinguish the extent of the verse by the conclusion of the sentence, lest the lines, by running into each other, should become altogether implicated and confused. (47)

When translated, this quasi virtual meter yields the pleasant surprise of a much closer faithfulness than is possible in translating Greek meter, which depended on syllabic count:

[A] poem translated literally from the Hebrew into the prose of any other language, whilst the same forms of the sentences remain, will still retain, even as far as relates to versification, much of its native dignity, and a faint appearance of versification. This is evident in our common version of the Scriptures, where frequently

"The order chang'd, and verse from verse disjoin'd,

"Yet still the poet's scatter'd limbs we find." (47–8)

Lowth thus revealed to his readers that versification was not the defining principle of Hebrew poetry, and consequently, prose translations of the Bible closely approximated the original. These two statements ran contrary to traditional conceptions of poetry and the belief in its untranslatability. If versification was not consubstantial to Hebrew poetry, how could the latter be distinguished from prose? For Meschonnic, Lowth invented the notion of "parallelism" as a strategy of substitution for the impossibility of finding meter and distinguishing prose from verse: "L'invention (plus que la découverte) du *parallélisme des membres*, dans le verset, en 1753, par Robert Lowth ... visait non à repérer des parallélismes rhétoriques, mais à fournir un critère formel, rhétorique—faute de métrique— pour distinguer entre une 'poésie' et une 'prose.'" [Lowth's invention (rather than discovery) in 1753 of a parallelism between segments in biblical verses did not aim to identify rhetorical parallels, but to provide a formal, rhetorical criterion—in the absence of a metric system—to distinguish "poetry" from "prose."][28]

Lowth's description of the different nature of Hebrew prose and poetry uncovered another revelation as to how Hebrew poetry functioned in ways

---

any thing be certainly known concerning the nature and principles of this versification or not." (38) This is a clear example of Lowth's deductive method, which could justly be criticized for its *a priori*. In fact, the very nature of Hebrew's meter defies and annuls Lowth's *a priori* on versification.

[28] Meschonnic and Dessons, *Traité du rythme*, 108. See also Meschonnic, *Les États de la poétique*, 113.

absolutely contrary to classical tenets of symmetry, regularity, concentration, closure, and polish:

> It is impossible to conceive of any thing more simple and unadorned than the common language of the Hebrews. It is plain, correct, chaste, and temperate; the words are uncommon neither in their meaning nor application; there is no appearance of study, nor even the least attention to the harmony of the periods. The order of the words is generally regular and uniform ... But in the Hebrew poetry the case is different, in part at least, if not in the whole. The free spirit is hurried along, and has neither leisure nor inclination to descend to those minute and frigid attentions. Frequently, instead of disguising the secret feelings of the author, it lays them quite open to public view; and the veil being as it were suddenly removed, all the affections and emotions of the soul, its sudden impulses, its hasty sallies and irregularities, are conspicuously displayed. (191–92)

For us modern readers, the description strikingly recalls Wordsworth's "spontaneous overflow of powerful feelings."[29] Ancient Hebrew poetry did not depend on versification, but on a stylistic disorderliness ("désordre"), reflective of a mind in a great state of agitation. Both Batteux and Lowth returned to the old notion of poetic enthusiasm to account for the jolts peculiar to lyrical poetry. In his appreciation of "that vivid and ardent style, which is so well calculated to display the emotions and passions of the mind," Lowth acknowledged the barrier that a classical mind encountered when confronted with such stirring effects:

> Hence the poetry of the Hebrews abounds with phrases and idioms totally unsuited to prose composition, and which frequently appear to us harsh and unusual, I had almost said unnatural and barbarous; which, however, are destitute neither of meaning, nor of force, were we but sufficiently informed to judge of their true application. (198)

The intimation of poetry's "wild" side no doubt came too early to be put into application, but it prepared the way for the success of Ossian's poems, soon to be praised and criticized for their non-classical, "oriental" poetics. The following observation on "the genius and character of Hebrew poetry" anticipated what later became the gist of the backlash against neoclassical poetics:

> It is unconstrained, animated, bold, and fervid. The Orientals look upon the language of poetry as wholly distinct from that of common life, as calculated immediately for expressing the passions: if, therefore, it were to be reduced to the plain rule and order of reason, if every word and sentence were to be arranged with care and study, as if calculated for perspicuity alone, it would be no longer what they intended it, and to call it the language of passion would be the grossest of solecisms. (203)

Lowth not only exposed his readers to radical poetics—acceptable because its matrix was the Bible—he helped them witness a no less radical interaction between prose

---

[29]   Wordsworth, Preface, *Lyrical Ballads*, 173.

and poetry. On several occasions, Lowth referred his readers to examples where poetry relayed prose, a fruitful coexistence that participated in the "sublimity of expression." Lowth's reminders about the interconnection between prose and poetry helped ennoble prose as poetry's worthy companion, even if Lowth did not pursue a more systematic appraisal of the occurrences and impact of this commingling between the two modes, leaving it up to authors like Rousseau to experiment with both prose poetry (*Le Lévite d'Éphraïm*) and poetic prose (*Les Rêveries*).

The alliance of prose and poetry in the Scriptures is a tempting justification to regard the sacred text as the ideal horizon of Enlightenment prose poems. Further, the Scriptures offered not only a unique alloy, but, according to Lowth, the most precious poetical essence, condensed in the "sublimest species," the ode (378). I would like to suggest that, given the context of a crisis of poetry in search of rejuvenation, the biblical text Lowth revealed came to represent "le suc concret, l'osmazôme de la littérature, l'huile essentielle de l'art" [literature's concrete pith, its nectar, art's essential oil]—des Esseintes's definition of the prose poem in Joris-Karl Huysman's *À Rebours* (1884). My hypothesis rests on Lowth's "metamorphosis" of the Bible into a non-classical but quintessential model of poetic diction, and simultaneously his elevation of the ode as the most condensed and essential poetical genre.

This will be more evident with a brief recapitulation of the history and generic status of the ode. Once the highest form within lyrical genres, the ode had evolved in the course of centuries, to celebrate the most sacred but also the most profane matters. In 1587, Ronsard prefaced his *Odes* by telling his readers about topics fit for lyrical poetry: "l'amour, le vin, les banquets dissolus, les danses, masques, chevaux victorieux, escrime, joutes et tournois, et peu souvent quelque argument de philosophie" [love, wine, dissolute banquets, dance, masks, victorious horses, fencing, jousts and tournaments, and rarely some philosophical argument.][30] The rapid drifting from high to low subjects prompted seventeenth-century authors to justify or protest the fit-for-all quality of the ode.[31] All agreed, however, that the ode had to present an apparent disorderliness, as Boileau famously explained: "Son style impétueux souvent marche au hasard./ Chez elle un beau désordre est un effet de l'art" [Its impetuous style often walks randomly/ Its beautiful disorder is an artistic effect.][32] To support their claim in favor of the ode's sublime character, Batteux and Lowth had to counter a long tradition that had trivialized the ode's original significance. While poets like Jean-Baptiste Rousseau and Klopstock reinvested the ode with sacred content, Batteux retraced the literary history of the

---

[30]   Cited by Guy Riegert ed., in Boileau, *L'Art Poétique*, 140.

[31]   Like Ronsard's preface, Boileau's twenty-three verses on the ode in the second canto of his *Art poétique* (lines 58–81) insisted on the ode's versatility, as did definitions of the ode by du Bellay, Peletier du Mans, and Guillaume des Autels. Ibid., 139–41. This wide interpretation of the ode in the seventeenth century derived from Horace's description in the *Art poétique* (line 53 and following). Ibid., 54n98.

[32]   Boileau, *Art poétique*, 55, lines 71–2.

form, and Lowth provided indisputable critical and historical evidence. Batteux succinctly formulated four phases germane to the development of the ode: first, the origin of language is equated with the origin of lyric expression ("La première exclamation de l'homme sortant des mains de Dieu, fut une expression lyrique" [The first exclamation of man when he rose from God's hand was a lyric expression] (277); second, musical genres (sacred songs, hymns, odes) were adopted to convey wonder and gratitude toward the Creator and his Creation; third, David and the prophets continued the ode's religious tradition; subsequently, the ode was appropriated for pagan celebrations of wine and love. Batteux's brief history of the ode made clear that the evolution of the form accounted for its present versatility. But amongst its various kinds (sacred, heroic, moral, Anacreontic), Batteux finds the ideal realized in the sacred not profane, lyric ode, which he illustrates with a close analysis of David's Psalm 103 to single out its "noble sublime" and fire, its beautiful irregularities and singular turns.[33]

Lowth's treatise relegated late derivations of the ode to the margins, then unequivocally ascertained its superiority over other poetical genres by underlining the exceptional character of the ode's origin.[34] The ode stood for the expression of "man on his first creation," "the offspring of the most vivid, and the most agreeable passions of the mind, of love, joy, and admiration" (351). Lowth's rehabilitation of the lyric ode hinged on the conclusion that it was poetry's original mode: "Thus the origin of the ode may be traced into that of poetry itself, and appears to be coeval with the commencement of religion, or more properly the creation of man" (353). Lowth in effect demonstrated that embedded at the core of the Bible was a poetic utterance dating back to the divine creation of man. Lyrical expression, therefore, carried with it the memory of its origin. The symbolic return to the origins (of mankind, of poetry) through lyricism is a defining trait of lyric prose writers like Rousseau and Chateaubriand. Why, one might ask, should the form of the ode be relevant to these prose authors? Classical versification impinged on the return of the lyric ode to its natural origins in a way that encouraged experimentations in prose to capture this poetic ideal. It is not a coincidence that two key players in the emergence of the prose poem foresaw that prose's redefinition was connected to the ode: before translating the *Iliad* in prose, Anne Dacier had translated in prose Anacreon and Sappho's odes, seeking to capture their inspiring enthusiasm; and La Motte dared write the first "ode en prose" of French literature, challenging his contemporaries to improve on his experiment.

The final element I wish to recover from Batteux and Lowth's examination of lyrical poetry also relates to its origin: not its utterance, just examined, but its performance; not its words, but its music. Authors in search of a new harmony in verse and meter lent an appreciative ear to the manifestation of yet another trait unique to lyrical poetry. Batteux began his treatise with the etymological reminder

---

[33]   Batteux, "Traité de la Poësie lyrique," in *Principes de la Littérature,* 277.

[34]   "Of all the different forms of poetical composition, there is none more agreeable, harmonious, elegant, diversified, and sublime than the ode." Lowth, *Lectures,* 355.

that the lyre gave its name to performances originally sung.[35] It followed that lyrical poetry and music cultivate a natural, organic relation with each other:

> la Poësie lyrique & la Musique ont entre elles un rapport intime, fondé dans les choses mêmes; puisqu'elles ont l'une & l'autre les mêmes objets à exprimer. Et si cela est, la Musique etant une expression des sentimens du cœur par les sons inarticulés, la Poësie musicale, ou lyrique, sera l'expression des mêmes sentimens par les sons articulés, ou, ce qui est la même chose, par les mots. L'une doit être l'interprete, & comme la traduction de l'autre. (270)

> [Lyric poetry and music have an intimate connection with each other, founded in the very order of things, since they have each the same objects to express. If so, music being an expression of the heart's feelings through inarticulate sounds, musical or lyric poetry must be an expression of the same feelings through articulate sounds, or, which is the same thing, through words. The former must be the interpreter, almost the translator, of the latter.]

One can see the formidable impact of this simple definition—even though practice lagged behind Batteux's theoretical inroads into a genre promising a great development.

Lowth contributed to the equation between lyrical poetry and music by anchoring his own definition into biblical history.[36] Though he could not give his readers a description of the music for evident reasons, Lowth provided a historical context that explained the development of the genre, and reminded readers that there once was a golden age for the arts of poetry and music, under David's governance (354–5). The sacred bard David, his lyre and Psalms came to symbolize a lost golden age. From the mid-century on, this emblematic biblical figure and his musical instrument guided many poetic dreams in prose, including those of Rousseau and Chateaubriand.

Rousseau's *Le Lévite d'Ephraïm*: "Une manière de petit poëme en prose"

> Et vous trop doux la Motte, et toi touchant Voltaire,
> Ta lecture à mon cœur restera toujours chére.
> Mais mon goût se refuse à tout frivole écrit,
> Dont l'auteur n'a pour but que de plaire à l'esprit.
> Il a beau prodiguer la brillante Antithése,
> Semer par tout des fleurs, chercher un tour qui plaise,
> Le cœur plus que l'esprit a chez moi des besoins,
> Et s'il n'est attendri, rebute tous ses soins.

---

[35] Batteux, "Traité de la Poësie lyrique," in *Principes de littérature*, 270.

[36] "The Hebrews cultivated this kind of poetry above every other. ... It was usual in every period of that nation to celebrate in songs of joy their gratitude to God, their Saviour, for every fortunate event, and particularly for success in war. Hence the triumphal odes of Moses, of Deborah, of David." Lowth, *Lectures*, 354.

[As for you, too sweet La Motte, and you, touching Voltaire/ Reading you will always be dear to my heart./But my taste refuses any frivolous writing / Whose author only seeks to please the mind./Though he lavishes brilliant antitheses,/ Seeds flowers all around/ Seeks a pleasing turn of phrase,/ My heart has greater needs than my mind,/And if unmoved, will reject all its cares.
Jean-Jacques Rousseau[37]

The heterogeneous nature of Gessner's *La Mort d'Abel*, part pastoral, part drama, with a biblical subject matter treated in prose, contributed to the implosion of strict generic definitions, and further liberated creative impulses ill at ease within constricted generic fields. It may be surprising that Gessner influenced none other than one of the eighteenth-century's most accomplished prose writers, Jean-Jacques Rousseau. As evidenced by his correspondence, Rousseau gave high marks to Gessner's biblical poem and eagerly awaited his collection of idylls. When Huber sent him his translation at the end of 1761, Rousseau wrote back a thank-you letter from Montmorency dated December 24, 1761. The *Idylles* worked like a therapeutic, distracting Rousseau from his physical pain, and soothing his mind with the congenial thoughts of a fellow spirit. Pastorals, which Rousseau "the man of nature" liked so well, represented his century's literature of escapism, and he delighted in Gessner's renovation of the genre in favor of simplicity and sentiment: "Je vous sais en particulier un gré infini d'avoir osé dépouiller nôtre langue de ce sot et précieux jargon qui ôte toute vérité aux images, et toute vie aux sentimens. Ceux qui veulent embellir et parer la nature sont des gens sans ame et sans goût qui n'ont jamais connu ses beautés" [I am particularly and infinitely grateful that you dare remove from our language this silly and precious jargon that removes any truth from images and life from sentiments. Those who wish to embellish and adorn nature are people without soul and taste, who have never known its beauties.][38] The best evidence of Rousseau's admiration came in the form of a biblical prose poem, *Le Lévite d'Ephraïm*, written in the spirit of Gessner's *La Mort d'Abel*. Rousseau wrote very few verses, and considered the practice a mere pleasurable "jeu d'esprit" that lacked the ambition and meaningfulness of his prose writing, meant to have an impact on society.[39] *Le Lévite d'Ephraïm* and a lyric drama I consider its

---

[37] Jean-Jacques Rousseau, "Le Verger de Madame de Warens," *Œuvres Complètes*, vol. 2, 1129.

[38] *Correspondance complète de Jean-Jacques Rousseau* (Madison, 1969), Lettre 1607, vol. 9 (June–December 1761), 349–50.

[39] See the Pleiade edition of Rousseau's complete works in the category "Ballets, Pastorales. Poésies" (1049–176). See also Rousseau's revealing remarks on versification as a mere pastime in the Avertissement preceding his few poems: "On ne manquera pas de s'écrier. Un malade faire des vers! Un homme à deux doigts du tombeau! *C'est précisément pour cela que j'ai fait des vers: si je me portais moins mal, je me croirois comptable de mes occupations au bien de la société; l'état où je suis ne me permet de travailler qu'à ma propre satisfaction*" [People will surely cry out. A sick man who writes verses! A man with one foot in the grave! *This is precisely why I composed verses. If I were feeling better, I would feel the need to account for my occupations to improve society. My current state only*

companion piece, *Pygmalion,* occupy an essential position in Rousseau's œuvre between the great philosophical and fictional works of the period 1757–1762, and the autobiographical *Confessions. Pygmalion* is subtitled "Scène lyrique en un acte;" *Le Lévite d'Ephraïm* is a sixteen-page biblical "poëme en prose" published posthumously in 1781. The two works have never been read nor analyzed as a pair, although both were composed the same year in 1762, and both illustrated aesthetic ideas Rousseau developed in his *Essai sur l'origine des langues* published a year earlier in 1761.[40] Just as Montesquieu sought to convey his personal ethics through a more reader-friendly format—*Le Temple de Gnide*—than his larger historical and philosophical works, Rousseau's two hybrid texts bear an intimate relation with his philosophy of language and music. The kinship between *Pygmalion* and the *Lévite* also resides in their ambiguous generic classification. In the Pléiade edition of Rousseau's *Œuvres complètes,* the two texts follow one another in the category "Contes et apologues," a narrow, inadequate classification given their nature: a lyrical drama and a (mini) religious epic poem.[41] Though each text sought legitimization through a connection with a canonical work—Ovid in the case of *Pygmalion,* the Bible in the case of *Le Lévite*—they escaped generic classification by virtue of their hybridity. Modern critics have discarded *Le Lévite d'Ephraïm* with terms reminiscent of the negative judgment passed on Montesquieu's *Temple de Gnide*: stifled, artificial, "weak," the "failed poem of a genius," "uninteresting" because "pseudo-classical" according to Suzanne Bernard, in other words, un-Rousseau-like.[42] Rousseau himself eventually marginalized *Le Lévite d'Ephraïm* as a "bagatelle," but left much evidence that he held the piece in high regard. [43] Notwithstanding its critical failure and exclusion from the Rousseau canon, the prose poem offers fresh insights on the poetics of his works.

---

lets me work for my own satisfaction.] "Le verger de Madame la Baronne de Warens" [pub. 1739], in *Œuvres complètes.* vol. 2, 1123 (emphasis added).

[40] Only Jechova, Mouret, and Voisine point at the parallelism between the two stories: "le *Pygmalion* de Rouseau ... introduit la prose dans le drame lyrique: expérimentation parallèle à son *Lévite d'Ephraïm*, mini-épopée religieuse en prose. ... La prose émotionnelle du *Pygmalion* entrecoupée de ruptures, est celle du sentimentalisme, et rappelle certaines lettres de la *Nouvelle Héloïse*. Dans le *Lévite* en revanche il s'agit d'une prose nombreuse, oratoire" [Rousseau's *Pygmalion* ... introduces prose into lyrical drama—an experiment parallel to his *Lévite d'Ephraïm*, a mini religious epic poem in prose. ... *Pygmalion*'s emotional prose, interrupted with breaks, belongs to sentimentalism and is reminiscent of certain letters from the *Nouvelle Héloïse*. On the contrary, the *Levite*'s prose is rhythmic, oratorical.] *La Poésie en prose des Lumières au romantisme,* 76.

[41] Rousseau, *Œuvres complètes,* vol. 2, 1205–31.

[42] Jean Starobinski, "Rousseau's Happy Days," *New Literary History* 11 (1979), 161; François Van Laere, *Jean-Jacques Rousseau, du phantasme à l'écriture: les révélations du Lévite d'Ephraïm* (Paris: 1967), 63; Bernard, *Le Poème en prose de Baudelaire jusqu'à nos jours,* 29–30n48; see also Marcel Thiry, "Rousseau et son Lévite," 78–80.

[43] Rousseau, "Second projet de préface," *Le Lévite d'Ephraïm,* 1206.

"Le *Lévite d'Ephraïm*, s'il n'est pas le meilleur de mes ouvrages, en sera toujours le plus chéri" [The *Lévite d'Ephraïm*, though not the best of my works, will always be the most cherished], Rousseau declared in the *Confessions*.[44] Why did the slim volume stand so close to Rousseau's heart? Book Eleven of the *Confessions* recalls in detail the unusual circumstances of its genesis.[45] Shortly after censorship seized and forbade *Émile*, the French Parliament issued an order for Rousseau's arrest; fleeing the order, Rousseau spent three days on the road where, to distract himself from his ordeal, he composed the first three cantos of *Le Lévite d'Ephraïm* by bringing together the memory of Gessner, whose *Idylles* he had recently read in translation, and the Old Testament's book of Judges, which he was reading the night he learnt about his impending arrest. Rousseau took great pride in this accomplishment in the face of adversity.[46] His overcoming fear and anguish through writing is the sole merit most critics have bestowed upon this unusual piece. For Aubrey Rosenberg, this "effort d'écriture" while in the direst circumstances reveals the unique character of its author but not the exact place of his prose narrative: "quoiqu'il y ait des correspondances indubitables entre la personnalité et la vie de Rousseau et l'histoire du Lévite, on a du mal à situer l'ouvrage dans le contexte de ses écrits politiques et philosophiques" [Though there are unquestionable correspondences between Rousseau's personality and life and the Levite's story, one has difficulty situating this work in the context of his political and philosophical writing.][47] Most critical interpretations have focused on biographical and psychoanalytical, not literary aspects, confirming that the work is thought to have slight aesthetic merit.

I argue the contrary and claim *Le Lévite d'Ephraïm* a daring, misunderstood experiment, though Rousseau documented its genesis and wrote two prefaces. In the first one (1763) Rousseau called his piece "une maniére de petit poëme en prose" [a kind of short poem in prose.][48] It has never been noted that Rousseau's terminology of "petit poëme en prose" prefigured Baudelaire's title to the *Spleen de Paris*, perhaps because it seems more evident and easier to acknowledge the influence on Baudelaire of the poetic prose and thematics of Rousseau's *Rêveries du promeneur solitaire* than that of an uncomfortably neoclassical, biblical imitation. What can the story of the Levite tell us that the *Rêveries* omitted? What does Rousseau's "petit poëme en prose" say in relation to Baudelaire's and his successors' modern poetics? The designation "prose poem" was doubly justified if one considers antecedents in the eighteenth century as well as Rousseau's theories on language. First, the term suggests to the reader a framework, albeit an unstable one. By the 1760s, readers had enjoyed enough prose poems sharing neoclassical poetic diction, following Fénelon's, to recognize the famous new genre.

---

[44]   Jean-Jacques Rousseau, *Confessions* (Paris, 1973), 696.

[45]   Ibid., 688–96.

[46]   Ibid., 695.

[47]   Aubrey Rosenberg, "Le Lévite d'Ephraïm," in *Dictionnaire de Jean-Jacques Rousseau* (Paris, 1996), 545.

[48]   Rousseau, "Premier projet de préface," *Œuvres complètes*, vol. 2, 1205.

But Rousseau gave the experiment a new twist, an internal justification as it were: his prose poem would embody some of his key concepts on the origin of language and on social theory. Naming his biblical fiction a prose poem went beyond generic classification to the core of his philosophy, of which it embodied key concepts.

Staging Passions: "Amour de soi" and "Amour propre"

Rousseau's aesthetic choice in prose poetry echoed his philosophy of language. In the *Essai sur l'origine des langues,* figurative language, poetry, precedes prose. Prose evolved with the faculty of reasoning: "Les premières histoires, les premières harangues, les premières loix furent en vers; la poésie fut trouvée avant la prose; cela devoit être, puisque les passions parlèrent avant la raison" [The first stories, the first harangues, and the first laws were in verse; poetry was discovered before prose; this had to be so, since the passions spoke before reason.][49] As we will see, the writing of the Levite story illustrates this dual evolution from poetical to prosaic and from passion to reason: the first canto celebrates the poetry of love; the subsequent cantos convey the prose of war. The first canto emulates the primitivism of original poetry, the last three express the ensuing modernity of prose.

At the same time, Rousseau's social theory finds ground for application in a biblical story. According to Rousseau, "l'amour de soi" was the first passion experienced by men and women. It remained a dominant passion but evolved as men formed societies and societies beget inequalities. "Amour-propre" resulted from the social development of "amour de soi": the latter leads to benevolence toward others whereas the former engenders comparisons and jealousy.[50] The story of *Le Lévite d'Ephraïm* captures a turning point in this social evolution of sentiments. Set during a golden age before laws have been instituted, the first canto is a pastoral celebrating the love of the Levite and his bride as a time of innocence and quiet happiness.[51] Theirs was a "passion douce et affectueuse"

---

[49] Rousseau, *Essai sur l'origine des langues,* in *Œuvres complètes* (Paris, 1964), vol. 2, 410. *Essay on the Origin of Languages,* ed. and trans. John T. Scott, in *The Collected Writings of Rousseau* (Hanover and London, 1998), vol. 7, 318.

[50] On "amour de soi" vs. "amour propre," see Rousseau, *Émile ou l'éducation,* livre IV, 493.

[51] "Dans les jours de liberté où nul ne régnoit sur le peuple du Seigneur, il fut un tems de licence où chacun, sans reconnoitre ni magistrat ni juge, étoit seul son propre maître, et faisoit tout ce qui lui sembloit bon. Israël, alors épars dans les champs, avoit peu de grandes villes, et la simplicité de ses mœurs rendoit superflu l'empire des loix" [In the days of freedom in which no one reigned over the people of the Lord, there was a time of license in which each, without recognizing either magistrat or judge, was alone his own master and did all that seemed good. Israel, then scattered in the fields, had few great cities, and the simplicity of its morals rendered superfluous the empire of laws.] Rousseau, *Le Lévite d'Ephraïm.* In *Œuvres complètes* (Paris: 1964), vol. 2, 1208–9. *The Levite of Ephraïm,* ed. and trans. John T. Scott, in *The Collected Writings of Rousseau* (Hanover and London: 1998), vol. 7, 353. Original and translation hereafter cited in text.

[a sweet and affectionate passion], but the idyll ended soon: the woman grew bored with the Levite "peut-être parce qu'il ne lui laissoit rien à désirer" [perhaps because he left nothing for her to desire] (1210).[52] Like Émile and Sophie, the lovers are enslaved by their solipsistic love, and separation becomes necessary. Setting family duties above love, the wife returns home to her parents and sisters, only to find lost illusions as childhood and innocence cannot be recaptured. The wife's dissatisfaction with her husband, then with the paternal home exposes the degradation of pure and simple feelings of a lost pastoral era Rousseau invented to open the story.

The Levite eventually resolves to fetch his wife. After two days of endlessly postponed farewells to the father, the couple leaves but must soon find shelter for the night in the town of Gibeah. There, no one offers hospitality, except an old man. Horror strikes after the friendly meal between the host and his guests. Lusting after the handsome Levite, a group of Benjamites demands that he be released to them. The host offers his daughter in exchange but is rebuffed. The Levite preserves his virtue by deciding to forfeit his wife. Gang-raped all night she expires in the morning just as the Levite opens the door. The Benjamites' concupiscence represents a new step in the evolution of passions: fueled by vanity, their desire is aggressive, uncontrollable and transgresses the social order and the sacred law of hospitality. Thus begins "le commencement de la fin de l'innocence" [the beginning of the end of innocence], the end of the golden age of sentiments and the beginning of the decadence of passions.[53]

Out of despair and fury, the Levite cuts up his wife's body in twelve parts and sends them to the twelve tribes of Israel. Rising in anger, the tribes massacre the tribe of Benjamin after it refuses to deliver the rapists. Only six hundred men survive. Suddenly stunned by the prospect of losing one of their tribes, the sons of Israel decide to find virgins to wed the survivors and save the tribe from extinction. They murder the men of the tribe of Jabès (as a punishment for not having participated with them in the massacre), and give all their virgin daughters

---

[52]   Thomas Kavanagh points out that Rousseau's version is "a substantial deviation from the biblical explanation. The Ostervald Version offers 'she committed an impurity'; whereas Chouraqui, in his recent translation priding itself on fidelity to the original Hebrew, chooses to render this as '*sa concubine putasse.*'" Thomas Kavanagh, "Rousseau's *Le Lévite d'Ephraïm*," 152. In fact, Rousseau implied the cause of the woman's boredom in the next paragraph, with the phrase "sa volage épouse" [his fickle spouse] and "l'infidèle" [the unfaithful one].

[53]   See Rosenberg's conclusion in "Rousseau's *Lévite d'Ephraïm* and the Golden Age" and his entry on *Le Lévite d'Ephraïm* in *Dictionnaire de Jean-Jacques Rousseau*, 546. Rousseau's first draft for a preface underscored a parallelism with his own life spent amidst endless persecutions: Rousseau contrasts the cruelty brought about by his contemporaries' vanity vs. a virtuous "amour de soi" and escape from "le tourment de haïr" (1205). See also the *Rêveries*'s sixth promenade: "Je m'aime trop moi-même pour pouvoir haïr qui que ce soit" [I love myself too much to be able to hate anyone else.] *Œuvres complètes*, vol. 1, 1056.

to the surviving Benjamites. Because two hundred brides are still missing, it is decided that more virgins will be captured during a festival. Though previously engaged, the young women are asked to sacrifice themselves willingly. Adding to the biblical narrative, Rousseau closed in on Axa and her husband-to-be, Elmacin. Both eventually obey the father's will: sacrificing her love, Axa faints in the arms of a Benjamite; Elmacin takes a vow of chastity. The narrative ends with the celebration of the virtues left in Israel as all young women follow Axa's example. The synopsis alone suggests why the story has never been part of the canon.

The final note of optimism, coming after such delirious escalation of violence, differs from the biblical original. But the end, in keeping with Rousseau's philosophy, illustrates the development of the tribes' social conscience over their original reaction to seek revenge. The moral of this brutal tale is that the destruction of the self-centered couple, symbolized by the ficticious Axa and Elmacin, was necessary for the community to reform itself after so much evil. The social pact called for the submission of the individuals to the general will, hence the exuberant "cries of joy" ringing at the end of the story as all sheep re-join the flock.

A Tale of Prose and Poetry

In his *Confessions,* Rousseau awarded his narrative "le mérite de la difficulté vaincue" [the merit of vanquished difficulty] (696). As I have shown, the tell-tale phrase belonged to a discourse on value, according to which overcoming the difficulty of verse ennobled poetry: the more difficult the versification, the better the poem and the more merit for the poet. Rousseau turned the phrase on its head: prose, no longer verse, was overcome—that is conquered—to rise to poetry. Rousseau confronted a double challenge: expressing the poetic language of sentiments through the medium of prose; and combining the poetic pastoral age of love with the prosaic, historical evolution of mankind toward increased violence.

Rousseau rewrote the story of the *Lévite d'Ephraïm* so as to highlight the double nature of the Bible as an historical document and a poetic text. The hybridity of prose poems lent itself perfectly to Rousseau's project as poet-historian who could moralize upon the end of the Golden Age: the disjunction between the poetic and the prosaic mimics the fracture between a lost primitive purity and modern decadence. But if a return to the past was not possible (just as man could no longer be a noble savage), establishing distance from modernity was critical to the Enlightenment philosopher. When elevating prose to "make" it poetry (and when imagining a nobler savage than the first human), he created this critical space for himself and his readers, precisely as a perspective from within modernity critiquing itself, its past and its future.

Le Lévite d'Ephraïm features familiar poetic elements that elevate the status of the prose text, four of which almost systematically appear in eighteenth-century "poëmes en prose." We already encountered the division into cantos. Here the structure of the four cantos, instead of the three biblical chapters, is meant to evoke the orality of primitive poetry—to which I will return in my last chapter. A second convention is the invocation of a muse to help the poet sing his song. Rousseau began with an apostrophe to virtue—"Sainte colere de la vertu, vient animer ma voix" [Sacred wrath of virtue, come animate my voice] (1208)—followed by subsequent apostrophes to men, then to innocence, a rhetorical gesture that allows the poet to introduce the theme of his song. This summary, given by Rousseau in the first three paragraphs, extrapolates from the Bible so as to frame the poem. The third characteristic poetic flourish—epic similes running three to four lines—work as elaborate comparisons imbued with classical, Homeric overtones, anchoring prose in ancient poetic tradition. Two examples:[54]

> [I]ls entourent la jeune fille à demi-morte, la saisissent, se l'arrachent sans pitié; tel dans leur brutale furie qu'au pied des Alpes glacées un troupeau de loups affamés surprend une foible genisse, se jette sur elle et la déchire, au retour de l'abreuvoir. (1214)

> [They surrounded the half-dead young woman, seized her, and fought over her without pity; in their brutal fury, they were like a pack of hungry wolves returning to a watering place at the foot of the icy Alps which surprises a weak heifer, throws itself on her and tears her to pieces.] (trans. 358)

> On voyoit les forts d'Israël en déroute tomber par milliers sous leur épée, et les champs de Rama se couvrir de cadavres, comme les sables d'Elath se couvrent des nuées de sauterelles qu'un vent brulant apporte et tue en un jour. (1217–18)

> [The routed able-bodied of Israel were seen falling by the thousands beneath their swords, and the fields of Ramah were covered with corpses, as the sands of Elath are covered with the grasshoppers' shells that a burning wind brings and kills in one day.] (trans. 360)

Finally, the fourth characteristic of prose poems such as Rousseau's is a distorted temporality, transporting readers outside realism and verisimilitude. Three typical distortions underscore the ubiquity of the poet narrator: condensation of time—the adverb *meanwhile* or *in the mean time* ("cependant"), used systematically in lieu of transition, gives an impression of immediacy and simultaneity;[55] acceleration of time—the adverb *already* ("déjà") hastens events;[56] and suspension of time, when the author uses expressions such as *sometimes ... sometimes* ("tantôt ... tantôt").[57]

---

54   See also *Le Lévite d'Ephraïm*, 1220–21.

55   Ibid., 1216 and 1219.

56   The second canto begins: "Le jeune Lévite suivoit la route avec sa femme, son serviteur et son bagage ... Déjà l'on découvroit la ville de Jébus à main droite." Ibid., 1212. [The young Levite followed his route with his wife, his servant, and his baggage ... Already the city of Jebus was spied on the right hand] (trans. 356).

57   The opening canto dwells on the suspension of time characteristic of blissful love. The repetition of temporal phrases or adverbs gives an impression of timelessness: "*Combien de fois* les côteaux du mont Hébal retentirent de ses aimables chansons? *Combien de fois* il la mena sous l'ombrage, dans les vallons de Sichem, cueillir des roses champêtres et goûter le frais au bord des ruisseaux? *Tantôt* il cherchoit dans les creux des rochers des

We should note, however, that the genre of the tale also relies on condensed and accelerated temporalities to achieve its effect, so in itself this attribute is not enough to distinguish poetic from prose fiction. But when accompanied by other poetic tropes, and found in combination with the slightly archaic, parallel temporal construction "tantôt ... tantôt," non-realist time helps the reader tune in on a different order of perception. Starobinski underlined the importance of these poetic temporal symmetries to describe Rousseau's happiness in the *Rêveries* and the couple's happiness in the Levite story:

> The expressions "*now... now*" and "*sometimes ... sometimes*" favored by Ronsard, Montaigne, and Diderot are the temporal organizers of an image of a leisurely, innocent, dreaming life, incapable by its very inconsistency of engaging in any sustained project. No future haunts a life devoted to an interchangeable present made up of instantly realized possibilities.[58]

The common denominators behind these four poetic devices are the Bible and Homer mediated through the prose of Fénelon's *Les Aventures de Télémaque*. The use of poetic diction signaled the departure from the forms of the novel or the tale and the invention of a nostalgic space within which to analyze the emergence of evil and modernity.

Didactic intentions prevailed in *Le Lévite d'Ephraïm* as they did in Gessner and most eighteenth-century prose poems starting with *Télémaque* and lasting beyond Chateaubriand's *Atala*. The prose poem originally transgressed genres to follow more effectively the classical injunction of instructing while entertaining. Moral purpose explained why Gessner and Rousseau chose dark, biblical episodes instead of, for instance, the more aesthetically pleasing lyricism of the Song of Solomon or the mysticism of the book of Job. Furthermore, Rousseau took special pride in the difficulty of unveiling the hidden poetry of this tale of rape, murder, and war. For example, he did not modify the long scene of the couple's separation from the father, postponed three times: its repetition added poetic merit. Similarly, Rousseau faithfully reproduced the poetry of numbers (in the mathematical count of the troops and casualties) because biblical numbers opened up the realm of the symbolic to convey the enormity of the massacre.[59] The comparison with the

---

rayons d'un miel doré dont elle faisoit ses délices; *tantôt* dans le feuillage des oliviers, il tendoit aux oiseaux des pieges trompeurs et lui apportait une tourterelle craintive qu'elle baisoit en la flattant." Ibid., 1209 (emphasis added). [How many times did the slopes of mount Hebal ring with his lovely songs? How many times did he lead her into the shade, into the valleys of Sichem, to cut the country roses and to taste the freshness by the shores of the streams? Sometimes he sought in the hollows of the rocks the combs of a golden honey from which she made her sweets; sometimes in the foliage of the olive trees he set deceptive traps for birds and he carried for her a fearful turtledove which she kissed while stroking it.] (trans. 353–4).

[58] Starobinski, "Rousseau's Happy Days," 150.

[59] Rousseau, *Le Lévite d'Éphraïm*, 1217 and 1219.

biblical text shows that Rousseau used his poetic license to flesh out the beginning and end of the story, namely the pastoral love of the Levite and the cruel solution found to redeem the massacre. Dwelling on the happy times of the Levite's love and inventing characters to embody the sacrifices of love, Rousseau in effect added the very lyricism that was present in other biblical passages but was missing in this particularly violent episode, offsetting the prose of war with the poetry of love.

Did Rousseau know Lowth's treatise when he composed his prose poem? Lowth made a single reference to this biblical passage, or more precisely to the last line of the book of Judges (xxi, 25): "In those days *there was* no king in Israel: every man did *that which was* right in his own eyes." Lowth remarked in a footnote that this was one of only two examples he found where a future tense (untranslated here) designated past events in a *prose* passage. Lowth interpreted the peculiar and puzzling usage of the future to convey the past as the distinctive evidence of *poetic* passages in the Hebrew original, a stylistic feature misunderstood and erased by translators. After giving examples of future tense invoking past events in the Bible, Lowth concludes that this "unusual" construction, this "singularity," is a poetic marker:

> Now, if, as I have stated, this unusual form of construction be the effect either of some sudden emotion of the speaker, of some new and extraordinary state of mind; or if, on any other account, from the relation of the subject, or the genius of the language, it be possessed of some peculiar force or energy; it will obviously follow, that it must more frequently occur in poetry than in prose, since it is particularly adapted to the nature, the versatility, and variety of the former, and to the expression of any violent passion; and since it has but little affinity to that mildness and temperance of language, which proceeds in one uniform and even tenour. Thus if we attend diligently to the poetry of the Hebrews and carefully remark its peculiar characteristics, we shall hardly find any circumstance, the regular and artificial conformation of sentences excepted, which more evidently distinguishes it from the style of prose composition than the singularity which is now under consideration. For though it be allowed, that this idiom is not so entirely inconsistent with prose, but that a few examples of it might be produced, on the whole I am convinced, that the free and frequent use of it may be accounted as the certain characteristic of poetry. [60]

One can infer from Lowth's remark that the exceptional use of the future tense to conclude the Hebrew prose narrative of the Levite story conferred poeticity to an otherwise matter-of-fact narration. Therefore, when Rousseau decided to begin his prose poem with this very sentence in the "future past" and expand it into a poetic invocation of a pastoral golden age, he reappropriated the poetic nature conveyed by the original biblical Hebrew line. Whether Rousseau was aware of the original construction or not, his poetic rendering shows a striking symbiosis with its biblical matrix.

---

[60] Lowth, *Lectures*, 211–12. In a footnote, Lowth refers to the passage from the book of Judges as one of only two examples of past future tense: "Hitherto I have only met with the following: Judg. ii 1... and xxi.25]." Ibid., n17.

The Language of Signs

I shall turn again to the *Essai sur l'origine des langues* to examine the narrative from the perspective of Rousseau's theory of language. At the beginning were needs, Rousseau tells us, and the first needs dictated the first gestures. Then sentiments drew the first voices. For Rousseau, neither physical needs nor thoughts stirred man into articulating words but the necessity of communicating sentiments. Parallel to the antinomy between needs and sentiments Rousseau sets up an antinomy between gesture and voice. The essay emphasizes the language of gesture as a language of action. Easier, more expressive, less dependent on convention, gestures say more in less time. Yet despite (or perhaps because of) the significance and weight of gestures, only voice can adequately transmit sentiments. The story of *Le Lévite d'Ephraïm* (as well as *Pygmalion*) tells the tale of this linguistic progression from body language to articulated language.

The Levite represents the language of gesture. From beginning to end, speech is rare in the story as it moves from one action to the next. A smile concludes the Levite's first encounter with the young woman. In the happy times of their reciprocal love, songs of praise and token gestures, such as the present of a dove to his beloved, convey the Levite's feelings. During the fateful trade of his wife's virtue against his own life, the Levite does not say a single word.[61] Then comes the most eloquent of all gestures. The Levite translates his desperate rage by cutting up his wife's dead body and sending the twelve body parts to the twelve tribes of Israel: body language at its most literal. The mutilation is replicated so that each body part will speak of the violence done to the woman: "the message is dispersed by synecdoche, each twelfth representing the whole."[62] These were times when tropes and figurative language were invented, preceding the invention of literal language.[63] It is important to remark here that the Levite's silent speech act is the very example Rousseau gives at the beginning of the *Essai sur l'origine des langues* to illustrate the expressivity of gestures in ancient times: "Ce que les anciens disoient le plus vivement, ils ne l'exprimoient pas par des mots mais par des signes; ils ne le disoient pas, ils le montroient" [What the ancients said most vividly they expressed not by words, but by signs; they did not say it, they showed it] (376; trans. 290). Drawing from other examples in the Bible, Rousseau insisted that "le langage le plus énergique est celui où le signe a tout dit avant qu'on parle" [the most energetic language is the one in which the sign has said everything before one speaks] (376; trans. 290). The twelve body parts performed as signs

---

[61] Rousseau, *Le Lévite d'Éphraïm*, 1214.

[62] Judith Still, "Rousseau's *Lévite d'Ephraïm*: the Imposition of Meaning (On Women), *French Studies XLIII*, 1 (1989), 27.

[63] See Rousseau, "Que le premier langage dut être figuré," in *Essai sur l'origine des langues*, chap. III, 381–2.

and signaled the tribes to rise and respond to the affront.[64] Only after the message had been sent and the tribes had gathered in response, did the Levite let out cries and lamentations, which in turn gave way to words of anger and calls for revenge. Similarly, the bloody massacre of the men of Jabès who had refused to partake in the extermination of the Benjamites is a silent, swift and potent collective gesture to indicate that dissidence will be punished. Giving away the surviving virgins sends a message to the remaining Benjamites that they must again reproduce. The abduction of the virgins of Silo is similarly expedited as decreed by the elders, until the fathers' anguished voices cry out for their daughters' freedom of choice. The reunion of the imaginary characters Axa and Elmacin took place in silence: neither could speak save for the mute eloquence ("éloquence muette") of their gaze.[65] We hear Axa's voice only once, when she murmurs her lover's name. It is as if, to express her other feelings (resignation, obedience, despair), she had not a voice, but only her body with which to speak. Her formerly promised husband, overwhelmed by his love to the exclusion of other feelings, eventually speaks up, raising his voice as he vows to embrace priesthood and chastity to preserve his faithfulness. The story ends with a cry of joy as the people witness all the virgins willingly sacrificing themselves to the Benjamites. Body language as synecdoche dominates the narrative of *Le Lévite d'Ephraïm* as the most powerful trope, but Rousseau introduced the spoken word in those instances wherein passions overwhelm the characters: opening with the musical but wordless happiness of the Levite and his bride, the story ends loudly with Elmacin's passionate solemn vows of eternal love. *Le Lévite d'Ephraïm* recounts an ancient biblical story with epic Homeric accents echoing modern and future tales of murder, vengeance, and war. A paradox emerges when one considers the timelessness of *Pygmalion*: though featuring a lyrically modern love-struck artist, it replicates not only Ovid's myth,

---

[64]   Kavanagh offers a convincing interpretation of this crucial episode in light of Rousseau's preoccupations: "If ... Rousseau was obsessed with the problem of semiology, it was because he felt so acutely the need for some other system of signs which, breaking through the endless lies spoken and written about him, might at last figure forth and adequately represent the full horror of his victimization. Rousseau's abstract reflection on the degeneration of human sign systems within progressively more elaborate forms of social organization must, in fact, be read as an attempt to arrive at some sort of coherent explanation of how it came to be that, in spite of his many repeated messages, his truth continued to go unrecognized." In "Rousseau's *Le Lévite d'Ephraïm*: Dream, Text and Synthesis," 156–7. For Starobinski, "[Rousseau] too would have liked to speak in signs and did so without, however being able to do more than reshape his way of dressing. Forced to use a language he believed less strong ... he writes letters, ... court-style speeches. ... He thus had to perform the discursive task of composition, the very opposite of the language of division, the dismemberment performed by the Levite, who lived in another historical age, one of different discourse." Starobinski, "Rousseau's Happy Days," 164.

[65]   See the complex web of visual and auditory exchanges between Axa, her father and her lover. Rousseau, *Le Lévite d'Éphraïm*, 1223. On silent eloquence, see Rousseau, *Essai sur l'origine des langues*, 377–8.

the statue Galatée coming to life, but also the archetypal biblical story of Adam and Eve, as Adam fell in love with a being created out of himself. *Pygmalion* and *Le Lévite d'Ephraïm* transgress time and history by building a dystopia where prose confronts poetry.

Though the Levite story has been mostly read in retrospect as illustrating the imperfections and awkwardness of a poetic mode in the making, I have argued that it already understands and uses prose poetry as the self-reflexive, dystopic mode that would become one of the most challenging genres of nineteenth and twentieth-century poetry. It is striking to compare this evolution with the downgrading of *Pygmalion*'s poetic mode. The original *Pygmalion* experimented successfully to associate text, music, and gestures to create a yet unheard-of language, which touched thousands of spectators in France and abroad, particularly Germany, where many representations were staged. However, in the wake of *Pygmalion*, the genre of the melodrama fell victim to its own success and degenerated into an exaggeration both of language and sentiments—hence the pejorative adjective "melodramatic." Sentimentality, already present in *Pygmalion* but kept within bounds, eventually turned into hyperbolic emotionalism. My goal has been to show that Rousseau was not only the lyrical prose poet whom posterity remembers for his effusions, but also a modernist prose poet, who had anticipated the limitations of lyricism and understood the poetic shock value of the prosaic. *Pygmalion* and *Le Lévite d'Ephraïm* embody this double nature of Rousseau's poetics. In the preface to *Petits poëmes en prose (Spleen de Paris)*, Baudelaire described his project to translate the "mouvements lyriques de l'âme" [the lyrical movements of the soul] and his dream of a "une prose poétique, musicale sans rythme et sans rime" [a poetic prose, musical without rhythm and rhyme.][66] Yet Baudelaire questioned and departed from lyricism and musicality in many prose poems. Rimbaud went even further in undoing lyrical subjectivity and exposing readers to the shock of prosaism, as can be seen also in the works of the next generation of prose poets, notably Huysmans, Mallarmé, Laforgue, Michaux, and Ponge. Therefore, although we prefer to embrace Rousseau's lyrical poetic prose (as in the "Fifth Promenade"), Rousseau himself constructed a more complex and modern framework for reading poetry.

Biblical Epics in Prose

In this final section, I focus on the vein of epic prose poems that allowed a religious spirit to find an outlet during the heyday of rationalist philosophy and, after the Revolution, during the reign of ideologues. Christian authors, when choosing the vehicle of prose poems, countered both the dominant ideology of the century and competed with novelists to develop and disseminate their vision of a fragile but good-natured mankind. The common denominator of the few biblical prose epics which saw light in the second half of the eighteenth century was a highly strained

---

[66]   Baudelaire, "A Arsène Houssaye," *Petits poëmes en prose (Spleen de Paris)*, 22.

style, possibly the most self-conscious of all the prose poems under consideration. For instance, Chateaubriand loads his prose epic *Les Martyrs* with an abundance of poetic tropes so that it be worthy of its biblical subject matter and characters. Rhetorical devices proliferate (prosopopœia, apostrophes, periphrases, epic similes, allegories, emphatic negations, among others), as well as formal features (systematic division into cantos, invocation) meant to signal unequivocally the poetic value of the texts.[67] In all cases, the style is riddled with a profusion of tropes, traditional comparisons, classical allegories, in short the same neoclassical poetic diction minus verse as eighteenth-century poetry. When the Miltonic model predominates, allegories and descriptions are legion, as in La Baume Desdossats's *La Christiade*. When Gessner is invoked, the prose poem takes a more pastoral turn, as in Le Clerc's *Tobie, poëme en quatre chants* (1773) and abbé Reyrac's various prose poems.[68] Whereas Christian authors struggled to put in practice the stylistic ideal of biblical poetry, they exploited the Bible's rich, thematic fund with greater ease. Despite their affected style, biblical prose poems are interesting in so far as they try to weave together or embroider upon some of the Bible's multiple narrative strands: pastoral, sentimental, didactic, heroic or sublime.[69] For instance, in the invocation opening his *Joseph* (1767), Bitaubé aspires to sing both epic and pastoral tunes, to follow both Milton and Gessner.[70] Bitaubé's *Joseph*, predominately a pastoral narrative, owed its considerable success to the same idyllic representation of sentiments as Gessner's poems: innocence, virtue, naïveté, and sensitivity in the face of adversity distinguish Joseph. In the same pastoral spirit, nature is sentimentalized, as in the opening canto where a melancholy Joseph, who has been sold to slavery, reminisces about his past happiness, in a scene echoing Rousseau, and most likely an inspiration to Bernardin de Saint-Pierre and Chateaubriand:

> Il arrive dans une forêt sombre, séjour de la nuit & de la mélancolie; il s'y arrête; ce lieu plaît à sa douleur. Deux palmiers antiques, qui, courbés l'un vers l'autre, confondoient leurs branches entrelacées, attirent tout à coup ses regards; ils avoient cru dans cet étroit embrassement; leur rameaux s'étendant à l'entour touchoient la terre & formoient comme d'eux-mêmes une cabane. ... Il unit facilement les rameaux flexibles, qui, croissant l'un vers l'autre, sembloient tendre à cette union.[71]

---

[67] For other examples, see P.-D. Dugat, *La mort d'Azaël ou le rapt de Dina* (1798) and Sophie Cottin, *La Prise de Jéricho* (1803).

[68] Louis-Claude Le Clerc, *Tobie; poëme en quatre chants* (1773); Reyrac, *Hymne au soleil, Suivi de plusieurs morceaux du même genre qui n'ont point encore paru* (1782).

[69] For example, see La Baume Desdossat, Preface, *Christiade*, xl, which insists that the Bible was replete with "fictions," notably parables.

[70] Bitaubé, *Joseph*, 3.

[71] Ibid., 14–15. One also finds in *Joseph* a passage on the concomitant birth of music and "sensibilité" evocative of Rousseau's linguistic theories, and in keeping with the importance of the biblical lyre: "Le bonheur & la vertu appellent dans ce séjour l'harmonie des chans: née au milieu des hameaux, elle y reparoît dans sa simplicité touchante. D'abord les bergers imitent la mélodie des oiseaux: bientôt formant des sons plus relevés, ils

[He arrives in a dark wood, the sojourn of night and melancholy; he stops there, the place suits his pain. His gaze is suddenly drawn toward two ancient palm trees, bent toward each other, their interlocking branches confounded; they had grown in this tight embrace; their spread out branches touched the ground and formed a cabin. ... He easily joined the supple branches, which, growing toward one another, seem to press for this union.]

In *Joseph*, Bitaubé developed psychological portraits of biblical figures, even inventing characters with which to contrast them. More precisely, the theme of female seduction and jealousy, so admired in Virgil's Dido (and famously taken up by Fénelon in the Calypso episode), proved an irresistible attraction for authors of biblical prose poems. Bitaubé invented the regal Zaluca who discovers Joseph, listens to his tale of woe, falls in love, is rebuffed, tries to seduce him to no avail, and finally claims to have been insulted or violated ("outragée"), which lands Joseph in jail. While in prison, the virtuous Joseph resists and remains faithful to Sélima—another invented character, Zaluca's counterpoint. In *Tobie*, Le Clerc yielded to the temptation to titillate readers with risqué situations, notably when Satan tempts his protagonist into seducing his bride, Sara, who had asked him to sacrifice the pleasures of their wedding night to God. The third canto builds up a strangely prurient narrative around Tobie's difficult resistance to sexual temptation, concluding the suspense with the triumph of chastity and love (for the sake of reproduction).[72] No matter how often Christian moralists vilified the dangerous character of novels, they too sought to attract readers with "realist" descriptions and situations typical of novels.[73]

Chateaubriand's Les Martyrs

In 1809, when Chateaubriand published his biblical epic poem in prose, *Les Martyrs*, only a handful of authors had dared develop in a long prose narrative a biblical theme, and all had felt obligated to defend their Christian epic in a lengthy preface. Chateaubriand, mindful of the critics, struggled to justify his

---

enseignent à leur tour leurs maîtres. Ils se font des lyres rustiques dont ils accompagnent leurs voix. Avec l'harmonie se réveille la sensibilité des cœurs, & l'on voit naître un amour vertueux & délicat" [Here, happiness and virtue call for the harmony of songs: born in villages, it returns with touching simplicity. First, shepherds imitate bird melodies. Soon with more elaborate sounds, they teach their masters. They make rustic lyres with which they accompany their voices. With the birth of harmony, sensitive hearts wake up and a virtuous, delicate love is born]. Ibid., 26.

[72] Le Clerc, *Tobie* (1773), 163–4.

[73] In the emerging genre of the novel, the treatment of love differs from the long tradition of sensuous pastorals, which idealized innocent female and male types, hence the greater public tolerance for representations of love in pastorals. A later pictorial equivalent can be found in the violent reactions to Edouard Manet's realist "Olympia" in contrast to public acceptance of more lascivious but idealized representations of Venus in academic paintings.

choice of prose to deflect criticism of treating an elevated, sacred subject in this lower medium. He criticized the "common, artificial" poetic prose of authors like Bitaubé, but also his own endeavor: "mon poème se ressent des lieux qu'il a *fréquentés*: le classique y domine le romantique" [my poem feels the effect of the places it visited: the classical dominates the Romantic.] [74] Chateaubriand's art mirrors his position in letters, poised on the brink of Romanticism, but steeped in classicism. His anatomy of criticism itself reflects this division: whereas the above late judgment from the aging Chateaubriand's *Mémoires d'outre-tombe* faulted his domineering classical heritage for stifling his Romantic impulses, the earlier "Examen des *Martyrs*" (published with the third edition in 1810) insisted on the poem's conformity with classical rules and the subordination of its Romantic elements. As I will now show, the author of *Les Martyrs* fundamentally hesitated between allegiance to the ancients or to the new school of Romanticism, a hesitation staged as a *mise en abyme*. While relating the Christian martyrs' ordeal, the poem seems to wonder if Romanticism is a Fall and classicism a paradise lost, therefore whether prose is a Fall and poetry a paradise lost. Further, *Les Martyrs* shows that by 1809 the value of the "poëme en prose" remained unresolved. The new contest between Romanticism and classicism in *Les Martyrs* fed into the old debate prose vs. poetry. In the wake of the *Génie du Christianisme*'s success, Chateaubriand envisioned an epic poem to boost his fame, and decided to pursue a Christian epic on the persecution of the first martyrs under the reign of Diocletian, at the end of the third century. The project materialized after a string of unhappy events: the arbitrary execution of the Duke d'Enghien in March 1804 by Napoleon's orders and the death of two beloved women—Pauline de Beaumont on 4 November 1803 and his sister Lucile a year later on 10 November 1804. Before Chateaubriand ventured on a yearlong journey to the Orient, which lasted from 13 July 1806 until 5 June 1807, he had the manuscript printed, probably as a "deposit" to secure funds for the trip. One copy of this primitive version, *Les Martyrs de Dioclétien*, as the story was then titled, resurfaced in 1932, revealing, by comparison, the transformations Chateaubriand made after his return to France in August 1807 when he rewrote the whole text, and published it as *Les Martyrs ou le triomphe de la religion chrétienne* in 1809. [75] This genesis, together with an "Examen des *Martyrs*" and remarks Chateaubriand added in defense of the text for its third edition in 1810, provide a telling example of the paratextual, intertextual and metatextual propensities of early prose poems.

Les *Martyrs* opposes pagans and Christians. But on a symbolic level, their ideological and religious confrontation unfolds as an ideological and aesthetic conflict between poetry and prose. The second book of *Les Martyrs* stages a

---

[74] See Chateaubriand's "Remarques" prefacing his translation of *Paradise Lost*, 103. Also Chateaubriand, *Mémoires* I, 637. His evaluation of *Les Martyrs* equally applies to *Les Natchez*.

[75] See Chateaubriand, *Les Martyrs de Dioclétien*, ed. Béatrice d'Andlau (Paris, 1951).

musical contest between Cymodocée, related to Homer through her lineage, and Eudore, a converted Christian. The scene symbolizes the contest opposing paganism to Christianity, each youth playing the lyre and singing stories from respectively Homer and the Old and New Testament. First, we hear Cymodocée's lyrics on wonders and myths, then the narrator condenses the biblical text sung by Eudore who ends with praises to the Lord.[76] In his zealous defense of the poem, Chateaubriand added a note to this passage, referencing the entirety of the Bible, as if to ensure that readers would not miss his intertext: "Pour le chant d'Eudore voyez toute la Bible" [For Eudore's song, see the whole Bible.][77]

On an allegorical level, the dual musical performances clearly stage the competition between poetry and prose: when Cymodocée stops singing, her proud father requests in vain from his Christian hosts a toast to Homer—"une coupe pour faire une libation au *dieu des vers*" [a cup to offer libations to *the god of verse*] (39, emphasis added). Cyrille, Lacedaemon's martyr bishop, breaks the silence of his fellow Christians to explain why they object to ancient poetry and its store of myths and fables as dangerous, irrational lies, though they remain touched by music and harmony (39). Cyrille presses Eudore to demonstrate how sacred songs can reach the elevated rank of "belle poésie" by singing lyrical fragments from the Scriptures (40). Chateaubriand reveals the exact nature of this new sacred and beautiful poetry through the special attributes and origin of Eudore's lyre: its Hebrew source, its large size, and the reference to David's harp suggest a poetry in prose, not verse:

> Aux branches d'un saule voisin étoit suspendue une lyre plus forte et plus grande que la lyre de Cymodocée: c'étoit un cinnor hébreu. Les cordes en étoient détendues par la rosée de la nuit. Eudore détacha l'instrument, et, après l'avoir accordé, il parut au milieu de l'assemblée, comme le jeune David prêt à chasser par les sons de sa harpe l'esprit qui s'était emparé du roi Saül. (*Martyrs*, Livre II, 40)

> [A stronger and larger lyre than Cymodocée's was suspended on the branches of a nearby willow: it was a Hebrew cinnor. Its strings were distended by the night's dew. Eudore picked up the instrument and after tuning it, appeared at the center of the assembly like young David, ready to chase with his harp's sounds the spirit that inspired King Saul.]

A final comparison relies on familiar, gendered metaphors between two competing poetic modes: "Cet hymne de Sion retentit au loin dans les antres de l'Arcadie, surpris de répéter au lieu des sons efféminés de la flûte de Pan, les mâles accords de la harpe de David" [This hymn of Scion echoed far in Arcadia's caves, surprised to repeat the masculine chords of David's harp instead of the feminine notes of Pan's flute] (41). In keeping with the critical discourses on poetry and prose examined in Chapter 2, ancient (pagan) poetry is gendered as feminine, and modern (Christian)

---

[76]   Chateaubriand, *Les Martyrs*, in *Œuvres complètes* (Paris, 1859), vol. 4, Livre II, 38 and 40–41. Hereafter cited in text.

[77]   Chateaubriand, *Remarques*, in *Les Martyrs*, 365n50.

poetry in prose as masculine. David's metaphorical harp and its virile accents echo through "Arcadian caves"—a leitmotiv harking back to Fénelon's prose poetry filling Calypso's cave, here christianized by Chateaubriand in keeping with his biblical subject.

At the very end of *Les Martyrs*, the pagan Cymodocée readies herself for baptism (book XVIII). Here again the baptism scene not only symbolizes a religious conversion but allegorizes prose conquering poetry. When Cymodocée expresses her love for her father, as well as her regret that she will not be able to visit his house again (the house of poetry), the gendered metaphor of the two lyres returns:

> On reconnaissoit dans son langage les accents confus de son ancienne religion et de sa religion nouvelle: ainsi, dans le calme d'une nuit pure, deux harpes suspendues au souffle d'Éole, mêlent leurs plaintes fugitives: ainsi frémissent ensemble deux lyres dont l'une laisse échapper les tons graves du mode dorien, et l'autre les accords voluptueux de la molle Ionie. (257)

> [One recognized in her words the blurry accents of her former religion and her new religion: just as, in the calm of a pure night, two harps suspended on Aeolus's breath mix their fugitive laments, so two lyres quiver together, one letting the low tones of the Dorian mode escape, the other the voluptuous chords of soft Ionia.]

Pervasive dualism now divides the world: ancient/modern, pagan/Christian, voluptuousness/gravitas, and Ionic/Doric, superimposed over the dichotomy feminine/masculine. But the rest of the sentence features a surprise reversal. Unexpectedly and abruptly, the gendered metaphor of dual lyres/poetics gives way to a startling comparison: it transcends rigid dualistic oppositions by invoking a completely different time and locale, the North American universe:

> [A]insi, dans les savanes de la Floride, deux cigognes argentées, agitant de concert leurs ailes sonores, font entendre un doux bruit au haut du ciel; assis au bord de la forêt, l'Indien prête l'oreille aux sons répandus dans les airs et croit reconnoître dans cette harmonie la voix des âmes de ses pères. (257)

> [Thus in Florida's savannahs, two silver-colored storks, flapping their sonorous wings in concert, make a gentle noise high in the sky. Sitting at the forest's edge, the Indian listens attentively to the sounds spreading in the air and thinks he recognizes in this harmony the voices of his ancestors' souls.]

Suddenly, neoclassical poetic diction recedes behind the distinctive rhythm of Chateaubriand's melodic phrasing, fraught with favorite echos ("argentées/forêts;" "airs/pères"), poetical cadences and themes, as he invokes the American wilderness and, characteristically, its birds—not their songs, but the more subtle and mysterious fluttering of their wings. The poetic image contrasts with the previous dogmatic lyres: the new symbol of the new poetry should not be a lyre, but a bird with musical wings. New harmony will connect the reader to another soulful universe if he or she can learn to listen like the Indian. At the very moment that the text formulates a comparison for prose poetry, its prose turns into poetry.

This epiphany does not last. On the contrary, the text's internal resistance to a new order of musical harmony appears on every page. *Les Martyrs* exhibits the author's attempts to overwrite the free and spontaneous expression of his emotions with rhetorical figures for the sake of literary convention. There is clear evidence that the narrative was originally conceived as a novel and later edited and revised to turn it into an epic poem, partly under the influence of the critic Fontanes's traditional views and advice (also Chateaubriand's mentor). This radical editing did not involve versification, which would have been a clear indicator of the text's poetic status; instead revisions consisted in integrating epic tropes into prose, such as prosopopœia and allegory, and making the action and characters more epic worthy. The resulting "poëme en prose" evidences *a posteriori* poeticization. It also exposes the dichotomy between the prosaic and poetic modes by staging their conflict within the story, as seen above. Chateaubriand's struggle is evident: second-guessing his original style, he disguised it in an epic garb, but not fully. Modern, Romantic prose infiltrates the classic poetry of the epic.

Chateaubriand's ambivalence toward *Les Martyrs* is noticeable in the preface to the first edition and in the "Examen des *Martyrs*" appended to the third edition. Of particular relevance to my problematic are Chateaubriand's comments on the "genre of this work." Far from being original or innovative, his commentary simply summarizes eighteenth-century discourses on prose poems, yet as such it confirms the significance of the ideological struggle tied to the aesthetic choice of the prose poem. First, Chateaubriand simply refused to take a position on the genre: "Je ne prendrai aucun parti dans une question si longtemps débattue; je me contenterai de rapporter les autorités" [I shall not take any side in a question debated for so long. I shall simply refer to the authorities] (10). Then he dismissed the issue as a banal question of terminology: "On demande s'il peut y avoir des poëmes en prose: question qui au fond pourroit bien n'être qu'une dispute de mots" [One asks if there can be prose poems? This question could very well be, in the end, a disagreement over words] (10). His genealogy of criticism, however, told otherwise. After beginning with the ancients, who treated prose and poetry as equals (Aristotle, Denys d'Halicarnasse, and Strabo), it focused on the pivotal role of *Télémaque* as prose epic, quoting the favorable opinion of contemporary authorities (Boileau, Louis de Sacy, Ramsay, etc.), before concluding on its status as an epic poem: "Enfin, écoutons Fénelon lui-même: 'Pour *Télémaque*, c'est une narration fabuleuse en forme de poëme héroïque, comme ceux d'Homère et Virgile.' Voilà qui est formel" [Finally, let us listen to Fénelon himself: 'As for *Télémaque*, it is a fabulous narrative in the form of a heroic poem, like those of Homer and Virgil] (10–11).[78] Chateaubriand then quotes the negative judgments of Faydit, Gueudeville, Voltaire and La Harpe, whose dismissal of *Télémaque* resulted, he believed,

---

[78] A note to this passage quotes the English critic Hugh Blair: "In reviewing the epic poets, it were unjust to make no mention of the amiable author of the *Adventures of Telemachus*. His work, though not composed in verse, is justly entitled to be held a poem. The measured poetical prose in which it is written, is remarkably harmonious; and gives the style nearly as much elevation as the French language is capable of supporting, even in regular verses" (11n4).

from their shared disgust toward the proliferation of bad imitations, an abuse of the genre of prose poems (12). Chateaubriand's genealogy of criticism concludes on a terminological impasse and his own critical withdrawal: "Si le *Télémaque* n'est pas un poëme, que sera-t-il? Un roman? Certainement le *Télémaque* diffère encore plus du roman que du poëme, dans le sens où nous entendons aujourd'hui ces deux mots. Voilà l'état de la question: je laisse la décision aux habiles" [If *Télémaque* is not a poem, what shall it be? A novel? Certainly, *Télémaque* differs even more from the novel than from a poem, in the way we understand these two words today. This is where the question stands now: I leave the decision to cleverer persons] (12). The terminological shortcoming betrayed impatience at having to justify his own "poëme en prose" and reluctance to engage in a critical debate. As the "Examen des *Martyrs*" confirms, Chateaubriand was not interested in becoming a theoretician of the prose poem, neither did he construe the "poëme en prose" as a challenge to existing generic categories.[79] His defense of *Les Martyrs* rested on conservative principles governing the separation of poetry and prose, respect for the hierarchy of genres, and references to authorities. Yet, Chateaubriand cites at length Faydit's critique of *Télémaque* so his readers can see "une conformité incroyable" [an amazing conformity] between the reproaches once leveled against *Télémaque* and attacks against *Les Martyrs* in terms of style, subject, and reception: "galimatias ... caractères ridicules, péril pour les mœurs et la religion, profanation, scandale" [nonsense, ridiculous characters, danger for morality and religion, profanation, scandal].[80] Chateaubriand clearly places his work in the lineage and under the auspices of *Télémaque*. In the end, his conclusion reminds us of Voltaire's: reiterating a topos, both assimilated prose poems to pseudo-translations—a cautious, rather reductive appreciation of the prose poem's driving force.[81] If translation was a useful trick to introduce innovation at the beginning of the eighteenth century, it had certainly been outgrown a hundred years later. The argument that *Télémaque* was best understood as a translation from the Greek confirms Chateaubriand's attachment to the ancients and the conservative bent of his aesthetic theories. He accommodated himself to existing structures, whether at the micro-level of the sentence, with a preference for classical periods, or at the macro-level of genre, with a respect for traditional forms. Paradoxically, his respect for formalism enabled him to renew content in favor of Romantic themes. The most revealing moment comes at the conclusion of his discussion of the prose poem, which coincides with the end of the preface:

> Je passerai, si l'on veut, condamnation sur le genre de mon ouvrage; je répéterai volontiers ce que j'ai dit dans la préface d'*Atala*: vingt beaux vers d'Homère, de Virgile ou de Racine, seront toujours incomparablement au-dessus de la plus belle prose du monde. Après cela, je prie les poètes de me pardonner d'avoir invoqué les Filles de Mémoire pour m'aider à chanter les Martyrs. Platon, cité par Plutarque, dit qu'il emprunte le nombre à la poésie, comme un char pour

---

    79   Chateaubriand, "Examen des *Martyrs*," in *Les Martyrs*, 593.
    80   Ibid., 572–5.
    81   Ibid., 593.

s'envoler au ciel: j'aurais bien voulu monter aussi sur ce char, mais j'ai peur que la divinité qui m'inspire ne soit une de ces Muses inconnues sur l'Hélicon, qui n'ont point d'ailes, et qui vont à pied, comme dit Horace: *Musa pedestris.*[82]

[If they want, I will condemn the genre of my work; I will gladly repeat what I said in *Atala*'s preface: twenty beautiful lines from Homer, Virgil or Racine, will always be beyond compare above the world's most beautiful prose. And so, I ask poets to forgive me for invoking the Daughters of Memory to help me sing the Martyrs. Plato, quoted by Plutarch, says that he borrows rhythm from poetry like a chariot to fly toward the sky. I would have liked to climb into this chariot too, but I am afraid that the divinity who inspires me is a Muse unknown on Mount Helicon, one with no wings and who walks, as Horace said, *Musa pedestris.*]

The superiority of classical verse over "the most beautiful prose in the world" and the allegory of prose as a pedestrian muse who cannot fly—unlike the winged muse of poetry— encapsulated Chateaubriand's vision of the status of prose: compared with poetry, it was always already a Fall. If prose was a Fall, then poetry represented, for Chateaubriand, a paradise lost. By association, Romanticism too was a Fall and classicism a paradise lost. Chateaubriand's spleen over the evolution of literature in response to modernity came to light in his considerable efforts to revive the classical epic genre, his ideological stance on the lowly character of prose, his misgivings about the "deplorable school" of Romanticism he had started, and his inability to classify *Les Martyrs*.[83]

If authors of biblical prose epics tended to vacillate between the competing aesthetics of the emerging novel and the long-standing epic poem, their ideological positioning remained unambiguous. All eighteenth-century prose poems composed from biblical sources exhibit a distinctive stance against rationalist philosophy. In the *Christiade*, Satan approaches Jesus "sous la forme d'un grave philosophe" [under the guise of a grave philosopher].[84] In the invocation opening *Tobie*'s first

---

[82] Chateaubriand, *Les Martyrs*, in *Œuvres romanesques et voyages* (Paris, 1969), vol. 2, 40.

[83] "Veut-on que ce soit un *roman*? je le veux bien; un *drame*? j'y consens; un *mélodrame*? de tout mon cœur; une *mosaïque*? j'y donne les mains. Je ne suis point poëte, je ne me proclame point poëte, pas même littérateur, comme on me fait l'honneur de me nommer; je n'ai jamais dit que j'avois fait un poëme, j'ai protesté et je proteste encore de mon respect pour les Muses. Rien ne m'enchante comme les vers. Et n'ai-je pas passé une grande partie de ma jeunesse à ranger deux à deux des milliers de rimes qui n'étoient guère plus mauvaises que celles de mes voisins?" [Do you want it to be a *novel*? I accept; a drama? I agree; a *melodrama*? with all my heart; a *mosaic*? I join in. I am not a poet, I do not proclaim myself to be a poet, not even a littérateur, as I have been called; I never said I wrote a poem, I protested and I protest again that I respect the Muses. Nothing delights me more than verse. Besides, did I not spend a great part of my youth pairing thousands of rhymes that were not any worse than my neighbors'?] Chateaubriand, "Examen des *Martyrs*," *Les Martyrs*, 593.

[84] La Baume Desdossats, *La Christiade*, 19.

canto, Le Clerc's apostrophe rebuffs two forms of vanity—power and philosophy: "Lorsque je chante cet homme juste [Tobie], éclipsez-vous, ambition guerrière, orgueil philosophique; c'est à la solidité des vertus morales à faire disparaître vos vains fantômes" [Vanish, warlike ambition, philosophical pride, when I sing this just man. The solidity of moral virtues will make your vain ghosts disappear.][85] The author seeks guidance and inspiration from Nature, to reach the wisdom of the heart, not of the mind: "[D]éfends-moi de cet esprit factice qui flatte le goût des nations trompées par un vain luxe" [Protect me from this artificial mindset, which flatters the taste of nations misled by vain luxury.][86] In the preface to *Les Martyrs* Chateaubriand justified his characterization of Hiéroclès, "sophist, writer, orator and persecutor," by citing the portraits of two other anti-Christian sophists, the first "a professional philosopher," the second a judge, and indicting their duplicity and cowardice (32). As the offensive portraits might draw objections, Chateaubriand quickly declared his respect and honor for "la vraie philosophie," which he saw as a moral attitude. Regardless, the backlash against the philosophy and rhetoric of the Enlightenment was unmistakable, particularly in book XVI, when Hiéroclès, seconded by "le Démon de la fausse sagesse, sous la figure d'un chef de l'école" [the Demon of false wisdom, disguised as a leader of the school], pronounced his harangue in favor of persecution (219). While it seemed logical for Christian authors like Chateaubriand and Le Clerc to want to denounce the excesses of philosophic mindsets (rationalism, materialism, and sensualism) the better to extol moral values and virtues praised by the Scriptures, the question of their choosing prose poems to do so remains intriguing. Neither verse, perhaps too seductive and manipulative, nor novels, reformed and adopted by the Moderns to further their progressive agenda, fitted the goals of the minority of authors under consideration in this chapter. Staking anti-rationalist ground in defiance of the Age of Reason, theirs was a spiritual quest which found refuge in a new, albeit imperfect, poetic genre.

---

[85] Le Clerc, *Tobie*, 2.

[86] Ibid., 3.

Chapter 6
The Reformation

Une analyse est critique si elle porte à découvert son enjeu. Seulement alors on peut dire qu'elle vise à produire une crise. Mais ce n'est plus selon l'idée naïve d'une discontinuité, d'une rupture. Plutôt la mise à jour des intérêts. Du rapport interne, par la théorie du langage, entre poétique et politique. Du conflit incessant.

[An analysis is critical if it exposes what is at stake. Only then can we say that it aims to provoke a crisis. But it is no longer according to the naïve idea of a discontinuity, a rupture. Rather an unveiling of interests. Of the internal relationship, through language theory, between poetics and politics. Their incessant conflict.]

Henri Meschonnic[1]

In earlier chapters, I tied criticism of verse to a critique of absolutism, imperialism and formalism in the French ancien régime. In that respect, the offensive against versification, although limited in scope and controversial, belongs to the same agenda as the Enlightenment's advocacy of reform, justice and freedom. But alongside this political activism under the symbolic guise of an aesthetic rebellion against verse—a struggle, I repeat, in the spirit of the Enlightenment—a second struggle, spiritual in nature, emerged that directly challenged the values and principles of rationality held highest by philosophers. Historians of ideas often characterize this combat as counter-Enlightenment, but this label fails to capture the fact that it took place from within, and could not be reduced to a pro/con dualism. If one returns to the multiple pronouncements on poetry made by critics and authors, it becomes obvious that qualities associated with the best French versification (codified by Boileau in the previous century) and the best prose, namely clarity, rigor, and logical accuracy, corresponded to the same qualities advocated by Enlightenment thinkers. In addition, if the classification of genres had long pre-existed their efforts to organize and categorize, nevertheless, in the end, such classification perfectly matched those efforts and only reinforced their philosophical doctrine. Thus most poets during the Age of Reason composed rational, albeit very diverse, poetry: this obvious connection reminds us that the Enlightenment enrolled poets in its vast movement. By contrast, authors who explored the Bible poetically, those who avoided versification by writing poetic narratives in prose, and ventured into a hybrid genre, in other words writers of prose poems, directly questioned the epistemology of Enlightenment philosophers like d'Alembert, d'Holbach, and to a certain extent Voltaire and Diderot, whose drive to divide, describe and categorize was perceived as not only limiting but

---

[1] Meschonnic, *Critique du rythme*, 20.

distorting, and whose struggle against the irrational had left scant room for the spiritual. In lieu of the "anti-" or "counter-"prefixes often used to characterize authors like Rousseau or Saint-Martin, I prefer to consider them reformers of the Enlightenment. I use here the term "reformation" in its widest, most generic sense, with only a tangential reference to Luther's Protestant schism with the Catholic Church in the sixteenth century. The spiritual reformation to which I refer took place in the eighteenth century when some Christian authors questioned the credo and dogma of the dominant discourse on rationality to restore a lost unity and a lost faith.

This questioning occurred within two religious movements, which I will now examine chronologically: quietism and illuminism. I first return to Fénelon's choice of prose poetry, this time in light of his interest in quietism, an unorthodox Christian movement also about reform, just as I examined *Télémaque* in view of Fénelon's political wish for reform. Then, from the mid-century to the Revolution, one encounters a few resisters who quietly pursued a double quest for spirituality and poetry in reaction to their century's scientific and philosophic enthusiasm.[2] Of all the authors assembled under the banner of spiritualist renewal in the second half of the century, a significant number penned "poëmes en prose," notably Bernardin de Saint-Pierre, Mme de Genlis, Chateaubriand, Nodier, Ballanche and the lesser known Cousin de Grainville and Boiste. The most striking feature of this spiritual vein in prose—nourished and sustained by new readings of the Bible as examined in the previous chapter—consists in its gradual revival of poetic affect and its invention of powerful poetic images. Finally, I will conclude with another important spiritual current, illuminism, in some ways a Christian mystical derivative of the former, to highlight Saint-Martin's contribution to prose poetry— the self-proclaimed "unknown philosopher" being one of the most outspoken disseminators of illuminism.

Quietism

When the Persian Rica visited the library of a convent in Montesquieu's *Lettres persanes*, his guide began the tour with religious writings, immediately followed by the works of mystics, "c'est-à-dire des dévots qui ont un cœur tendre" [namely pious people with a tender heart]; the inquisitive Rica asked for more information on devotion, to which his guide replied that it often degenerated in quietism, adding knowingly: "vous savez qu'un quiétiste n'est autre chose qu'un homme fou, dévot et libertin" [You know that a quietist is nothing but a mad, pious and libertine man.][3] The exchange captured the public perception of mystics as tender hearts, therefore not very dangerous, and misgivings regarding adepts of quietism, who had lost their reason by dint of excessive free-thinking and devotion. Fénelon never became a mystic or a "fou" but remained consistently devout *and* critical of the Church, which led him to espouse the mystical doctrine of quietism, a vision

---

2   See Delon, Mauzi, and Menant, *Histoire de la littérature française*, 154–76.
3   Montesquieu, *Lettres persanes* (Paris, 1995), Letter CXXXIV, 263–4.

as much at the heart of his aesthetics as the humanist principles I emphasized in Chapter 1.[4] Under Mme Guyon's impulsion, quietists preached that Christian perfection resided in a continual state of "quiétude" and union with God.[5] Calm, simplicity, and peace were sought to bring the soul in unison with God. Bossuet and the Jansenists sternly and relentlessly fought against the doctrine. Understanding Fénelon's Christian humanism and quietism reveals new stakes behind the quarrel between verse and prose triggered by *Télémaque*. In addition to its political overtones, the aesthetic dispute exposed deep philosophical and religious differences: a divergent view of God, the world, man's place, redemption, and salvation. The fierce quarrel between Jansenists and quietists exposed two opposing, irreconcilable sensibilities: on the Jansenist side stood Puritanism, austerity, rigor, and rigidity—a constant preoccupation with form leading to a staunch defense of verse. On the quietists' side, mysticism, love, and freedom prevailed—a concern with essence leading to the choice of prose, as we will see. The former had a school: Port Royal; the latter a temple: Nature. Reason reigned supreme on one side, imagination on the other. The concern for the people ("la multitude") that Fénelon expressed when advocating poetry and religion equally accessible to all, contrasted with the goal to identify an elite, a goal implicit in the Jansenist doctrine based on grace and predestination.

Fénelon delineated his literary principles and recommendations in the "Projet de poétique" inserted in his *Lettre à l'Académie* (1714).[6] By staying clear of radical extremes, he avoided the dichotomy of Ancient vs. Modern, yet his groundbreaking *Télémaque* had already rekindled the battle. Fénelon stated his aesthetic preferences simply and clearly: "Ce n'est ni le difficile, ni le rare, ni le merveilleux que je cherche. C'est le beau simple, aimable et commode que je goûte. ... Je veux un beau si naturel qu'il n'ait aucun besoin de me surprendre par sa nouveauté" [I do not seek the difficult, the rare or the marvelous. It is a simple, pleasing and effortless beautiful that I seek. ... I want a beautiful so natural that it does not need to surprise me with its novelty] (78). Fénelon disliked the precious and the marvelous (for instance the Scuderian novel), the difficult (rhyme), and the brilliant (wit). The heart must prevail over the mind. Fénelon's aesthetic vision favored simplicity, ease, and beauty that were natural, not artificial: "Tout ornement qui n'est qu'ornement est de trop" [Every ornament that is only an ornament is one too many] (75). With *Télémaque* he had offered an imaginary alternative to Louis XIV's reign, a return to substance and a rejection of ornament, spectacle, and fabrication for their own sake. The beautiful, however, could not be reserved to an elite, it must be universal: "Le beau ne perdroit rien de son prix, quand il seroit commun à tout le genre humain; il en seroit plus estimable. La rareté est un défaut et une pauvreté

---

[4]   See François-Xavier Cuche and Jacques Le Brun eds, *Fénelon. Mystique et Politique (1699–1999)* (Paris, 2004).

[5]   Jeanne-Marie Guyon (1648–1717), whose best known writing was *Le Moyen court et très facile de faire oraison que tous peuvent pratiquer très aisément et arriver par là dans peu de temps à une haute perfection* (1682).

[6]   Fénelon, *Lettre à l'Académie* (Geneva, 1970). Hereafter cited in text.

de la nature. Les rayons du soleil n'en sont pas moins un grand thrésor, quoiqu'ils éclairent tout l'univers" [The beautiful would not lose its price if it were common to the whole human race; it would be more esteemed. Rarity is a flaw and a poverty of nature. The sun's rays are no less a great treasure, even though they light up the entire universe] (78). A humanist promoting universalism, Fénelon advised to avoid rarity, singularity and elitism. The poet should not write for a privileged group of readers, but reach out to the "multitude," that is humanity: "en fait de langue on ne vient à bout de rien sans l'aveu des hommes pour lesquels on parle. On ne doit jamais faire deux pas à la fois et il faut s'arrêter dès qu'on ne se voit pas suivi de la multitude. La singularité est dangereuse en tout" [In terms of language, one does not go anywhere without the recognition of men for whom one speaks. One should not take two steps at a time and one must stop as soon as one realizes that the crowd is not following. Singularity is dangerous in everyway] (71). Contrary to aesthetic stances later in the nineteenth century, Fénelon rejected hermeticism as an obstacle to reaching out to the multitude: "le premier de tous les devoirs d'un homme qui n'écrit que pour être entendu est de soulager son lecteur en se faisant d'abord entendre" [the very first duty for a man who writes to be heard is to help his reader by making himself understood first] (72). All the principles announced above—simplicity, universal beauty, and accessibility—translated into a political and religious cause. Fénelon's originality in an age of absolutism consisted in his advocacy of a return to humanist principles governing the poet's mission as well as guiding the mode and subject of his writing. Embodied by *Télémaque*, prose would be the vehicle to connect with more readers, an optimistic gesture destined to revitalize French poetry, though writers such as Voltaire vigorously resisted it. Ironically, Fénelon's humanist lead when initiating prose poetry reversed itself when prose poets entered the nineteenth then the twentieth century. As political governance became more democratic and the bourgeois sphere safer and more comfortable, the genre narrowed its accessibility and readership, and endorsed a reputation of difficulty and elitism.

Fénelon's view of the poet also contrasts significantly with both classical and future Romantic and modern definitions. The poet, Fénelon believed, is not a superior genius, but a mortal among mortals, albeit a more disinterested one: "Je demande un poète aimable, proportionné au commun des hommes, qui fasse tout pour eux et rien pour lui" [I ask for an amiable poet, on a par with average men, who does all for them and nothing for himself] (75). "All for them and nothing for himself": the concise phrase gave the essence of the poet's mission, to be the voice not of God but of Jesus, that is, his image made flesh among humans, a divine man who spoke, lived, and suffered like mortals. In terms of writing: the prose of Jesus vs. the poetry of God. Jesus seems the very incarnation of the "sublime doux et familier" Fénelon so famously advocated: "Je veux un sublime si familier, si doux et si simple que chacun soit d'abord tenté de croire qu'il l'auroit trouvé sans peine, quoique peu d'hommes soient capables de le trouver" [I want a sublime so familiar, sweet, and simple that everyone will think at first that they would have found it easily, though few men are capable of actually finding it] (75). Today, the phrase "sweet sublime" rings as an unintelligible oxymoron in comparison to the more familiar Romantic sublime. Fénelon's sublime was not based upon awe, but upon recognition, hence its sweetness.[7] Because biblical scriptures contained the most sublime of all poetry in its recounting the origin of the world and God's wonders, the best subsequent poetry would strive to attain a similar sublime, the sublime of the original Word. The first pages of Fénelon's "Projet de Poétique" unite poetry with religion. Poetry civilized and pacified the first men, gave them laws and art. This powerful language, defined by Fénelon as "la parole animée par les vives images, par les grandes figures, par le transport des passions et par le charme de l'harmonie" [voice animated by vivid images, great figures of speech, outbursts of passion, and charming harmony] was called the language of the gods (64). As a sacred language, it ought to be at the service of wisdom, virtue, and the spiritual, in lieu of being reduced to a witty contest among versifiers.

After praising the sacred poetry of Moses' *Cantiques*, the book of Job, the Song of Solomon, and the Psalms, Fénelon shifted his focus to ancient Greek and Latin poets, in particular Virgil, whom he quotes extensively, to link them with biblical writing via their similar depiction of the pastoral age. The citations from the *Buccolics* and the *Georgics* illustrated the "naïveté champêtre" of these primitive times as well as a "simplicité passionnée" unmediated (so it seemed) by rhetoric (88). In descriptions, Fénelon favored the plain, down-to-earth realities of the natural world, in dialogues, the direct expression of passions. It goes without saying that both the Virgilian pastoral world and the Greek characters' blunt speech were highly constructed: the former invoked an imaginary Golden Age, the latter followed the rules of the Greek rhetoric of passions. Like all his contemporaries, Fénelon (con)fused Nature with the natural.[8] The proximity, almost equivalence, between ancient mores and nature paralleled the union that Fénelon sought to establish between men and God, readers and poet. The sublime "doux, familier, simple" that defined Fénelon's vision proposed an unmediated relation to nature, to poetry, and to God.

In sum, the ins and outs of Fénelon's religious and political creed cast him as a humanist at odds with the Jansenists' defense of aristocratic principles in religion and literature, and thus ahead of his times. Notwithstanding Germaine de Staël's vindication of Bossuet's prose (Fénelon's arch enemy), Bossuet did not depart radically from classicism, remaining within its traditional realm, eloquence, aloof in the precision and clarity of its rhetoric, whereas Fénelon's prose sought to conquer the realm of poetry to build a discursive, "quietist" space of intimacy and communion between poet and reader.[9] For example, Fénelon's poetic description of the Elysium fields where good kings reside after their death (book XIV), while reminding readers of Calypso's enchanted island in *Télémaque*'s incipit, develops an extended metaphor of light familiar to readers of the book of Revelations to

---

[7]   See also "ce je ne sais quoi si admirable, si familier et si inconnu ne peut être que Dieu" in Fénelon's *Traité de l'existence et des attributs de Dieu* (1713). Cited by Scholar, *The* Je-Ne-Sais-Quoi *in Early Modern Europe*, 68n127.

[8]   See Albert Chérel, introduction to *Fénelon au XVIII siècle en France*, xiv.

[9]   Germaine de Staël, Preface to the second edition, *De la Littérature considérée dans ses rapports avec les institutions sociales*, 1800 (Paris, 1991), 55.

translate a spiritual realm—a passage also infused with some of Mme Guyon's mystical phrases:

> Une lumière pure et douce se répand autour des corps de ces hommes justes, et les environne de ces rayons comme d'un vêtement. Cette lumière n'est point semblable à la lumière sombre qui éclaire les yeux des misérables mortels, et qui n'est que ténèbres; c'est plutôt une gloire céleste qu'une lumière: elle pénètre subtilement les corps les plus épais, que les rayons du soleil ne pénètrent le plus pur cristal; elle n'éblouie jamais; au contraire, elle fortifie les yeux, et porte dans le fond de l'âme je ne sais quelle sérénité. C'est d'elle seule que les hommes bienheureux sont nourris ... Ils sont plongés dans cet abîme de joie, comme les poissons dans la mer. Ils ne veulent plus rien. Ils ont tout, sans rien avoir, car ce goût de lumière pure apaise la faim de leur cœur ... (Fénelon 317–18)

> [A pure delightful stream of light diffuses itself round the bodies of these just men, and encompasses them with its rays, as with a garment. It is not like that gloomy gleam which enlightens the eyes of the wretched mortals, and is, indeed, naught else but darkness visible. It is rather a celestial glory, than that we call light, penetrating with more subtlety the densest bodies, than the rays of the sun pervade the purest crystal; never dazzling, but on the contrary strengthening the eyes, and diffusing a serenity into the inmost recesses of the soul. By this alone, the blessed are nourished. ... In this abyss of pleasure are they immersed as fishes in the sea; they desire nothing further; and, without having anything, enjoy every thing: the sweets of the pure light gratifying every wish of their hearts.] (Smollett 229)

The critic Gueudeville targeted the "amphibious light" in this passage as borderline sacrilegious, too equivocal to be intelligible, "la vision d'un Poëte non rimant qui béatifie les bons Princes à la mode" [the vision of a non-rhyming poet who beatifies good, fashionable princes.][10]

The very recent reprint of Henri Brémond's ambitious comprehensive history of religious sentiment in French literature, carried through to the early seventeenth century, provides crucial historical and textual evidence, and now makes available a fuller background to situate and understand the aesthetic undertaking of authors like Fénelon within a religious perspective.[11] His first volume, for instance, distinguishes between devout and Christian humanism, the former being more "speculative, populist and practical" than the latter—characteristics common to Fénelon's vision.[12] I acknowledge that my attempt to link Fénelon's poetics to quietism is here incomplete and insufficient, but the purpose of my brief sketch on the religious underpinnings of Fénelon's choice of prose poetry has been to suggest that the prose poem served as a crucial spiritual channel and to encourage further research.

---

[10]   Gueudeville, *Le Critique ressuscité ou fin de la Critique des Aventures de Télémaque* (1704), 48–51.

[11]   Henri Brémond, *Histoire littéraire du sentiment religieux en France* (Paris, 2006).

[12]   On the link between the spiritual and prose poetry, see "Progrès et manifestations diverses de l'humanisme dévot," ibid.

The spiritualist vein in poetry widened geographically and shifted content as the century progressed: Hana Jechova, François Mouret, and Jacques Voisine concluded their study with a significant chapter on "irrational experiences in literary prose," which traces "la quête d'un irrationnel porteur de révélations" [the quest of an irrational that carries revelations] in France, England, and Germany.[13] The authors linked new poetic creations in literary prose to the importance of dreams and *rêveries*, the interest in madness, and drug-induced visions. In this context, the tradition of mysticism and the illuminist movement represented one aspect of the irrational experiences pursued around the turn of the century. While this is persuasively demonstrated, the authors' comparative approach does not allow the specificity of the French literature under question to clearly emerge. Furthermore, they dismiss the crucial issue of the choice of prose, arguing that such formal preoccupation was irrelevant to writers focused on higher realities.[14] Far from absurd in the French case, the question of a link between spiritual and poetic expression can be answered categorically in favor of a deliberate choice of prose over verse during the Enlightenment. Fénelon's quietism partly drove his choice of prose just as, a hundred years later, Chateaubriand's religious preoccupation found its natural expression in prose. Such was also the case of Rousseau's "religion naturelle," Bernardin de Saint-Pierre's pastoralism, and Saint-Martin's "illuminisme."[15] Jechova, Mouret and Voisine's assumption that spiritual pursuit in eighteenth-century France precluded an involvement with society is proven wrong by Fénelon, Chateaubriand, and their fellow prose poets, who, like the illuminist Saint-Martin, constantly moved in social circles and were particularly eager to propagate their vision with the most efficient medium. They did, therefore, greatly preoccupy themselves with formal choices. In effect, though the eighteenth century bore religious poets in verse, their verses had a lesser impact in addressing the crisis of poetry than the "poëmes en prose" of contemporary Christian authors.

Jechova, Mouret and Voisine's conclusion on the impact of the "nouvelle orientation spirituelle et thématique" in the second half of the century helps summarize three crucial aesthetic developments that accompanied this spiritual current: a shift in the object of poetry from the "instructing while pleasing" motto to a personal vision of the world; an alteration of generic borders; and a displacement from analysis and synthesis toward fragmentation and hybridity.[16] These new features, which profoundly alter the face of poetry, clearly emerge from

---

[13]   Jechova, Mouret and Voisine eds, *La Poésie en prose des Lumières au romantisme*, 125–83.

[14]   Ibid., 137.

[15]   Montesquieu, too, finds a place in this intriguing genealogy. In 1787 an anonymous editor bound together the *Lettres persanes*'s utopian Troglodyte episode, Moutonné Clairfons's *Les Iles fortunées*, and four other stories. The editor published this compilation under the evocative title: *Voyages imaginaires, romanesques, merveilleus allégoriques, amusans, comiques et critiques. Suivs des songes, visions, et des romans cabalistiques.* See "Avertissement de l'éditeur des Voyages imaginaires," vii–xii.

[16]   Jechova, Mouret and Voisine eds, *La Poésie en prose des Lumières au romantisme*, 175.

the writings of Saint-Martin and Cousin de Grainville, which I will explore now, and from Parny and Chateaubriand's poetics analyzed in the next chapter.

Illuminism

> Qui l'eût dit, qu'après les encyclopédistes viendraient les martinistes? Ceux-ci n'ont aucun trait de la physionomie propre à la hautaine secte philosophique. Je ne sais comment le clergé, le gouvernement et la littérature s'arrangeront un jour avec eux. La secte qui vit dans un monde intellectuel ne paraît pas vouloir recourir à ce qui choque les hommes. Elle n'ambitionne ni pouvoir, ni richesse, ni renommée; elle rêve, elle cherche la perfection; elle est douce et vertueuse, elle veut parler aux morts et aux esprits.

> Cela n'est pas dangereux.

> [Who would have thought that after the Encyclopedists the Martinists would come? The latter have none of the physiognomic traits inherent to the haughty philosophical sect. I do not know how the clergy, the government and literature will one day accommodate themselves to them. The sect that lives in an intellectual world does not seem to want to shock men. It has no ambition for power, wealth, or fame; it dreams, it seeks perfection, it is sweet and virtuous, it wants to speak to the dead and to spirits.

> None of this is dangerous.]

Sébastien Mercier[17]

Saint-Martin's life and work are not well-known today though his writing played a considerable role before and after the Revolution, including a sharp critique of the Enlightenment's philosophes.[18] His mysticism later inspired numerous Romantic and post-Romantic authors throughout Europe (Germaine de Staël, Louis-Sébastien Mercier, Jacques Cazotte, Charles Nodier, Ballanche, Guérin, Lamartine, Joseph de Maistre, Lamennais, Sénancour, Sainte-Beuve, Balzac and Baudelaire).[19] Saint-Martin belonged to the generation who turned a page of history as it witnessed the end of the ancien régime and survived

---

[17]   Sébastien Mercier, *Tableau de Paris* (Paris, 1994), vol. I, chap. DCIX, 1427–8.

[18]   This analysis of Saint-Martin's work is adapted from my article "The Crocodile Strikes Back. Saint-Martin's Interpretation of the French Revolution," *Eighteenth-Century Fiction* 19:1–2 (October, 2006), 71–97.

[19]   See Auguste Viatte, *Les Sources occultes du Romantisme. Illuminisme, théosophie. 1770–1820.* Vol 1, *Le Préromantisme* (Paris, 1979); Paul Bénichou, *Le Sacre de l'écrivain. Essai sur l'avènement d'un pouvoir spirituel laïque dans la France moderne* (Paris, 1973); Brian Juden, *Traditions orphiques et tendances mystiques dans le romantisme français, 1800–1855* (Geneva, 1984), 174; Maurice Roche, *Balzac et le Philosophe Inconnu* (Tours, 1951); Anne-Marie Amiot, *Baudelaire et l'illuminisme* (Paris, 1982); and Fabienne Moore, "Baudelaire et les poëmes en prose du dix-huitième siècle," *Bulletin Baudelairien* (January, 2006).

revolutionary turmoil.[20] His was the rare case of an aristocrat who lost his fortune but saved his head, genuinely embracing the Revolution as revealed by his *Lettre à un ami*, an extraordinary anti-clerical document vindicating the revolutionaries for having eliminated the "gangrène" of aristocrats and priests.[21] Simultaneously, Saint-Martin wrote his only work of fiction about the Revolution, a sprawling allegory quickly exiled from the canon: *Le Crocodile, ou la guerre du bien et du mal, arrivée sous le règne de Louis XV*, composed in 1792.[22] Waiting until 1799 to publish it, he wrote an anonymous article, praising his own fiction as "un ouvrage extraordinaire dans lequel l'auteur, sous le voile d'une allégorie toujours soutenue, développe des vérités très hautes, et jette çà et là les germes d'une philosophie absolument neuve, ou qui du moins n'a été connue jusqu'à présent que d'un bien petit nombre de personnes" [an extraordinary work, in which the author, under the veil of a sustained allegory, develops high truths, and here and there sows the seeds of an absolutely new philosophy, or at least known until now only by very few people.][23] This mysterious philosophy is "illuminisme," based on divine revelation and the search for spiritual regeneration.

The *Encyclopédie*'s philosophers and the fin-de-siècle ideologues worked under the aegis of "les Lumières." The metaphor of light stood for human reason and intelligence penetrating experience to reveal our universe. For proponents of "illuminisme," light came from above as an illumination, namely a divine, supernatural light. Saint-Martin, the most outspoken disseminator of "illuminisme," devoted his life to the study of humanity, appearing in many ways a humanist in the tradition of the preceding century. Yet France's "Philosophe inconnu," the pseudonym under which Saint-Martin published his writings, thrust open the doors left ajar by such humanists turned quietist as Fénelon, advancing and developing the mystical writings of Martinès de Pasqually (1710?–1774), the Swedish author Swedenbörg (1688–1772), and most importantly, the German Jacob Bœhme (1575–1624). Saint-Martin shunned miraculous operations, prodigies, and other marvelous communications (as showcased by Cagliostro and Messmer), to turn inward, relying on will and desire to reach spiritual knowledge—an inner course in keeping with Bœhme's teachings. Saint-Martin turned his attention away from external "magical" demonstrations to observe instead history's upheavals. To the

---

[20] See Louis-Claude de Saint-Martin, *Mon Portrait historique et philosophique*, ed. Robert Amadou (Paris, 1961), and Charles Augustin Sainte-Beuve, "Saint-Martin, le Philosophe inconnu," *Causeries du lundi* (Paris, 1855), vol. X, 190–225. On Saint-Martin's behavior under the Revolution, see Mieczyslawa Sekrecka, *Louis-Claude de Saint-Martin, le philosophe inconnu. L'homme et l'œuvre* (Wroclaw, 1968), 161–73. For recent work on Saint-Martin, see Nicole Jacques-Lefèvre, *Louis-Claude de Saint-Martin, le philosophe inconnu (1743–1803). Un Illuministe au siècle des Lumières* (Paris, 2003).

[21] Saint-Martin, *Mon Portrait*, 230.

[22] Louis-Claude de Saint-Martin, *Le Crocodile ou la guerre du bien et du mal arrivée sous le règne de Louis XV. Poème épico-magique en 102 chants,* ed. Simone Rihouët-Coroze (Paris, 1979).

[23] Cited by Robert Amadou, preface to *Le Crocodile* by Saint-Martin, 15.

tempting gratification of a symbolic union with the eternal promised by esoteric practices, he preferred the more arduous quest for meaning: in his quest to reach spiritual enlightenment, "allegorèse" prevailed over symbolism, prefiguring the same shift in his writing.

Saint-Martin the theosophist was overshadowed by the "idéologues," his contemporaries in the last quarter of the eighteenth century: then and now his mysticism challenges the nature of modernity and progress associated with the Enlightenment and the Revolution. European Enlightenment's "other side," whether qualified as occult, enthusiastic, mystical or theosophical, calls for renewed interpretation. Though these inspired, spiritualist discourses exerted considerable influence throughout Europe, they now generate critical discomfort: not only are visionary writings perceived as antithetical to the Age of Reason but they also appear too esoteric to warrant serious academic investigation.[24]

Saint-Martin's importance cannot be measured simply according to its later impact—although it is a telling measurement. His works represent a laboratory of ideas—philosophical, political, social, religious, and linguistic—in search of answers to the same questions that eighteenth-century philosophers examined.[25] They met at certain junctures: both expressed their contempt for a corrupted clergy; both put reason and nature center stage, and elevated man, "l'homme-Dieu" as Saint-Martin sometimes called him.[26] They most often clashed radically because they differed on the goal of scientific pursuit and on the importance accorded to matter. Saint-Martin believed in the unity of all things as opposed to the fragmentation observed by contemporary philosophers.[27]

Saint-Martin had written and published his most acclaimed work, *L'Homme de désir,* before the Terror, in 1790, a year after his discovery of Bœhme's writings. This prose poem ignored the mold of neoclassical poetry and alexandrine verses, and shunned the straightforward prose style of the emerging novel, to create unusual prose stanzas, suffused with poetic lyricism. "L'homme de désir" heralds the poetic creative power and prophetic mission of men and women. Offering new and fresh insights into man's nature, sung in an original, accessible voice, *L'Homme de désir* caused a sensation. Today excerpts are included in poetry anthologies and

---

[24] For exceptions, see Jonathan Irvine Israel, *Radical Enlightenment: Philosophy and the Making of Modernity, 1650–1750* (New York, 2001); Margaret Jacob, *The Radical Enlightenment: Pantheists, Freemasons, and Republicans* (Boston, 1981); and Paula McDowell, "Enlightenment Enthusiasms and the Spectacular Failure of the Philadelphian Society," *Eighteenth Century Studies* 35:4 (Summer, 2002), 528.

[25] See Mario Matuci ed., *Lumières et illuminisme. Actes du colloque international.* Cortona, 3–6 October, 1983.

[26] Louis-Claude de Saint-Martin, *L'Homme de désir* (Paris, 1994), 192, 223. Hereafter cited in text, the first number referring to the stanza and the second to the page.

[27] Juden, *Traditions orphiques,* 175.

it is the only work by Saint-Martin one can find in a French bookstore, albeit in the "esoteric" section.[28]

L'Homme de désir's polished stanzas contrast with the composite one hundred and two songs of *Le Crocodile*, yet both pursued an identical goal: a reform both spiritual and linguistic. This aspect of Saint-Martin's thought seems the most ignored in current eighteenth-century studies. His contribution to debates on language and his experimentation in prose and poetry offer a privileged window into the competition between rationalists and spiritualists, philosophers and theosophists, positivists and idealists, in other words, between divergent visions of the world and interpretations of man's essence. Yet all looked for the mystery of man's essence in the mystery of the origin of his language. Saint-Martin's passionate effort at understanding the problem of language integrated aspects of Condillac and Rousseau's theories, while establishing a dialogue with more mystical linguists such as Court de Gébelin and Fabre d'Olivet later on.[29] His trials and errors in prose and poetry reflect the difficult passage from theory to practice.

A brief summary of Saint-Martin's key concepts regarding the origin of language helps foreground the two prose poems under examination. Saint-Martin embraced Rousseau's paradoxical admission that by necessity language pre-existed the institution of language —"la parole avait été nécessaire pour l'institution de la parole" [speech had been necessary to institute speech].[30] Although Saint-Martin regretted that Rousseau could not unveil this mystery further because he did not have its "key," the citation is read as an insight into the source of speech (la parole) which was always already there, like a seed already sowed that germinates and bears fruit.[31] This "luminous principle," to quote Saint-Martin, brings down the scaffold of human sciences and its systems. Saint-Martin makes a second point concerning speech, the source of which we can infer from the fact that idea precedes speech, in other words that we think before we speak. Scientists who are looking for the source of voice in words are mistaking the means—"secondary mechanical means"—with the origin, they wrongly believe the production of speech to be the source of voice.[32] Finally, to account for the origin of language, Saint-Martin establishes an essential distinction between *words* and *parole.* Words are only "agents" or vectors conveying parole/speech while parole/speech

---

[28] See *Anthologie de la poésie française du dix-huitième siècle*, ed. Delon (297–300), and *Anthologie de la poésie française du XVIIIᵉ siècle, XIXᵉ siècle, XXᵉ siècle*, eds Bercot, Collot, and Seth, 1–436. See also Laudyce Rétat, "*L'Homme de désir*: Louis-Claude de Saint-Martin et la 'parole vive,'" in *Aux Origines du poème en prose français*, eds Bernard-Griffiths, Pickering and Vincent-Munnia, 316–27.

[29] Antoine Court de Gébelin, *Monde Primitif* (1813) and *La Langue hébraïque restituée* (1815).

[30] Louis-Claude de Saint-Martin, *Cahiers des langues*, in *Les Cahiers de la Tour Saint-Jacques* VII (Paris, 1962), 182.

[31] Ibid.

[32] Ibid., 165.

conveys thought. This privileged nature of parole/speech is further emphasized by the synonym Saint-Martin uses to develop his analysis. It is both a linguistic and an extra-linguistic term, which one is not surprised to find in the writings of an illuminist: "verbe"—translated in English as The Word. Two quotations define The Word as a power unique to man as well as the source of language: "Le verbe est la faculté prééminente de l'homme, celle qui le distingue si fort des autres êtres qu'on ne peut en rien les comparer avec eux" [The Word is man's preeminent faculty, which distinguishes him so completely from other beings that they cannot be compared with him in any way]; and "Le verbe est cette parole conçue en nous avant qu'aucun mot l'exprime, c'est l'émanation de l'âme" [The Word is speech conceived within us before our first expression, it is the soul's emanation.][33] True to the belief in divine illumination from within, true to the Christian equation of God with The Word, Saint-Martin's approach to the problem of language is a coherent, elegant, highly unscientific (but that is also its point), rebuttal of skeptics and materialists. The different languages are generated by speech/parole, itself a reflection of The Word. Thereby Saint-Martin redeems what had been lost through Enlightenment rational, linguistic speculations: the sacredness of language. A concise, poetic definition encapsulates the nature of language, without revealing its mystery "la langue est le caractère et le hiéroglyphe du Verbe" [language is the character and hieroglyph of The Word.][34]

As with Rousseau, Saint-Martin's theory of language determined his literary aesthetic: in his case, both are spiritualist and symbolist. The most radical consequence of the belief that divine inspiration unfolds through language leads to the superiority of thought over matter, hence the breaking of forms and genres to accentuate the triumph of idea at all costs, to liberate a pure voice.[35] In three hundred and two prose stanzas, *L'Homme de désir* exalts the living light of God, nature's visible light, and the invisible, sacred light within man's soul.[36] Without a preface, without rhyming twelve-syllable verses or neoclassical tropes, this unusual prose poem reads like a book of hymns, sounds like a song of praise ("cantiques"), and resembles a prophetic performance. Its dominant stylistic feature is a paratactic style characteristic of the Scriptures, without coordination or conjunction, but rapid succession of multiple apostrophes, exclamations, interrogations, short declarative sentences, creating an unusually syncopated rhythm.[37] I have already signaled this paratactic poetic diction in previous authors, and will return to it when contrasting Parny and Chateaubriand. Whereas comparisons tended to dominate the sacred poetry of eighteenth-century French poets such as Jean-Baptiste Rousseau, Saint-Martin innovated with correspondences and symbols, some of which he reconnected to their religious roots, such as light, darkness, and spark, so often

---

[33]　Ibid., 160, 164.
[34]　Ibid., 195.
[35]　Juden, *Traditions orphiques*, 299.
[36]　Saint-Martin, *L'Homme de désir*, st.2, 22–3.
[37]　Ibid., st.81, 119.

invoked by the Encyclopedists. [38] Most Saint-Martinist symbols link spiritual and natural worlds, such as "semence" [seed/semen], "germe" [germ], "sève" [sap], the roots and branches of trees, torrent, stars, and rainbows (st.47, 80–81). Symbols of salt, oil (st.29, 57), wheat, wine (st.219, 247), sulfur, wax, and honey (st.223, 250) also abound.

Form and content are freed from expectations and rules in *L'Homme de désir*, a singular contrast with contemporary poetry, whether sacred or descriptive. Descriptive poetry could not satisfy Saint-Martin's imperative that natural beauty be celebrated not in and of itself, but for its Creator. Alluding to descriptive poets like Saint-Lambert and Bernardin de Saint-Pierre, the Man of Desire admits their talent but points at its artifice: "cette nature désavoue elle-même la plus grande partie de vos délicieux tableaux ... Et malgré le doux empire de vos séduisants pinceaux, elle se repose sur une main plus puissante, qui un jour voudra bien réparer ses désastres" [nature disavows most of your exquisite pictures ... And despite the sweet power of your seductive paintbrushes, nature trusts a more powerful hand which one day shall repair such disasters.][39] The Man of Desire also chides scientists, naturalists, and philosophers who seek to describe and explain nature, to decompose and examine its parts, just as linguists try to break down and analyze parole/speech:

> Mortels, la lyre harmonieuse de la nature est devant vous; tâchez d'en tirer des sons, et ne consumez pas vos jours à en décomposer la structure.

> Verbe sacré, ils te font injure par leurs recherches, comme s'ils ne savaient pas que c'est par leur parole que tout se crée et s'anime autour d'eux.[40]

> [Mortals, nature's harmonious lyre is before you: make an attempt to play it and do not spend your days decomposing its sounds.

> Sacred Word, their scholarship insults you, as if they did not know that through their voice all is created and animated around them.]

Such interjections bind the indicative and the imperative, celebration and injunction. The preachy side of the Man of Desire, although it might bother us today, blends in with its inspired enthusiasm: it remains a speech act, not a catechism. The originality and sincerity of this unmediated parole, delivered in prose, in the first person (in a dialogue with a second person, "tu" being God or man) captured the desire of contemporaries for a poetry no longer societal but spiritual.[41]

---

[38] "La lumière rendait des sons, la mélodie enfantait la lumière, les couleurs avaient du mouvement, parce que les couleurs étaient vivantes; et les objets étaient à la fois sonores, diaphanes et assez mobiles pour se pénétrer les uns les autres, et parcourir d'un trait toute l'étendue" [Light produced sounds, melody gave birth to light, colors moved because colors were alive; and objects were at the same time sonorous, transparent and mobile enough to penetrate one another and travel the expanse in a flash]. Ibid., st.46, 79.

[39] Ibid., st.210, 240.

[40] Ibid., st.88, 126.

[41] Ibid., st.68, 106.

Le Crocodile

As if to challenge readers, Saint-Martin abandoned lyricism and turned to the epic genre with a mock-heroic poem in prose, *Le Crocodile ou la guerre du bien et du mal arrivée sous le règne de Louis XV* [see Figures 9 and 10].

The subtitle of *Le Crocodile* subverts any appropriation based on genre—it is a "poème épico-magique en 102 chants"—and the pseudonym, "par un amateur de choses cachées," points at the esoteric, secret design behind the burlesque appearance of the evil crocodile. While the prose poem continuously plays with literary conventions through mystifying and witty stylistic and thematic parodies, it also directly engages a dangerous subject. The story allegorized the Revolution at a time when most contemporaries shied away from fictionalizing its traumatic violence. The *Crocodile* raised a few eyebrows but otherwise failed to attract notice or praise. It was too extravagant; the narrative and didactic episodes were too repetitive and roughly stitched together. Saint-Martin himself admitted it would have benefited from tighter editing.[42] Midway between the fantastic novel and Romantic epic poetry, its place in literary history remains undetermined.[43] How does a sweeping allegory such as *Le Crocodile* combine a political, social, and poetic vision of the war, and to what effect? Within this "poëme hiéroglyphique et baroque," snubbed on account of its outlandish excesses, lie perhaps the most searing indictment of intellectual and moral irresponsibility and the most hopeful expectations about regeneration written just before the onset of the Terror by any of its witnesses.[44] Yet one fellow poet-philosopher across the Channel was writing, at the same time, an equally eclectic work, featuring "the sneaking serpent," mixing prose and verse, satire and paradox, epigrams and visions: William Blake's *Marriage of Heaven and Hell* offers surprising parallels with *Le Crocodile*, with regard to its heterogeneous form but also context, source, and substance. Inspired by the French Revolution with which Blake sympathized, *Marriage of Heaven and Hell* is filled with references to Bœhme as well as a critique of Swedenbörg in the same disillusioned vein as Saint-Martin's. Like the "philosophe inconnu," Blake promoted a spiritual vision that condemned materialism (the Newtonian world and Locke's empiricism), rejected priesthood and dogma, but extolled energy and desire. In the absence of firm evidence, one can only suggest that Saint-Martin be included

---

[42]   See Saint-Martin, *Mon Portrait historique*, 394.

[43]   Robert Amadou, Preface, *Le Crocodile*, 24. See also Nicole Jacques-Chaquin, "Le *Crocodile* de Louis-Claude de Saint-Martin: le Paris fantastique d'une Révolution figurée," in *Studia Latomorum et Historica. Hommages à Daniel Ligou*, ed. Charles Porset (Paris, 1998), 183–202; and Sekrecka, *Louis-Claude de Saint-Martin*, 185–90.

[44]   Sainte-Beuve, "Saint-Martin," 210. Sainte-Beuve criticized the epic prose poem as "une plaisanterie lourde le plus souvent et du plus mauvais goût ... Le rire, en général, va peu aux mystiques ... Saint-Martin ne gagne rien à s'approcher du genre de son compatriote Rabelais" [a joke most often heavy-handed and in the worst taste ... Laughter as a rule does not suit mystics ... Saint-Martin does not gain anything by imitating his fellow countryman Rabelais.]

LE CROCODILE,

OU

LA GUERRE

DU BIEN ET DU MAL,

ARRIVÉE SOUS LE RÈGNE DE LOUIS XV;

POÈME ÉPIQUO-MAGIQUE

EN 102 CHANTS,

Dans lequel il y a de longs voyages, sans accidens qui soient mortels ; un peu d'amour sans aucune de ses fureurs ; de grandes batailles, sans une goutte de sang répandu ; quelques instructions sans le bonnet de docteur ; et qui, parce qu'il renferme de la prose et des vers, pourroit bien en effet, n'être ni en vers, ni en prose.

OEUVRE POSTHUME D'UN AMATEUR DES CHOSES CACHÉES.

A PARIS.

De l'Imprimerie - Librairie du CERCLE - SOCIAL,
Rue du Théâtre - Français , n°. 4.

AN VII de LA RÉPUBLIQUE FRANÇAISE.

Fig. 9   Title-page. Louis-Claude de Saint-Martin, *Le Crocodile, ou la guerre du bien et du mal, arrivée sous le règne de Louis XV; Poème épico-magique en 102 chants*. 1799.

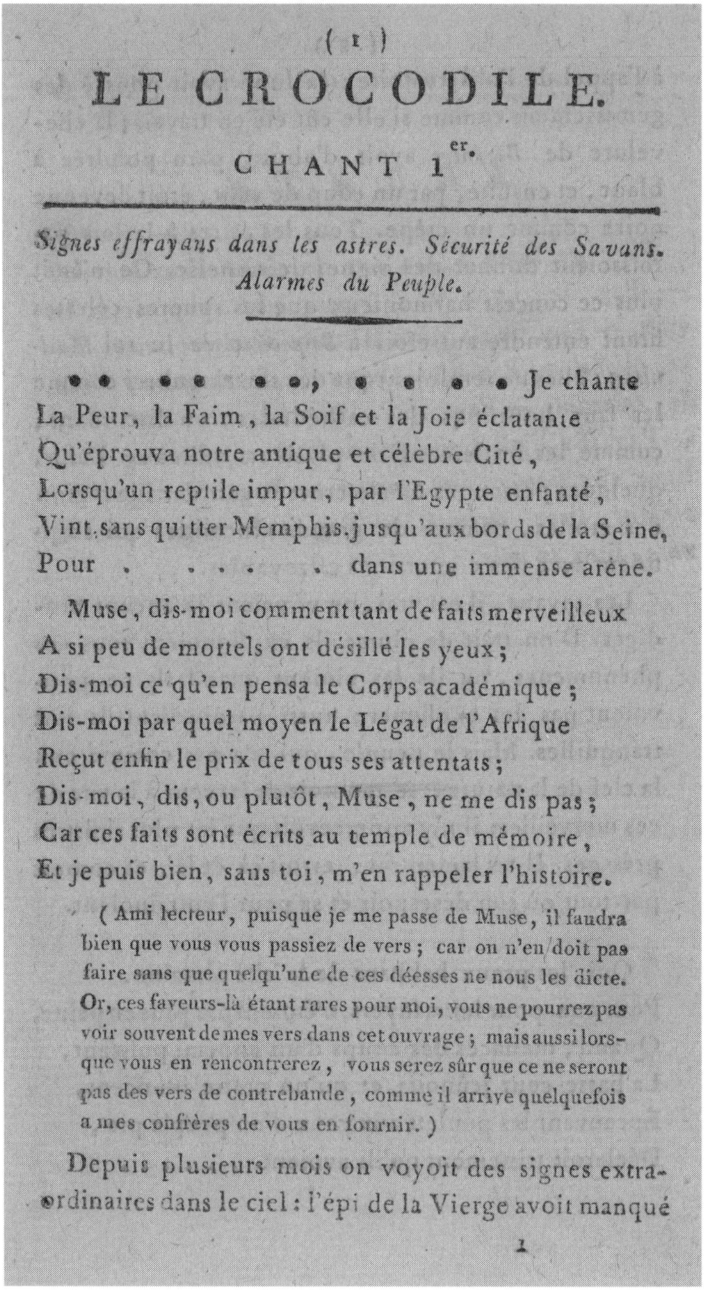

(1)

LE CROCODILE.

CHANT 1ᵉʳ.

Signes effrayans dans les astres. Sécurité des Savans.
Alarmes du Peuple.

• • • • • • •, • • • • Je chante
La Peur, la Faim, la Soif et la Joie éclatante
Qu'éprouva notre antique et célèbre Cité,
Lorsqu'un reptile impur, par l'Egypte enfanté,
Vint sans quitter Memphis, jusqu'aux bords de la Seine,
Pour . . . . . . dans une immense arène.

Muse, dis-moi comment tant de faits merveilleux
A si peu de mortels ont désillé les yeux ;
Dis-moi ce qu'en pensa le Corps académique ;
Dis-moi par quel moyen le Légat de l'Afrique
Reçut enfin le prix de tous ses attentats ;
Dis-moi, dis, ou plutôt, Muse, ne me dis pas ;
Car ces faits sont écrits au temple de mémoire,
Et je puis bien, sans toi, m'en rappeler l'histoire.

(Ami lecteur, puisque je me passe de Muse, il faudra
bien que vous vous passiez de vers ; car on n'en doit pas
faire sans que quelqu'une de ces déesses ne nous les dicte.
Or, ces faveurs-là étant rares pour moi, vous ne pourrez pas
voir souvent de mes vers dans cet ouvrage ; mais aussi lorsque vous en rencontrerez, vous serez sûr que ce ne seront
pas des vers de contrebande, comme il arrive quelquefois
a mes confrères de vous en fournir.)

Depuis plusieurs mois on voyoit des signes extra-
ordinaires dans le ciel : l'épi de la Vierge avoit manqué

1

Fig. 10   First page. Louis-Claude de Saint-Martin, *Le Crocodile, ou la guerre du bien et du mal, arrivée sous le règne de Louis XV; Poème épico-magique en 102 chants.* 1799.

in Jon Mee's assessment that "Blake's prophetic radicalism has features in common with a whole range of texts produced from a broader culture of enthusiasm."[45]

Saint-Martin recorded precisely his completion of *Le Crocodile*, on 7 August 1792 on the same week as the 10 August uprising that brought the King to prison three days later and signaled the foundation of the Republic.[46] But the diary entry raises more questions regarding the connection between the text and its historical context than it answers. The very nature of allegory prevents readers from pinning down its exact referent, multiplying instead interpretative layers that fluctuate with time. Walter Benjamin in his study of the German baroque drama, linked allegory with ruins and the fragmentation of reality. Benjamin famously contrasted the symbol, which offers a glimpse of nature's "transfigured face," to allegory displaying history's "*facies hippocratica*," that is, its death head: "This is the heart of the allegorical way of seeing, of the baroque, secular explanation of history as the Passion of the world; its importance resides solely in the stations of its decline."[47] Allegory conveys historicity and temporality, whereas the symbol encapsulates immediacy and makes it seem eternal. A symbol functions like a revelation, a lightening flash, whereas allegory is always a construction. A symbol fuses the signifier and signified, whereas allegory separates them. As Todorov explained, "the symbol is, allegory signifies."[48] Saint-Martin built the allegorical framework most relevant to the period 1789–1799, ten extraordinary years of destructive as well as constructive warfare that changed the course of every reader's life and French history. Yet, as François Furet writes, "il existe ... une histoire de l'histoire de la Terreur, liée aux vicissitudes de l'histoire politique française depuis deux cents ans" [there is a history of the history of the Terror, linked to the turmoils of French political history in the past two hundred years], thus making it impossible and unwise to give a definitive, "eternal" meaning to the revolutionary Terror.[49] Whatever revisions Saint-Martin may have made to

---

[45] See Jon Mee, *Dangerous Enthusiasm. William Blake and the Culture of Radicalism in the 1790s* (Oxford, 1992), 51. Had Saint-Martin heard about Blake during his six-month stay in London, from January to July 1787? Was Blake aware of Saint-Martin's *Des Erreurs et de la vérité* (1775) and *L'Homme de désir* (1790) directly or indirectly through his circle of friends or perhaps Johnson's *Analytical Review*? Though further research is necessary to ascertain textual references that would link the two authors, theirs were kindred spirits participating in a "radical Enlightenment." Mee argues that "bricolage" (the incorporation of elements from various discourses) is "a striking feature of the organization of Blake's poetry, a feature shared by many whose writing responded to and was shaped by the Revolution controversy" (10). The circulation of Saint-Martin's works in Europe suggests the possibility that Blake's "bricolage" may include Martinist elements.

[46] Saint-Martin, *Mon Portrait*, 315.

[47] Walter Benjamin, *The Origin of German Tragic Drama* (New York, 1990), 166. It is noteworthy that Benjamin considered Jacob Bœhme "one of the greatest allegorists," ibid., 201.

[48] Tzvetan Todorov, *Théories du symbole* (Paris, 1977), 251.

[49] François Furet, "Terreur," in *Dictionnaire critique de la Révolution française*, ed. François Furet and Mona Ozouf (Paris, 1988), 165.

his prose poem until 1799, his allegory encourages readers to work within their own temporality and historicity to build transitory meanings. For most critics, *Le Crocodile*'s happy ending trumps the violent revolutionary context during which it was composed and revised, emphasizing instead the context of millenarianism and its hopeful expectations:[50] the strength and reach of Saint-Martin's message not to forsake the spiritual in favor of the rational effaces all traces of disappointment or disillusion the author may have experienced as the Terror unfolded. To the contrary, I wish to underline that Saint-Martin's prophetic rhetoric exhibits and represses the experience of violence and death.

Le Crocodile, as allegory, dissolves all suspension of disbelief. The reader's task is not to empathize, as was customary with contemporary sentimental novels, but to decipher. Names are encrypted: the main character is Sédir, an anagram for "désir;" the protagonist Eléazar, a Spanish Jew (like Pasqually), has a Hebrew name revealing his connection with God; Rachel, his daughter in the story, is a biblical figure; the benevolent Madame Jof represents "la Foi;" her husband, the jewel maker, bears all the attributes of Jesus. In the opposite camp of evil forces, nefarious geniuses appear alongside three agents of the crocodile: conspirators named "la femme de poids" who dresses like a man; "le grand homme sec," closely resembling Cagliostro; and the shouting and violent general Roson (anagram of "sonore") who leads the evil rebellion. In choosing a crocodile to embody the forces of evil, Saint-Martin subverted a sacred Egyptian symbol into a parodic reference to the rites of supposedly Egyptian origins introduced in France by Cagliostro.[51] The crocodile, which burst from the underground one day in Paris, proclaims itself the expression of universal matter: its objectives are to corrupt human intelligence through lies and confusion, and to foment human extermination through self-destruction. The war between good and evil forces is fought through several battles, each allegorical as well.[52]

The description of revolutionary Paris borrows a few realist touches (topographical for instance), but Saint-Martin's goal was not historical, his story not about facts but meaning. Thus the shortage of wheat, people's hunger, and the spreading famine, while reflecting the food crisis actually suffered by Parisians, illustrate as well people's hunger for knowledge and for some understanding of the confusing events rocking the capital. Saint-Martin translated the power of revolutionary crowds into images of war-like column formation, and its anarchical impulse into a torrent flowing into the streets. One scene briefly sketched the confusing heterogeneity of the crowd:

> On voyait donc l'ennemi sortir par colonnes des différentes rues de la ville et des faubourgs, comme autant de torrents, et venir se jeter en foule vers l'endroit où il

---

[50]   Simone Rihouët-Coroze, "Analyse du Crocodile" in *Le Crocodile ou la guerre du bien et du mal* by Saint-Martin, 59–61.

[51]   On Masonic symbolism, see Jean-Louis Ricard, *Étude sur le* "Crocodile ou la Guerre du bien et du mal" *de Louis-Claude de Saint-Martin* (Paris, 1996).

[52]   See Rihouët-Coroze, "Analyse du Crocodile," 29–61.

trouvait le plus d'espace. Chaudronniers, maîtres à danser, cuisiniers, ramoneurs, fiacres, poètes, tout était pêle-mêle dans cette horrible confusion ... (114)

[We could see the enemy come in column formation out of the various streets of the city and its suburbs, like so many torrents, and flocking toward the side where there was the most space. Coppersmiths, dance instructors, cooks, chimney sweeps, carriages, poets, all was jumbled up in this awful confusion.]

This humorously eclectic enumeration juxtaposed with hints of horror is a good example of the text's destabilizing effect, always working against readers' expectations. Similarly, in a canto titled "Fureurs du peuple contre le contrôleur général," a hungry people, looking for a culprit, storm the *contrôleur général's* house to punish him for his mismanagement. But the dramatic, potentially bloody, outburst hits against six alexandrine lines mimicking the *contrôleur's* insouciance:

Le peuple, que la faim travaille de plus en plus, et que les discours des savants ne soulagent point, cherche enfin à connaître l'auteur de tous ces désastres; ou plutôt, il cherche à assouvir sur lui sa vengeance. ... On court en foule à son hôtel, qu'on entoure; on enfonce la porte, et l'on entre: que trouve-t-on?

Dans ce temps désastreux, dans ce temps d'indigence,
Où chacun, malgré soi, fait entière abstinence,
Le ministre est à table, entouré de perdrix,
De pain frais, de gâteaux, de vins les plus exquis;
Et pour mieux oublier la misère publique,
Il appelle au festin le Dieu de la musique. (152)

[The people, starving more and more, and not at all relieved by scholarly speeches, finally seek to discover the author of all these disasters; or rather, they seek to satisfy their vengeance on him. ... The crowd runs to his residence, surrounds it, forces the door open and enters: what do they find?

In this disastrous time, this time of indigence/ When all, against their will, practice total abstinence/ Mr. Secretary is eating, surrounded by partridges/ Fresh bread, cakes, the most delicious wines;/ And to forget more easily the misery of the public,/ He invites to the feast the God of music.]

As the text returns to prose, the crowd resumes its destructive mission, yet its prey unexpectedly escapes and damages are only material. Stylistically (verse vs. prose), semantically ("temps desastreux" vs. "perdrix, pain frais, gâteaux, vins;" "terreur" vs. "lumière"), the allegorical epic poem represents the insurgency at the same time as it contains its furor. Though its aesthetic effect might feel like an artifice, allegory is able here to signify the violence while keeping it at a distance. Moreover, the lilting alexandrines of time past surrender to the prose of revolutionary history, an emblematic victory.

Any reader of *Le Crocodile* will be struck, no doubt surprised, by the omission of blood and death in this war story. Does it cast Saint-Martin as a pacifist, or perhaps an early proponent of non-violence? The author does not explicitly oppose war; violence, fighting and armed conflicts appear but no bloodshed, and remarkably no death in *Le Crocodile*.[53] Paris police lieutenant Sédir orders his troops to preserve life, and urges combat without killing: when they capture their enemies at the end of the story, they receive "ordre de ne leur faire aucun mal, jusqu'à ce que les lois aient décidé de leur sort" [orders not to hurt them until laws decide their fate] (242). Their fate is prison, not execution. Under Saint-Martin's pen, even the crocodile does not sacrifice life but temporarily suspends it, as when the monster swallows the two opposing armies at the beginning, and then throws them up so violently at the end that they find themselves in the skies among stars and planets. There, the two armies resume their fighting as mighty cosmic spheres that collide violently. Instead of exploding as one might expect, they bounce off one another. Drawn back to earth, the two armies eventually reconcile, becoming "une famille de frères" [a family of brothers] (243). As for the vanquished crocodile, he is engulfed back into the earth, to be more tightly pinned under one of Egypt's pyramids. In keeping with his stance against the death penalty, Saint-Martin consistently refused to portray death as punishment, shunning historical evidence and gothic pyrotechnics, to embed the more subtle conviction that neither evil nor goodness ever completely disappears. Saint-Martin's characters escape the dichotomy of invincible superheroes and hapless victims, reflecting his belief that people could rise from their fallen station in life if they turned to faith and inner strength. Saint-Martin always allows the option of spiritual regeneration, and when people stumble because of their vices, they retain their virtues and always have the potential for redemption (232). In a manner as surprising as in *Lettre à un ami*, Saint-Martin did not frame the revolutionary conflict as a bloody class confrontation, the Third Estate opposing aristocrats and the clergy. Nor did he fictionalize in any way the political battle between the Girondins and Jacobins factions as he could have before publishing the story in 1799. As in his essay, "the unknown philosopher" painted a completely alternative picture to sociopolitical and historical representations of the revolutionary crisis, offering instead a vision of apocalyptic spiritual and ethical transformation.

Similar revolutionary crises are the source of the numerous national wars mentioned in the course of the allegory, each historical occurrence being linked to

---

[53] See the subtitle, itself a metatextual parody mocking conventional genres (picaresque, sentimental, and epic) and preparing readers to enter a fantastic epic where no blood is spilled: "Poëme épico-magique en 102 chants, Dans lequel il y a de longs voyages, *sans accidens qui soient mortels*; un peu d'amour, sans aucune de ses fureurs; de grandes batailles, *sans une goutte de sang répandu*; quelques instructions sans le bonnet de docteur; et qui, parce qu'il renferme de la prose et des vers, pourrait bien en effet, n'être ni en vers, ni en prose" [Epic and magic poem in 102 cantos ... where there are long journeys *without fatal accidents*; some love without any of its furors; great battles with *no bloodshed*; some instructions without the scholar's hat; and containing verse and prose, which means it might neither be in verse nor prose.] (emphasis added).

the crocodile's evil momentum, evidenced in his speech to the Parisians and the discourse and behavior of the captives in his entrails. For instance, in his belly, figures play a political game of cards wherein each card stands for a kingdom—an explanation for the perpetual shuffling of empires (178). Saint-Martin suspended the narrative from canto 30 to 35 to transcribe the "discours scientifique du crocodile," a lengthy chronicle of the reptile's involvement in historical events, a parallel history to the official version, revealing the agency of evil at work from the beginnings of the world and throughout time.[54] But the point of Saint-Martin's allegory lies beyond the conviction that evil originates war, it concerns his answer to the difficult question of the origins of evil itself. Where does evil come from? Though Saint-Martin adhered to the Christian belief in humanity's original fall, the text implies a concomitant origin as well as responsibility: evil grows within us. The principle that derives from this inner proclivity is that freedom means the capacity to choose between good and evil. Several prototypes illustrate this choice. On the positive side, the historical figure of Las Casas and the fictional characters Rachel and Ourdeck choose to follow benevolent influences and internal predilection. By contrast, the rebel general Roson and "the tall bony man" exercised their freedom in favor of evil impulses, opposing their heritage of goodness: in a moment of remorse the tall bony man reveals that his enlightened, virtuous mother tried to steer him onto the path of wisdom and virtue, but he chose to follow other masters and let himself be subjugated (155–56). As for Roson, Eléazar laments the criminal and disorderly life that this former acquaintance chose to lead, driven by pride and arrogance (101). The crucial definition of freedom as a choice between good and evil mirrors the striking metaphor of the "carte noire" given by aerial enemies to their delegate in order to exterminate Eléazar (212). The "carte noire" is the obverse of the "carte blanche," the French idiomatic phrase synonymous with free choice or doing what one pleases: as one exercises freedom, the options always include a black card, because freedom for Saint-Martin is not a blank slate but a choice between the negative and the positive, darkness and light.

Nations face similar choices, but with the added perverse effect that evil begets evil, or, in Saint-Martin's metaphor, that the crocodile lends for the sake of usury, as was the case with Spain's murderous conquest of the Americas: "les Espagnols trouvèrent la mort dans leurs plaisirs en Amérique, après y avoir cherché l'or dans le sang de ses habitants, et chez eux je leur ai donné l'Inquisition, qui est comme l'abrégé et l'élixir de toutes mes industries" [In America the Spaniards found death in their pleasures after looking for gold in the blood of its inhabitants, and at home I gave them the Inquisition, which is the synthesis and quintessence of all

---

[54] Saint-Martin gives voice to the evil crocodile for the same reason that Blake transcribes "the voice of the devil" in *The Marriage of Heaven and Hell*—"the Proverbs of Hell shew the nature of Infernal wisdom better than any description of buildings or garments." *The Complete Poetry and Prose of William Blake*, ed. David V. Erdman, 35. Charles Baudelaire also let the devil speak in his prose poem "Le Joueur généreux," yet another allegory of evil with hard to verify yet plausible connections with Saint-Martin. Blake's subversive inversion of good and evil seems much closer to Baudelaire's own understanding of evil.

my efforts] (132). Not only was Saint-Martin more straightforward in his critique of colonialism than most contemporaries, but he understood colonialism as the onset of globalization, with its inherent danger of explosive conflicts in a world interconnected by relationships of power and dominance, as in a chess game:

> [L]e profit que j'ai fait à la découverte des Indes et de l'Amérique, c'est qu'actuellement il ne me faut qu'une allumette pour embraser le globe. Ainsi la politique, sur toute la terre, est devenue, par mon ministère, comme une partie d'échecs qui commence toujours et qui ne peut plus finir, parce que les puissances qui en forment les diverses pièces, peuvent bien se prendre les unes les autres, mais elles ne peuvent me prendre moi, qui en suis roi, et elles ne savent pas me faire mat; aussi les génies, mes adversaires, sont-ils entièrement déroutés aujourd'hui. (132)

> [The benefit I made from discovering India and America is that now I only need a match to set the planet on fire. Thus politics all over the earth has become through my ministry like a chess game that starts repeatedly but can never end, because the powers which compose its various pieces can overtake each other but cannot capture me who is king, and that they do not know how to checkmate me. That is why geniuses, my adversaries, have nowadays completely gone astray.]

Thus the crocodile strikes back: imperialism bears violent (terrorist?) fruit, which we do not yet know how to checkmate.

In addition to wars, the manifestation of evil upon which the allegorical epic insists the most concerns the distortion of truth. Whereas Saint-Martin primarily targeted the Church in his *Lettre à un ami*, his prose poem focuses on two sets of equally manipulative characters: magicians and scholars. Saint-Martin's denunciation of false prophets, such as Cagliostro, placed him at the heart of the Enlightenment's critique of abusers of faith, whether they plied their mystification as clergy members or phony clairvoyants. Yet the relentless accusations directed against scholars, scientists, philosophers, and academicians of all stripes gave Saint-Martin his counter-Enlightenment reputation. In lieu of an oversimplified classification as "anti-Lumières," a nuanced reading can offer a more progressive orientation for a "philosophe inconnu" whose priorities regarding truth and knowledge mirror the Enlightenment's credo after all. By nature heavy-handed, allegory emphasized scholarship's blind spots and shortcomings, thereby raising concerns and warnings reverberating to this day.

Eléazar warns the police chief Sédir that the tall bony man from Egypt (alias Cagliostro) is the state's most terrible enemy (108). This shady individual admits that he "rules in a zero," hence the need to capture and retain people's minds (160). But his magic is a lie:

> Il soutient, tant qu'il peut, la révolte, par les moyens qui lui sont connus; il souffle dans les conjurés l'esprit de vertige ... [mais] il ne peut conduire aucune entreprise jusqu'à un heureux terme, parce qu'il ne connaît pas ses propres correspondances avec la porte de la nature, et quand il veut en essayer la clef, qui en effet se trouve partout, il la tourne toujours à contre-sens. (109)

[He supports the rebellion as much as possible, with means known to him; he inspires the rebels with the spirit of errors ... [but] he cannot bring any project to fruition because he does not know his own correspondences which open nature's door, and when he tries the key, which indeed is all around, he always turns it the wrong way.]

Instead of unlocking nature's mysteries, this nefarious character turns the key the wrong way, to confuse scholars' minds, destroy their books, starve Parisians, and entice them to crime (157). Beyond the imposture perpetrated by Cagliostro and the like, Saint-Martin seems to be warning his readers against the power of religious sects to blind their flocks (108). In another episode, deep in the crocodile's entrails, the reader sees alchemists promising treasures, "pendant que la seule alchimie et les seuls trésors qui soient véritablement utiles pour nous, c'est la transmutation ou le renouvellement de notre être" [whereas the only alchemy and sole treasures truly useful to us are transmutation or the renewal of our being] (226). Other creatures dwelling inside the beast include fanatics who massacre their fellow beings "au nom d'un Dieu de paix" [in the name of a God of peace] and writers who do not pursue truth but vainglory (226–7).

Like his agent the tall bony man, the crocodile seeks to distort truth, but the animal represents an even more insidious threat. This reptile can distend itself to reach the four corners of the globe, as well as metamorphose into different forms. In the genealogy of evil that he chronicles before a dumbfounded crowd of Parisians and scholars, the crocodile particularly rejoices at the help he received from the invention of the printing press and the swift dissemination of books under the reign of Louis XV, as useful to this current destructive ambition as canon powder had been in the previous century.[55] Although lamenting a lack of funding, which restricted the range of its circulation, the crocodile singles out Diderot's famous *Encyclopédie* for how it might have promoted and expanded its reign, namely the reign of matter and materialism: "quels fruits n'aurais-je pas retirés de cette Encyclopédie animée, qui, pullulant sans cesse, eût successivement étendu mon règne sur toute la terre!" [I would have picked so many fruits from this lively Encyclopedia which, always proliferating, would have progressively extended my reign on earth!] (134). Exaggerating the spread of noxious or empty works and their authors' misguided scholarship, the narrative introduces two more allegorical scenarios, the plague of books and the sciences held in captivity, thus targeting

---

[55]   Blake's third "Memorable Fancy," in *The Marriage of Heaven and Hell* mysteriously begins with a "Printing house in Hell" where the poet sees "the method in which knowledge is transmitted from generation to generation." *The Complete Poetry and Prose of William Blake*, 40. Blake's imagery of caves, dragons, and vipers in association with books and libraries bears an uncanny resemblance to Saint-Martin's, though Blake's netherworld allegorizes the creative process while Saint-Martin deplores the overproduction of books. I have not been able to establish if Saint-Martin knew the *Marriage of Heaven and Hell*, but the limited circulation of Blake's work makes this conjecture unlikely.

the core of what is usually considered Enlightenment's success: its formidable philosophical and scientific advances.

One of the most sensational episodes illustrates the ineptitude and impotence of scholars when confronted with a catastrophic threat requiring immediate action. When an academic decree orders them to search all libraries to explain the apparition of the crocodile, "une plaie tomba subitement sur tous les livres" [a plague fell on all books], a mysterious humidity turning all books, all over France, into a gray, soft mush (136). At the same time, a legion of women looking like wet nurses appears in every scholarly meeting place. Armed with spoons, they feed the mushy paste to the voracious scholars. The scholars react, says the narrator, "avec une telle confusion de pensées et de langage, que la tour de Babel, en comparaison, était un soleil de clarté; parce que tous parlaient ensemble, et que chacun parlait de toutes les sciences à la fois" [with such confusion of thought and language that the tower of Babel by comparison seemed a sun of clarity, because all spoke together and everyone spoke at the same time of all the sciences] (137). A member of the Academy, who may have eaten more than his colleagues, begins an apparently incoherent speech: for a dozen pages, readers are treated to a Rabelaisian parody of scholarly discourse merging the scientific and literary, in a burlesque collage of references (138–49). Although language seems to collapse into gibberish, the narrator has warned us that one may glimpse truth amid the academician's ramblings. For instance, the latter interjects that man's soul, though immortal, has become a night moth consumed by anxiety (142). He describes three afflictions impeding action, three metaphoric obstacles to eliminating the beast and cleansing the mirror of truth: people are sleepwalking (the crocodile keeps their heads under their wings—"la tête sous l'aile"); philosophers are babbling; and scientists are blind (145). Several episodes in the story parody the scientific obsession with description and measurement.[56] Naturalists, for instance, only describe the visible in nature and fail to satisfy our need to understand the invisible (104). Whereas the search for origins should prevail, scientists have hidden nature behind abstract scaffolding (225). We have learnt that the crocodile's belly holds a menagerie of phony scholars (housed in chicken pens), who have mutilated the sciences and deceived men; the crocodile employs them to perpetrate lies (177). As he boasted in his scientific discourse upon his appearance in Paris:

---

[56]   As early as 1761, when he published in French his *Essai sur l'étude de la littérature / An Essay on the Study of Literature* (London, 1994), a young Edward Gibbon cautioned against the tendency of the French "esprit philosophique" to drift toward an "esprit géomètre" (88–9). When Gibbon pitched Montesquieu against d'Alembert (109–10), or when he urged a middle ground between equally extreme philosophical speculations that view mankind as "either too systematical or too capricious," governed solely by geometric reason or by caprice (110–12), he was defending a conception of "l'esprit philosophique" whose moderation, penetration and attention to origins might have appealed to Saint-Martin (89–90). Gibbon later favored the French Revolution before denouncing its destructive violence.

[J]'ai fait professer aux philosophes de ce siècle toutes ces doctrines qui ont appris aux hommes que tout n'était rien; que les corps pensaient, et que la pensée ne pensait point; que l'on n'avait pas besoin de recourir à un sens moral pour expliquer l'homme; mais qu'il fallait seulement lui apprendre à faire des idées. (133)

[I made this century's philosophers profess all those doctrines that taught men that all was nothing, that bodies were thinking, and minds were not; that we did not need to invoke moral sense to explain humankind but that men could simply be taught to produce ideas.]

The doctrines of materialism, sensualism, atheism, and *encyclopédisme* are conflated in a systematic accusation (void of nuance), confirming Robert Amadou's verdict that the book mainly sought to denounce "les erreurs de la pensée moderne."[57] A particularly self-deprecating comment in the mouth of an academician encapsulates Saint-Martin's illuminist view that his century was extinguishing the light: "Car nous sommes un peu semblables aux rats, qui s'introduisent dans les temples, qui y boivent l'huile des lampes, et détruisent par là la lumière qu'elles pouvaient répandre; et puis nous disons qu'on y voit pas clair" [For we are somewhat similar to the rats that crawl inside temples, drink the lamps' oil and thus destroy the light they shed; then we say we cannot see clearly] (145). Yet, this also grants scholars the power of self-criticism, opening the door to reform.[58] Saint-Martin, while he was indeed combating the eighteenth century in its materialist naïveté, also borrowed from the Enlightenment's philosophes.[59] Confining his position to an anti-modern, anti-rational stance counter to the Enlightenment's thrust (even if the parody at work in the allegory might encourage it) does not represent his contribution to the debate on modernity. Insofar as he adopted the same discursive pugnacity as the philosophes, Saint-Martin participated in the dynamic of the Enlightenment to escape what Kant famously defined as "un état de minorité."[60]

Silence is recommended to the wise few. One character's most hopeful academic experience is the revelation of an academic "chaire de silence" in the imaginary city of Atalante. The evil effects of misguided scholarship are one of the primary concerns of the allegory. Did the obsession for rationality lead to revolutionary excesses? Saint-Martin's more subtle answer is that alienation results from the "faux usage de la liberté de l'homme" and induces violence (225). One of allegory's strongest assets is the ability to reveal and conceal simultaneously,

---

[57]   Amadou, preface to *Le Crocodile*, 23.

[58]   The same self-critical academician admits that his colleagues are probably not so much against the name and idea of God, than they are against its "teinte capucineuse" [its Capuchin layer], from "capucin," the Franciscan religious order whose corruption tainted the sacred name. Saint-Martin, *Le Crocodile*, 149.

[59]   See Sekrecka, *Louis-Claude de Saint-Martin*, 45.

[60]   Immanuel Kant, "Réponse à la question 'Qu'est-ce que les Lumières?'"(1784), in *Œuvres philosophiques* (Paris, 1985), vol. 2, 209–17.

as evident in the evocation of Atalante. Among the persons frozen in time whom Ourdeck discovers, their words inscribed above their heads, are a preacher in a temple and a hierophant in his cave, located "rue des Singes." The visitor Ourdeck realizes that the preacher was a hypocrite whose double-speak he can see as a dual stream of words which he follows through the littered and narrowing street to the hierophant's chair in an underground temple of symbolic proportions and ritual objects, including chained iron monkeys on an altar (203). A horrified Ourdeck understands that the hierophant's goal consisted in "faire anéantir l'ordre de toutes choses, et d'établir à sa place un ordre fictif, qui ne fût qu'une fausse figure de la vérité" [to annihilate the order of all things and establish in its place a fictitious order, which would be a false image of truth] (205). A soon as Ourdeck reads that a holy and respectable man will overthrow the scheme of these enemies, he desires to know his identity so much that, as the name Eléazar appears, it brings to life the two iron monkeys who in a few minutes multiply, devour the assembled disciples and the hierophant (after plucking out his eyes), then devour one another without leaving traces (205).[61] Such an extraordinary scene is open to interpretation, for the hierophant and his initiated could equally represent priests, black magicians, rationalists, or revolutionary ideologues, with the latter's reciprocal extermination during the Terror a possible referent for this suggestive, cataclysmic ending.

If the Apocalypse according to Saint-Martin leads eventually to redemption, credit must be given to the forces of goodness and their pacific weapons. Wisdom, desire, faith, and knowledge constitute four constitutive virtues that help the characters triumph over the crocodile. Eléazar "le digne Israélite" who often cites Solomon, embodies wisdom. Particularly noteworthy is the clue that Eléazar was formerly an intimate friend of an Arab scholar "de la race des Ommiades réfugiés en Espagne, depuis l'usurpation des Abbassides" and that one of his Arab friend's ancestors had known Las Casas who transmitted him secret powers.[62] The text insists on the essential confluence of Hebrew, Arab, and Christian heritage within the story's most sacred and spiritual protagonist, whose mysterious magical powder was invented by the Arab scholar (219). Eléazar's wisdom rests in this triple religious and cultural heritage, a significant message on Saint-Martin's part

---

[61] See striking similarities between this episode and the end of Blake's fourth "Memorable Fancy" in the *Marriage of Heaven and Hell*: "in it [one of seven brick houses] were a number of monkeys, baboons, & all of that species chaind by the middle, grinning and snatching at one another, but withheld by the shortness of their chains: however I saw that they sometimes grew numerous, and then the weak were caught by the strong and with a grinning aspect, first coupled with & then devourd, by plucking off first one limb and then another till the body was left a helpless trunk. this after grinning & kissing it with seeming fondness they devourd too; and here & there I saw one savourily picking the flesh off of his own tail; as the stench terribly annoyed us both we went into the mill, & I in my hand brought the skeleton of a body, which in the mill was Aristotle's Analytics." *The Complete Poetry and Prose of William Blake*, 42.

[62] See Ricard, *Étude sur le Crocodile*, 25. According to Diderot's *Encyclopédie*, the "Ommiades" was the name of princes from an ancient Arabic dynasty.

concerning his belief in the peaceful coexistence and reciprocal enrichment of faiths and cultures.

Desire, incarnated by Sédir, is Saint-Martin's code word throughout his mystical writings to urge us to seek truth. Desire is expression as well as action, the aspiration to be intimate with and understand the human spirit. When the mysterious jewel maker/invisible man proclaims, "Sédir, levez-vous" [Rise, Sédir], Sédir rises to defeat the monster, free the sciences, thus returning peace and abundance to Paris (233). The traveler Ourdeck, who courageously volunteered to defend Paris, embodies another manifestation of desire as a slow process of initiation and awakening for those who were initially skeptical. Tellingly, the antepenultimate canto celebrates the end of Ourdeck's journey toward faith and knowledge. As a reward, the magic power of his desire draws Rachel near him, happily ending the story with their marriage's celebration (245).

Madame Jof, as the incarnation of Faith, sustained and supported Ourdeck during his trials. Faith offers the possibility of belief in higher truths, invisible to the naked eye. Her ubiquitous powers make her "une veritable cosmopolite" [a genuine cosmopolitan] (87), another reminder that the spiritual trumps cultural and religious particularisms. The Society of Independents, which she heads, is a virtual assembly whose members communicate and see one another regardless of distance (87). Her speech to the Society's fellows didactically rephrases the various points illustrated by the story. Paris is punished by shortages and famine because her citizens ignored a more essential and spiritual hunger; prodigies have dazzled and scared them because Parisian scholars and doctors neither are searching for genuine knowledge nor have the right minds to do so: they can contemplate the universe's marvels but not unlock the secret of its existence (88). Madame Jof laments atheists, who do not recognize a divine principle, and false prophets, but reserves her harshest blame for priests (90). She remarks that writers who are the friends of truth have had to hide it under emblems and allegories "tant ils craignaient de la profaner et de l'exposer à la prostitution des méchants" [because they fear so much to desecrate and expose it to the prostitution of the wicked], thereby revealing the reason behind Saint-Martin's hermetic fiction and its singular allegorical framework (90).

The ill-received *Le Crocodile* has suffered from comparison with Saint-Martin's most acclaimed work, *L'Homme de désir*. In a retrospective self-critique, Saint-Martin pitched the cold, methodic rigor and logic at play in *Le Crocodile* against the lively enthusiasm of *L'Homme de désir*.[63] This admission of failure, however humble, has a lacuna. Saint-Martin does not invoke the Revolution as the historical event that prompted *Le Crocodile* in the first place. "L'enthousiasme" of *L'Homme de désir* (begun in 1787, finished in 1788, and published anonymously in 1790) is pre-Revolutionary, whereas the sprawling allegory of the war between good and evil was composed in 1792—the only fiction Saint-Martin wrote after 1789 taking the Revolution as its source as well as its subject. Could not

---

[63] Saint-Martin, "Du style en général," *Œuvres posthumes*, 2 vols (Paris, 1986), 120–21.

allegory, in its supposed chilliness, be the sole available poetic device capable of confronting the systematic spirit and crimes of the Terror? Could the optimistic, enthusiastic poetic prose of *L'Homme de désir* convey fury, bloodshed, hunger, or mere academic obtuseness? Faced with the very modern question of how poetry confronts disaster, Saint-Martin chose allegory to convey what Maurice Blanchot calls "l'ébranlement de la rupture" [the jolt of rupture], to speak of absence, and to capture an event, imperfectly, without guaranteed meaning.[64]

Le Crocodile addresses the fragmentation and destruction of the totality of history. By contrast, the pre-revolutionary *L'Homme de désir* carries the hope of a true totality of experience, as suggested by its unifying symbolism. The Revolution was a rupture, the Terror devastating. In their wake, Saint-Martin no longer chose symbolism but allegory. Paul de Man envisions symbolism and allegory as two discursive strategies available to modernist poets: he showed how the Romantic poets reacted to the rupture of modernity not only with the rhetorical choice of symbolism, to capture a lost unity for which they yearned, but also with allegories that represented and emphasized the experience of laceration. Allegory as "an alternative rhetorical procedure to symbolism ... renounces any nostalgic attempt at recomposition, is bitterly pessimistic, [and] lucidly catastrophic."[65] Saint-Martin's theosophy should not be confined to its illuminist sphere but extended to encompass a darker, allegorical world, for each conveys wisdom, each offers a road to knowledge. Is Enlightenment a symbol or an allegory? We tend to interpret the Enlightenment as a symbol of the triumph of knowledge and reason. But we know there co-existed a less-rational, *allegorical* Enlightenment, full of disruptions and disunities, the most irreversible and traumatic being the Revolution itself.

Eschatology

The call for spiritual reformation at the core of quietism and illuminism turned more somber at the dawn of the nineteenth century, when eschatology made a striking comeback. The Enlightenment's fascination with mythology continued, except that myths now related the end of the world, not its creation or Golden Age, the destruction of humanity not its fulfillment, and the overcoming of life by death. If in Genesis, death enters the world when man oversteps the confines of his knowledge, eschatological visions seem to present the extreme consequences of the knowledge unbound by Enlightenment thinkers. Once again, the question of an appropriate form to convey a message neither fit for a novel or neoclassical verse gets resolved with the choice of prose poetry. Reminiscent of Milton's epic tone, Pierre-Claude-Victor Boiste's *L'univers poëme en prose en douze chants* (1801)— it became *L'univers, narration épique* in 1804 with 30 books—seeks to integrate

---

[64]   Maurice Blanchot, *L'Écriture du désastre* (Paris, 1980), 155.

[65]   On allegory, see Benjamin, *The Origin of German Tragic Drama*; and Paul de Man, "The Rhetoric of Temporality" in Charles S. Singleton ed., *Interpretation: Theory and Practice* (Baltimore, 1969), 173-209.

history, religion, ethics, poetry and the sciences, a formidable ambition that makes it one of the richest and most challenging prose poems. Unusual features include footnotes and endnotes explaining various scientific, philosophic, moral or religious issues; explicit references to the Revolution and the Terror; vivid descriptions of natural phenomena and wonders; graphic violence mixed with allegorical figures; dichotomies such as spirit vs. matter, peace vs. war, good vs. evil, eternity vs. contingency; and a didactic message of anti-materialism, anti-atheism, anti-terrorism, *and* universalism. This epic on chaos and death attempts to answer the question of how to represent and make sense of violence in nature and among human beings, but the sheer accumulation of events in the seemingly endless narrative suggests a baroque fascination of the kind analyzed by Benjamin in German baroque dramas. The epic ends quite abruptly in a paradise of immortality thanks to religion which comes to the rescue of reason. The happy endings of Saint-Martin's and Boiste's prose poems could be interpreted as a strategy to contain both violence and a *parole* out of control.

Let us turn to a final example, Cousin de Grainville (1746–1805), who fought relentlessly against the philosophes, was bankrupt by the Revolution, "one of the clergy who were forced to marry during the Terror, and under the Empire ... suffered the social ostracism experienced by the priests who had broken their vows."[66] He committed suicide after composing *Le Dernier homme*. General indifference greeted the book when published posthumously in 1805, and again in 1811 when recovered and prefaced by an admirer, Charles Nodier.[67] Sharing the fate of other Enlightenment prose poems, it now rests in oblivion, despite its fascinating subject, imaginative narrative, and vivid imagery. In Nodier's view, the text's complete lack of paratext and generic indeterminacy explains public disregard;[68] this confirms the amphibious existence ("existence amphibie") that threatens such works, to quote once more the journalist/critic Bitaubé. Nodier underlines how Grainville's prose narrative is eminently poetic by virtue of a unique kind of "merveilleux" and an entirely original premise, "un sujet ... échappé [à la poésie], et qu'elle n'avoit même pas semblé prévoir" [a subject escaped from poetry, which poetry did not seem to have anticipated]: the fate of the last man and woman left on earth (Omégare and Sydérie), the death of humankind, and the destruction of the planet—an imaginary representation of the Apocalypse mirroring Milton's representation of Genesis (ix–x). To compensate for Grainville's absent paratext, Nodier situated the text "just below Klopstock,"

---

[66]   Clayton, *The Prose Poem in French Literature of the Eighteenth Century*, 95. See also 96–7.

[67]   Jean-Baptiste-François-Xavier Cousin de Grainville, *Le Dernier Homme* (1805; 2nd ed., 1811), ed. Charles Nodier (Geneva, 1976). See also Charles Nodier, *Les Méditations du cloître* (1803) in *Romans de Charles Nodier* (Paris, 1850) for an example of lyrical, philosophical meditation on ruins.

[68]   Charles Nodier, "Observations préliminaires du nouvel éditeur," in Grainville, *Le Dernier Homme*, vj–vii. Hereafter cited in text.

then carefully delineated the work's position with respect to sources (Milton), generic affiliation (an epic poem), and indispensable fictional elements such as the marvelous (vj–viii). Readers are left to discover on their own the more radical aspects of *Le Dernier homme*. Cosmic presages announce earth's last day: "Toutes les comètes ... se rapprochent de la terre et rougissent le ciel de leurs chevelures épouvantables; le soleil pleure, son disque est couvert de larmes de sang" [Comets are all getting closer to the earth and their dreadful plumes redden the sky; the sun is crying, its disk covered with tears of blood] (79–80). The first canto ends with foreboding suspense: "Le soleil commençoit à s'élever sur l'horizon, aucun nuage ne voiloit l'azur du firmament, et cette journée étoit belle pour la décadence du monde" [The sun was rising on the horizon, no clouds veiled the azure of the sky, and it was a beautiful day for the world's decadence] (32). Allegories no longer seem classical but vividly tragic. In Death's cave, the narrator sees Time personified: "A ma droite, aux pieds d'une colonne de diamant, est enchaîné un vieillard robuste dont les épaules sont mutilées et qui regarde avec douleur les éclats d'une horloge brisée, et deux ailes sanglantes sur la terre étendue" [To my right, at the foot of an adamantine column, a strong old man is held in chains, his shoulders mutilated, who looks sorrowfully at the fragments of a broken clock and two bloodied wings spread on the ground] (5). Classical and biblical sources echo in the characters' tragic fate: Omégare, the last man, cannot bear to sacrifice the last woman who is bearing his child despite a prediction of parricide. He meets Adam, who, knowing the fateful consequence of this progeny, is prey to unbearable suffering: "son corps à demi renversé par les souffrances, et sa bouche ouverte, comme s'il exhaloit des cris, il l'entend prononcer d'une voix lamentable ces paroles: *Je recommence des siècles de tourmens*" [His body, half-bent with suffering, his mouth open, as if exhaling shouts, he heard him pronounce this pitiful lament: *I begin anew centuries of torments*] (74). Disaster is represented with striking sobriety: "Paris n'étoit plus: la Seine ne couloit point au milieu de ses murs; ses jardins, ses temples, son louvre ont disparu. D'un si grand nombre d'édifices qui couvroient son sein, il n'y reste pas une chétive cabane où puisse reposer un être vivant. Ce lieu n'est qu'un désert, un vaste champ de poussière, le séjour de la mort et du silence" [Paris was no longer: the Seine no longer ran through her walls; her gardens, temples, Louvres museum had disappeared. From the great number of buildings that covered her heart, not even a fragile cabin remains where a living being could find shelter. This place is but a desert, a vast field of dust, the sojourn of death and silence] (85). Sterility and death reverse the common trope of *locus amoenus*:

> De quel étonnement le père des humains [Adam] est frappé, lorsqu'il voit les plaines et les montagnes dépouillées de verdure, stériles et nues comme un rocher; les arbres dégénérés et couverts d'une écorce blanchâtre, le soleil, dont la lumière étoit affaiblie, jeter sur ces objets un jour pâle et lugubre. Ce n'étoit point l'hiver et ses frimas qui répandoit cette horreur sur la nature. Jusque dans cette saison cruelle, elle conservoit une beauté mâle, et cette vigueur qui promet une fécondité prochaine, mais la terre avoit subi la commune destinée. Après

avoir lutté pendant des siècles contre les efforts du temps et des hommes qui l'avoient épuisée, elle portoit les tristes marques de sa caducité. (20–21)

[How astonished was the father of mankind when he behold valleys and mountains stripped of greenery, sterile and barren like a rock; degenerated trees, covered with whitish bark; and the sun whose light had weakened, casting a pale, dismal light on these objects. It was not wintry weather that cast such horror upon nature. Even in this cruel season, she kept a manly beauty and vigor that promised future fecundity. But the earth had succumbed to the general destiny. After fighting for centuries against the efforts of time and men which exhausted it, she carried the sad bearings of its decay.]

The end is announced with tragic eloquence: "Il dit d'une voix triste: *le dernier jour de la terre commence* ... le temps, après avoir tout dévoré, va finir et céder à l'éternité" [He said with a sad voice: *the last day of the earth is beginning* ... time, after consuming everything, is about to end and yield to eternity] (102); "On entend dans l'air une voix lugubre qui s'écrie: Le genre humain est mort" [you can hear in the air a dismal voice shouting: Humankind is dead] (167). There is great shock value to Grainville's narrative as it appropriates the set pieces of the Fénelonian prose poem to serve the most dismal story lines, substituting the soothing vision of a Golden Age for its antithesis: the torment, not of the Fall, but of mankind's disappearance, which prefigures Grainville's own suicide. Édouard Guitton's incisive judgment understands both the unusual and brilliant character of this forgotten work: "Cet ouvrage, épopée en prose bizarre et échevelée, traversée de visions eschatologiques (la mort de la lune, le refroidissement du soleil, la décadence de la terre, la disparition de la vie, la conflagration finale), est une des productions les plus originales de l'époque impériale" [This work, a wild and bizarre epic poem in prose, filled with eschatological visions (the moon's death, the sun's cooling off, earth's decadence, life's disappearance, and the final conflagration) is one of the most original productions of the imperial era.][69] Grainville subverted the aesthetic attraction of graveyard poetry and ruins, which prevailed at the end of the century: earth's decay, general and inescapable, implied decadence, mortality and mankind's disappearance. On earth's last day, no more ruins remain, only ashes. Unlike ruins, which still preserve interpretable traces, ashes bespeak the obliteration of signs, the demise of the Enlightenment's epistemological project, the annihilation of meaning. Like Saint-Martin's and Boiste's allegories of disaster, though in a more pessimistic vein, Grainville channeled his eschatological vision through a poetic genre that dissented from philosophical and aesthetic positivism.

---

[69] Edouard Guitton, *Jacques Delille (1738–1813) et le poème de la nature en France de 1750 à 1820* (Paris, 1974), 461–2.

Chapter 7
New Rhythms

Le sauvage est plus avancé que toi dans l'ordre éternel des choses;
il appelle l'écriture, *le papier qui parle*, et toi, tu ne veux pas que les mots
parlent.

[The savage is more advanced than you in the eternal order of things;
he calls writing *paper that speaks*, but you do not want words to speak.]

Louis Sébastien Mercier[1]

Enlightenment prose poems have been off limits to recent scholarship because
their neoclassical aesthetic clashes with an established canon of daring eighteenth-
century fiction and drama. While seemingly "kitsch" and self-conscious from a
post-Romantic perspective, their poetics embodies the development of a different
kind of Enlightenment critique from the one with which we are familiar, a critique
carried through the prism of a heavy classical heritage. This study would not be
complete without the inclusion of three authors whose theory and practice of prose
poetry first assimilated then outgrew their century's classical proclivities: Évariste
Parny, François René de Chateaubriand, and Sébastien Mercier. My close readings
of Parny and Chateaubriand will elucidate the above epigraph, Mercier's praise
of primitive ("sauvage") eloquence and his periphrasis of writing as "paper that
speaks"—the dream of a voice no longer reading verses publicly in a salon, but
speaking directly and intimately from the page. Though still admired, the precision
of scientific prose or classically polished poetic diction lacked inspiration for
the fin de siècle. Oral cultures had more appeal than volumes of rhetoric as a
new fount of eloquence, prompting Mercier to interrupt the narrative of literary
progress: "le sauvage est plus avancé que toi dans l'ordre éternel des choses."
The quest for a voice instead of stylistics has direct implication on the standing of
prose, poetry, and verse, as Meschonnic suggests: "L'oralité comme subjectivité
neutralise également l'opposition entre prose et poésie. Elle permet de mieux
distinguer la poésie et le vers ... Si quelque chose distingue la poésie, ce n'est pas
la métaphore, mais le mode d'oralité" [Orality as subjectivity also neutralizes the
opposition between prose and poetry. It allows a better distinction between poetry
and verse ... If something distinguishes poetry, it is not metaphor but the mode of
orality.][2] Paradoxically, the oral performance delivered by authors who declaimed
their verses or read their prose in the semi-public space of the salon had become
so scripted as to be more written than spoken, more objective than subjective.

---

[1] Louis Sébastien Mercier, *Néologie ou vocabulaire de mots nouveaux, à renouveler,
ou pris dans des acceptions nouvelles* (1801), vol. 1, xx.

[2] Meschonnic, *Les États de la poétique*, 145.

It is a new kind of orality, therefore, toward which Parny, Chateaubriand, and Mercier were dreaming, tied to faraway lands and "primitive" cultures. Their new rhythms are a *provocation* aimed at re-energizing the Enlightenment—from the Latin *provocatio*, to call out.[3]

In 1770, the poet Jean-François de Saint-Lambert introduced lyrical songs in a prose narrative published anonymously, "Les Deux Amis: conte iroquois," featuring three short "chansons" couched in a style strikingly similar to the songs later showcased in Marmontel's *Les Incas; ou la destruction de l'empire du Pérou* (1777), Évariste Parny's *Chansons madécasses* (1787), and Chateaubriand's *Atala* (1801).[4] Instead of his familiar descriptive verses (see *Les Saisons*), which were falling short of his lyrical ideal, Saint-Lambert inserted Indian songs to construct a "primitive" utterance as a source of natural, spontaneous, metaphoric, and rhythmic poetry. As Roger Little pointed out, repetition, symmetry, refrains, and typographical markers (indentation and quotation marks) compensated for the absence of rhymes, a license imputable to pseudo-translation.[5] In addition to poetic diction, the subject matter of Saint-Lambert's three songs likely helped shape the lyrics sung by Marmontel's Inca characters, Parny's islanders, and Chateaubriand's Indians, undeniably similar in form and inspiration to Saint-Lambert's. In the three authors, one hears an echo of the farewell song from Saint-Lambert's Iroquois woman to her suitors, the prisoner's song, and a young man's melancholy love song.[6] What was the origin of the commonly held belief in the ease and natural talent that all primitives supposedly share for poetry? The notion of primitive eloquence had long been part of rhetoric (to say more with less), and as we have seen, a renewed poetic reading of the Old Testament brought forth a respected example in mid century. The evolution of travel literature from narrating exploratory ventures to an ethnographic and encyclopedic recording based on methodical observation and archeological digs also fueled the fascination with native oral cultures. A new era began when authors drew examples of primitive eloquence from a more direct experience with non-European civilizations: Chateaubriand explored the American wilderness, while Parny hailed from one of France's colonial territories, Bourbon island (nowadays Reunion). Contrary to the celebrated exotic descriptions of Bernardin de Saint-Pierre's *Paul et Virginie*, which have led us to ignore the conventional propriety of his characters' dialogues,

---

[3]   Diderot had searched for new rhythms in antiquity: cf. his attempt at rhythmic translation and his endorsement of Bouchaud's distinction between rhythmic vs. metric poetry. Diderot, "L'Essai sur la poésie rythmique de Bouchaud" 1er janvier 1744, in ed. Jean Varloot, *Œuvres complètes*, vol. XIII *Arts et Lettres* (Paris 1980), 420–26.

[4]   Jean-François de Saint-Lambert, *Contes américains*, ed. Roger Little (Exeter, 1997). See also Roger Little, "Quelques poèmes en prose de Saint-Lambert," *Revue d'histoire littéraire de la France* 1 (January–February 1997), 113–18.

[5]   Little, Introduction to *Contes américains*, xxx–xxxii; and Little, "Quelques poèmes en prose de Saint-Lambert," 115–17.

[6]   *Les Deux Amis. Conte iroquois*, in Saint-Lambert, *Contes américains*, 30; 42–3; 49.

Parny's *Chansons madécasses* attempted to transcribe a new mode of expression, not a new landscape. The acknowledged originality of *Paul et Virginie* should not erase Parny's contribution to the emancipation of French prose and poetry: his construction of a primitive "parole" invented a modern voice that questioned traditional poetics as radically as Bernardin de Saint-Pierre's "peintures." Yet Parny's poetic legacy has been eclipsed by French Romantics. He has been long relegated to the shadows of those he inspired the most, namely Chateaubriand, who knew his elegies by heart, and Lamartine, who composed verses *à la* Parny for ten years then later burnt them—"the great elegiac poet who dethroned Parny" according to Sainte-Beuve.[7] Specialists of eighteenth-century poetry (Menant, Delon) and theorists of French prose poetry (Bernard, Vincent-Munia) have acknowledged the importance of the *Chansons madécasses*, notably within the genealogy of the French prose poem, but few have interrogated in detail the work's singular poetics to understand how and for whom it resonated.[8]

Évarise Parny: Orality

Published in 1787, Parny's *Chansons madécasses* (i.e., from the island of Madagascar) echoed his earlier, mildly erotic, elegies. However, the *Chansons madécasses* stood out among the poet's œuvre and contemporary poems by a radically original form and content: a short, structured, non-versified poem celebrating love and denouncing the evils of war and colonialism.[9] This political message struck home again in the 1920s when two artists rediscovered Parny. In 1920, the writer Jean Paulhan published the *Chansons* in the *Nouvelle revue française* in the midst of a post-WWI craze for African culture. In 1926, the composer Maurice Ravel discovered a copy of Parny's complete works at a bookstall along the Seine, and around the same time, accepted a commission to compose a cycle of songs accompanied by flute, piano, and cello. Taking advantage of this coincidence, he set to music three of Parny's twelve songs. Paulhan and Ravel's interest in Parny underscores the interrelation of four artistic and political spheres within the *Chansons madécasses*: a poetic form new to European literature yet akin to the native ("primitive") poetry of the island; an affinity between prose poetry and

---

[7]   See Chateaubriand, *Mémoires d'outre-tombe*, vol. 1, 139. Chateaubriand also quoted lines from Parny's *Chansons* in a note to the first edition (1802) of the *Génie du Christianisme* (1934, note *a*), and borrowed a scene and exotic color for *Les Natchez*, 368–70. Charles Augustin Sainte-Beuve, "Parny," in *Portraits contemporains* (Paris, 1870), vol. 4, 440.

[8]   An exception is Catriona Seth, "Les *Chansons madécasses* de Parny: une poésie des origines aux origines du poème en prose," in eds Bernard-Griffiths, Pickering and Vincent-Munnia, *Aux Origines du poème en prose français*, 447–57.

[9]   Parny's views against slavery establish another link with the poet Saint-Lambert, who authored an anti-slavery North American tale, *Zimeo,* more somber than *Les Deux Amis.* On Saint-Lambert's importance in the abolitionist movement, see Michèle Duchet, *Anthropologie et histoire au siècle des Lumières* (Paris, 1995), 166–70 and 177–93.

music; an ambiguous exotic appeal; and lastly, a political denunciation of colonial oppression and exploitation. The first realm was brought to light by Paulhan, who had lived in Madagascar from 1908 to 1910, studied the language, and collected several hundred *hainteny*, a poetic form unique to the island.[10] Ravel, particularly drawn to the music of prose poetry, captured the second, musical realm. (He also composed a "sonatine" from three prose poems from Aloysius Bertrand's *Gaspard de la Nuit*.). Finally, the songs' exoticism attracted Paulhan and Ravel (also the famous composer of the *Boléro*, a *Spanish Rhapsody*, *Tzigane*, and Greek popular melodies) at a time when the "black continent" was rediscovered as the cradle of art, while being simultaneously subjugated and plundered by colonial rule.

One could argue that the (dis)harmony of these politico-aesthetic spheres was specific to the early twentieth century, not the Enlightenment, yet this modernist legacy helps evaluate the parallels between two periods equally eager to confront a dominant discourse, be it political or literary: both times, the point was to rejuvenate poetry with a more "authentic" voice and expose the outrageous consequences of colonial expansion, as if to offset the latter with the former. In addition, eroticism and exoticism united in a yet unheard, elegiac song, voiced in a short prose poem. Parny's "exo/poétique" juxtaposed a lyrical celebration of love and leisure with an eloquent denunciation of the evils of colonialism. This paradoxical combination of good and evil, pleasure and pain, ideal and reality—a paradox underscored by form—translated the fate of Madagascar's Creolized natives.

Creolization

Parny was Creole by birth, white by race, and French by education. During the eighteenth and nineteenth centuries, the noun and adjective *Creole* designated a white person born on the American continent or in the tropics.[11] This definition, which excluded other races, was eventually contested in the famous 1989 manifesto *Éloge de la créolité*, signed by Jean Bernabé, Patrick Chamoiseau, and Raphaël Confiant: in reality, anyone, white or black transplanted onto the islands was a Creole. Traditional definitions had drawn up lists of the Creole character's paradoxical qualities and flaws: indolence and lively imagination, languor and vivacity, idleness and passion—clichés echoed by Chateaubriand in his portrait of Parny. [12] Although the *Chansons madécasses*'s characters seem to match these stereotypical representations, Parny unfolded a more problematic picture before his readers, the complex socio-cultural process of "Creolization." As defined by Bernabé, Chamoiseau, and Confiant, Creolization corresponds to a double process

---

[10]   See Jean Paulhan, *Les Hain-teny merinas.* 1913 (Paris, 2007). For a comprehensive study, see Leonard Fox, *Hainteny. The Traditional Poetry of Madagascar* (Lewisburg, 1990).

[11]   See article "Créole" in Diderot's *Encyclopédie*, which indicts the dangers of social inequality bred by colonialism (vol. 4, 453–4).

[12]   See the ethnocentric article "Créole," in Pierrre Larousse's *Grand dictionnaire universel du XIXeme siècle* and Chateaubriand, *Mémoires d'outre-tombe*, vol. 1, 139.

"d'adaptation des Européens, des Africains et des Asiatiques au Nouveau Monde; de confrontation culturelle entre ces peuples au sein d'un même espace, aboutissant à la création d'une culture syncrétique dite créole" [the adaptation of Europeans, Africans, and Asians to the New World; and their cultural confrontation within the same space, leading to the creation of a syncretic culture called Creole.][13] With radical modernity, the *Chansons madécasses* explored the suffering and hardships created by this confrontation, the difficulty of speaking as a master while being a victim, the disturbing paradoxes of cross-cultural exchange. Uniting Rousseau's uncorrupted *bon sauvage* and Bernardin de Saint-Pierre's Occidentalized characters, Parny created a Creolized persona shaped by a lingering primitivism and contaminating European influence. Torn by joy and sorrow, good and bad fortunes, pleasure and pain, the hybrid, Creolized character, oscillating between nature and culture, figured the Enlightenment's divided subject. Further, the irreversible losses and dubious gains at the core of *créolité* [Creoleness] combined in an equivocal pleasure similar to the mixed pleasure experienced amid ruins and graveyards, of which the late eighteenth century was so fond. But the poet subsumed these divisions and tensions by choosing a poetic form itself hybrid and "bastard." In sum, Creolization stands as a metaphor for the aesthetic mutations provoked by the emergence of prose poetry in French literature. I adapt here the concept of the process of Creolization from the *Éloge de la créolité* to turn it into a metaphor for the poeticizing of prose.

A revealing detail has escaped most commentators: the frontispiece of the first edition of *Poésies érotiques* mentioned the Bourbon island as the place of publication, and such was the case again in the 1780 edition: "A l'Ile de Bourbon, chez Lemarié, libraire, sur le sommet des Trois Salasses" [Published on the Bourbon island, at the librarian's Lemarié, on top of the Three Salasses mountain.] This discreet and fictitious geographical precision testified, better than any exotic detail, to Parny's intention of grounding his first collection of poems to the very location where he conceived them, on the island where he met his beloved Éléonore. Like an umbilical cord, the inscription linked the manuscript to the island that engendered and nourished it. As in the case of Macpherson's *Ossian*, veracity mattered less than the appearance of authenticity. Besides a fictitious publishing location, the mention "translated into French" followed the title *Chansons madécasses*, a translation further confirmed by the "Avertissement": "J'ai recueilli et traduit quelques chansons qui peuvent donner une idée de leurs usages et de leurs mœurs. Ils n'ont point de vers; leur poésie n'est qu'une prose soignée. Leur musique est simple, douce et toujours mélancolique" [I collected and translated a few songs, which can give an idea of their customs and mores. They do not have verses; their poetry is but a polished prose. Their music is simple, sweet and always melancholy.] [14]

---

[13] Jean Bernabé, Patrick Chamoiseau, and Raphaël Confiant, *Éloge de la créolité* (Paris, 1989), 31.

[14] Évariste Parny, *Chansons madécasses*, in *Anthologie de la poésie française, XVIIIe siècle, XIXe siècle, XXe siècle*, eds. Bercot, Collot, and Seth, 335. Hereafter cited in text.

Parny, a native of the Bourbon Island, lived there until nine years old, though he returned periodically after settling in France. Since it is likely that Parny knew the traditions of the large, neighboring island, Madagascar, his transcription of the lyrics of some native songs remains plausible. Sainte-Beuve rejected this hypothesis in favor of the explanation that Parny simply invented this pseudo-native form and its exotic content, driven by his rivalry with Bernardin de Saint-Pierre—a view initially propagated by Chateaubriand.[15] The affinity between the *Chansons madécasses* and *hainteny*—so far unexplored—reveals a much more complex process whereby Parny reappropriated and transformed a native poetic heritage for a contemporary French readership. A brief definition of the main characteristics of *hainteny* will put in perspective the connection between "this extremely subtle poetic form" and Parny's *Chansons madécasses*:

> In terms of content, the majority of *hainteny* are concerned with love in all its forms and stages ... *hainteny* also treat many other universal themes, such as good and evil, wisdom and foolishness, parental love, filial devotion, war, and death. ... In general, *hainteny* are composed of lines whose meter is not determined by number of syllables, but by number of temporal accents, counted beginning with the first accented syllable. The line usually ends with a pause, but sometimes with a silence that completes the metrical foot; its length is added to the normal pause at the end of the line. Although rhyme is almost never used, assonance plays a major role in the poetic techniques of *hainteny*.[16]

Though the *Chansons madécasses* do not faithfully mirror this non-Western aesthetic, I believe the poetic horizon of *hainteny* accounts for the *Chansons*'s startling originality. In the *Chansons madécasses*, Parny established a pact with readers similar to other pseudo-translations seeking to defamiliarize them with a new mode of writing: the mediation of translation authorized a poetic genre that was not versified, as well as allowed for the author's risky, in this case anti-colonialist, opinions to be attributed to another voice. Further, unlike his fellow prose poets who imagined and "translated" virtual poetry to compose unversified poems, Parny anchored his *Chansons madécasses* in the specific, long-established, poetic tradition of Madagascar's *hainteny*. This original source not only distinguishes the *Chansons* from previous endeavors, but also explains why Parny's prose poem appears, in the corpus of the present study, as the most emancipated from classical rules, and the achievement closest to modern prose poetry. However unsettling its message, the poetic voice gained authenticity by espousing the orality common to the *hainteny* tradition and Creole culture:[17] "L'oralité créole, même contrariée

---

[15] Chateaubriand implied in a note to the *Essai sur les Révolutions* (1470, note *c*) that Parny's jealousy toward Bernardin de Saint-Pierre compelled him to write the exotic *Chansons*. Sainte-Beuve elaborated on this rivalry in his *Portraits contemporains* (vol. 4, 448). Raphaël Barquisseau reestablished the anteriority of Parny's elegies over Bernardin de Saint-Pierre's representation of love in *Les Chevaliers des îles* (Ile de la Réunion, 1990), 65.

[16] Fox, *Hainteny*, 40–41.

[17] See "Oral literature," in Fox, *Hainteny*, 34–40, and the section entitled "L'enracinement dans l'oral" in Bernabé, Chamoiseau, and Constant, *Éloge de la créolité*, 34–7.

dans son expression esthétique, recèle un système de contre-valeurs, une contre-culture; elle porte témoignage du génie ordinaire appliqué à la résistance, dévoué à la survie" [Creole orality, even when its aesthetic expression is thwarted, conceals a system of counter-values, a counter-culture; it bears testimony to ordinary genius applied to resistance, devoted to survival.][18] My claim is that in their resistance against verse, the *Chansons madécasses* promoted the counter-culture of prose and the counter-value of orality versus the written word.

A close textual study brings forth three thematic and stylistic moments in Parny's twelve cantos. "Love songs" (1, 2, 7, 8, and 12) develop an aesthetic of pleasure and leisure, and experiment with an oral poetic style. These love songs celebrate sensuality and sexuality: they were Chateaubriand's source of inspiration. By contrast, "war songs" (3, 4, 5, 6, 9, and 10) are openly political and very close to a tradition of eloquent, oratory prose. Depicting a universe mired by conflict and death, they are the sites of an ethical questioning. Eros and Thanatos alternate throughout the collection and coexist in two songs (4 and 6). Two other songs (7 and 11), invoking higher powers, escape the love/war dichotomy by turning into hopeful and anguished "prayer songs."

Love Songs

The *Chansons madécasses* open at dusk when the chief Ampanini welcomes a white stranger with a simple meal of rice, milk, and ripe fruit served on large banana leaves. Ampanini also offers his daughter for the nightly pleasures of his guest. The bed is prepared, her loincloth undone. The loincloth, made of tree leaves, becomes the last layer of the lovers' leafy bed. This image recurs in the last song when Nahandove's lover prepares his bed in the same fashion: "Le lit de feuilles est préparé; je l'ai parsemé de fleurs et d'herbes odoriférantes; il est digne de tes charmes, Nahandove, ô belle Nahandove!" [The leafy bed is ready; I have sprinkled flowers and scented herbs; it is worthy of your charms, Nahandove, o beautiful Nahandove] (183). Senses awaken at nightfall: the scented leafy bed and the gentle sounds of breathing and walking are precursors of the pleasures to come. Parny's last song is more naïve, and more directly physical than Chateaubriand's subsequent imitation: "Tes baisers pénètrent jusqu'à l'âme, tes caresses brûlent tous mes sens: arrête, ou je vais mourir. Meurt-on de volupté, Nahandove, ô belle Nahandove!" [Your kisses penetrate my soul, your caresses are burning all my senses: stop, or I shall die. Does one die of pleasure, Nahandove, o beautiful Nahandove?] (183).[19] The experience of the "petite mort," climax, is conveyed

---

[18]   Ibid., 34.

[19]   Chateaubriand transposed this scene in the second part of his novel *Les Natchez*. He intensified it by showing the naked body of the beloved emerging from the waters. He heightened the sacredness of the feminine mystery by portraying the male lover wishing to devour the leafy bed, thus penetrating the secret of the nest. But, as customary, Chateaubriand's pen stayed shy of a more detailed erotic representation. Imaginary kisses are blown in the wind, as if the power of desire escaped words. Chateaubriand, *Atala, René, Les Natchez*, 370.

with candor and simplicity. Sainte-Beuve remarked: "La passion chez Parny se présente nue et sans fard. Il n'y ajoute rien; il n'y met pas des couleurs à éblouir et à distraire du fond, il ne pousse pas non plus de ces cris à se tordre les entrailles" [Parny presents passion naked and unvarnished. He adds nothing, no splashy colors that distract from the content, nor does he shout heart-rending cries.][20] This alluded to Byron's, Chateaubriand's, and Musset's characters and their ambition to seize the impossible, embrace the infinite. Comparing Parny to the Romantics, Sainte-Beuve concluded: "Parny est moins violent et plus simplement amoureux; il est amoureux d'une personne, nullement d'un prétexte et d'une chose poétique" [Parny is less violent and more simply in love; he is in love with a person, not at all with a pretext or a poetic object.][21]

In contrast to the Christian melancholy sentiments and attitude of Chateaubriand's characters, Parny celebrated an Epicurean philosophy evident in the eighth song, which begins, "Il est doux de se coucher durant la chaleur sous un arbre touffu, et d'attendre que le vent du soir amène la fraîcheur" [It is sweet to lie down when it is hot under a leafy tree, and wait for the evening breeze to bring coolness back] (339). The rhythm of the song is punctuated by internal rhymes (chaleur/fraîcheur; baiser/volupté), repetitions ("arbre touffu'), apostrophes and imperatives addressed to women ("Femmes approchez ... occupez mon oreille ... répétez la chanson ... Allez, et préparez le repas"), and by the return of the evening breeze (339–40). To lie down, to wait, to rest: the passive verbs express the sweetness, languor, and idleness of masculine life under hot climates, while women labor to entertain and feed the hedonist beneath his tree. An economic hedonism derives from Epicurean philosophy, the pursuit of maximum satisfaction with minimum effort—even though the last song contains a warning: "Le plaisir passe comme un éclair" [Pleasure goes by in a flash] (342).

Parny, who founded a small coterie of Epicurean advocates in Paris, cherished a natural simplicity, which distinguished his poetic style. In Bernardin de Saint-Pierre's *Paul and Virginie*, the precision of exotic details in descriptions contrasts with the idealization of the discourse, always proper, courteous, sincere, and uniform.[22] On the contrary, the décor of the *Chansons madécasses* remains vague, almost stylized—a mountain range, a plain—closer to an image of eternity than "tropicality." But the "lyrics" of the *Chansons madécasses* are always direct, precise, with variable tone colors, in turn realist, loving, violent, sensuous, tragic, and passionate. The exotic character of the *Chansons madécasses* does not reside in rare descriptions, but in speech acts: local color is nested in dialogues and monologues.

---

[20]   Sainte-Beuve, Preface to *Œuvres de Parny. Élégies et poésies diverses* (1862), xvii–xviii. This preface is included in the fifteenth volume of the *Causeries du lundi*, 285–300.

[21]   Ibid., xii–xiii.

[22]   Chateaubriand erased references to Parny's *Chansons madécasses* in favor of Bernardin de Saint-Pierre's *Paul and Virginie* the better to illustrate his apology of religion in subsequent editions of the *Génie du Christianisme*. *Paul et Virginie* stood as the epitome of a Christian fiction thanks to its topic, characters, morality, and tragic denouement, unlike the happy Epicurean sensualists of the last "chanson madécasse." Chateaubriand thought that Bernardin owed to Christianity his talent to paint nature. *Génie du Christianisme*, 706.

Since the female body is the avowed site of desire, the surrounding landscape is not the pretext for subconscious projections, as is famously the case in *Paul and Virginie*. Beauty, desire, and pleasure are openly celebrated, in harmony with the surrounding nature. Chateaubriand, for his part, later pushed the symbiotic universe of the songs toward symbolism, multiplying comparisons, which slowly edged toward metaphors. By contrast, Parny turned his back on rhetoric for the sake of greater effects, hence the striking sobriety of his songs. Apostrophes are all directed at persons, not the abstract, allegorical entities of contemporary poetry. Syntactical structure is simplified to the extreme, with no subordinate constructions and rare conjunctions. Sentences remain short; pauses are frequent and marked by a strong punctuation, which gives each song a rhythm in accord with its subject. For instance, the couplets in the twelfth song are balanced by the echo of internal rhymes ("sommeil/réveil," "languir/désir") and repetitions: "Que le sommeil est *délicieux* dans les bras d'une maîtresse! moins *délicieux* pourtant que le réveil. Tu pars, et je vais *languir* dans les regrets et les désirs; je *languirai* jusqu'au *soir*; tu reviendras ce *soir*, Nahandove, ô belle *Nahandove*!" [Sleep is so *sweet* in the arms of a lover! yet less *sweet* than waking up. You leave, and I will *languish* with regret and desire; I will *languish* until *tonight*. You will return *tonight*, Nahandove, o beautiful Nahandove!] (342, emphasis added).

The strophic arrangement, the periodic return of the apostrophe "Nahandove," and the echoing name of the beloved, structure the text like a poem. The musical effects of the *Chansons madécasses* invalidate Sainte-Beuve's criticism against Parny, unfavorably compared with Chateaubriand: "c'est un poëte que Parny, ce n'est pas un enchanteur: il n'a pas la magie du pinceau. Il n'est pas de force à créer son instrument" [Parny is a poet, not an enchanter; he does not have a magic brush. He does not have the vigor to create his instrument.][23] The comment, grounded in the classical conception of poetry as painting, failed to perceive Parny's originality. Parny did not paint like Bernardin de Saint-Pierre or Chateaubriand; he conceived poetry as akin to music. "Like music, prose" and no longer *ut pictura poesis*. The reader sees less than he hears: when Ravel transposed the text into a musical score, he took the title "chansons" literally.

The relationship between the sexes in the *Chansons madécasses* is loving but also conflicted. In the second song, the father uses his daughter as an object of exchange, a gift of welcome in his dealing with the white stranger, like Orou offering his daughters to the priest in Diderot's *Supplément au Voyage de Bougainville*. The power exerted by men over women is center-stage in songs VII and X, which conclude with opposite results. The seventh song is the collection's turning point. Charmed by the prisoner Vaïna's beauty, the king Ampanini wants to become her lover. Touched by her tears, he renounces his desire and lets her go. Ampanini's kindness contrasts with his cruelty toward his lover Yaouna, whom he catches in the arms of another man (song X). The chief punishes the affront by killing the two lovers. The violent and barbarous crime of jealousy questions

---

[23] Sainte-Beuve, Preface to *Œuvres de Parny*, xvii.

anew the conciliatory attitude of the king in the preceding songs, as well as the atmosphere of internal peace that seemingly prevailed among his people in the first songs. The vengeful act opens up a breach in a society one might have believed to be so far harmonious. In a primitive society, fidelity is not a requisite, jealousy unknown, and marriage an aberration. How did jealousy infiltrate the society of the Madécasses?

It is obvious from the first song onward that the universe of the Madécasses is neither a utopia nor a pastoral. The simple welcome, rudimentary comfort, sparse words, and the familiar "tu," coexist within a segregated, hierarchical society. The first song mentions a king, a royal hut, a chief, and then slaves who are ordered to serve. Equality no longer exists among the Madécasses, their community is divided among free and obedient individuals. No equality but no anarchy either: everyone stays in his or her own place. In addition to class differences, racial differences become explicit in Ampanini's first words, "Homme blanc, je te rends ton salut!" [White man, I return your salute!] The distrustful initial questioning— "Viens-tu la main ouverte?" "Que cherches-tu?" [Do you come with an open hand? What are you looking for?]—suggests a past fraught with antagonisms and false promises (335). Yet, unlike the Tahitian chief's message asking Bougainville to leave in Diderot's *Supplément*, chief Ampanini offers his hospitality and remains respectful of his guest's freedom—"tes pas et tes regards sont libres" [Your steps and your gaze are free] (335).

War Songs

The young girls' songs and dances mute these subterranean conflicts, which spring up again in war songs: each stages an aspect of how exterior forces contaminate the Madécasses society, either directly in wars, or indirectly through internecine conflicts. The fifth song, the only one recounting the past, is also the only one to use a metaphor ("bouche d'airain" for cannon), marking a turn toward a more oratorical style, culminating with the eloquent repetition of the slogan "Méfiez-vous des blancs, habitants du rivage" [Beware of the white men, people of the shores] (337). The song tells the sad story of a breach of confidence leading to a war of conquest and extermination lost by the Whites. "Ils ne sont plus, et nous vivons, et nous vivons libres" [They are no longer, and we are alive, alive and free] (358). Parny expressed in this song his anti-colonialist and anti-slavery opinions without concession or compromise.[24] Ravel chose to set it to music, creating a scandal on its first performance in Paris in 1926 as Parny's perceived anti-patriotism triggered the indignant protests of 1920's venture colonialists.

Parny staged another prevailing theme of anti-slavery literature, the wars between tribes to capture prisoners for sale to Europeans.[25] The third song recounts

[24] Christian Leroy reads "Méfiez-vous des blancs" as a metapoetical denunciation of "vers blanc" [blank verse]. In *Aux origines du poëme en prose français*, eds. Bernard-Griffiths, Pickering and Vincent-Munnia, 71.

[25] See Léon-François Hoffmann, *Le Nègre romantique. Personnage littéraire et obsession collective* (Paris, 1973), 75.

such fratricides. Ampanini's swift victory is told in a few words, emphasizing the absurdity of the war: no one knows how or why it started in the first place and who the enemies are. The simplicity of the vocabulary—blood, vengeance, fall, fear, death, and ashes—endows the message with universal value (all wars resemble this one) as well as ironic skepticism (all wars are absurd). The vanity of victory is underscored by the strange final procession where the king pushes ahead mooing cattle, followed by chained prisoners, then crying women.

Father and son, mother and daughter, all fall victims to the contamination propagated by the Whites. The ninth song introduces another common theme of anti-slavery literature: a mother remains deaf to her daughter's plea because blood ties are no longer honored under the influence of the Whites who encourage parents to sell their children.[26] The dry, ineluctable concluding verdict contrasts with the filial prayers meant to soften the heart, to restore the reason and nature of a de-natured mother whose maternal instinct has been corrupted by greed.

Another pernicious and unhappy consequence of the introduction of slavery on the island of Madagascar is pictured in the enigmatic eleventh song. From the mother's tearful monologue to the god Niang, the reader guesses an infanticide, which, along with abortion, was commonly practiced by female slaves. The text does not give the explicit reason for the gesture, possibly the belief that death was better than slavery. The female voice is only heard in this eleventh song as she laments the god Niang's cruelty, god of unhappiness, catastrophe, and evil. The first prayer song, an invocation to the divinities of good and evil, had announced the fate of the unfortunate mother's child. Parny's Madécasses no longer live in a golden age: the confrontation with colonial powers has led to the perpetration of evil deeds undermining the social fabric of the family and the tribe; and the emergence of fidelity and jealousy threatens frank, natural sexuality.

In conclusion, the elegiac voice of Parny's Madécasses transformed the hackneyed theme of the Epicurean Creole into songs simpler and subtler than the rhetorical speeches of the eighteenth-century idealized "bons sauvages." Parny's "exo/poétique" explored the conflicted nature of the pleasure so often celebrated in the primitive character, and brought to the fore an intimate experience of loss and death. As the process of Creolization loosens ties with one's origins, it engenders melancholy. The young Chateaubriand experienced a similar disenchantment when he discovered America's already "corrupted" Indian savages, and the ruins of the so-called New World. But before continuing with Chateaubriand, I wish to probe briefly Parny's return to formal conservatism, and reflect on what happened to the lyrical "I" in search of a voice.

La Guerre des dieux anciens et modernes

When Voltaire returned to Paris in 1778, a few months before his death, he bestowed a public compliment onto Parny, greeting him as "mon cher Tibulle." While I have emphasized the ambivalent modernity of the *Chansons madécasses*, Voltaire

---

[26] Ibid.

and his contemporaries simply read Parny's *Poésies érotiques* as a successful revival of a classical vein. Parny shocked his admirers by publishing afterward an irreverent, anti-Christian, mock epic poem in verse, *La Guerre des dieux anciens et modernes* (1799). The year 1789 had provoked a complete reversal of fortune for Parny, the loss of financial and class privileges. Far from being a political activist, Parny avoided the revolutionary turmoil and reemerged with the publication of *La Guerre des Dieux*, an anti-clerical epic poem that went through six editions the first year, and spurred the indignation of Chateaubriand, who admittedly reacted by writing his *Génie du Christianisme*. But Parny received a "succès de scandale," not critical acclaim. A contemporary, the abbé de Féletz judged it as "le poëme le plus monstrueux et le plus révoltant qu'aient produit l'impiété, la corruption et l'immoralité" [the most monstrous and revolting poem ever invented by impiety, corruption and immorality.][27] Narrated by the Holy Spirit, the poem stages the arrival of Christian gods on Mount Olympus and their overcoming the pagan gods' resistance and opposition. Why was verse and mythology better suited than prose to convey Parny's anti-clerical audacity? To put it differently, how did Parny's choice of poetic genre and form (innovative in the case of the *Chansons*, conservative for *La Guerre*) relate to the "message" he sought to convey in these works? As with Saint-Martin, Parny's divergent poetic strategies are a direct response to their pre- and post-revolutionary context.

At first, *La Guerre des Dieux* seems proof of the crisis of verse in the eighteenth century, to borrow the phrase Mallarmé applied to his own century. Parny, who had avoided neoclassical subject matter and poetic diction in his first collection, went backward, so to speak, with a mock epic genre, a traditional versification (decasyllables) and an allegorical theme that seem to contradict or renounce his previous aesthetic forays. But Parny's second academic or conservative manner perfectly matched his didactic message, allowing him to strike harder blows in his anti-clerical fight. Therefore it is both right and wrong to speak of a crisis of verse: there was crisis in the sense that Parny's epic decasyllable was not original but often awkward like many similar contemporary poems. But the adequation of versification with message appears obvious when one focuses on its subject matter. *La Guerre des Dieux*, as an allegory, functions in an ironic mode, like Voltaire's *La Pucelle*, the model that inspired Parny: such irony thrived within traditional decasyllables and would have been incompatible with the light, lyrical and musical rhythm of his love poetry. Whether lyricism and irony are compatible is one of the great questions raised by Baudelaire's *Petits Poëme en prose* (*Spleen de Paris*) and prose poetry in general. Parny's choice to allegorize violence, vengeance, and fanaticism should be compared to Saint-Martin's similar decision for his epic *Crocodile*. In both cases, the Revolution and systematic spirit of the Terror mandated a rhetorical trope, allegory, as more fitting to speak to reason than new rhythms meant to awaken imagination and the senses (Saint-Martin's *L'Homme de désir* and Parny's *Chansons*).

---

[27] Cited by Jacques-Charles Lemaire, Introduction to *La Guerre des dieux (1799)* by Évariste de Parny (Paris, 2002), 15.

Chateaubriand's *Atala*

In the manner of Bernardin de Saint-Pierre's *Paul et Virginie* embedded in the larger, non fictional work of the *Études de la nature*, but soon published independently, Chateaubriand inserted in the *Génie du christianisme* the stories of *Atala* and *René* as "illustrations" of his main thesis and easily extracted them the better to promote their originality and showcase his talent.[28] *Atala* appeared in 1801, a year earlier than the publication of the *Génie*, and twenty-five years earlier than *Les Natchez*, its original framework. This complex genealogy—from an episode within an epic-like narrative to an illustration of an aesthetic treatise on religion, then an autonomous (and unclassifiable) story—announced as well as participated in the composite nature of *Atala*. It also shares with the lyrical punctum of the *Essai sur les revolutions*, known as "the American night," a similar source of inspiration in Chateaubriand's American journey and a common origin in his American manuscript. As an autonomous narrative it brings to light the ambivalent modernity of Chateaubriand's prose. *Atala* was composed, read, and judged as a "poëme," unlike its original companion story, *René*. Chateaubriand's formalist concerns in *Atala* may explain the different posterity of the twin stories: he attempted in *Atala* to capture the "parler sauvage," by means of what turns out to be, ultimately, a tightly controlled rhetoric; then he shifted to an unbridled expression of sentiments, embodied by René's voice. Atala did not become a prototypical Romantic character like René, despite her Romantic attributes. She is alienated like René, she commits suicide like Werther, but she has remained other, foreign, and strange in an even stranger land, the North American wilderness. Atala as a "métisse" represents a modern split subject, a new kind of heroine whose voice Chateaubriand struggled to capture. I read the conflicted poetics at the heart of the narrative, which I will now examine, as an aesthetic translation of "métissage."

Who is Atala? She is the daughter of an Indian woman who had tasted the fruit of knowledge with the Spaniard Lopez: "Avant que ma mère eût apporté en mariage au guerrier Simaghan trente cavales, vingt buffles, cent mesures d'huile de glands, cinquante peaux de castors et beaucoup d'autres richesses, elle avait connu un homme de la chair blanche" [Before my mother brought the warrior Simaghan her marriage offering of thirty mares, twenty buffaloes, a hundred measures of acorn oil, fifty beaver skins and many other riches, she had known a man of white flesh.][29] The fruit of this union—of the sin—Atala was born with a double nature, "fière comme une Espagnole et comme une Sauvage," a double heritage that remained unreconciled (127). I want to argue that the story of *Atala* allegorizes "métissage" as a fall from primitive innocence caused by the snake of colonialism. Originally published within the *Génie du christianisme* to illustrate

---

[28]   *René* belonged to *Génie du christianisme,* Part II, "Poétique du christianisme" and concluded Book III. *Atala* concluded Part III, "Beaux-Arts et Littérature."

[29]   Chateaubriand, *Atala, René, Les Natchez*, ed. Jean-Claude Berchet (Paris, 1989), 127. *Atala. René.* Trans. Irving Putter (Berkeley, 1980), 45. Hereafter cited in text.

"les harmonies de la religion chrétienne avec les scènes de la nature et les passions du cœur humain" [harmonies of the Christian religion with nature's scenes and the passions of the human heart], *Atala* paradoxically and contrary to this authorial claim, stages the *lost* harmony at the heart of Christianity, following the original sin and the fall from Paradise:[30] in lieu of classical harmony, the narrative conveys a modern hybridity.

Dual at its core, the story pitches descriptions against dialogues: innovative, original compositions translate the song of nature heard in the American wilderness (to which I will return), which vividly contrast with the characters' artificial, so-called primitive eloquence. Chateaubriand, who often referred to himself as a "sauvage," sought to recreate a sacred, inherently poetic, unmediated language in which versification had no part, particularly in *Atala*'s Indian songs: like Parny's Madécasses, their "orality" was meant to reinforce the spontaneity of the primitive voice. But Chateaubriand's attempt to confer authenticity to this voice produced a very different result, almost a mirror opposite to Parny's.

In its struggle to define the genre of the story, the preface to *Atala*'s first edition offered two apparently contradictory claims, both commonly found as justifications for breaching tradition: a claim of radical novelty, which precludes any existing category or label, and a tie to the classics and ancient tradition:

> Je ne sais si le public goûtera cette histoire qui sort de toutes les routes connues, et qui présente une nature et des mœurs tout à fait étrangères à l'Europe. Il n'y a point d'aventures dans *Atala*. C'est une sorte de poème, moitié descriptif, moitié dramatique: tout consiste dans la peinture de deux amants qui marchent et causent dans la solitude; tout gît dans le tableau des troubles de l'amour, au milieu du calme des déserts, et du calme de la religion. J'ai donné à ce petit ouvrage les formes les plus antiques; il est divisé en *prologue, récit* et *épilogue*. ... c'était ainsi que dans les premiers siècles de la Grèce, les Rhapsodes chantaient, sous divers titres, les fragments de l'*Iliade* et de l'*Odyssée*. Je ne dissimule point que j'ai cherché l'extrême simplicité de fond et de style, la partie descriptive exceptée; encore est-il vrai que dans la description même, il est une manière d'être à la fois pompeux et simple. ... Depuis longtemps je ne lis plus qu'Homère et la Bible. (43–4)

> [I do not know if the public will taste this story far from the beaten path, which shows nature and mores very alien to Europe. There are no adventures in *Atala*. It is a kind of poem, half-descriptive, half-dramatic: everything consists in the painting of two lovers who walk and talk in solitude; everything rests in the picture of troubled love, in the midst of the calm wilderness and the calm of religion. I gave this small work the most antique forms; it is divided into a prologue, narrative, and epilogue. ... this is how, in Greece's first centuries, rhapsodists sang under various titles fragments from the *Iliad* and *Odyssey*.

---

[30] See the title of Book Five, Part III of the *Génie*, 873. *Atala ou les amours de deux sauvages dans le désert* originally constituted the last chapter of Book Five. See also reference to "l'antique tradition d'une dégradation originelle," Chateaubriand, Preface to the first edition, *Atala*, 46.

I do not conceal that I sought an extreme simplicity of content and style, except for descriptions. Yet, it is true that even with descriptions, there is a way to be at the same time pompous and simple. ... For a long time I have only been reading Homer and the Bible.]

Chateaubriand introduced *Atala* as both an exotic and familiar text: the settings and characters are not European but foreign and the plot is not that of a modern novel ("point d'aventures"); however, its structure, its spare story line and alternating styles emulate classical and biblical models. This "defamiliarization" coalesces with a fragmentation of the narrative. Reference to the rhapsode's songs invokes the figure of the bard who played a central role in Chateaubriand's imagination. The bard, whose memory stores lengthy narratives, has a unique, fragmented manner of delivery, hence the name "rhapsode" used by Chateaubriand to preface a narrative fragmented in several sections ("The hunters," "The tillers"), genres (descriptive, dramatic) and discourses (primitive, modern), and itself a fragment from two larger texts (the *Génie* and *Les Natchez*). Thus the "poëme" seeks to synthesize opposite tensions (an epic-like trajectory, lyrical outbursts, descriptions) within the narrative. If this disjunction allows for stylistic plurality, akin to the multiplicity found in the Bible (*ta biblia*: les livres), the lack of cohesion in this hybrid mélange allows for a bracing stylistic experiment to reveal Chateaubriand's novel mythopoetics.

A Primitive Voice

The epilogue begins with the following remark by the narrator: "Quand un Siminole me raconta cette histoire, je la trouvai instructive et parfaitement belle, parce qu'il y mit la fleur du désert, la grâce de la cabane, et une simplicité à conter la douleur, que je ne me flatte pas d'avoir conservées" (160) [I was told this story by a Seminole, and I found it highly edifying and surpassingly beautiful, for he had put into it the flower of the wilderness, the grace of the cabin, and a simplicity in describing sorrow which I cannot boast of having preserved] (trans. 76). The sentence is a *mise en abyme* of the linguistic and aesthetic conflict at the heart of the story. The narrator's praise draws on a quintessentially classical principle, the Horacian precept of instructing while pleasing—"une histoire instructive et belle." But this is linked to two cryptic metaphors borrowed from the Indians—"la fleur du désert, la grâce de la cabane." This hybrid language, part European, part "sauvage," is meant to re-create a primitive language the ambivalence of which I will now examine in the Indian songs and dialogues in light of three commentaries: Chateaubriand's prefatory justifications, the abbé Morellet's remarks in his stinging criticism of *Atala,* and an anonymous sequel entitled *Résurrection d'Atala* (1802).[31]

---

[31] Morellet, *Observations critiques sur le roman intitulé: ATALA* (an IX). Among *Atala*'s flaws: "l'affectation, l'enflure, l'impropriété, l'obscurité des termes et des expressions, l'exagération dans les sentimens, l'invraisemblance dans la conduite et la situation des personnages, les contradictions et l'incohérence des diverses parties de l'ouvrage; enfin, et en général, tout ce qui blesse le goût et la raison" [affectation, bombast,

In his 1801 preface, Chateaubriand justified *Atala*'s composite style, or rather the storyteller's primitive voice (since the narrative was a transcription of Chactas's confession), by explaining that Chactas's "style mêlé" mirrored his equipoise "entre la société et la nature."[32] The author alternates emphasis on the social (European) and the natural (Indian): in dialogues, Chactas speaks in his native idiom whereas he narrates in his adoptive French language (the musical compositions I will soon examine belong to this second "European" style). Out of concern for his readers, the author chose not to sustain the Indian style throughout: "si je m'étais toujours servi du style indien, *Atala* eût été de l'hébreu pour le lecteur" [if I had used the Indian style throughout, *Atala* would have sounded like Hebrew to its readers] (46). There is more to this metaphor than meets the eye. Indeed it proves to be less of a metaphor (Hebrew as a metaphor for difficulty) than a motivated linguistic comparison: the Indian style was similar to Hebrew—the orientalism signaled by Lowth—the language set apart in the *Génie* as "concis, énergique." The exotic was construed like the primitive. Criticizing both Chateaubriand's goal and the phrasing of this goal, "fondre les couleurs d'Homère et de la Bible dans les teintes du désert" [merge the colors of Homer and the Bible with the shades of the wilderness], the critic Morellet exclaimed: "C'est, sans doute, un hébraïsme, et je n'entends pas l'hébreu" [It is probably a Hebrew neologism, and I do not understand Hebrew.][33] The metaphoric concision of Hebrew on which Chateaubriand based his Indian style made for an "unintelligible language" according to the critic Morellet.[34]

The problematic nature of this language drew apparently contradictory statements in Morellet's criticism: he objected to the so-called savage eloquence as "un galimathias vuide de sens, et qu'on ne peut regarder que comme le begaiement de l'enfance" [a meaningless gibberish that can only be seen as childhood babbling],[35] yet assimilated it with the most sophisticated and elaborate stylistic mannerism, "precious style."[36] The contradiction reflected Chateaubriand's own antithetical claim to be simultaneously "pompeux et simple" [pompous and simple] (44). The connection between precious and primitive styles, however paradoxical, is a key to understanding the special effects of Chateaubriand's Indian style. Both precious and primitive styles were highly figurative, for opposite reasons: in the case of *precious* language, the wealth of concrete (low) words propels a periphrastic turn of speaking; in the case of *primitive* language, a lack of conceptual words results in periphrases inspired by concrete situations. In Morellet's eyes, figurative language,

---

impropriety, obscure words and turns of phrase, exaggerated feelings, lack of verisimilitude in the characters' behavior and situation, contradictions and incoherence between the book's various sections; in sum, everything that shocks taste and reason] (5–6). A reference to Richardson's *Clarissa* and Rousseau's *Nouvelle Héloïse* placed *Atala* squarely within the context of sentimental fiction.

32   Chateaubriand, Preface to the first edition, *Atala*, 46.
33   Morellet, *Observations*, 55.
34   Ibid., 60.
35   Ibid., 65–6.
36   Ibid., 13.

regardless of its cause, had but one consequence: an exaggerated, affected style, on the brink of absurdity. In one passage (among the scores Morellet criticized) an older Chactas thus explained his shyness toward Atala: "je crois que j'eusse préféré d'être jeté aux crocodiles de la fontaine, à me trouver seul ainsi avec Atala" [I think I would have preferred being thrown to the crocodiles in the stream to being alone with Atala] (107, trans. 26). Morellet remarked sarcastically: "se donner en pâture aux crocodiles plutôt que d'éprouver l'embarras de dire, *je vous aime*, est une hyperbole amoureuse, dont on ne trouveroit pas le pendant dans tous les romans de la Calprenède et de Scudéry" [to be devoured by crocodiles rather than experience the embarrassment of saying *I love you*, is a hyperbole of passion whose equivalent could not be found in all Calprenède's and Scudéry's novels] (15).[37] The comparison with the "precious" Scudéry might seem incongruous when considering Chateaubriand's style (based on volume and rhythm), yet it captured the artificial, periphrastic quality of the recreated Indian voice, which brought later generations of readers to dethrone *Atala* in favor of *René*. It also brings attention to the unseemly yet indisputable influence of Scudéry on Chateaubriand: let us remember that his mother knew *Le Grand Cyrus* by heart.[38]

At the core of the primitive language elaborated by Chateaubriand as well as his predecessors (including Parny) laid a paradox: metaphors and periphrasis, which were believed to abound in primitive language due to its limited vocabulary and proximity to nature, eventually became rhetorical figures of speech, which retrospectively made primitive voices seem supremely eloquent. Witness Parny's "bouche d'airain" [bronze mouth] for cannon. Attempts at reconstructing a primitive, natural idiom were bound to seem contrived: "the natural" was an artificial, illusory, construction. Morellet tore the veil of illusion by asking bluntly: "N'est-on pas tenté de prier l'auteur de se *démétaphoriser?*" [Are we not tempted to ask the author to *demetaphorize?*][39] The question betrayed the critic's conception of poetic eloquence and his misunderstanding of Chateaubriand's purpose. Analyzing primitive language, Max Milner explained how it had the potential to upset the traditional theory and practice of poetry considered as "une forme raffinée du bien-dire: l'art d'agrémenter et d'ennoblir, à l'aide de figures choisies et de sonorités harmonieuses, l'expression de pensées ou de sentiments correspondant à une réalité épurée ou idéale" [a refined form of eloquence: the art of embellishing and ennobling, with chosen figures and harmonious tones, the expression of thoughts or feelings corresponding to an ideal or purified reality.][40] By contrast,

> l'idée d'une langue primitive, exprimant d'instinct le sens sacré des choses, naturellement anthropomorphique, parce que la vie du primitif est encore à moitié engagée dans la nature, devait donner l'idée d'une poésie où l'expression

---

[37]   Jean-Claude Berchet cites part of Morellet's comment in a note to the passage, and concurs with the comparison to precious style. Chateaubriand, *Atala*, 617n107.

[38]   Chateaubriand, *Mémoires*, I, 16.

[39]   Morellet, *Observations*, 24.

[40]   Max Milner, *Le Romantisme, 1820–1843* (Paris, 1973), 105.

figurée ne serait pas le fruit d'un raffinement de civilisation, mais la traduction d'un rapport substantiel entre l'homme et la réalité transcendante. ... Le mythe, la personnification des forces de la nature, le symbole, la métaphore ne résultaient donc pas d'un jeu de l'esprit, mais d'une saisie intuitive de la situation de l'homme dans le monde.[41]

[the idea of a primitive language—naturally anthropomorphic because primitive life is still half ensconced in nature— expressing the sacred meaning of things, was meant to give an idea of a poetry where figurative expression would not be the fruit of a refined civilization, but the translation of a substantial relationship between man and transcendent reality. ... Therefore myths, the personification of the forces of nature, symbols, metaphors, did not result from a mental play, but from an intuitive perception of man's situation in the world.]

The warrior's song on his way to meet his beloved illustrated the ideal of primitive "poetics":

Je devancerai les pas du jour sur le sommet des montagnes, pour chercher ma colombe solitaire parmi les chênes de la forêt.

J'ai attaché à son cou un collier de porcelaines; on y voit trois grains rouges pour mon amour, trois violets pour mes craintes, trois bleus pour mes espérances.

Mila a les yeux d'une hermine et la chevelure légère d'un champ de riz; sa bouche est un coquillage rose, garni de perles; ses deux seins sont comme deux petits chevreaux sans tache, nés au même jour d'une seule mère.

Puisse Mila éteindre ce flambeau! Puisse sa bouche verser sur lui une ombre voluptueuse! Je fertiliserai son sein. L'espoir de la patrie pendra à sa mamelle féconde, et je fumerai mon calumet de paix sur le berceau de mon fils!

Ah! laissez-moi devancer les pas du jour sur le sommet des montagnes, pour chercher ma colombe solitaire parmi les chênes de la forêt! (110–11)

[I will hasten before the steps of day to the mountain top to seek out my lonely dove among the oaks of the forest.

I have hung about her throat a necklace of shells; there are three red beads for my love, three purple ones for my fears, three blue ones for my hopes.

Mila has the eyes of an ermine and the flowing hair of a field of rice. Her mouth is a pink shell set with pearls. Her two breasts are as two spotless kids, born the same day of a single mother.

May Mila put out this torch! May her mouth cast over it a voluptuous shadow! I will make fertile her womb. The hope of a nation shall cling to her plenteous breast, and I will smoke my calumet of peace by the cradle of my son.

---

[41]   Ibid.

Ah! Let me hasten before the steps of day to the mountain top to seek out my lonely dove among the oaks of the forest!] (trans. 30)

References to two artifacts and to a Native American custom anchor the song in its geographic locale: the inevitable peace pipe, the color-coded necklace of shells and grains (uniting water and earth), and the sexually symbolic courting ceremonial, whereby a virgin accepts a future husband by blowing out the flame of his torch, or rejects him by letting the flame burn. These three indications confer an exotic flavor to the otherwise familiar biblical style of the Song of Solomon: the "verset"-like structure, the framing of the song with a chorus, metaphors based on nature's wonders, such as "ma colombe solitaire" [my solitary dove] for his beloved. The four comparisons describing Mila's eyes, hair, mouth, and breasts, borrowed from the world of nature, indirectly praise the Creator as living through his human, animal, and vegetal creations.[42] Perhaps the most recognizable aspect of primitive voice is the short, syncopated rhythm of the song, its "style coupé" (parataxis) so contrary to the characteristically ample rhythm of Chateaubriand's descriptions. *Atala*'s hybridity derives in part from the juxtapositions of two writing styles: the biblical, rhapsodic parataxis—the staple of eighteenth-century prose poems— and Chateaubriand's highly periodicized style. It is not a coincidence that the impersonal parataxis was easily copied, whereas the new and unique rhythmic character of Chateaubriand's personal style escaped imitation.[43] The self-reflective, self-conscious moments when the author's prose claims a poetic status by duplicating the poetic cadences of the Bible are, expectedly, the least "natural" to the author's style. If they seem artificial to a modern reader, they nonetheless pleased contemporaries whose appreciation for Chateaubriand's original genius coexisted with enjoyment of variations on classical themes, genres, and styles.[44]

---

[42] The comparisons are repeated almost verbatim at the beginning of the anonymous sequel, *Résurrection d'Atala* (1802) where they serve to identify the young woman who has just appeared as the real Atala. But their transposition in a description (in lieu of an Indian song as in Chateaubriand) destroys the illusion of a native voice (vol. I, 7–8).

[43] See the imitation of Atala's song in *Résurrection d'Atala* (vol. I, 170–73), which begins: "Bienheureuse la fille du désert qui ne quitta jamais la hutte de son père, et jamais ne chercha, hors du sein de sa mère, les embrassemens qui brûlent le cœur!" [Happy is the daughter of the wilderness who never left her father's hut, and never sought outside of her mother's bosom embraces that burn the heart.] Atala is later asked to sing her "chanson du retour," which also imitates Chateaubriand's primitive style (with echoes of Parny's *Chansons madécasses*). Anon., *Résurrection d'Atala*, vol. II, 18–20.

[44] The infatuation for this new voice is parodied in the *Résurrection d'Atala*. In concluding her praise of the "resurrected" Atala in a letter to a friend, the main protagonist exclaimed: "Je finirai, je crois, si Atala me reste, par devenir sauvage et parler comme elle; je te dirai alors que tu es belle comme le désert, et que tu chantes comme la Nonpareille des Florides" [If Atala stays, I think I will end up becoming an Indian and speaking like her; then I will tell you that you are beautiful like the wilderness and that you sing like the bunting of the Floridas] (vol. I, 43).

Like the warrior's song, Atala's second song (about the "absent motherland")
integrates a few exotic traits—"le geai bleu du Meschacebé," "la nonpareille des
Florides," "le soleil de ma savane" [the blue jay of the Meschacebe, the bunting
of the Floridas, the sun of my savannah]—within a biblical incantation ("Heureux
celui qui ...") punctuated by a refrain, couplets, repetitions, and metaphors.[45]
Parataxis predominates, evidenced by repeated, generic substantives, often
introduced by the universalizing definite article ("le voyageur," "la cabane"),
identical subject-verb-complement order, minimal transitions, and verbs of action
in the present tense. There are few epithets, in sharp contrast to Chateaubriand's
inclination for multiple adjectives. The effort to render a primitive style is palpable
since this style decidedly differs from Chateaubriand's classical period, as this
second stanza shows:

> Après les heures d'une marche pénible, le voyageur s'assied tristement. Il
> contemple autour de lui les toits des hommes; le voyageur n'a pas un lieu où
> reposer sa tête. Le voyageur frappe à la cabane, il met son arc derrière la porte,
> il demande l'hospitalité; le maître fait un geste de la main; le voyageur reprend
> son arc, et retourne au désert! (124)

> [After wending his painful way many hours, the traveler sits down quietly. He
> contemplates about him the roofs of men; the traveler has no place to rest his
> head. The traveler knocks at the cabin, he places his bow behind the door, he
> asks for hospitality. The master makes a sign with his hand; the traveler takes up
> his bow and returns to the wilderness!] (trans. 42)

The subject matter, exile from the motherland, relates to the Homeric tradition.
Inhospitality toward the traveler recalls biblical examples of rejection gestures
toward the exiled (including the plight of the Levite of Ephraïm in Rousseau's
prose poem), as well as the endless wandering of the tribes of Israel.[46] The detail of
the bow in lieu of the customary walking stick is enough to transpose the Homeric
and biblical *topoi* into an Indian context.

The most revealing transposition occurs in the epilogue, when the narrator's
voice turns native, so to speak, when he greets an Indian traveler: "Frère, je te
souhaite un ciel bleu, beaucoup de chevreuils, un manteau de castor, et l'espérance.
Tu n'es donc pas de ce désert?" [Brother, I wish you a blue sky, many roes, a
beaver mantle, and hope. Are you not from this wilderness?] (162; trans. 78)
The Indian replies straightforwardly: "Non ... nous sommes des exilés, et nous
allons chercher une patrie" [No ... we are exiles in search of a homeland], but

---

[45]   Chateaubriand, *Atala*, 123–4. Trans. 42. The refrain is repeated three times, at the
beginning, middle, and end of the song: "Heureux ceux qui n'ont point vu la fumée des
fêtes de l'étranger, et qui ne se sont assis qu'aux festins de leur pères!" [Happy are they who
have never seen the smoke of the stranger's celebrations and have sat only at the festivals
of their fathers!] Ibid.

[46]   See Chateaubriand, *Œuvres romanesques et voyages*, vol. 1, 1175n1. Maurice
Regard notes that it is a reminiscence from Saint Matthew (VIII, 20).

the narrator continues in a symbolic vein: "Voulez-vous me permettre d'allumer votre feu cette nuit?" [Will you allow me to light your fire this night?] (162; trans. 78). What does it mean for the European narrator to appropriate or imitate the primitive voice of an exiled people driven to extinction by European colonialism? Baudelaire, a great admirer of Chateaubriand's "cosmopolitan style" quoted the metaphors of "la fleur du désert" and "la grâce de la cabane" to describe the beauty of a Delacroix painting. It seems puzzling at first that the poet of modern life and big cities be touched by "la fleur du désert" et "la grâce de la cabane." Yet these expressions capture what Baudelaire said he was always searching for in literature: "une antiquité nouvelle" [a new antiquity.][47] Both metaphors illustrate the combination of simplicity and artifice in the supposedly American paradise visited and romanticized by Chateaubriand, simultaneously antique (a primitive continent and its natives) and modern (corruption and massacre brought by European colonization). In other words, the Indian heroine with her mixed blood and the narration that stages her tragedy in a "style mêlé" [mixed style] are both *métisses*, a cross-breeding of nature and culture.[48] Chateaubriand's "new antiquity" (to adopt Baudelaire's phrase) namely his modernity, resides in this "métissage" [cross-breeding] diluting idealized purity, the spleen of the Enlightenment.

The Letter A

I wish to examine now another aspect of Chateaubriand's "antiquité nouvelle," by reading very closely the prose of his poem. Let us begin with the title *Atala*. Let us consider other names: "la grande savane Alachua," "Apalachucla," "Cuscowilla," "Mila," and "Celuta."[49] Chateaubriand favored the letter *a*, a letter that typesetters needed to replace systematically so worn it became in the process of printing his works.[50] It would remain an anecdotal idiosyncrasy if it were not for a long and curious footnote in the *Génie du christianisme* explaining Chateaubriand's predilection for this vowel. On the occasion of his commentary on Theocritus's poem, *The Cyclop and Galathea*, Chateaubriand remarked on the frequency and poetry of the letter *a* found especially in substantives and adjectives linked to the countryside. This observation is further developed in the following footnote:

> La lettre *A* ayant été découverte la première, comme étant la première émission naturelle de la voix, les hommes, alors pasteurs, l'ont employée dans les mots qui composaient le simple dictionnaire de leur vie. L'égalité de leurs mœurs, et le peu de variété de leurs idées nécessairement teintes des images des champs,

---

[47] Baudelaire used the phrase in his notes describing the aesthetics of the baroque Belgian church of Namur, *Œuvres complètes*, II, 952. See Moore, "Baudelaire et les poëmes en prose du dix-huitième siècle."

[48] Chateaubriand, Préface de la première édition, *Atala*, 46.

[49] See also the Ossianic characters of Malvina, Morna, Galvina, Comala, Lorma, Vinvela, Minina, Darthula, Oïchoma, etc., and the locations of their tales, Selma, Temora, Lutha, Duthula, Lona, etc., familiar to all eighteenth-century readers.

[50] Mourot, *Génie d'un style*, 227.

devaient aussi rappeler le retour des mêmes sons dans le langage. Le son de l'*A* convient au calme d'un cœur champêtre et à la paix des tableaux rustiques. L'accent d'une âme passionnée est aigu, sifflant, précipité; l'*A* est trop long pour elle: il faut une bouche pastorale, qui puisse prendre le temps de le prononcer avec lenteur. Mais toutefois il entre fort bien encore dans les plaintes, dans les larmes amoureuses, et dans les naïfs *hélas* d'un chevrier. Enfin, la nature fait entendre cette lettre rurale dans ses bruits, et une oreille attentive peut la reconnaître diversement accentuée, dans les murmures de certains ombrages, comme dans celui du tremble et du lierre, dans la première voix, ou dans la finale du bêlement des troupeaux, et, la nuit, dans les aboiements du chien rustique. (*Génie* 702–3nA)

[The letter *A* being discovered first, as the first natural emission of voice, men, who were then shepherds, used it in the words that formed the simple dictionary of their lives. Their tranquil mores and the small variety of their ideas necessarily colored with rural images, must also have recalled the return of the same sounds in language. The sound of *A* suits a calm pastoral heart and peaceful, rustic scenes. The accent of a passionate soul is high-pitched, hissing, breathless; the *A* is too long for it. It needs a pastoral mouth which can take the time to pronounce it slowly. However, it is still part of complaints, tears of love, and the goatherd's naïve *alas*. Finally, nature makes this rural letter heard through her sounds, and an attentive ear can recognize its various accents in the murmurs of certain shady trees, such as the trembling poplar and the ivy; in the first voice or in the lingering bleating of a flock; and at night in the barking of the country dog.]

The letter *a* belonged to an onomastic tradition particularly prized at the turn of the century,[51] but Chateaubriand's note left aside proper nouns, focusing instead on common names to look for the origins of this "rural letter," a quest reminiscent of the Platonic dialogue *Cratylus*, and Rousseau's theories on the origin of language.[52] Chateaubriand envisioned the simplicity and naïveté of an early pastoral age when the repetition of the letter *a* reflected a limited horizon, a slow pace, peaceful mores and a restricted, agriculture-based *prosaic* vocabulary. In this golden language of

---

[51] "La finale *a*, dans l'onomastique littéraire du XIXe siècle, confère à l'héroïne un prestige d'exotisme ou d'antiquité, l'entoure même d'une *aura* religieuse (quand Nerval fait de l'actrice dont l'image l'obsède une abstraction mystique, l'Aurélie de *Sylvie* devient Aurelia)" [The ending *a* in nineteenth-century literary onomastics, confers exotic or antique prestige to the heroine, it even surrounds her with a religious aura (when Nerval turns the actress, whose image obsesses him, into a mystical abstraction, the Aurélie in *Sylvie* becomes Aurelia.] Ibid.

[52] Socrates argued that one must begin with the letter, then the syllable, then the word, to analyze how the essence of each thing is expressed in its name: "where does the imitator begin? Imitation of the essence is made by syllables and letters. Ought we not, therefore, first to separate the letters, just as those who are beginning rhythm first distinguish the powers of elementary and then of compound sounds, and when they have done so, but not before, proceed to the consideration of rhythms?" Plato, *Cratylus*, in *The Collected Dialogues*, 459.

few words and fewer concepts, semantic density made up for the lack of variety, and the letter *a* could convey sorrow as well as more earthy realities. The letter *a* evoked a mythic time when signifier and signified were one. Its frequency in Greek and Latin vocabulary and grammar testified to the ancients' proximity to these primitive times. The letter *a* was not only pastoral and rural but *antique*. It was therefore an important vowel for Chateaubriand's project of bringing literature back to "ce goût antique, trop oublié de nos jours" [this antique taste, too often forgotten nowadays], which *Atala* represented.[53]

It is therefore the symbolic, not scientific value of Chateaubriand's speculation that is of interest to this analysis: the letter *a* discloses a "prosaïcs" (under its antique patina), but also a whole poetics, as the end of the footnote confirms. The alpha of language, the letter *a* is the alpha of poetry: moving easily from the pastoral age to the world of nature, Chateaubriand took an anthropomorphic view of nature and animals as emitting a linguistically identifiable *a*. Chateaubriand let his ear guide the flight of his poetic imagination in perceiving articulated sounds in the faintest "bruits" ("les murmures de certains ombrages ... du tremble et du lierre" [the murmurs of certain shady trees ... the trembling poplar and the ivy]) as well as in familiar rural noises (bleating sheep, barking dogs).[54] The traditional definition of poetry as imitation of a beautiful nature, in which Chateaubriand believed, is here transposed from the pictorial to the musical realm: a Chateaubrianesque imitation of nature will be first and foremost based on sonority, not images, or allegories. In turning to *Atala*, we can now explore the sounds recorded in descriptions.

The Song of Nature

The descriptive passages interspersed in the narrative of *Atala* elicited great praise for their representation of the American wilderness. The "tableaux" are visually striking and symbolically charged. Yet it was not as pictorial masterpieces that these descriptions broke the conventional mold, but (paradoxically) as musical numbers. By this, I do not mean the complex, overall rhythmic effect of Chateaubriand's musical prose, but literally the deep semantic field of acoustics, which lifts the descriptions from pictorial stasis into a symphony of sounds:

> Si tout est silence et repos dans les savanes de l'autre côté du fleuve, tout ici, au contraire, est mouvement et murmure: des coups de bec contre le tronc des chênes, des froissements d'animaux qui marchent, broutent ou broient entre leurs dents les noyaux des fruits, des bruissements d'ondes, de faibles gémissements,

---

[53] Preface from 1801, *Atala*, 47. For Mourot, a natural predilection for the "couleur vocalique" *e* - *ę* was the hallmark of Chateaubriand's style. Mourot, *Génie d'un style*, 227–36.

[54] I leave aside the comic aspect of Chateaubriand's poetic enthusiasm, which verges on the ridiculous when invoking the onomatopoeic "ouah, ouah" of the country dog at night. Despite its imitative and apparently universal nature, onomatopoeia is a highly idiosyncratic linguistic phenomenon, as speakers of foreign languages well know.

de sourds meuglements, de doux roucoulements, remplissent ces déserts d'une tendre et sauvage harmonie. Mais quand une brise vient à animer ces solitudes, à balancer ces corps flottants, à confondre ces masses de blanc, d'azur, de vert, de rose, à mêler toutes les couleurs, à réunir tous les murmures; alors il sort de tels bruits du fond des forêts, il se passe de telles choses aux yeux, que j'essaierais en vain de les décrire à ceux qui n'ont point parcouru ces champs primitifs de la nature. (99–100)

[While in the savannahs beyond the river everything is permeated with silence and calm, here, on the contrary everything stirs and murmurs. Beaks pecking against the trunks of oak trees, the rustle of animals moving about or grazing or grinding fruit stones between their teeth, the rippling of waves, feeble moanings, muffled bellowings and gentle cooings, all fill this wilderness with a primitive and tender harmony. But should any breeze happen to stir up these solitudes, rocking these floating forms, confusing these masses of white and blue and green and pink, mingling all the colors and combining all the murmurs, then there emerges from the depths of the forest such sounds, and the eyes behold such sights, that it would be futile for me to attempt their description to those who have never themselves passed through these primeval fields of nature.] (trans. 19)

In the concluding phrase—"ces champs primitifs de la nature"—the homonyms "champs"/"chant" emphasize the layering of spatial and auditory fields. The challenge that Chateaubriand set himself in his descriptions was to express noises and cries, a more ground-breaking and paradoxical endeavor than the expression of visual details, the staple of eighteenth-century descriptive theory and practice. To reflect this focus on listening, I therefore propose to qualify Chateaubriand's descriptive passages as *compositions* rather than descriptions, as Chateaubriand treated sounds as identifiable individual notes and measures participating in the concert of nature. Animal cries and natural sounds are transcribed successively in the above composition before cohering as "une tendre et sauvage harmonie." The epithet "sauvage," imbued with connotations of violence, unlike its synonym "primitive," creates an antithesis, which adds further mystery to this music of the wilderness.

The description ends with preterition, a statement about the impossibility to tell, to describe the visual and auditory spectacle set in motion by the breeze. The invisible hand of the wind animates the scenery in ways that a realistic description cannot account for, which is why it ends abruptly: first, the breeze merges colors and collides sounds, thereby overwhelming the senses that preside over the description; then, the strangely animated nature draws the describer face to face with an inexpressible, sacred mystery ("de tels bruits," "de telles choses" [such sounds, such sights]). This progression, from realism to animism, is characteristic of the descriptions in *Atala* and is particularly striking in sound mimesis. Certain paragraphs read like a score, creating the musical equivalent of an ekphrastic moment: "Tout était calme et superbe au désert. La cigogne criait sur son nid, les bois retentissaient du chant monotone des cailles, du sifflement des perruches, du mugissement des bisons et du hennissement de cavales siminoles" [All the wilderness was calm and glorious. The stork was calling from its nest. The woods echoed with the monotonous song of the quail, the whistling of the parakeets, the bellowing of the bison, and the whinnying of Seminole mares.] (109, trans. 28).

Another example:

> les serpents à sonnettes bruissaient de toutes parts; et les loups, les ours, les carcajous, les petits tigres, qui venaient se cacher dans ces retraites, les remplissaient de leurs rugissements. ... du milieu de ce vaste chaos s'élève un mugissement confus formé par le fracas des vents, le gémissement des arbres, le hurlement des bêtes féroces, le bourdonnement de l'incendie, et la chute répétée du tonnerre qui siffle en s'éteignant dans les eaux. (126)

> [everywhere rattlesnakes were hissing, and wolves, bears, little tigers, and wolverines, coming to take refuge, filled these retreats with their roars. ... From the midst of this vast chaos rose a confused uproar formed by the crashing winds, the moaning trees, the howling of fierce beasts, the crackling of the conflagration, and the constant flashing of the lightening hissing as it plunged into the waters.] (trans. 44)

In contrast to these realistic recordings, other descriptions lead into another reality via auditory flashes. This magical effect happens when sounds, no longer perceived as a succession of noises, merge into a melodic ensemble: "Aucun bruit ne se faisait entendre, hors je ne sais quelle harmonie lointaine qui régnait dans la profondeur des bois: on eût dit que l'âme de la solitude soupirait dans toute l'étendue du désert" [No sound could be heard, save some vague far-away harmony permeating the depths of the woods. It was as though the soul of solitude were sighing through the entire expanse of the wilderness] (110, trans. 29). The moment when sounds are perceived as musical and no longer cacophonic, there automatically appears an animist impulse: a voice chants the song of nature. This transmutation of natural sounds into a song occurs in two instances: the "Bocages de la mort" [the Groves of Death] and the scene of Atala's burial. In the first instance, the nature of the site—a sacred burial ground—is enough to transform indistinct noises into the vibrations of an instrument, and the birds' chirrup into a hymn: "il y régnait un bruit religieux, semblable au sourd mugissement de l'orgue sous les voûtes d'une église; mais lorsqu'on pénétrait au fond du sanctuaire, on n'entendait plus que les hymnes des oiseaux qui célébraient à la mémoire des morts une fête éternelle" [The atmosphere was permeated with a religious resonance like the muffled roar of the organ beneath the vaults of a church. But within the depths of the sanctuary, nothing could be heard but the hymn of the birds glorifying the memory of the dead in eternal celebration] (135–6, trans. 53) In the second instance, a mix of individualized sounds (birds, water, and a bell) join the hymn sung by the Père Aubry to form a celestial chorus:

> Ainsi chantait l'ancien des hommes. Sa voix grave et un peu cadencée, allait roulant dans le silence des déserts. Le nom de Dieu et du tombeau sortait de tous les échos, de tous les torrents, de toutes les forêts. Les roucoulements de la colombe de Virginie, la chute d'un torrent dans la montagne, les tintements de la cloche qui appelait les voyageurs, se mêlaient à ces chants funèbres, et l'on

croyait entendre dans les Bocages de la mort le chœur lointain des décédés, qui résonnait à la voix du Solitaire. (156–7)

[Thus sang the ancient among men. His grave, rhythmical voice reverberated out into the silence of the wilderness, and the name of God and the tomb echoed back from all the waters and all the forests. The cooing of the Virginia dove, the falling of the mountain torrent and the tolling of the bell to summon wayfarers, all mingled with these funeral chants, while from the Groves of death the far-away choir of the departed could almost be heard replying to the voice of the hermit.] (trans. 73)

In the first instance the comparative "semblable" introduces the assimilation between natural sounds, then the comparison dissolves ("on n'entendait plus que") in favor of the birds' melodies. The movement is reversed in the second instance: the sounds of nature retain their specificity and realism until the expression "l'on croyait entendre" signals a shift to a purely imaginative realm where voices, not noises, are heard, where music, not sounds, resonate. The exchange between physical and symbolic worlds is, ultimately, an interplay between the prosaic and poetic—taken as stylistic as well as metaphoric modes. Sounds in *Atala* reveal Chateaubriand's approach to writing: words expressing sounds, often based on onomatopoeia, carry a prosaic weight when taken literally; yet simultaneously, their figurative possibilities prove highly poetical. Only prose could allow Chateaubriand this ideal combination of the prosaic and poetic within the specific semantic field of acoustics.

As might have been noticed in the above citations, one feature stands out in the enumeration of sounds: clusters of substantives with sibilant *s*'s and the "-ement" suffix create a poetic effect. The list of these substantives in *Atala* alone speaks for itself: "froissement; bruissement; frémissement; gémissements (twice); meuglements; roucoulements; mugissements (five times); tintement (twice); rugissements (twice); sifflement; hennissement; roulement; hurlement; bourdonnement" [wrinkling, rustling, trembling, moaning, mooing, cooing, bellowing, tinting, roaring, hissing, whinnying, rumbling, howling, buzzing.] Such a list violated the principles that had long guided versification, and by extension poetry itself: the "oreille" would have rejected this accumulation of polysyllabic nouns with repetitive, masculine endings, and taste would have condemned the base semantic register of animal sounds. Chateaubriand's prose, on the contrary, artfully blends in clusters of animal names and sounds to increase the poetic density of his compositions. In the following example, the short, abstract, verse-like first sentence with feminine endings is counter-balanced by a longer segment rich in visual and auditory clues (specific animal names and sounds): "Tout était calme et superbe au désert. La cigogne criait sur son nid, les bois retentissaient du chant monotone des cailles, du sifflement des perruches, du mugissement des bisons et du hennissement de cavales siminoles." (109) By giving life to this "calm and superb" totality, the enumeration disturbs the conventional, natural harmony that the first sentence had seemed to set in place: real harmony is in the juxtaposition of the sounds of life, and true calm teams with the peaceful energy of nature's creatures, not silence.

The list of sound words perfectly reflects Chateaubriand's poetic sensibility. A seemingly anti-poetical noun, the bovine "mugissement" [bellowing] in fact epitomizes his poetics. Chateaubriand uses it five times, applied to the bull, the buffalo, the storm, the organ, and Niagara Falls. Obviously a favorite of Chateaubriand, the word "mugissement," a reminiscence from Virgil's *Georgics*, retains its onomatopoeic origin and pastoral sources, but Chateaubriand changes its connotations of felicitous country life into a signifier of emotional and metaphysical wilderness connected to the author's obsessions. "Mugissement," by extension, refers to any deep and profound sound, a cry of elemental depth and intensity associated with violence and the sublime (tempests, thundering). In contrast to the positive, sweet reminiscences conveyed by the letter *a*, "mugissement" expresses horrific memories, unfathomable despair, and immense sorrow in Chateaubriand's mythopoetics. In the epilogue, we learn that the narrator has followed a wandering couple mourning their dead child, and empathized with the mother's grief. After contemplating the awesome Niagara Falls, he learns of the tragedy that has befallen René (the woman's father), Father Aubry, and his utopian community. The "affreux mugissements" of the cataract, itself a colossal veil of tears, echo and sublimate the repressed wailing of the Natchez tribe's last survivors and the melancholy of the exiled narrator (162). The "mugissement" of the Niagara Falls could be read as the young Chateaubriand's sonorous coat of arms: it condenses themes (exile, melancholy, nature, the sublime), and effects (spatial and temporal volume and echo) essential to his poetic imagination. It stands for the commingling of the prosaic and the poetic in an original synthesis of the physical and symbolic, the natural and ontological, united by the New World's double mirror of the exotic and the primitive.

Sébastien Mercier: Visions

It is now easy to understand why Mercier enjoyed *Atala* so much: Chateaubriand's writing was "le papier qui parle" [paper that speaks]. Mercier's views on French language and literature place him today at the forefront of his century's movement to modernize the field of Belles Lettres.[55] His relentless crusade to free poetry and drama from versification[56] and rhyme,[57] welcome modern foreign literature,[58]

---

[55] See Jean-Claude Bonnet, ed. *Louis Sébastien Mercier (1740–1814): un hérétique en littérature* (Paris: 1994).

[56] "La poésie audacieuse est la vraie poésie. La poésie élégante n'est que de la versification" [Bold poetry is genuine poetry. Elegant poetry is only versification.] Sébastien Mercier, *Discours sur la lecture*, in *Dictionnaire d'un polygraphe, Textes de Louis-Sébastien Mercier* (Paris, 1978), 330.

[57] Mercier, "Rime" and "Impitoyables versificateurs," *Tableau de Paris*, vol. 2, 449–54 and 1485–8.

[58] "Ce divin Homère nous ennuie. ... notre Homère à nous sera Richardson; notre Théocrite, Gessner; notre Théophraste, Fielding" [This divine Homer bores us. Our Homer shall be Richardson, our Theocritus, Gessner, our Theophrastus, Fielding.] Mercier, "Contre l'Homère traduit en français," *Mon Bonnet de nuit*, 205.

supplant epic poems with novels,[59] renew the French language, and defy "la langue monarchique" with "neology"[60] represents the most comprehensive effort to revolutionize prose and poetry at the end of the century. Ill-regarded by fellow critics, Mercier the *provocateur* did not build a consensus around his program, which fell upon the critics' deaf ears. His voice, however, expressed the concerns and frustrations of fellow prose writers in a straightforward and articulate manner unparalleled at the time.

Like the majority of authors cited in previous chapters, Mercier produced works of fiction that appear to clash with his theories. The most eloquent and perceptive defender of prose was a conflicted practitioner of the "poëme en prose," like Chateaubriand after him. At the beginning of his career, in 1767, he penned a prose poem, *Les Amours de Cherale, poëme en six chants*, a lyrical interior monologue and a hymn to love and self-overcoming, later erased from the list he drew of his complete works.[61] This paradox, as much as his provoking ideas, makes him an emblematic figure for his century's struggle with neoclassicism. Though Mercier's complex work deserves a more thorough approach, I will circumscribe my analysis to one of the most avant-garde aspects of his theory, namely his pronouncements on prose. Mercier's virulent attacks against the mediocrity of contemporary French poetry resulted in a heightened appreciation for France's prose masterworks.[62]

---

[59]   "Tandis que d'un côté on rend un hommage sans borne au poëme épique, qui n'est qu'une fiction plus ou moins heureuse; de l'autre, on a voulu humilier le roman, qui au fond est la même chose, ayant la même marche, la même étendue, & le même but. Il ne seroit pas difficile de prouver que le roman est souvent plus ingénieux, plus varié et plus moral que le poëme épique; mais parmi les ouvrages comme parmi les hommes, les titres en imposent beaucoup à l'imagination, & les dénominations sont encore aujourd'hui ce qui détermine le jugement des esprits, qui croient avoir le plus renoncé à l'ascendant des préjugés" [While on the one hand, one pays endless homage to epic poems, which are but more or less felicitous fictions; on the other hand, one has tried to humiliate the novel, which in the end is identical to the former, having the same pace, breath and goal. It would be easy to prove that the novel is often wittier, more varied and moral than epic poetry; but among books as among men, titles impress the imagination a great deal and today labels still determine the judgments of minds who think they have renounced the influence of prejudice.] Mercier, "Des jugements littéraires," *Mon Bonnet du matin*, 25.

[60]   Mercier, *Néologie*, lxxiij. Mercier brought in the open the interconnection between reforming language and political reform.

[61]   A more comprehensive study of Mercier's œuvre would also draw connections between his theories and practice, with an emphasis on the importance of his early "héroïdes" and the unclassifiable *L'An deux mille quatre cent quarante*, his predilection for fragmentary writing (*Mon Bonnet de nuit, Bonnet du matin*), his groundbreaking journalistic work for the *Tableau de Paris*, and his redefinition of drama.

[62]   "Ajouterai-je que je ne puis lire la prose des écrivains du dernier siècle, excepté celle de la Bruyere & de Pascal, & que Montesquieu, l'abbé Raynal, Voltaire, Diderot, Buffon, & J.J. Rousseau, Paw, &c. contrebalancent à eux seuls, dans mon esprit, tout le siècle de Louis XIV, qui n'a eu que des poëtes & pas un seul écrivain qu'on puissent méditer, soit en

Cette pauvreté de la langue poétique n'empêche pas les poètes d'être en foule parmi nous; mais si nous en avons en vers, nous en avons aussi en prose; sûrement Bossuet, Fénelon, Buffon, J.-J. Rousseau, étaient poètes en prose. Les traductions poétiques de Le Tourneur partagent le charme et l'harmonie des vers. Là sont peut-être nos richesses poétiques réelles.[63]

[This poverty of poetic language has not prevented a throng of poets among us: but if we have poets in verse, we also have poets in prose; surely Bossuet, Fénelon, Buffon, and J.-J. Rousseau were poets in prose. Le Tourneur's poetic translations share the charm and harmony of verses. Therein are perhaps our true poetic riches.]

Given how weighty the phrase "poètes en prose" had become after decades of disquisition, Mercier's choice of words was important: it intimated that the nature of poetry did not depend on verse. A section on French verse in *Mon Bonnet du matin* similarly addressed and resolved the question of prose poems:

Peut-il y avoir des poèmes en prose? Cette question ne pourrait-elle pas être proposée sous d'autres termes: si la qualité de poète est inséparable de celle de versificateur? On regarde aujourd'hui comme certain que l'on peut être versificateur sans être poète: témoin M. l'abbé Delille. Un ouvrage, quoiqu'écrit en vers, mais sans épisodes, sans figures, sans mouvement, sans images, ne serait point l'ouvrage d'un poète. Mais admettez du génie, de la force, de l'imagination, de la variété en prose; cet auteur-là sera poète sans être versificateur.[64]

[Can there be prose poems? Could this question not be raised in different terms: whether a poet's qualification is inseparable from that of a verse writer? Today we take for granted that one can versify without being a poet: witness M. Abbé Delille. A work, albeit in verse but without episodes, figures, movements, images, would not be the work of a poet. But include genius, strength, imagination, variety in prose, and this author will be a poet without writing verse.]

Mercier's definition did not anticipate the aesthetic of modern prose poems as such, but simply restated the dissociation between verse and poetic essence. The repetition of this evidence as late as 1784 by Mercier himself proves the permanence of an insufferable frustration with contemporary poetical productions, and the dismissal of descriptive verses as the solution to the current crisis. Mercier adopted Fénelonian accents to invoke his ideal: "Et les vers? ... pour qu'on les pardonnât,

---

morale, soit en politique" [Shall I add that I cannot read the prose of last century's writers, except la Bruyère and Pascal, and that Montesquieu, abbé Raynal, Voltaire, Diderot, Buffon, J.J. Rousseau, Paw, etc. counterbalance in my mind the whole Louis XIV's century, which only had poets and not a single author upon whom one can meditate either about morals or politics.] Mercier, "Des jugements littéraires," *Mon Bonnet du matin*, 29.

[63] Mercier, *Tableau de Paris*, vol. 2, 1488. Madame de Staël's groundbreaking *De la Littérature* owes an important debt to Mercier's modern views.

[64] Mercier, "Vers français," *Mon Bonnet de Nuit*, 462.

il faudrait qu'ils se rapprochassent de la prose, c'est-à-dire, qu'ils fussent doux, simples, faciles, et naturels" [How about verses? ... To be forgiven, they should come closer to prose, in other words be pleasant, simple, easy and natural.][65] There were still no examples to illustrate this new poetry: Mercier disliked Homer and castigated "rimailleurs" and the literary institutions and periodicals that contributed to their proliferation. [66] He found "genius, strength, imagination, and variety" in prose only: he admired English novels and praised contemporary French *prosateurs* and translators like his friend Le Tourneur. Another source important to Mercier, though less remarked upon, sprung from historical examples of primitive eloquence. They appeared in two telling fragments from the *Mon Bonnet du matin* (1787), which expound respectively on "le style figuré" and "l'éloquence des choses," two essential notions for Mercier's new poetics. Adopting Rousseau's description of the origin of language, Mercier insisted on the natural genius and strength of primitive expression:

> Toutes les langues naissantes qui touchent au berceau des nations ont un style figuré: elles empruntent ces images sensibles qui peuvent seules représenter l'esprit à lui-même, de là ces métaphores qui animent & colorent les idées: cette simplicité énergique annonce la vigueur d'un peuple encore entre les mains de la nature. Ce peuple n'anatomise point de petites sensations avec des expressions fines & délicates: il a le stile hardi, qui élève l'ame & qui occupe toute sa capacité; il parle, il entraîne, il subjugue: loin de ces entraves arbitraires qui sont une suite de nos frêles institutions, il ne voit que les grands traits, que les traits caractérisés qui forment la physionomie des choses sublimes.[67]

> [All beginning languages that are connected to the cradle of nations have a figurative style: they borrow sensitive images which can only represent the mind to itself, hence metaphors that animate and color ideas. This energetic simplicity announces the vigor of a people still in the hands of nature. Such a people do not anatomize small sensations with refined and delicate phrases: they use a bold style, which elevates the soul and fills it wholly; they speak up, they carry away, they subjugate. Far from the arbitrary fetters that are a consequence of our weak institutions, they only see major traits, the characteristic traits that form the physiognomy of sublime things.]

As a confirmation, Mercier cited the "sublime harangue" of an Indian chief to an Englishman. The natural eloquence of Native Americans matched in strength examples from Greek and Roman antiquity, but its novelty and ingenuity reinvented rhetoric. Mercier also developed this point in a subsequent segment, illustrated with the oft cited example of the Scythes:

---

[65]   Mercier, "Nouvel examen de la tragédie française," *Dictionnaire d'un polygraphe*, 330.

[66]   Mercier, "Contre l'Homère traduit en français," *Mon Bonnet de nuit*, 206.

[67]   Mercier, "Du style figuré," *Mon Bonnet du matin*, 112.

De l'éloquence des choses. Combien elle est supérieure à celle des mots! Elle rejette le luxe de la parole pour étonner l'ame par la fréquence de ses images & de ses vérités nues. Elle laisse à sa rivale le vain étalage de phrases nombreuses & cadencées, de mots pompeux, sonores & symétriques, qui cachent la stérilité des idées. Voyez dans le discours suivant la mâle simplicité des Scythes, & sous quel jour ils ont mis le tableau de la fureur d'Alexandre pour les conquêtes; comme le style en est plein, & quel sens profond il offre à la méditation; c'est un des plus beaux morceaux que nous offre l'histoire, ou, si vous l'aimez mieux, le génie de l'historien.[68]

[On the eloquence of things. How superior it is to the eloquence of words! It dismisses the luxury of speech to astonish the soul with the recurrence of its images and naked truths. It leaves to its rival the vain display of rhythmical and cadenced sentences, pompous, sonorous and symmetrical words, which hide sterile ideas. See in the following speech, the Scythes' male simplicity, and the light under which they have cast the picture of Alexander's passion for conquests. How the style is filled with it and what profound meaning it offers for meditation. It is one of the most sublime pieces that history offers us, or if you prefer, the genius of the historian.]

The dissociation between the eloquence of things and the eloquence of words clearly separated "primitive" language from more elaborate, accomplished, and "civilized" writing. The former rang true, the latter seemed artificial. The reference to number, cadence, sonority, and symmetry as part of the eloquence of words suggests that Mercier had in mind versified poetry and possibly prose poems *à la* Bitaubé. Conceptualizing prose as "eloquence of things" and poetry as "eloquence of words" was an insightful response to the theoretical impasse of contemporary writers when it came to define the essential difference governing the two modes. The "éloquence des choses" defined the figurative style emblematic of oral cultures, which so fascinated translators (Anne Dacier, Le Tourneur), novelists (Mme de Graffigny), poets (Saint-Lambert, Parny), and prosateurs (Marmontel, Chateaubriand). The purpose of this oxymoron was not to throw a linguistic challenge by dissociating sign ("le mot") and referent ("la chose")—however problematic this gesture obviously was—but to mirror the chasm between expression and reality in contemporary letters. Simply put, the eloquence of things and the eloquence of words used to be one and the same but disunited in the passage from oral to written culture, and the ensuing pressure to refine language, which eventually reached an unprecedented level of preciousness, abstraction, and artifice.

Mercier stands out from the gallery of prose authors assembled in this book: his outspoken defense of prose, his perception of poetic genius, and his vision for a new literature reveal a *consciousness* about prose thus far unsurpassed (the obverse of Monsieur Jourdain's "prose-sans-le-savoir"). His entry on "prose poétique" in the *Néologie* is a refreshing and buoyant manifesto, or more precisely a prescription to cure the ills of French literature:

---

[68]   Mercier, *Mon Bonnet du matin*, 121–2.

Qui n'aurait pitié de tous ces jeunes gens perdus, abymés dans la versification française, et qui s'éloignent d'autant plus de la poésie! Je suis venu pour les guérir, pour dessiller leurs yeux, pour leur donner peut-être une langue poétique; elle tiendra au développement de la nôtre, d'après son mécanisme et ses anomalies. Médecin curateur, je veux les préserver de la rimaille française, véritable habitude émanée d'un siècle sourd et barbare; monotonie insoutenable, enfantillage honteux, qui, pour avoir été caressé par plusieurs écrivains, n'en est pas moins ridicule. La prose est à nous; sa marche est libre; il n'appartient qu'à nous de lui imprimer un caractère plus vivant. Les prosateurs sont nos vrais poètes; qu'ils osent, et la langue prendra des accens tout nouveaux.[69]

[Who would not feel sorry for all these lost young men, overwhelmed with French versification and getting all the farther from poetry! I came to cure them, to open their eyes, perhaps to give them a poetic language; it will be related to the development of ours, in its mechanism and anomalies. Healer and doctor, I want to preserve them from bad French rhymes, a habit coming from a deaf and barbarous century; insufferable monotony, shameful nonsense, which is no less ridiculous for having been indulged in by several writers. Prose is ours; its pace is free; it behooves us alone to impart to it a more lively character. Prose writers are our true poets. Let them dare, and our language will take wholly new accents.]

Mercier advocated the following steps: "dévoiler l'ossature de notre langue" [to unveil the skeleton of our language], "délivrer le versificateur français de pénibles et ridicules entraves—'le masque de la rime'" [to free French verse writers from painful and ridiculous fetters—the mask of rhymes], "remanier ... tout ce qui forme la contexture de notre langue, en la refusant sans la décomposer; examiner l'ordre et la génération des idées intellectuelles, pour courir aussi rapidement qu'elles" [to reshape ... all that forms the contexture of our language, by refusing it without decomposing it; to examine the order and formation of intellectual ideas to run as fast as they do].[70] Unlike powerless diagnosis and vague remedies offered by contemporary critics, Mercier's program resembles a dissection of the French language. His attention to the organic body of the language, his listening to its beat, and his sensitivity to linguistic alteration, gave Mercier exceptional prescience. His jubilant appreciation of Chateaubriand's first-born, *Atala*, rightly conjectured the successful deliverance of prose from its neoclassical womb:

[J]e souris de voir s'accréditer des licences qui tourneront à la plus grande gloire de la langue; j'aime le style d'*Atala*, parce que j'aime le style qui, indigné des obstacles qu'il rencontre, élance, pour les franchir, ses phrases audacieuses, offre à l'esprit étonné des merveilles nées du sein même des obstacles. Allez vous endormir près des lacs tranquilles ou des eaux stagnantes; j'aime tout fleuve majestueux qui roule ses ondes sur les rochers inégaux, qui les précipite par torrens de perles éclatantes, *qui emplit mon oreille d'un mugissement harmonieux*, qui

---

[69]   Mercier, *Néologie*, xliv–xiv, n1

[70]   Ibid., xiv–xlvij.

frappe mon œil d'une tourmente écumeuse, et qui me rappelle sans cesse près de ce magnifique spectacle, toujours plus enchanté des concordantes convulsions de la nature. Allumez-vous au milieu de nous, volcans des arts![71]

[I smile when I see the acceptance of licenses that will turn into the greatest glory of our language; I love *Atala*'s style because I love a style that, indignant from the obstacles it encounters, casts audacious sentences to surmount them, and offers to the astonished mind, marvels born of these very obstacles. Go and fall asleep near quiet lakes or stagnant waters! I love any majestic river that billows upon uneven rocks, rushes down in torrents of dazzling pearls, *fills my ear with harmonious roaring*, catches my eye with foamy rapids, and draws me over again near this magnificent spectacle, always more enchanted by nature's concordant convulsions. Light up amongst us, volcano of the arts!] (emphasis added)

This enthusiastic celebration meshes *Atala*'s opening and closing descriptions— the Mississippi river banks and Niagara Falls—by adopting a rather amusing imitative style (e.g., "concordante convulsions"). These spirited excesses— Mercier's famed extravagance—should not detract from the remarkable accuracy of Mercier's poetic perception: the invocation of one of Chateaubriand's most personal and revealing phrases, the "mugissement harmonieux," aptly concludes Mercier's segment on "Prose poétique," and opens a new chapter in the emergence of prose poetry.

---

[71] Ibid., xlvij–xlviij.

Conclusion
The Farewell of Telemachus
and Eucharis

The journey from Fénelon's ancient Greece to Chateaubriand's New World, from Calypso's tantalizing island to the mysterious banks of the Meschacebé, via the *terra incognita* of eighteenth-century prose poems, allows for the reappraisal of a poetic genre invented in the Enlightenment as an instrument of critique and rebellion—literary, religious, and socio-political. Mapping this voyage did not reveal a linear trajectory from a postclassical to a lyric Enlightenment, as the dawn of Romanticism might have tempted us to read retrospectively, but rather the complex ebb and flow of the tide of modernity reshaping classical shores. Before Mentor pushed Telemachus off a cliff into the ocean's "bitter waters" to wake him up from his infatuation with Eucharis's beauty and to cause him to resume his search for Ulysses, the young hero had begged for a final farewell to the nymph whom he loathed to abandon. While Fénelon denied his characters their last intimate encounter, it is this melancholy moment that Jacques-Louis David chose to represent in 1818 in a painting that I read symbolically as capturing the essence of Enlightenment prose poems: the brush of the modern through the classical, animated by the tension between freedom and formalism. "The Farewell of Telemachus and Eucharis" (see Figure 11), which Dorothy Johnson describes as "David's most lyrical and melancholy mythological masterpiece," translates on canvas the literary history, evolution, and tropes that I have drawn out in the course of this study.[1]

First, the painting illustrates a scene from the inaugural text that famously launched prose poems. Further, David translated pictorially the neoclassical style that characterizes Fénelonian prose and subsequent imitations. The ambivalence one feels in contemplating the painting, in reading "poëmes en prose," and in

---

[1] Dorothy Johnson, *The Farewell of Telemachus and Eucharis* (Los Angeles, 1997), 8. My interpretation is meant to complement Johnson's examination of David's painting from an artistic and historical perspective. Johnson argues for an interpretation of the scene as a positive representation of the virtue and purity of adolescent love, whereby David transformed Fénelon's episode of destructive passion into an idealized moment of innocence: "For he does not represent the loves of Telemachus and Eucharis as loathsome or morally reprehensible; on the contrary, he presents the lovers very sympathetically, with great tenderness and poignant affection" (Ibid., 49–50). I prefer to read the painting as a literary allegory of the tension between Prose and Poetry, in the same vein as another allegory representing aesthetic values, the last painting of David's life, *Mars disarmed by Venus and the Graces* (1824), "a seriocomic work that subverts accepted conventions and norms by combining the parodic and the sublime, realism and idealism ... his final aesthetic manifesto." Ibid., 8.

Fig. 11   Jacques-Louis David, *Adieux de Télémaque et d'Eucharis.* 1818. Oil on canvas, 34 ³/₈ x 40 ¹/₂ in. Los Angeles, The J. Paul Getty Museum.

deciding how to appreciate their value and form is part of the mystery of neoclassical aesthetic and its long-standing appeal in the Age of Reason, the story of which I wanted to tell in the present book. Finally, I interpret the lovers' farewell scene chosen by David as emblematic of the never-ending, always postponed, farewell to classical versification begun by Fénelon: Eucharis's shapely arms locked in embrace around Telemachus's neck, her bent head and closed eyes, contrast with Telemachus's straight gaze directed at the viewer, his hand resting on Eucharis's thigh, in the posture of someone ready to rise and leave. I propose to interpret their interaction as an allegory of the muse Poetry retaining Prose, whose virility is symbolized by the vertical spear. Cupid's arrows are stashed away in the quiver on Eucharis's back, as if intimating the end of Poetry's mythological *merveilleux*. By contrast, Telemachus's horn is strategically placed, suggesting the new songs Prose will soon sing. Eucharis's clasped fingers symbolize the chain of verse from which prose is freeing itself, with nostalgia. The royal blue and gold colors of the cloak (artistically folded to reveal Telemachus's young, heroic nude body) are symbolic of his nobility—a nobility, which, associated with strength, energy, and virility, is characteristic of the qualities of Prose as represented in the Enlightenment.[2] While the painting captures metaphorically the languid state of Poetry's verse and the moment just before Prose's emancipation, it reveals a tension between two characters who also embody the tension between two modes in prose poetry.[3] That David set the adieux in a cave reminds us of Calypso's grotto, so famously described by Fénelon as a fascinating, utopian space escaping representation where art and nature commingle and opposites unite.

It might come as a surprise to discover that Baudelaire praised David's painting as "a charming picture" and disapproved of his young contemporaries' dismissive smiles (and perhaps ours too), "adeptes de la fausse école romantique en poésie" [adepts of the false Romantic school in poetry.] Baudelaire made clear that Romanticism's filiation ought to be traced back also to the severity and austerity of David's formalism.[4] Baudelaire then professed a preference that is even more revealing in light of my allegorical interpretation: "Des deux personnages, c'est Télémaque qui est le plus séduisant. Il est présumable que l'artiste s'est servi pour le dessiner d'un modèle féminin" [Telemachus is the most seductive of both characters. We can presume that the artist used a female model to draw him.][5] Baudelaire found Telemachus/Prose the most attractive of David's characters, but on account of his androgyny. Sexual ambivalence, tellingly detected by Baudelaire, symbolizes the generic indeterminacy of prose poems. David's Telemachus is the pictorial equivalent of Baudelaire's own rendition of Franz Liszt's music in "Le Tyrse": the poetic arabesque of the feminine flowing around the prosaic.

The last word is best left to the exiles who lifted the lyre of prose to sing poetry's metamorphosis: in 1723, Rousseau coined the verb "prosaïser;" in 1810, de Staël minted "dépoétiser," and in 1848 Chateaubriand reinvented the meaning of "poétiser" to signify "giving a poetic character," and no longer "writing verse."[6] The three neologisms convey the dialectics behind the invention and development of Enlightenment prose poems.

---

[2]   "Telemachus's semidraped form belongs more to the convention of the heroic nude, emblem of strength, virtue, and truth, rather than to that of the soft, sensual male nudes, objects of sexual desire, that abounded in French art from the 1790s to around 1820." Ibid., 45.

[3]   Johnson notes that Telemachus's spear "functions as a counterbalance to the leaning figures, whose configuration is not completely stable." Ibid., 43.

[4]   "[ils] ne peuvent rien comprendre à ces sévères leçons de la peinture révolutionnaire, cette peinture qui se prive volontairement du charme et du ragoût malsains, et qui vit surtout par la pensée et par l'âme—amère et despotique comme la révolution dont elle est née. ... La couleur les a aveuglés, et ils ne peuvent plus voir et suivre en arrière l'austère filiation du romantisme, cette expression de la société moderne" [They cannot understand anything of the severe lessons of revolutionary paintings, a painting which deliberately deprives itself from unhealthy charm and relish, and which mostly live through the mind and the soul—bitter and despotic like the revolution from which it is born. ... Color has blinded them, and they can no longer see and trace in the past the austere filiation of Romanticism, the expression of modern society.] Baudelaire, *Œuvres complètes*, vol. 2, 409.

[5]   Ibid., 583.

[6]   Oresme had invented "poétiser" in 1372. *Dictionnaire historique et étymologique de la langue française* (Paris, 1993), 593, 623.

Appendix 1
Abbé Fraguier,
"A Discourse to shew that there can be no Poems in Prose"

By Mr. L'Abbe Fraguier.
Read to the French Academy of Belles Lettres, August 2d, 1719[1,2]

To displace the Land-marks erected by our Fathers to distinguish the Heritages of Families, has always been punished in Society as a very heinous Crime. The *Romans* made it a Part of their Religion not to touch them: They adored as a God the Mark which limited their Possessions: It was a sure Way of avoiding all Contests and Confusions;

> Omnis erit sine te litigiosus ager. Ovid. Fast. 1.2.

And of maintaining Justice and Property, by preserving the certain Knowledge of every one's Possessions.

> Limes agro positus, litem ut discerneret arvis. Virg. Aeneid.1.12.v.898.

Throughout the vast Field of Human Science, in the Partition of the ingenious Arts, each has its Boundaries: The Intelligence which animates them all, and gives them Fecundity, presides over their several Productions; *Spiritus intus alit.* The same Spirit watches likewise over the Preservation of the Limits which separate them; none of them can be dislodged out of its proper Place, without being culpable in its Eyes: It is to disturb the Order it has established, it is to create Disorder and Confusion where Harmony and Tranquility ought to reign.

If certain Wits, who confound Poetry with Prose, had well considered the Nature and Consequences of their Enterprize, they would have contented themselves with

---

[1]   "A Discourse to shew that there can be no Poems in Prose. By Mr. L'Abbé Fraguier. Read to the French Academy of Belles Lettres, August 2nd, 1719," in Académies des inscriptions & belles-lettres, *Select discourses read to the Academy of Belles Lettres and Inscriptions at Paris. Translated from the memoirs of the Academy.* London, 1741, 80–95. Abbé Fraguier, "Qu'il ne peut y avoir de Poëmes en Prose," in *Memoires de litterature tirez des registres de l'academie royale des inscriptions et belleslettres depuis l'année M. DCCVII jusques & compris l'année M. DCCXXV.* Tome sixieme. Paris: Imprimerie royale, M. DCCXXIX. Brackets indicate text from the original French. The lettered footnotes are in the English translation.

[2]   *Memoirs of Literature, T.6. p. 265. [Footnote from the original.]

excelling in either, without removing the unalterable Boundaries by which they are essentially separated. But let us search into the Origin of such an Innovation.

The Poet, whose Art consists wholly in Imitation and Painting, will find, say they, in Prose, and there more abundantly than in Verse, all that is necessary for Painting and Imitation. Wherefore, without subjecting the Liberty of his Genius to the Constraints and Fetters of Verse, which always too straitly confine the Imagination, he will attain to the End of his Art; and his Compositions, tho' in Prose, will notwithstanding be in Reality excellent Poems.

In answer to this Reasoning, I say, that a Poet is not naturally an Imitator only, since he hath the free Choice of the Means he employs in imitating: But that he is tied down to verse in his Imitations.

The Painter, the Musician, and the Poet, have equally for their End and Object Imitation: The Musician imitates by Sounds, the Painter by Colours; and the Poet by chosen Words, the different Union of which, within the Bounds of an unvaried Measure, produce an infinitely diversified Harmony. This is what is called Verse: And because by the Aid of this Harmony the Poet, more hardy than either the Musician or the Painter, makes Images pass which are far more lively and grand than any Prose can admit, and thus gives an original Air to his Copy; his Imitation is termed in one Word *Poem, i.e.* Work; and he himself, the Author of such a wonderful Imitation is denominated, by Way of Eminence, *The Worker*, ποιητής. Hence the Authority of the first Poets over the human Mind.

> Sylvestres homines sacer interpresque Deorum
> Caedibus, & fœdo victu deterruit Orpheus. Hor. Art. Poet.

For most assuredly it was not by Odes in Prose, that *Orpheus* tamed Lions and Tygers.

> Dictus ob hoc lenire tigres rabidosque leones.

Nor that *Amphion* raised the Walls of *Thebes*.

> Dictus & Amphion, Thebanae conditor arcis,
> Saxa movere sono testidunis, & prece blanda,
> Ducere quo vellet.

'Twas by the magical Power of fine Verse,[3] that both getting fast hold of the human Heart, led Men to Virtue; insomuch that the glorious Name of Poet being due to the Admiration with which Men were struck by their Verse, it could never after be acquired or preserved but by Means of the same enchanting Versification which gave Birth to it. The Poet, then, has Measures and Numbers for every Kind of Imitation.

> Res gestae regumque ducumque,& tristia bella,
> Quo scribi possint numero monstravit Homerus.

---

[3]   Canto quae solitus.——Amphion Dircaeus. Virg. Ec. 2.

Versibus impariter junctis querimonia primum,
Post etiam inclusa est voti sententia compos. Hor. Ibidem.
[Archilochum proprio rabies armavit ïambo.
Hunc socci cepere pedem, grandesque cothurni ...
Musa dedit fidibus divos, puerosque Deorum,
Et pugilem victorem, & equum certamine primum,
Et juvenum curas, & libera vina referre.]

Each Subject, in general, demands the Kind of Verse suitable to its Nature and Genius: And it is the Poet's Business to find within the Confines of each particular Measure, all the various Cadences proper to set before the Reader's Eyes, Images traced from the most beauteous Nature and from Fancy. This is the masterly Power of Poetry, to which Prose can never arrive; *Odi prosanum vulgus & arceo.*

Verse may be a Subjection to one of an ordinary Genius; to a Poet it is Sport, it is Pleasure: He is at no Loss to find those fine Arrangements of Words which enchant the Ear: Words flow at his Command, and as it were voluntarily take their Places. Out of them he forms an exquisite Melody: He glides from one Sound to another: Some he sinks and enfeebles, on purpose to raise and strengthen others: And if in all this he finds any Difficulty, that Labour enhances the Merit of his Works: The Efforts he makes to surmount it, and the Fire with which he is inflamed, awaken Ideas and Expressions in a Mind glowing with the Sense and Love of Glory, much more beautiful and striking than any Prose can suggest with all its boasted Freedom. *Virgil* explains himself on this Subject most admirably.

Nec sum animi dubius, verbis ea vincere magnum
Quam sit, & augustis hunc addere rebus honorem.
Sed me Parnassi deserta per ardua dulcis
Raptat amor: juvat ire jugis qua nulla priorum
Castaliam molli divertitur orbita clivo. Georg.1.3.v.289.

And elsewhere,

Tentanda via est, qua me quoque possim
Tollere humo, victorque virûm volitare per ora. Ibid. v.8.

The Vulgar of Mankind, dazled by the Lustre of such a rare Talent, have ascribed it to Divine Inspiration, which makes the Poet an Instrument to *Apollo* and the Muses.

Sic honor & nomen [divinis] vatibus, atque Carminibus venit. Hor. Art Poet.

Sing Muse, says[4] *Homer*: And *Virgil* cries aloud,

Pandite nunc Helicona deae, cantusque movete. Aeneid 7. v.641.

"I sing, *Homer* wrote, says *Apollo*."

---

4   Iliad & Odyss.

Ἡειδον μέν ἐγών, ἐχάρασσε δέ θειος' Ὁμηρος. Antho. Graeca.

The Oracle to give itself a more Divine Air, expressed itself in Verse.

Dictae per carmina sortes. Hor. Art Poet.

Whatever Eloquence any Orator may have had, hath he been ever the Interpreter of the Gods? And can we debase Poetry more than to transform it into Prose? Add to this that Poetry is adapted to singing.

Musa lyrae solers & cantor Apollo. Hor. Ibid.

The different Species of it had anciently a Relation to the respective Instruments which were the distinguishing Symbols of the Muses, and to various Modes of harmonical Composition.

Ye Songs, which regulate my Lyre, says Pindar, Olymp.2.

And Horace,

Verba Lyrae motura sonum.Hor. Ep.2.1.2.

Suffer Prose but to enter into the Ode, and what will become of its poetical Fire and Enthusiasm? To sing Prose, some perhaps will say, A fine Employment!

———O testudinis aureae
Dulcem quae strepitum, Pieri, temperas.Hor. Od.3. 1.5.

Muse, whose Lyre brings forth such delightful Sounds, shall you be reduced to elevate the Merit of your Enemy, and in Prejudice of the Language of the Gods, to give a Value to that of Mortals?

What, say they, Is not Prose susceptible of Cadence and Harmony? It is undoubtedly. Nothing is more evident from the Writings of the famous Orators: The ancient Teachers of Eloquence prescribe Rules for attaining to it. But one essential Rule relative to Prose in all Languages and in Stile of every Kind, is that in seeking for the Harmony of Words, and the Riches of Numbers, one cannot be too attentive to keep at a Distance from those Sounds and Numbers, which, being peculiar to Poetry, would render Prose in some Measure poetical.

As for the true Harmony of Prose, to whatever Degree of Perfection *Demosthenes* and *Cicero*, *Balzac* and *Patru* may have carried it, they will never be brought into Competition with *Homer*, nor with *Virgil*. And how far do they fall below *Pindar* and *Horace*, *Malherbe* and *Sarazin*? But as we have already said, 'tis from the Enchantment of Harmony, so infinitely diversified amidst the Uniformity of Verse, that the Poet owes his Name, and the Glory annexed to it.

Which is more, the Poets of every Country have made a particular Language for themselves, consisting partly of antique Words, Words transferred from their primitive to another Signification, Words more figurative and more energetick, Words either more soft or more rude than those employ'd to mark the same Things in common Discourse. The Gods, says *Homer*, call such a Thing so; Men give it another Name: We may say precisely the same of Prose and Poetry. The Difference in Language lies no less in the Construction, than in the Turns and Figures. The Poet and the Orator, says *Anthony* in *Cicero*, seem not to speak the same Language. *Poetas*, ———*quasi alia quadam lingua locutos*. A *Greek* would have said the same of the *Roman* Poets: We say so every Day of the *Italian*, *Spanish* and *English* Poets. If this Difference of Stile be less sensible in the *French* Tongue, it however takes place in it likewise, and is very distinguishable by those who thoroughly understand the Genius of the Language. But were it less remarkable in it than it is in other Languages, is this a Reason for utterly effacing and destroying it? for passing the Plow over the dividing Land-marks, and giving to Prose what hath always belonged to Poetry; and thus making, of two distinct Heritages, one and the same common Field?

Malherbe did not use them in this Manner; he could cultivate both without confounding them. His Stile in Prose is masculine and nervous [noble]; but in order to manage poetical Subjects as they ought, he had formed to himself an elevated, rich and harmonious Language.

Despreaux says justly of him,

> Fit sentir [dans] le[s] vers une juste cadence,
> D'un mot mis en sa place enseign[a] le pouvoir. L'Art Poet.[5]

He made Rhime contribute to render his Compositions yet more precious and beautiful. This is the Road chalked out by the great Masters for rising to the Perfection of Art, and rendering one's Name respectable to latest Posterity. All this poetical Equipage is not less interdicted Prose, than Prose is Poetry [Tout cet appareil poëtique n'est pas moins interdit à la Prose, que la Prose elle-même est défendue à la Poësie]; and I know not which is most blame-worthy, the poetick Prose, or the prosaick Poetry. However that be, does not Prose over-charged with poetical Ornaments, seem to labour to destroy, by its great care to embellish, that particular Beauty naturally belonging to it?

> Naturaeque decus mercato perdere cultu,
> Nec sinere in propriis membra nitere bonis. Prop. l.I. Eleg.2.

Perhaps not so good natured a Critick might call it a ridiculous Mascarade, compare it to an old Country Comedian, who the more she is dressed out, the more ridiculous she is; and address her in this rude Manner with the Rustick in *Plautus*: *Do you fancy yourself handsomer because you have Bracelets and Jewels, and have given your Robe and your Face a new Dip?*

> An eo bella es, quia accepisti armillas & virias?
> Quia tibi insuaso fecisti, propudiosa, pallulam?
> Quiaque istas buccas tam belle purpurissatas habes? Plaut. Truciol. 2. Act. Sc.2.

---

[5]　[Malherbe] made us sense a just cadence in verses and taught us the power of a word well placed.

Let not Prose, which hath its own special Beauty, go about to beg a Foreign one; and above all, let it not flatter itself with the Hopes of ever equaling Poetry by the Aid of borrowed Embellishments.

Let us call to Mind the Pleasure good Verses afford us, when the Truth and Beauty of Sentiments supported, nay enhanced by the Charms of Numbers and Harmony, take powerful Hold of our Soul and entirely possess it: When the Enthusiasm of the Poet seizes the Actor, and passes from him to the Hearer. If so much as one Word is displaced; if but one Syllable is out of Order; if the Harmony be broken in the smallest Degree by negligent Pronunciation, all our Pleasure evanishes. What must then be the Case, if the Verse is wholly destroyed, and reduced to mere prose? Nothing would remain but, at most, what *Horace* calls *Disjecti membra Poetae*, the shattered Members of a disjointed Poet, which can no more make a Poem, than severed, scattered Limbs a Body.

Because after having destroyed the Versification, which being very like to Prose, is proper to Comedy, nothing remain'd but mere Prose, without one Spark of that divine Fire which is the Soul of true Poetry; *Horace*, a great Poet and an able Critick, seems to approve the opinion of those who refused Comedy a Place amongst the poetical Compositions.

> Quidam Comoedia nec ne Poema
> Esset, quaesierat; quod acer spiritus, ac vis
> Nec verbis, nec rebus inest, nisi quod pede certo
> Differt sermoni sermo merus. Hor. l. I. Sat.4.

However, says he, we often find in Comedy a provoked angry Father, reproaching his Son for his Extravagancy and Irregularities, in Terms full of Fire and Passion.

> ————————————At pater ardens
> Saevit, quod meretrice nepos insanit amica,
> Filius uxorem grandi cum dote recuset, &c.

But to make a Work deserving to be called a Poem, it is not sufficient, says *Horace*, to express one's self in Terms, which if you but alter their Form and Arrangement a little, every angry Father would naturally use

> Non satis est puris versum perscribere verbis,
> Quem si dissolvas, quivis stomachetur eodem
> Quo personatus pacto pater.

But if Comedy in Verse, as it then always was, deserved not, in his Opinion, the Name of a Poem, What must he have thought of our Comedies in Prose? He would undoubtedly have looked upon them but as Dialogues, such as several other ancient Dialogues, which have never passed for Poems, and whose Authors have never been accounted Poets.

> Ingenium cui sit, cui mens divinior, atque os
> Magna sonaturum, des nominis hujus honorem.

This fine Genius [ce beau naturel], *ingenium,* this Divine Genius, *mens divinior,* this rich Vein of Harmony, *os magna sonaturum*: All this, according to *Horace,* is requisite to make a Poet, and belongs only to the Poet who speaks in Beautiful Numbers.

This would be the proper Place for replying to those, who, admitting no Difference between one Language and another, maintain, that Beauty of Sounds, and the Harmony resounding from thence, are but Chimæra: But the Question being about a Matter of Taste and Sentiment, which cannot be given to those who have not received it from Nature, let us satisfy ourselves with pitying them, and let us not insult their Misfortune. For ourselves, let us only entreat such not to condemn our Sensibility, but to suffer us to enjoy our foolish Fancy, if it be such, or to profit by a Sense which we have more than they. If there be indeed any reality in it.

> ————Si modo ego & vos ...
> Legitimumque sonum digitis callemus & aure. Hora.Art Poet.

It will, perhaps, be objected to me, that I make Poetry wholly to consist in Versification. Were I of this Sentiment I could support it by the Authority[6] of *Isaac Casaubon*[7]: I could likewise quote *Plato,* in whose Judgment, *Every Poetical Work, when considered abstractly from Harmony of Verse and Musick, is no more than a Face, which having no real Beauty, hath nothing to recommend it, but a certain Air of Freshness and Youth, which quickly passes away.* But I chuse rather to answer, that there may be Verses without any Poetry in them.

> ————Neque enim concludere versum
> Dixeris esse satis.

But there can be no Poetry without Verse.

In order to explain this Reply, let it be observed, that all the fine Arts have something in common, and something particular to each, that constitutes its proper and distinguishing Character. For Instance, the Painter and the Poet must be able to compose a beautiful Whole of the different Parts of Nature they study and copy, which often does not exist but in their Imagination.

> ————Poeta tabulas cum cepit sibi,
> Quaerit quod nusquam est gentium, reperit tamen. Plaut. Pseud. Act I. Sc.4.

Both must *design,* each in his own Manner, what they have invented, mark and distribute all the Parts, and all their Bearings, Relations and Dependencies. But when all this is done, if the Painter should not add Colours; and if the Poet should not add Versification, neither hath the one made a Picture, nor the other a Poem: For as Colours are essential to a Picture, so is Versification to Poetry.

---

[6]   Casaub. De Sat. Gr. Poes. &c.
[7]   De Rep.1.10.p. 601.

It will be said, is not a Poem transformed [traduit] into Prose a Poem still? Who will say it is not? Do not the Plan, the Ordonnance, the Thoughts, the Sentiments, the Descriptions still subsist; all in a Word one can desire to know and understand from the Original? I dare adventure to ask in my Turn, If a Print engraved after a Picture, is a Picture? If they agree it is not, I am ready, in favour of so beautiful and useful an Art, to let pass, without further Dispute, the whole Comparison between a Print in respect of a Picture, and a Prose Translation in respect to the Original in Verse.————I say, to let it pass without more Dispute; for there would even upon that Concession be room for a great deal. As then, the World is greatly obliged to the Labours of a *Marc Antonio*, that famous Engraver, which have put it in the Power of an Infinity of Persons to be acquainted with the Compositions of *Raphael*, of which they would, without such Help, have had no idea; so we cannot put too high a Value on the Labours of those happy Genius's, who possessing some Share of the Talents of the great Poets they have translated, have given some Idea of them in Prose to many who could never otherwise have known them. It is certainly a very meritorious Service, especially when their Translations are accompanied with learned Remarks and judicious Reflexions, by which, as much as can be, is restored to their Originals, of what they must necessarily lose in the best Prose Translations. Let us admire the fine Translations of the most renowned Poets, with which several illustrious Persons have enriched our Language and Age: Let us make a proper Use of them for our better understanding the ancient Originals: But after having rendered to every one his due Praise, let us agree, out of Regard to Truth, that Poems stripp'd of that Harmony peculiar to them, have no more that charming Complexion, that wonderful captivating Beauty, which according to *Plato*, makes them Poems. I am apt to think I cannot be charged with affirming any thing not agreeable to the Idea the Ancients had of Poetry. If the *Latin* Writers have never translated the *Greek* Poets into Prose, it was because their Verse being very like to that of the *Greeks*, it was not difficult for them to do it in Verse; and they thought they could not pretend to present their Countrymen with a Poem, if they gave them Prose.

And indeed no Writer ever assumed to himself the Name of a Poet, when he did not compose in Verse. Neither *Apuleius* nor *Lucian* are ranked in that Class: Yet the Metamorphoses of the former is a very poetical Work; and the History of *Psyche* would be a Poem, were it not in Prose. The Stile of *Apuleius* is florid enough to merit the new Name of Poetical-Prose. The Visions of *Lucian* in his *true History*, are of the same Kind: His Stile is gay and flowery; bedecked with the Flowers only to be gathered in the Garden of the Muses: But neither of them is classed with the Poets. And why? Because neither of them wrote in Verse. I might say the same of *Scipio's Dream*; the Beauty, the Sublimity of which Composition would have merited *Cicero* the first Rank among the Poets, if Prose could have gained that Prize.

The Verses Mr. *D'Urfé* has inserted into his *Astrea*, have given occasion to say of him, that as good a Writer of *Romance* as he was, he was not a good Poet. And therefore Romances have no better Title to be called Poems than other Prose-works. I am persuaded that the illustrious Author of *Telemachus* never intended to make it a Poem: He knew too well every part of the *Belles Lettres*, not to pay due Regard to the Limits which divide that Territory into different Provinces: He lov'd our Language too much to think of spoiling it; and Poetry too well to destroy it. He would have been sorry to have given a pernicious Example, that might, by its Effects, at last have reduced us to the Poverty of some Eastern Nations [Nations de l'Orient], which never produced true Poems. All their Poetry is nothing but high-sounding Prose [de la Prose cadencée au hazard, & sans nulle mesure certaine de Vers], and an enormous Assemblage of extravagant Metaphors, monstrous Hyperboles, and affected enigmatical Epithets. In one Word, their Poetry is like their Musick, which consists in a confused barbarous Arrangement of Words and Sounds, which having no Proportion, no Concord, cannot be reduced to Rules and Measures of Harmony capable of arithmetical Demonstration.

In fine, if one could merit the Name of Poet by writing in Prose, every one would aspire at the Character: A high-swoln Stile would hold the Rank of the true Sublime: An arbitrary Disposition of Phrases and Periods would hold the Rank of Harmony: And besides, the Ideas called Poetical being trite, and within the Reach of every one, every new Day would bring forth some new Monster call'd a Poem. Fine Poets, disgusted to see their Laurels thus prostituted to every Trifler, would abandon an Art from which formerly they derived real Honour; and ranking this pretended Poetry with the lowest Arts, they will say with Indignation,

> Frange leves calamos & scinde, Thalia, libellos;
> Si dare sutori calceus ista potest. Mart. I.9. Ep. 75.

Thus have I given you, Gentlemen, a slight Sketch of what might be said upon a Subject which it was of Importance to handle, lest if Poetry should come to change its Features amongst us, or to be entirely lost, other polite Nations and Posterity should impute it to the Silence of this Society.

Appendix 2
Bitaubé, *Guillaume de Nassau, or The Foundation of the United Provinces* (1775)[1]

Foreword on the following preface

We give this preface in the form of an imaginary dialogue between a journalist and the author because under this form it is easier and perhaps less boring to discuss several points related to this work.

Dialogue between the author and a journalist

The Journalist. You give the title *Guillaume* to your manuscript. Will you add nothing to designate more precisely the genre of the work?
The Author. I do not see its necessity.
The J. Did you not give yourself a goal? Did you not follow a model? Have you written a story? Is it a novel? Or is your work a new genre?
The A. I do not know. But let us suppose it is so, is it my role to name it, and is it not more modest and reasonable to let the public decide? Besides, I do not trouble myself with genre. Someone told me the only bad genre was the boring genre.
The J. Allow me to mistrust somewhat an author's modesty; and fear that ...
The A. Did my book bore you?
The J. I would like to know in which class to place it. Will you be happy if it has an amphibious existence? No one will talk about it for want of knowing how it calls itself.
The A. I shall be happy if it meets a certain number of readers like you who feel enough interest that they are concerned by the title it should receive.
The J. I am not the dupe of all these subterfuges. Admit that you wanted to write a poem in prose.
The A. I assure you that I planned nothing and that I let my mind follow the incline it pleased.
The J. You were well inspired. But in literature one is not satisfied by such a defeat; we want to give a title to a work, it is the first thing that strikes a reader. Despite yourself, they will say your work is a poem in prose.

---

[1]   Paul-Jérémie Bitaubé, *Guillaume de Nassau, ou La Fondation des Provinces-Unies. Nouvelle [Deuxième] Edition considérablement augmentée & corrigée.* Paris: Prault, Imprimeur du Roi, M.DCC.LXXV [1775].

The A. If they say it despite myself, I will have to bear it; but no one will be able to claim that I said it first.

The J. I admit I fear for you the critics' severity. The public has shown indulgence towards your *Joseph* and it has been generally considered a poem: the topic was familiar, it could adapt to prose's tone, and this attempt did not seem to be of any consequence. But now that you are writing a second work in this genre, in a higher style, and that you seem to aspire almost to be an epic poet, do you not fear to awaken the attention of the literary Republic's censors? Similar to old censors, they scream that one shall not innovate.

The A. In good faith, you frighten me when I hear that I wrote a poem in prose, and you seem to me at this moment an austere censor. What do you advise me to do? I do not have enough talent for versification, and even if I had, should I rewrite my whole work to put it into verse? I might as well withdraw it.

The J. The alternative is a bit harsh, and for several reasons I would like your attempt to see the light. But the critics ...

The A. You always come back to them. Since you do not want me to withdraw my work, my fate is apparently to write works that look like poems in prose.

The J. Would you like to discuss together this kind of writing?

The A. I do not object, provided you do not want to set traps for me now, and that you take into account my statement, namely that I did not pretend to write a poem in prose: if *Guillaume* resembles one in some respect, the harm is done.

The J. You distrust me? I accept your statement. Let us forget your work, and let us only speak of the genre with which it would seem to have the most affinities, if we absolutely had to find it a title. Do you not think that there is some contradiction in the terms poem in prose?

The A. The word poem should be taken here in a general sense and mean the story of a great, interesting action, etc.—a narrative that could be written either in verse or measured prose [prose mesurée]. Have we not prose comedies? It is true that when they began their Authors ran some risks and even saw their works denied the name comedies. Expectedly, people said they were a novelty and that, since it is easier to write comedies in prose instead of verse, they would only appear in prose from now on. However, comedies in verse have been written since then, and today one no longer denies the name of comedy to those written in prose.

The J. Though comedy sometimes inflates its tone, *tumido delitigat ore*, you will agree that the genre of epic poetry is higher.

The A. I do not care and I did not want to compare them. But you must agree in turn that an orator can reach the sublime, that he touches our hearts or dismays us, and that (putting aside the prestige of action) we are transported when reading Demosthenes, Cicero and Bossuet in the silence of our study.

The J. Who doubts it?

The A. Unquestionably, one can affect the soul powerfully, elevate and move it with the language of prose only. Poetic prose ...

The J. I stop you here: some people do not know what poetic prose is.

The A. You surprise me. There is, I believe, some difference between the prose of a simple letter, and the one used to translate poets. Poetic prose is as noble and sometimes bolder than oratorical prose: its inversions can be more frequent and audacious; its epithets more numerous and striking. Unlike oratorical style, it does not need to hide art as much: however, it would not suit it to wear all of poetry's ornaments; it would step out of its genre and become affected. We could place it between poetry and eloquence [genre oratoire], since it borrows something from each. Despite the opinion of those who want poets translated in verse, we read good prose translations with pleasure. It would not be impossible to write an original work in the style that gifted authors successfully used to translate poets.

The J. Such work would be more pleasing in verse.

The A. I feel like you. But if those who are able to read the originals sometimes read with pleasure a good translation despite the loss it suffered, one only has to look at the work about which I am speaking as the translation of an original that has been lost and with which it would not be unfairly compared. We prefer a beautiful painting to a print which is but its copy; but it does not make us reject all engravings, and I do not see that we despise those that have the merit of being originals.

The J. But would you like, for instance, that only tragedies in prose be written, and will you be, like La Motte, the apologist of a genre that is closer to dramas, which, it is said, infect literature?

The A. I am not surprised that you thus generalize my opinions: one should always expect it. One might inveigh against bad dramas as much as one pleases, I will add my voice to the critics'; but without deciding the rank it should occupy in literature, I dare maintain, since you address this point, that in itself the genre of bourgeois drama is not bad, and that a felicitous genius would know how to cultivate it. Legislators who want to establish despotic laws in the empire of Letters should not forget that events destroyed similar systems more than once: a lot has been written against the genre of the novel and none has produced so many bad books: it has been said, and there is nothing more likely, that it was tasteless, monotonous, that the ancients had not tried it, etc., and yet nature's great painters, the Fieldings and Richardsons, became immortal by writing in this genre. How many roads can genius take to please? Are there chains that can subject this Protheus? But such is our nature, so why would we treat books better than men? Did someone mislead us? It is not rare that we hold a grudge against a whole nation, and sometimes even the whole human race. However, I think that it is possible to write an interesting tragedy in prose, and I am far from touching with a sacrilegious hand the altars justly raised in memory of Corneille and Racine.

The J. La Motte did not defend his thesis well; for he wrote a tragedy in prose that lacked any interest and failed more from its content than its style. He did further harm: he put in prose one of Racine's scene, the most harmonious of our poets, the poet *par excellence*; it is as if, immediately after a delicious dish, we would be presented with it again but less seasoned and told that it was the same. After this sort of crime, I am no longer curious to read La Motte's verses, and I do not know what to think of his poetic genius. What one could say in favor of your statement is that a beautiful prose is worth more than harsh and neglected verses, and that the gist of situations and sentiments in *Inès* pleases a lot despite its faults. We read with delight Brumoy's translation of Sophocles' tragedies; if we would produce them on stage as translations of ancient tragedies (and I am surprised it has never been tried) perhaps they would succeed despite the differences between our mores and Athens.

Yet I admit that, either out of reason or habit, the idea of a tragedy in prose revolts me. Though you may say that I only judge post facto, I will wait to make up my mind for the publication of one that will be well received. I am less shocked by the idea of a prose poem; the length of a work can serve as an excuse; the enterprise is less slippery than theater, and besides, the innovation is less obvious since we have works that belong to this genre. But it was unknown to the ancients.

The A. Is this objection really philosophical? Shall we not be allowed to divert ever from the path they traced? Are we in the same circumstances? Have we the same language? Is it not at least probable that if the ancients had the yoke of rhyme as we do, there would have been several writers who, especially in works of some length, would have tried to free themselves? Even if they had not tried it, would their example have been an inviolable law? They did not have comedies in prose and we have some. But what do you mean? Does not Plato sometimes take poetry's elevated tone, and was he not considered the philosophers' poet? We doubt if our sacred poems, these odes unsurpassed by any poets, are written in verse; and it seems that David's language is, like Job's, the language of measured prose [prose mesurée], which, compared to meter, is halfway between ordinary prose and versification, but which can compensate what it is lacking with the greatness of its ideas. Those who praise the ancients most cannot flatter themselves to have studied them with more taste than Fénelon; and yet, when imitating beautiful passages in Homer, Sophocles and Virgil, he wrote in prose ...

The J. He did not claim that he wrote a poem.

The A. What does it matter, provided that when he surrendered to his genius he wrote a book that does not resemble a mediocre but the most excellent poem: while people argue about the class to which it belongs, more read it than numerous epic poems. Could not poetic prose replace blank verse, which we do not dare introduce in our language now, whereas most modern nations that cultivate letters have them, so that their poets can, according to their inclination, receive or reject rhyme?

The J. I have read somewhere that to take a different path than the great masters who preceded us, is to declare that we are not capable of walking in their footsteps.

The A. I have just shown you that the genre we are speaking about is not as new as we suppose. But were we to make the always modest and most often true confession that we cannot reach the same height as these great geniuses who opened steep and inaccessible paths, should we abandon cultivating plains or slopes according to one's strength? Are we sure that we follow their footsteps better by writing in verse? How many verse writers remain far behind them!

The J. I would be afraid that the flock of such works disfigure history.

The A. It is a false alarm. Who does not see that imagination plays a great role in these works? They can help disseminate major facts but what reader would want to draw deep in them for historical knowledge? We have never recognized that the prodigious fecundity of Greek tragic authors spread confusion in history.

The J. Fear you not yourself, given the genre's easiness, that we be inundated by prose poems? We can see quickly that such torrent would be muddy.
The A. What makes you think this genre is so easy? Is the number of great writers so huge? Do we have many good translations of poets, a genre close to the one we are discussing now, and do we not see writers, otherwise talented, fail at it? Cicero remarked that there were more great poets than great orators; however orators are not bound by poetry's chains. One cannot write well in a rhythmic and measured prose [prose nombreuse & cadencée] without experiencing the poet's enthusiasm. Those who did not try only see the absence of rhyme. According to them, thoughts and feelings flow on their own from the prose author's quill; they are ready to challenge you like *Crispin* in *Horace*; but if they took up their quill, they would be fast proven wrong. After *Racine* had written his tragedy in prose, he would say, *my tragedy is done*, which proves that the greatest obstacles he faced did not come from versification. M. de *Voltaire* observes that it is all the more difficult to aim high when using a simple, natural language that must replace the pleasure of rhyme with the strength and variety of ideas. I do not fear boring you by reading to you now several passages from Cicero which I transcribed and are related to this matter. *Esse in oratione numerum quemdam, non est difficile cognoscere. Judicat enim sensus: in quo iniquum est, quod accidit, non cognoscere, si, cur id accidat, reperire nequeamus. Neque enim ipse versus ratione est cognitus, sed natura atque sensu, quem dimensa ratio docuit, quid acciderit. Ita notatio naturae, & animadversio, perperit artem. Sed in versibus res est apertior: quanquam etiam a modis quibusdam, cantu remoto, soluta esse videatur oratio, maximeque id in optimo quoque eorum poëtarum, qui lyricoi a Graecis nominantur: quos cum cantu spoliaveris, nuda paene remanet oratio.*[2] Cicero observes that the best Greek lyrical verses, when removed from singing, were close to prose: he explains even better when he adds *nisi cum tibicen accessit.*[3] Doubtless, he does not mean *Pindar* or *Alcée*'s poems, and by the word *lyrical* we should understand here only ancient dramas whose meter was iambic and accompanied by singing. What will you say if I read to you one of Cicero's thought where he argues that it is more difficult to write in rhythmic prose [prose nombreuse] than in verse? I will simply quote the passage and let you judge it as you please. *Atque id in dicendo numerosum putatur, non quod totum constat e numeris, sed quod ad numeros proxime accedit: quo etiam difficilius est oratione uti, quam versibus: quod in illis certa quaedam & definita lex est, quam sequi sit necesse: in dicendo autem*

---

[2]   Ciceron, L'Orateur, chap. 55. "S'il existe un nombre oratoire n'est pas difficile à résoudre. L'oreille a prononcé. On n'a pas le droit de nier un fait, par la raison qu'on en ignore la cause. Connaît-on mieux la cause du plaisir que procure le nombre poétique? Non. C'est la nature et le sentiment qui ont fait le vers. La raison est venue en constater l'existence, et le mesurer. L'art n'a pas tardé à naître de l'observation intelligente de la nature. Le nombre se fait mieux sentir en poésie, bien que plusieurs espèces de vers ressemblent beaucoup à de la prose, quand on ne les chante point. Tels sont surtout les vers lyriques. Supprimez le chant, la prose se montre à nu."

[3]   Ibid., "si l'on retranchait l'accompagnement de la flûte."

nihil est propositum, nisi aut ne immoderata, aut angusta, aut dissoluta, aut fluens sit oratio. Itaque non sunt in ea tanquam tibicini percussionum modi, sed universa comprehensio & species orationis clausa & terminata est: quod voluptate aurium judicatur ...[4] *Quantum autem sit apte dicere, experiri licet, si aut compositi oratoris bene structam collocationem dissolvas permutatione verborum.*[5] I think you will allow me these quotations from the most harmonious orator who could be forgiven if he exaggerated the difficulties of his art.

The J. Then you do not know how much I love this philosopher-orator. It seems to me you felt like a certain journalist who puts the genre of prose poems on the same level as prose translations of poetry.

The A. Though producing such translations has more merit than we think, it seems to me it is not an accurate appreciation because invention is left out, which, I presume, should be put in the balance.

The J. Could not the success of a prose poem harm the art of verse?

The A. Such art will always garner the most flattering successes; and so many people rhyme despite Minerva that we should not fear that those truly born with the talent to compose verses, will ever try or succeed in stifling it.

The J. I noticed you like verses.

The A. When *La Motte* declaims against French verses, he proves that he lacked a poetic genius to feel their charm. We do not find our great Poets' verses monotonous: who gets tired of reading *Racine, Corneille, La Fontaine, Boileau*, etc.?

Such is not the case with mediocre poets; and it is quite possible that La Motte, surprised by the monotony of his own verses preferred to accuse art rather than the artist. You think this is a paradox: but the ending of Greek and Latin hexameters is perhaps no less monotonous that that of our heroic verses. The latter, aside from two different, alternating endings, constantly offer other rhymes and rhythms [nombres], whereas the former always end (with rare exceptions) with a dactyl and spondee. The poet has to eliminate monotony with rich tableaux, sentiments and style.

The J. I see that you are not one of those who elevate a genre by bringing down other genres.

---

[4]   Ibid., chap. 58. "Le nombre n'est pas une condition d'existence pour la prose comme pour la poésie. Un discours où tout serait soumis au nombre, serait un poème. Il lui suffit, pour être nombreux, d'avoir une allure égale et décidée, où rien de boiteux ne trahisse un défaut d'équilibre. Il ne sera pas entièrement composé de nombres, mais il se rapprochera de cette constitution. Et voilà pourquoi la difficulté d'écrire est plus grande en prose qu'en vers. Ici, des lois positives, invariables, nécessaires; là, des conditions de rythme vagues, arbitraires et négatives. Car il ne doit être ni trop étendu, ni trop resserré, ni trop négligé. La musique a des temps frappés, qui donnent à la mesure une précision parfaite. La prose n'a que des règles générales, des préceptes d'ensemble, qui la laissent sans guide pour les détails, et sans autre régulateur que le caprice de l'oreille qu'elle veut séduire."

[5]   Ibid., chap. 70. "Deux épreuves bien faciles vont nous mettre à même d'apprécier sans hésitation toute l'utilité de l'harmonie. La première consiste à changer l'ordre des mots dans une phrase bien construite."

The A. Could this be a merit?

The J. I think you have remarked that independently of our sacred poems, there are indeed prose poems.

The A. Gessner ...

The J. Naming this beautiful genius says it all. And what do you think of the *Temple of Gnidus*, given that we have already talked about *Telemachus*?

The A. If you promise me not to betray me in your paper ...

The J. I can guess your answer. Will it not be easy now for us to find a title for *Guillaume*?

The A. Let me remain silent on this issue.

The J. I press you no further. If we wanted to speak more on this topic, we would imitate these cataloguers who, in botanic, exhaust themselves creating systems to classify beings instead of spending their time studying them.

One more word. You are probably going to produce some other ... I almost said poem?

The A. It would not be prudent to speak always with the same tone to the public, especially when we should be inspired by imagination. We do not dare guarantee that we shall always be protected from the seductions of this temptress: but at least I intend not to yield to it any more.

Appendix 3
Collin d'Harleville,
"Dialogue between Prose and Poetry" (1802)[1]

POETRY

Prose, allow me have a few words.

PROSE

Ah! Poetry, it is you!

POETRY

One moment, without witnesses,
Let us talk.

PROSE

Gladly.

POETRY

We often see each other, but from a distance,
Almost in passing; never, it seems, have we
Spoken, conversed together
Dear Prose, let us give ourselves the pleasure this once:
Indeed, now that we both have the leisure.

PROSE

This is more than true.

POETRY

Do not fear my grand airs, my style; one knows, my dear,
"How to move from serious to sweet, and from pleasing to severe"
Without trying here to dazzle and shine,
I do consent to slip back into colloquial style.

PROSE

As you like. I too have more than one tone, and I will match mine to yours.

POETRY

With your modesty, fair and square, you amuse me:
From the cradle, raised to converse with the Muses
I took a noble flight: I know not what accent,
More fire, more spirit, a pressing, lively turn of phrase,
All put between us an immense interval.
Therefore, always my sister, never my rival,
Who of my courtiers defected to your side?

---

[1]   Jean-François Collin d'Harleville, "Dialogue entre Prose et Poésie," in *Œuvres de Collin-Harleville contenant son théâtre et ses poésies fugitives*. 4 vols. Paris: Delongchamps, 1828, vol. 4, *Poésies fugitives* [1802], 101–12.

PROSE

Who? Voltaire, for example.

POETRY

Do you believe his heart felt divided between us?
I still remember a certain epithet
So sly, between us, that I shall not repeat it.

PROSE

A bad joke. Did Voltaire lower himself when he wrote at my dictation *Zadig,*
l'*Ingénu, Candide* and so many other, more important, works?
Come, though each of us has her own visage and style, we are still both students
of grammar—a grammar, let us say in passing, whose lessons we have sometimes
forgotten; nevertheless we are sisters, twin sisters even.

POETRY

I am the elder.

PROSE

You, the elder? Your pretension is ridiculous.

POETRY

At least, it is new.
This is the first time that, even without witnesses,
Two ladies try to outdo each other to claim seniority:
But I am attached to my rank more than to my youth.
Twins! Prose, how could you have forgotten?
I sang, while you barely knew how to stammer;
Still obedient to the laws of cold grammar,
When I already inspired Moses, Orpheus, and Homer.
Who amongst us dared first open the skies?
Who sang first Mount Olympus and the Gods?
And brave heroes, almost all of whom my creation,
And whom my voice, as much as their courage, turned into Gods?
This is how my inspiration let its treasures flow,
And you, what were you doing then my poor Prose!

PROSE

I did what I am doing at present: I was less brilliant; yet I did exist. Amongst
sisters, one shines more, another is more useful. Without boasting, I sometimes
corrected your work, you had confused everything; I untangled this chaos; you
gave birth to fictions, I let the truth speak; you created fables, but one owes history
to me.

POETRY

Indeed! A nice present which men strangely put to use!
I said somewhere, "Error has its merits."
But yourself, ... and your naïveté makes me laugh,
It seems you never invented anything!
Have you not, by error or lapse of memory,
Often introduced fable into history?

Your Herodotus and yourself, without being more brilliant
Are neither more exact nor in better faith.

PROSE

You speak too rashly. And if I wanted to justify Herodotus ... but we are digressing. You really believe you are the world's first language? Come, sister! Was I not, before you, the interpreter of the soul's tenderest affections? Was I not the first who got a child to stammer the name of her father, inspired friendship's effusions, and whispered love's sweet words in one's ear?

POETRY

"Whispered love's sweet words in one's ear!"
I admire such a phrase in your mouth
Dear sister, believe me, speak more plainly
Deal thoroughly with science and reasoning:
Serve, I agree, as a channel to tender friendship;
But would you dare imitate me when I sing,
When I capture the accent, the cry of passions,
When with fire, wit and choice of words,
I paint the soul's deepest feelings?
Learn that the transports of a burning flame
And the charming art of verse were born the same day,
And that I hummed the first love song.

PROSE

Very well! You will see that one has never sighed but in verse, and that one must be a poet to say *I love you!* Dear sister, a word, a look have always been enough to be understood; they say everything. Silence is often most eloquent; and love could do without you and me. Come, he who sings and tells of his lover's favors and even her rigors, has not yet loved or no longer does.

POETRY

Heavens! If it is thus, the world is credulous indeed.
Anacreon, Terence and you, dear Tibullus,
All of you, whose sweet verse, shaped by the graces
Have painted love so well, you would have never loved!
Nor you, Virgil, nature's painter!
Sentiments, for you, were but impersonations;
And never, in a sincere, tender abandon
Did your heart share Dido's pain!

PROSE

Now you exaggerate as usual. I respect, nay I like Virgil, because he is enthusiastic as well as wise, harmonious and true; and *true*, do you hear me, sister? It is a rare merit among your favorites. You often sacrifice accuracy to grace, and reason to the desire to shine: you have not always trained Boileaus. But after all, perhaps it is the fault of verses themselves.

POETRY

Nice excuse indeed! The fault of verses themselves?
What? You repeat my enemies' blasphemes?

In a cold and ridiculous bout,
Would you like to recommence the trial of your La Mothe-Houdard
And by accusing me again of some fine crime
Have Rhyme and me banished forever?

PROSE

No, no. I criticize verses but I do not want to prohibit them: I do not hate my pleasures that much. I honor sweet prosody, harmonious diction, showy images, and bold inversions as well; but for the rest, of which you are so proud, your rhythm, your caesura, your sonorous and often meaningless rhymes, your resounding epithets, all these serious trifles ...

POETRY

Rhythm, caesura, oh heavens, *rhyme* especially, mere trifles!
You do speak like Prose. But all these ties,
Pleasing constraints and noble chains,
That I honor and love, and you defy,
Far from stifling poetry's meaning and expression
Give it more life, more precision:
But free, easy, in short with no excuse,
You let yourself go, languid and diffuse.
Is not your friend Cicero too verbose
With his periods and pompous style?

PROSE

I was fair to Virgil: speak with respect about Cicero—Cicero, eloquence's model, always pure, clear, and meaningful: quote me twenty lines that have such merit.

POETRY

To reply to your fine criticism,
I could quote all of Racine, and [Boileau's] Art poétique.
Try and name one of your dear prose authors,
Whose reason ... What am I saying? Despite your attitude
You sense only too well the value of noble poetry:
You may decry it, but it is out of jealousy.

PROSE

Who? Me, jealous? And of what? Did I not have, like you, successes, students, and friends? If you mention Homer, I shall name Plato and Plutarch; do you not think that Demosthenes and Tacitus counterbalance Sophocles' and Pindar's glory? That Corneille and Molière eclipse Pascal and Bossuet? Nowadays, you can boast almost only about Voltaire; whereas I count Montesquieu, Buffon, Bernardin de Saint Pierre; lastly, each of us has a Rousseau.[2]

POETRY

They are both mine: yes, noble interpreters
Of genius and taste, thou art both poets.

---

[2]   A reference to the poet Jean-Baptiste Rousseau and the philosopher Jean-Jacques Rousseau.

PROSE

Still more chimeras! This way, one would confuse everything. Jealous and ambitious sister! What if, in turn, I was going to contest your poets?

POETRY

I could part with more than one without regret:
The honor would be all mine; for I would take from you
All the sublime authors in your language,
And you would get from me only versifiers.

PROSE

Let us stop this debate: what fruit does it bear? Let us argue instead about who will be the most useful. Believe me, sister, quell your imagination's outbursts: it misled you more than once; retrace your steps.

POETRY

Courage! It suits you well to preach to me,
As if you had nothing to reproach yourself!
When you thus put on matronly airs,
You remind me even more of Petronius:
If sometimes I enlivened tales and couplets,
Did you not inspire Boccaccio and Rabelais?

PROSE

Yes, but you went even further. If only you had just dictated fables to your La Fontaine!

POETRY

Ah! It would be a pity: we admire his fables;
But he composed other very nice verses.

PROSE

Very nice, indeed. They are the picture of grace; or at least taste, even delicacy. But nowadays, with more license, we do not know how to get our digressions equally forgiven. No doubt, sister, that you still dictate charming verses: but how many more remain flat and mediocre! ...

POETRY

Perhaps I deserve this reproach somewhat:
But Prose, now that you mention mediocrity,
What about your novels? ... Ah, you lower your eyes:
You blush and remain silent; you become befuddled.

PROSE

I shall admit it, I could ill justify myself in this respect. But sister, let us not, by quarrelling with each other, become our common enemies' laughing stock. Instead, let us benefit from this precious encounter. Listen: you see it too much, bad taste is spreading and it is partly our fault. We allow ourselves often, more than ever, to say and even print what should remain silent. Restraint, delicacy, exquisite tactfulness, and a sense of propriety seem to have gone out of fashion; and it is a pity, for we will lose elegance, and the public will lose pleasure. Well then! Let us try to revive a modest tone and more decent attitude. Let us return to the pure, delicate language that used to be natural ...

POETRY

I would quite enjoy your project, dear sister:
But I fear falling into another misery;
Yes, to stop being licentious and then
Suffer the biggest wrong of all, to become dull.

PROSE

On the contrary, all this bad taste is boring: nothing makes one more blasé than indecency.

POETRY

Indeed, we must admit, evil has reached its peak
In madness as in immorality;
If we become wise again and with no hypocrisy,
We will have the merit of novelty:
Your own style would be noble, simple and eloquent,
My verses pure, true, and wise; it would be pleasing.

PROSE

I vouch for it. But if we publish this conversation, let us remember, sister, and let us say it one last time, each of us shall use her own style; let us not step on one another's toes any longer: let us agree on this point before we part.

POETRY

Yes, from now on, let us each speak our language.
First of all, had you written the most beautiful harangue,
It shall not be a poem, sister, unless written in verse.

PROSE

All the better: I will keep my Telemachus.

POETRY

Between us, I am losing a very beautiful work. But since it belongs to you …
Besides Telemachus is still quite far from the Cid and Andromaque.

PROSE

You want to start the quarrel again, but I do not have such leisure.

POETRY

Above all, do not affect in your pompous speeches,
My sublime and proud tone, my images, my diction;
And Prose, if I allowed you comedy,
Never raise yourself to tragedy.

PROSE

I promise. But sister, let me whisper a word in your ear as well. If you forbid me to usurp your domain, do not get too close to mine; and when you advise me not be too poetical, beware yourself not to become … you hear me. Adieu.

Appendix 4
"Dialogue entre la Prose et la Poésie" (1809)[1]

PROSE

Good morning, sister, I am at your service. How do you feel?

POETRY

Heavens, what language! In the name of the gods, in the name of harmony, do not be my servant, and do not sully your mouth with crude expressions that shock! As for me, oh sister, I bow low to you. I smile at you like the morning rose smiles at dawn's weeping, like the new bride smiles at her husband raising radiantly from her bed, or like the young mother at her first born.

PROSE

This is very lovely; but between sisters, it is somewhat ridiculous to greet one another in this manner; all your life you have shown a ridiculous affectation and exaggeration. I can see that you will not correct yourself, perhaps you would feel dishonored if you were to use the right word just once.

POETRY

Ah! For shame! Your proper word is the most disgusting thing in the world. You will never come out of your triviality and abjection. In truth, I can hardly believe we are daughters of the same mother, and were raised together.

PROSE

Do you know that I am your elder, and that, without flattery, I believe I was raised better than you? All your life you were but a spoiled child who was made to believe she was a great genius, and you took off from there to extrapolate ceaselessly, and to allow yourself only the shadow of common sense with your rhymes, caesuras, hemistiches, etc. I would be ashamed to use all this gibberish, all these childish games which chop speech into a regular number of syllables and interrupt one's breathing at the end of each line. I just say what I want to say, in the simplest, most natural order; I do not feel obliged to fill half of my talk with common places to make the other half wittier or louder! Yet I am not a stranger to the harmony of language; I elevate mine, when needed, to the height of great ideas. I know very well how to be poetical when I please, but it is not what I do best, and I sometimes feel ashamed to have been a sweet talker or a "précieuse ridicule" about history, mythology, astronomy or mathematics. Besides, I readily forgive your harmonious mistakes; forgive me my *triviality* and *proper words*. I wish nothing more than to live in peace with you: please, step down to join me, however vile I am, and let us talk as good friends.

---

[1]   Anon. "Dialogue entre la Prose et la Poésie," in *Almanach des prosateurs, ou recueil de pieces fugitives en prose*. Rédigé par M. Leclerc. Huitième année. Paris: Imprimerie de Le Normant, 1809, 1–13.

POETRY

Very well then, I accept. In truth, I am terribly fatigued from all the poetical efforts I have made for some time. I feel faint and ill at ease, I fear I will catch a serious illness; I have difficulty living, as my friend Fontenelle would say. Sometimes I have vertigo and flashes, and I do realize then that I am talking nonsense, that I am losing the thread of my conversation, and that I do not know what my point was.

PROSE

But you do not spare yourself; you work like a madwoman, without ever stopping, and taking time to breathe and eat some solid food. You drink fresh water only and eat only boiled food. You compose a great quantity of terrible lines that damage your character and health. You write on all occasions, about all kinds of topics, without consulting your strengths and means. You speak of a thousand things outside your domain that do not concern you. I do not despair that I shall see you one day put into verse Archimedes, Euclid, and Newton's works; and you will doubtless write a poem about a straight line, a curve, a parallelogram, or the square of the hypotenuse. In truth, you ought to stay quiet for a while. I venture further that, should you rest for a century or two without opening your mouth, it would do no harm. The world has a good enough provision of verse for men's consumption and for feeding everyone's mind. You do compose beautiful lines here and there, but there are so beautiful one has difficulty reading them. Besides, they are sometimes drowned among so many bad ones, that one hesitates to jump in and try to catch them.

POETRY

What do you expect me to do, sister, I must occupy myself and work. I feel a need to speak that is stronger than myself. If I were to remain without speaking for a while, I am sure that I would be even sicker. Besides, I am constantly obsessed by all that surrounds me. The beauty of nature, particularly, does not leave me in peace: meadows, woods, rivers, flowers, stones even, demand my verses. Love, friendship, heroes, beautiful ladies, and animals, all solicit my talent. Everywhere they beg me to sing; I do not like to be begged, I sing for everyone, this is how I exhaust myself and become hoarse out of courtesy and politeness.

PROSE

There is no question that the extreme weakness that makes you yield to every request will turn you into the most impossible chatterer and the most boring singer possible. There might even come a time when you will be asked in earnest to remain silent. This is all you will have gained.

POETRY

But you, sister, do not seem to rest more than me, and I could reproach you equally. You spoke before I did, and have not stopped chatting for six thousand years. What you say today is not better, I believe, than what you said in theory—or rather you simply repeat yourself.

PROSE

I agree with you that I speak a lot and have done so for a long time, but my words are somewhat without consequence. They take flight, as we say, and do not linger. Besides, I have a very robust constitution and excellent lungs. I too say silly things sometimes, but they are not as noticeable as yours, sister, because I do it with less affection and pretension, because it does not reveal uneasiness, labor or difficulty. Unlike you, I do not spend several days and nights composing a few lines for a small speech, and at least my works are worth what they cost me: they are not tiresome to read since they are ordinarily quite clear, and I do not seek divine or diabolical expressions in heaven or hell to say that two and two make four. People do not demand much of me because I do not pretend to express myself as elegantly as the gods when I only have to speak to men; therefore, men have been polite and honest with me, while they often stand away from you as from too noble a lady one no longer wishes to visit on account of her arrogance and haughtiness ... But what is the matter, sister, you are no longer listening to me, you are distracted.

POETRY

May the earth awake to the accents of my voice! ... what do I see! which divinity inspires me! ... which divinity animates me!

PROSE

You are returning to your familiar folly once again.

POETRY

My nerves are terribly frayed. I can feel I am composing an ode: it will not be serious.

PROSE

What do you mean, it will not be serious! You suffer horrible convulsions; your face is all altered! You seem to want to throw yourself at me like a fury ...

POETRY

Happy be the one who on s*oft grounds*, in *a flowery meadow, slowly walks*! Happy be the shepherd who, near a clear river, sitting beside his lover, can step upon green ferns and flowers.

PROSE

I am pleased to see you a little calmer.

POETRY

I sing the victor of all the earth's victors.

PROSE

Heaven have mercy! What furor of singing!

POETRY

O crime, O shame, O despair! come closer, follow me in the infernal darkness: for whom are *these serpents hissing on my head*? Hold me back, sister, I am afraid I might stab everyone; I will murder all of antiquity; I am mostly furious against Agamemnon's family ...

PROSE

Oh! Now, has she gone totally mad?

POETRY

How I enjoy the flattering respect paid to me here with such zeal!—Despite my yearning, despite my concern, Achilles has not yet appeared. There is but one evil and one good, it is to love or to love none.—Ah! Ah! tol-de-rol, fol-de-rol-de-rido ...

PROSE

In truth, I cannot stand it any more! I flattered myself in vain when thinking I could make her more reasonable. Sister, I wish you a good night.

POETRY

Adieu, O the first born of our chaste parents' love. Adieu: May the zephyr's breath caress you always and play with the flowing folds of your long tunic! May the morning dew moisten you at every dawn! May ... I fly back to Mount Olympus where I am expected at the gods' banquet.

PROSE

Bon voyage et bon appétit.

Bibliography

Primary Texts

Anon. "Dialogue entre la prose et la poésie," in *Almanach des prosateurs*. Paris, 1809, 1–13.

Anon. *La Pariséide ou les amours d'un jeune patriote et d'une belle aristocrate, poëme héroi-comi-politique, en prose nationale*. Paris, 1790.

Anon. *Résurrection d'Atala, et son voyage à Paris*. 2 vols. Paris, An X [1802].

Anon. "Sur la prose poétique, sur la prose rythmique et sur les poëmes en prose, à l'occasion d'un ouvrage de ce genre intitulé l'Univers, poëme en prose," in *Le Spectateur français au XIXe siècle ou Variétés morales, politiques et littéraires recueillies des meilleurs écrits périodiques* (1805–1812). Geneva: Slatkine Reprints, 1970, 606–11.

Anthologie de la poésie française du XVIIIe siècle, ed. Michel Delon. Paris: Gallimard, 1997.

Anthologie de la poésie française, XVIIIe siècle, XIXe siècle, XXe siècle, eds Martine Bercot, Michel Collot, and Catriona Seth. Paris: Gallimard, 2000.

Aragon, Louis. *Les Aventures de Télémaque*, 1922. Paris: Gallimard, 1966.

———. *The Adventures of Telemachus*, trans. Renée Riese Hubert and Judd D. Hubert. Boston: Exact Change, 1997.

Balzac, Honoré de. *Le Père Goriot*, in *La Comédie Humaine*, vol. 3. Paris: Gallimard, 1976.

———. *Père Goriot*, trans. A.J. Krailsheimer. New York: Oxford University Press, 1999.

Barthelemy, Jean-Jacques. *Les Amours de Carite et Polydore, roman traduit du grec*. Paris, 1760.

Batteux, Charles. *Les Beaux-Arts réduits à un même principe*, 1747, in *Principes de la Littérature. Cinquième édition*. 1775. Geneva: Slatkine Reprints, 1967.

———. *Principes de la littérature. Cinquième édition*. 1775. Geneva: Slatkine Reprints, 1967.

———. Trans. "Traité de l'arrangement des mots" (1788): avec des réflexions sur la langue françoise comparée avec la langue grecque; et les tragédies de Polyeucte de P. Corneille, avec des remarques trad. du grec de Denys d'Halicarnasse. Paris, 1783.

Baudelaire, Charles. *Petits poëmes en prose (Le Spleen de Paris)*. 1869. Paris: Gallimard, 1973.

———. *Œuvres complètes*. 2 vols. Paris: Gallimard, 1976.

Beaufort d'Hautpoul, Anne Marie de. *Zilia, roman pastoral*. Toulouse, 1789.

Bertrand, Louis, dit Aloysius. *Gaspard de la Nuit. Fantaisies à la manière de Rembrandt et de Callot*. 1842. Paris: Gallimard, 1980.

Bitaubé, Paul-Jérémie. *Guillaume de Nassau, ou la Fondation des Provinces-Unies*. Paris, 1775.

————. *Joseph, en neuf chants.* Paris, 1767.

Blake, William. *The Complete Poetry and Prose of William Blake*, ed. David V. Erdman. Berkeley: University of California Press, 1982.

Boësnier, *Le Mexique conquis.* Paris, 1752.

Boileau-Despréaux, Nicolas. *L'Art poétique.* 1674. Paris: Larousse, 1972.

Boiste, Pierre-Claude-Victor. *L'Univers, poëme en prose en douze chants, suivi de notes et d'observations sur le système de Newton et la théorie physique de la Terre.* 2 vols. Paris, 1801.

————. *L'Univers, narration épique; suivie de notes et d'observations sur le système de Newton et la théorie physique de la Terre.* 2nd edition. 2 vols. Paris, 1804.

Bonneville, Nicolas de. *De l'esprit des religions. Ouvrage promis et nécessaire à la confédération universelle des amis de la vérité.* Paris, 1792.

————. *Choix de petits romans, imités de l'Allemand. Suivis de quelques essais de poésies lyriques dédiés à la reine.* Paris, 1786.

Cazotte, Jacques. *Ollivier, poëme.* 1763. In *Œuvres Badines et morales, historiques et philosophiques.* 4 vols. Hildesheim: Georg Olms Verlag, 1976. vol.1, p. 1–263

Chabanon, Michel Paul Guy de. *Sur le sort de la poësie en ce siècle philosophe.* 1764. Geneva: Slatkine Reprints, 1970.

Chansierges. *Les Avantures de Néoptolème fils d'Achille. Propres à former les mœurs d'un jeune prince.* 1718. Leipzig, 1756.

Chastellux, François-Jean de. *Essai sur l'union de la poésie et de la musique.* 1765. Genève: Slatkine Reprints, 1970.

Chateaubriand, François René, vicomte de. *Atala. René. Les Natchez*, ed. Jean-Claude Berchet. Paris: Librairie générale française, 1989.

————. *Atala. René*, trans. Irving Putter. Berkeley: University of California Press, 1980.

————. *Essai sur les révolutions.* Paris: Gallimard, 1978.

————. *Génie du christianisme.* Paris: Gallimard, 1978.

————. *Les Martyrs de Dioclétien*, ed. B. d'Andlau. Paris: Belin, 1951.

————. *Mémoires d'outre-tombe.* 2 vols. Paris: Gallimard, 1951.

————. *Œuvres romanesques et voyages.* 2 vols. Paris: Gallimard, 1969.

————. *Œuvres complètes.* 32 vols. Paris: Ladvocat, 1826–1831.

————. *Œuvres complètes.* 12 vols. Paris: Garnier, 1859–1861.

François-René de Chateaubriand. Les Itinéraires du romantisme. L'Œuvre intégrale de Chateaubriand. CD-ROM. Paris: Acamédia, 1997.

[Chateaubriand, Lucile de] *Lucile de Chateaubriand. Ses contes, ses poèmes, ses lettres*, ed. Anatole France. Paris: Charavay frères, 1879.

————. *Œuvres de Lucile de Chateaubriand*, ed. Louis Thomas. Paris: Albert Messein, 1912.

Chenier, Marie-Joseph. *Tableau historique de l'état et des progrès de la littérature depuis 1789.* Paris: Maradan, 1816.

Chérade-Montbron, Joseph. *Les Scandinaves, poème traduit du swéo-gothique, suivi d'observations sur les mœurs et la religion des anciens peuples de l'Europe barbare.* 2 vols. Paris: an IX, 1801.

Collin d'Harleville, Jean-François. "Dialogue entre prose et poésie," 1802, in *Œuvres de Collin-Harleville contenant son théâtre et ses poésies fugitives*, vol. 4. Paris: Delongchamps, 1828, 90–99.

Coqueley de Chaussepierre, Charles-Georges. *Le Roué vertueux: Poëme en prose en quatre chants propre à faire, en cas de besoin, un Drame à jouer deux fois par semaine*. Lausanne, 1770.

Cottin, Sophie. *La Prise de Jéricho*, 1803, in *Œuvres complètes*, vol. 1. Paris: Librairie populaire et des campagnes, 1847.

Court de Gébelin, Antoine. *Monde primitif analysé et comparé avec le monde moderne considéré dans son génie allégorique et dans les allégories auxquelles conduisit ce génie*. 9 vols. Paris, 1773–1782.

Cousin de Grainville, Jean-Baptiste-François-Xavier. *Le Dernier Homme*, 1805, ed. Charles Nodier. 2nd edition. 1811. Geneva: Slatkine Reprints, 1976.

Dacier, Anne Lefèvre. *Des Causes de la corruption du goust*, 1714. Geneva: Slatkine Reprints, 1970.

———. *Homère défendu contre l'apologie du R. P. Hardouin. Ou suite des causes de la corruption du goust*. Paris, 1716.

———. *L'Iliade d'Homère traduite en français, avec des remarques*. 3 vols. 2nd edition. Paris, 1719.

———. *L'Odyssée d'Homère, traduite en français avec des remarques*. Paris, 1716.

———. *Les Poésies d'Anacréon et de Sapho traduites en français, avec des remarques*. 1681. Amsterdam, 1716.

D'Alembert, Jean Le Rond. *Eloge de M. Le Président de Montesquieu*, 1763, in *Encyclopédie, ou dictionnaire raisonné des sciences, des arts et des métiers, par une société de gens de lettres*. 1751–80. 35 vols, vol. 5. Stuttgart: Friedrich Frommann Verlag, 1966–1967, iii–xxiii.

D'Escherny, François-Louis. *Mélange de littérature, d'histoire, de morale et de philosophie*. 2 vols, vol. 2. Paris, 1811.

Desforges Maillard, Pierre Jean Baptiste. "Ode en prose à M. Houdart de la Mothe sur ce qu'il a prétendu qu'on pourroit faire d'aussi beaux ouvrages de Poësie en prose qu'en vers," *Mercure de France*, 1 août 1750, 127.

Diderot, Denis. "Carite et Polydore de Barthélemy" 1er mai 1760, in *Œuvres complètes*. 25 vols, eds Herbert Dieckmann, Jacques Proust, and Jean Varloot, vol XIII. *Arts et Lettres*, ed. Jean Varloot. Paris: Hermann, 1980, 148–60.

———. *De la poésie dramatique*, in *Œuvres complètes*. 25 vols, eds Herbert Dieckmann, Jacques Proust, and Jean Varloot, vol. X. *Le Drame Bourgeois*, eds Jacques Chouillet and Anne-Marie Chouillet. Paris: Hermann, 1980, 323–427.

———. *Essais sur la peinture*, ed. Gita May. Paris: Hermann, 1984.

———. "L'Essai sur la poésie rythmique de Bouchaud" 1er janvier 1744, in *Œuvres complètes*. 25 vols, ed. Jean Varloot, vol XIII *Arts et Lettres*. Paris: Harmann, 1980, 420–26.

Diderot, Denis and Jean Le Rond D'Alembert. *Encyclopédie, ou dictionnaire raisonné des sciences, des arts et des métiers, par une société de gens de lettres*. 1751–80. 35 vols. Stuttgart: Friedrich Frommann Verlag, 1966–1967.

D[ionis], Mademoiselle. *Origines des grâces*. Paris, 1777.

Dubos, Jean-Baptiste. *Réflexions critiques sur la poësie et sur la peinture* I–III. Geneva: Slatkine Reprints, 1993.

Ducasse, Isidore [pseud. Le Comte de Lautréamont]. *Les Chants de Maldoror. Poésies I et II*. Paris: Flammarion, 1990.

Dufresne, Mme. *Idylles et pièces fugitives trouvées dans un hermitage au pied du mont Ste. Odile*. Paris, 1781.

Dugat, P.-D. *La mort d'Azaël ou le rapt de Dina*. Paris: an VII [1798].

Escherny, François Louis de. "De la poésie et des vers," in *Mélanges de littérature, d'histoire, de morale et de philosophie*, vol. 2. Paris, 1811, 209–307.

Fabre d'Olivet, Antoine. *La Langue hébraïque restituée et le véritable sens des mots hébreux rétabli et prouvé leur analyse radicale*. Paris, 1815.

Faydit, abbé. *La Télémacomanie, ou la censure et critique du roman intitulé: Les Avantures de Telemaque Fils d'Ulysse, ou suite du quatrieme Livre de l'Odyssée d'Homere*. Eleuterople [Paris], 1700.

Fénelon, François de Salignac de la Mothe. *Les Aventures de Télémaque*, 1699, ed. Jacques Le Brun. Paris: Gallimard, 1995.

———. *The Adventures of Telemachus, the Son of Ulysses*, trans. Tobias Smollett, eds Leslie A. Chilton and O.M. Brack Jr. Athens and London: The University of Georgia Press, 1997.

———. *Lettre à l'Académie*. 1718. Geneva: Droz, 1970.

Fleury, Abbé. *Discours sur la poésie, et en particulier celle des anciens Hébreux*. Paris, 1713.

Florian, Jean-Pierre Claris de. *Estelle et Némorin*, 1788, in *Œuvres complètes. Nouvelle édition*, vol. 1. Paris: Ladrange, 1829, 147–277.

———. *Galatée*, 1788, in *Œuvres complètes. Nouvelle édition*, vol. 1. Paris: Ladrange, 1829, 27–123.

———. *Gonzalve de Cordou ou Grenade reconquise*, 1791, in *Œuvres complètes. Nouvelle édition*, vols 7–8. Paris: Ladrange, 1829.

———. *Guillaume Tell ou la Suisse libre*, 1802, in *Œuvres complètes. Nouvelle édition*, vol. 9. Paris: Ladrange, 1829.

———. *Numa Pompilius second roi de Rome*, 1787, in *Œuvres complètes. Nouvelle édition*, vol. 2. Paris: Ladrange, 1829.

Fontenelle, Bertrand Le Bovier de. *Rêveries diverses. Opuscules littéraires et philosophiques*, ed. Alain Niderst. Paris: Desjonquères, 1994.

———. *Discours sur la nature de l'églogue*, in *Œuvres complètes*, ed. Alain Niderst. 9 vols, vol. 2. Paris: Fayard, 1990, 381–409.

Fournier de Tony. *Les Nymphes de Dyctyme ou révolutions de l'empire virginal*. Paris, 1790.

Fraguier, M. l'abbé. "Qu'il ne peut y avoir de poëmes en prose," in *Memoires de litterature tirez des registres de l'academie royale des inscriptions et belles lettres. Depuis l'année M. DCCVII. jusques & compris l'année M. DCCXXV*, vol. 6. Paris: Imprimerie royale, 1719, 265–78.

———. "A Discourse to shew that there can be no Poems in Prose. By Mr. L'Abbé Fraguier. Read to the French Academy of Belles Lettres, August 2nd, 1719," in *Select discourses read to the Academy of Belles Lettres and Inscriptions at Paris. Translated from the memoirs of the Academy.* London, 1741, 80–95.

Fréron, Élie. *L'Année littéraire*, vol. XXII, 1775. Geneva: Slatkine Reprints, 1966.

Furetière, Antoine. *Nouvelle allégorique ou Histoire des derniers troubles arrivés au Royaume de l'Eloquence*, 1658, eds Mathilde Bombart and Nicolas Schapira. Toulouse: Société de Littératures Classiques, 2004.

Galtier de Saint Symphorien, Jean-Louis. *Les Céramiques ou les aventures de Nicias et d'Antiope.* Londres, 1760.

Gessner, Salomon. *Œuvres complètes.* 3 vols. n.d.

Gibbon, Edward. *Essai sur l'étude de la littérature/An Essay on the Study of Literature.* London: Routledge/Thoemmes Press, 1994.

Giraud, Claude Marie. *Diabotinus, ou L'Orvietan de Salins. Poëme héroicomique, traduit du languedocien.* Paris, 1749.

Gomez, Madeleine-Angélique Poisson de. *Lettre critique sur le livre intitulé, Le Temple de Gnide. Avec des reflexions sur l'utilité de la véritable Critique, & sur les Poëmes en Prose.* Paris, 1725.

Grainville, Jean-Baptiste-Christophe. *Ismene et Tarsis, ou la colere de Vénus, roman poétique; suivi d'une premiere traduction de quelques poésies légeres de Métastase.* Londres [Paris?], 1785.

Gueudeville, Nicolas. *Critique générale des Aventures de Télémaque.* Cologne, 1700.

———. *Le Critique ressuscité ou fin de la Critique des Aventures de Télémaque, Ou l'on voit le véritable portrait des bons & des mauvais Rois.* Cologne, 1704

Guiard de Servigné, Jean-Baptiste. *Le Rhinoceros, poëme en prose divisé en six chants. Par Mlle de ***.* Paris, 1750.

Houdar de La Motte, Antoine. *Œuvres Complètes*, 1754, 2 vols. Geneva: Slatkine Reprints, 1970.

———. *Textes critiques. Les Raisons du sentiment*, eds Françoise Gevrey and Béatrice Guion. Paris: Champion, 2002.

Huet, Pierre-Daniel. *Traité de l'origine des romans*, 1670. Genève: Slatkine Reprints, 1970.

Hugo, Victor. Preface. *Cromwell.* Paris: Garnier-Flammarion, 1968.

Huysmans, Karl Joris. *A Rebours.* Paris: Gallimard, 1977.

———. *Le Drageoir aux épices suivi de textes inédits*, ed. Patrice Locmant. Paris: Champion, 2003.

Irail, Simon-Augustin. "La versification et la rime," in *Querelles littéraires, ou Mémoires pour servir à l'histoire des révolutions de la république des lettres depuis Homère jusqu'à nos jours*, vol. 2. Paris, 1761, 257–74.

Jauffret, Louis-François. *Les Charmes de l'enfance et les plaisirs de l'amour maternel*, 1791. Paris, 1796.

Kant, Immanuel. "Réponse à la question 'Qu'est-ce que les Lumières?'"(1784), in *Œuvres philosophiques*, vol. 2. Paris: Gallimard, 1985, 209–17.

Klopstock, Friedrich Gottlieb. *On Sacred Poetry*, 1755, in *Eighteenth-Century German Criticism*, ed. Timothy J. Chamberlain. New York: Continuum, 1992.

La Baume-Desdossats, Jacques-François de. *La Christiade ou le paradis reconquis, pour servir de suite au Paradis perdu de Milton*. Bruxelles, 1753.

Lacépède, Bernard-Germain-Etienne de La Ville, Comte de. *La Poétique de la musique*. Paris, 1785.

La Harpe, Jean-François de. *Cours de Littérature ancienne et moderne*. 3 vols. Paris: Didot, 1847.

Le Bossu, René. *Traité du poëme épique*, ed. Volker Kapp. Hamburg: H. Buske, 1981.

Le Clerc, Louis-Claude. *Tobie; poëme, en quatre chants*. Paris, 1773.

Lenglet-Dufresnoy, Nicolas. *De l'usage des romans*, 1734. Geneva: Slatkine Reprints, 1970.

Le Suire, Robert Martin. *Les Noces patriarchales, poëme en prose en cinq chants*. Londres, 1777.

Le Tourneur, Pierre, trans. *Ossian, fils de Fingal, barde du troisième siècle: poésies galliques, traduites sur l'anglois de M. Macpherson*. 2 vols. Paris, 1777.

Longue, Louis-Pierre de. *Raisonnements hazardés sur la poésie françoise*. Paris, 1737.

Lowth, Robert. *Lectures on the Sacred Poetry of the Hebrews*, 1753, trans. G. Gregory. Boston, Buckingham, 1815.

Macpherson, James. *The Poems of Ossian and Related Works*, ed. Howard Gaskill. Edinburgh: Edinburgh University Press, 1996.

Malouet, Pierre Victor de. *Les Quatre parties du jour à la mer*. Amsterdam, 1783.

M[amin, Simon], *Aventures d'Ulysse dans l'isle d'Aeaea*. Paris, 1752.

Marcillac, Mise de. *Le Temple du destin, ou l'hommage des cœurs françois, à Madame la Dauphine. Poëme, en cinq chants, en prose*. Paris, 1770.

Marivaux, Pierre de. *Le Télémaque travesti*, 1775, ed. Fédéric Deloffre. Geneva: Droz, 1956.

Marmontel, Jean-François. *Bélisaire*, 1766, ed. Robert Granderoute. Paris: Société des textes français modernes, 1994.

———. *Eléments de littérature*, ed. Sophie de Ménahèze. Paris: Desjonquères, 2005. 1765.

———. *Les Incas; ou la destruction de l'empire du Pérou*. 2 vols. Paris, 1777.

Masson, John. *An Essay on the power and harmony of prosaic numbers: being a sequel to one on the power of numbers and the principles of harmony on poetic compositions*. London, 1749.

Mercier, Louis-Sébastien. *Les Amours de Cherale, poëme en six chants, suivi du Bon Génie*. Amsterdam, 1767.

———. *Dictionnaire d'un polygraphe. Textes de Louis-Sébastien Mercier,* ed. Geneviève Bollème. Paris: Union générale d'édition, 1978.

———. *Mon Bonnet de nuit suivi de Du Théâtre*, ed. Jean-Claude Bonnet. Paris: Mercure de France, 1999.

———. *Mon Bonnet du matin*. 2 vols. Lausanne, 1787.

———. *Néologie ou vocabulaire de mots nouveaux, à renouveler, ou pris dans des acceptions nouvelles*. 2 vols. Paris, 1801.

————. *Songes et visions philosophiques*, ed. Jean-Claude Bonnet. Paris: Éditions Manucius, 2005.

————. *Tableau de Paris*, ed. Jean-Claude Bonnet. 2 vols. Paris: Mercure de France, 1994.

Monneron, Marie-Uranie-Rose. *Annamire, poëme en trois chants*. Lausanne: Mourer, 1783.

Montesquieu, Charles-Louis de Secondat, baron de. *Lettres persanes*. Paris: Flammarion, 1995.

————. *Œuvres complètes*. 2 vols. Paris: Gallimard, 1949–1951.

————. *Œuvres diverses de Montesquieu*. Paris: Pourrat, 1834.

————. *Le Temple de Gnide*, eds Cecil P. Courtney and Carole Dornier, in *Œuvres et écrits divers. Œuvres complètes de Montesquieu*, ed. Pierre Rétat, vol. 8. Oxford: Voltaire Foundation, 2003, 323–427.

————. *Le Temple de Gnide*, ed. O. Uzanne. Paris, 1881.

————. *Le Temple de Gnide*, 1725, in *Œuvres complètes*, 2 vols, ed. Roger Caillois, vol. I. Paris: Gallimard, 1949, 387–413.

————. *The Temple of Gnidus, and Arsaces and Ismenia. Translated from the French of Charles de Secondat, Baron de Montesquieu*. London, 1797.

Morellet, André. *Observations critiques sur le roman intitulé: ATALA*. Paris: An IX.

Morelly, Etienne Gabriel. *Naufrage des Isles flottantes, ou Basiliade du célèbre Pilpai. Poëme traduit de l'Indien par Mr. M*******. 2 vols. Paris, 1753.

Moutonnet-Clairfons, Julien Jacques. *Les Îles fortunées, ou Les aventures de Bathylle et de Cléobule*, 1771, in *Voyages imaginaires, romanesques, merveilleux, allégoriques, amusans, comiques et critiques. Suivis des songes, visions, et des romans cabalistiques*. Amsterdam, 1787, 95–210.

Nodier, Charles. *Les Méditations du cloître*, 1803, in *Romans de Charles Nodier*. Paris: Charpentier, 1850, 77–86.

Parny, Evariste Désiré de Forges. *Chansons madécasses, traduites en français*, 1787, in *Anthologie de la poésie française, XVIIIᵉ siècle, XIXᵉ XIXᵉsiècle, XXᵉ siècle*, eds Martine Bercot, Michel Collot, and Catriona Seth. Paris: Gallimard, 2000, 334–42.

————. *La Guerre des Dieux (1799)*, ed. Jacques-Charles Lemaire. Paris: Champion, 2002.

————. *Œuvres de Parny. Élégies et poésies diverses*, ed. Sainte-Beuve. Paris: Garnier, 1862.

Pechméja, Jean de. *Télèphe, en XII livres*, 1784. Londres, 1785.

Perrot d'Ablancourt, Nicolas. *Lettres et préfaces critiques*, ed. Roger Zuber. Paris: Marcel Didier, 1972.

Philostrate, *La Galerie de tableaux*, ed. Pierre Hadot. Paris: Les Belles Lettres, 1991.

Plato, *Cratylus*, in *The Collected Dialogues*, eds Edith Hamilton and Huntington Cairns. Princeton: Princeton University Press, 1961.

Pope, Alexander, trans. *The Iliad by Homer*, ed. Steven Shankman. London: Penguin, 1996.

Puget de Saint-Pierre, Jean. *Les Aventures de Périphas descendant de Cécrops.* Amsterdam, 1761.

Racine, Louis. "Sur l'essence de la poësie," in *Memoires de litterature tirez des registres de l'academie royale des inscriptions et belles lettres. Depuis l'année M. DCCVII. jusques & compris l'année M. DCCXXV*, vol. 6. Paris: Imprimerie royale, 1719.

Rémond de Saint-Mard, Toussaint. *Examen philosophique de la poésie en général.* Paris, 1729.

Reyrac, François Philippe de Laurens de. *Hymne au soleil* [1777], *Suivi de plusieurs morceaux du même genre qui n'ont point encore paru.* 6th edition. Paris, 1782.

Rimbaud, Arthur. *Poésies. Une Saison en enfer. Illuminations.* Paris: Gallimard, 1984.

————. *Prose Poems from Les Illuminations of Arthur Rimbaud*, trans. Helen Rootham. London: Faber and Faber, 1932.

Rivarol, Antoine de. *L'Universalité de la langue française.* 1785. Paris: Arléa, 1991.

Rousseau, Jean-Jacques. *Les Confessions.* Paris: Gallimard, 1973.

————. *Correspondance complète de Jean-Jacques Rousseau*, ed. R.A. Leigh, vol. 9. Juin-décembre, 1761. Madison: University of Wisconsin Press, 1969.

————. *Dialogues. Rousseau juge de Jean-Jacques. Le Lévite d'Éphraïm*, ed. Érik Leborgne. Paris: Flammarion, 1999.

————. *Dictionnaire de musique.* 1768, ed. Jean-Jacques Eigeldinger. Genève: Minkoff, 1998.

————. *Émile ou de l'éducation.* Paris: Garnier, 1961.

————. *Emile or Education by Rousseau*, trans. Barbara Foxley. London: Dent, 1925.

————. *Essai sur l'origine des langues*, in *Œuvres complètes*, vol. 2. Paris: Gallimard, 1964.

————. *Essay on the Origin of Languages*, in *The Collected Writings of Rousseau*, ed. and trans. John T. Scott, vol. 7. Hanover and London: The University Press of New England, 1998, 289–332.

————. *Le Lévite d'Ephraïm*, in *Œuvres complètes*, vol. 2. Paris: Gallimard, 1964, 1205–23.

————. *Le Lévite d'Ephraïm*, ed. Frédéric Eigeldinger. Paris: Champion, 1999.

————. *The Levite of Ephraïm*, in *The Collected Writings of Rousseau*, ed. and trans. John T. Scott, vol. 7. Hanover and London: The University Press of New England, 1998, 351–65.

————. *Œuvres complètes.* 4 vols. Paris: Gallimard, 1964.

————. *Pygmalion, scène lyrique*, 1771, in *Œuvres complètes*, vol. 2. Paris: Gallimard, 1964, 1224–31.

————. *Les Rêveries du promeneur solitaire.* Paris: Flammarion, 1964.

————. *Reveries of the Solitary Walker*, in *The Collected Writings of Rousseau*, ed. Christopher Kelly, trans. Charles E. Butterworth, Alexandra Cook and

Terence E. Marshall, vol. 8. Hanover and London: The University Press of New England, 2000, 1–90.

Roussy, Jean. *Aurélia ou Orléans délivré, Poeme latin traduit en françois*. Paris, 1738.

Saint-Lambert, Jean-François de. *Contes américains*, ed. Roger Little. Exeter: University of Exeter Press, 1997.

Saint-Martin, Louis-Claude de. *Cahiers des langues*, in *Les Cahiers de la Tour Saint-Jacques VII*. Paris: H. Roudil, 1962, 139–200.

———. *Le Crocodile, ou la guerre du bien et du mal, arrivée sous le règne de Louis XV; Poème épico-magique en 102 chants. An VI* [1799], ed. Simone Rihouët-Coroze. Preface by Robert Amadou. Paris: Triades-Editions, 1979.

———. *L'Homme de désir*. 1790. Monaco: Éditions du Rocher, 1994.

———. *Mon Portrait historique et philosophique*, ed. Robert Amadou. Paris: Julliard, 1961.

———. "Du style en général," in *Œuvres posthumes*, vol. 2. Villeneuve-Saint-Georges: Éditions rosicruciennes, 1986, 120–21.

Saint-Pierre, Bernardin de. *Œuvres complètes*. 12 vols. Paris, 1818.

———. *Paul et Virginie*, 1788. Paris: Flammarion, 1992.

Sainte-Beuve, Charles-Augustin. "Parny," in *Portraits contemporains*, vol. 4. Paris: Levy, 1870, 423–70.

———. "Preface," in *Œuvres de Parny. Élégies et poésies diverses*, v–xxvi. Paris: Garnier, 1862.

———. "Saint-Martin, le philosophe inconnu," in *Causeries du lundi*, vol. X. Paris: Garnier, 1855, 190–225.

Seran de la Tour, Abbé. *Mysis et Glaucé, Poëme en trois Chants, traduit du Grec*. Geneva, 1748.

Staël, Anne Louise Germaine de. *De la littérature considérée dans ses rapports avec les institutions sociales*, 1810. Paris: Flammarion, 1991.

Valery, Paul. *Pièces sur l'art*, 1891. Paris: Gallimard, 1943.

Vernes, François. *La Franciade, ou l'Ancienne France. Poëme en seize chants*. Lausanne, 1789.

Voltaire, "Discours aux Welches," in *Mélanges*, ed. Jacques Van Den Heuvel. Paris: Gallimard, 1961, 685–708.

———. *La Fête de Bélesbat*, in Voltaire, *Œuvres complètes*, eds Roger J.V. Cotte and Paul Gibbard, vol. 3A. Oxford: Voltaire Foundation, 2004, 141–86.

———. *An Essay on Epic Poetry. Essai sur la poésie épique*, in Voltaire, *Œuvres complètes*, ed. David Williams, vol. 3B. Oxford: Voltaire Foundation, 1996, 117–575.

———. "Hémistiche," in *Œuvres alphabétiques*, ed. Jeroom Vercruysse, in Voltaire, *Œuvres Complètes*, vol. 33. Oxford: Voltaire Foundation, 1987, 152–7.

———. *Lettres philosophiques ou Lettres anglaises*, ed. Raymond Naves. Paris: Garnier, 1988.

———. *Questions sur l'Encyclopédie, distribuées en forme de dictionnaire*. 9 vols. Londres, 1771–1772.

————. *Le Temple du goût*, in Voltaire, *Œuvres complètes*, ed. O.R. Taylor, vol. 9. Oxford: Voltaire Foundation, 1999, 119–210.

————. Préface d'*Oedipe* de l'édition de 1730, in Voltaire, *Œuvres Complètes*, ed. David Jory, vol. 1A. Oxford: Voltaire Foundation, 2001, 260–83.

————. *Jules César. Tragédie de Shakespeare*, 1733, in *Œuvres complètes*, vol. 9. Oxford: Voltaire Foundation, 1999.

Watelet, Claude-Henri. *Silvie*, 1743. Paris, 1784.

Wordsworth, William. "Preface of 1800, With a Collation of the Enlarged Preface of 1802," in *Lyrical Ballads*. Oxford: Oxford University Press, 1969, 153–79.

Young, Edward. *Conjectures on Original Composition*, 1759. Manchester: The University Press, 1918.

————. *Night Thoughts on Life, Death, and Immortality*, 1742, ed. Stephen Cornford. Cambridge: Cambridge University Press, 1989.

Secondary Texts

Alter, Robert. *The Art of Biblical Narrative*. New York: Basic Books, 1981.

Amiot, Anne-Marie. *Baudelaire et l'illuminisme*. Paris: Nizet, 1982.

Andlau, Béatrix d'. *Chateaubriand et "Les Martyrs." Naissance d'une épopée*. Paris: Librairie José Corti, 1952.

Apostolidès, Jean-Marie. *Le Roi-machine. Spectacle et politique au temps de Louis XIV*. Paris: Minuit, 1981.

Baldner, Ralph W. *Bibliography of Seventeenth-Century Prose Fiction*. New York: Columbia University Press, 1967.

Barbéris, Pierre. "Télémaque/Modernité. Désir/Roman/Utopie et Langage de la Contre-Réforme," in *Je ne sais quoi de pur et de sublime ... Télémaque*, ed. Alain Lanavère. Orléans: Paradigme, 1994, 21–52.

————. *À la recherche d'une écriture, Chateaubriand*. Paris: Maison Mame, 1974.

Barquisseau, Raphaël. *Les Chevaliers des îles*. Ile de la Réunion: CRI, 1990.

————. *Les Poètes créoles du dix-huitième siècle: Parny, Bertin, Léonard*. Paris: J. Vigneau, 1949.

Beaujour, Michel. "Short Epiphanies: Two Contextual Approaches to the French Prose Poem," in *The Prose Poem in France: Theory and Practice*, eds Mary Ann Caws and Hermine Riffaterre. New York: Columbia University Press, 1983, 39–59.

Bebee, Thomas O. *The Ideology of Genre. A Comparative Study of Generic Instability*. Pensylvania Park: The Pennsylvania State University Press, 1994.

Becq, Annie. "La réflexion sur la poétique en France au XVIIIe siècle," in *Histoire des poétiques*, eds Jean Bessière, Eva Kushner, Roland Mortier, and Jean Weisberger. Paris: PUF, 1997, 219–39.

Bénichou, Paul. *Le Sacre de l'écrivain. 1750–1830. Essai sur l'avènement d'un pouvoir spirituel laïque dans la France moderne*, 1973. Paris: Gallimard, 1996.

Benjamin, Walter. *The Origin of German Tragic Drama*, trans. John Osborne. New York: Verso, 1990.

Benrekassa, Georges. *Montesquieu, la liberté et l'histoire*. Paris: Librairie générale française, 1987.

Berchet, Jean-Claude, ed. *Chateaubriand. Le Tremblement du temps*. Toulouse: Presses Universitaires du Mirail, 1994.

Berman, Antoine. "La traduction et la lettre—ou l'auberge du lointain," in *Les Tours de Babel (Essais sur la traduction)*, eds Antoine Berman, Gérard Granel, Annick Jaulin, Georges Mailhos, and Henri Meschonnic. Mauvezin: Trans-Europ-Repress, 1985.

———. *Pour une critique des traductions: John Donne*. Paris: Gallimard, 1995.

———. *L'Épreuve de l'étranger. Culture et traduction dans l'Allemagne romantique*. Paris: Gallimard, 1984.

Bernabé, Jean, Patrick Chamoiseau, and Raphaël Confiant. *Éloge de la Créolité*. Paris: Gallimard/Presses universitaires créoles, 1989.

Bernard, Suzanne. *Le Poème en prose de Baudelaire à nos jours*. Paris: Champion, 1959.

Besse, Henriette. "Galathée à l'origine des langues. Comments on Rousseau's *Pygmalion* as Lyric Drama," *Modern Language Notes* 93:5 (December, 1978): 839–51.

Blanchot, Maurice, *L'Écriture du désastre*. Paris: Gallimard, 1980.

Bonnet, Jean-Claude, ed. *Louis Sébastien Mercier (1740–1814): un hérétique en littérature*. Paris: Mercure de France, 1994.

Boucher, Gwenaëlle. *La Poésie philosophique de Voltaire. SVEC* 05 (2003), 1–286.

Brémond, Henri. *Histoire littéraire du sentiment religieux en France*. 5 vols. Paris: Éditions Jérôme Millon, 2006.

Brunot, Ferdinand. *Histoire de la langue française des origines à nos jours*. 13 vols. Paris: Armand Colin, 1966.

Bunuel, Pierre, ed. *Dictionnaire des mythes littéraires*. Paris: Edition du Rocher, 1988.

Candler Hayes, Julie. "Of meaning and modernity: Anne Dacier and the Homer Debate," *EMF: Studies in Early Modern France* 8 (2002): 173–95.

———. *Reading the French Enlightenment: System and Subversion*. Cambridge, New York: Cambridge University Press, 1999.

———. *Identity and Ideology: Diderot, Sade, and the Serious Genre*. Amsterdam, Philadelphia: J. Benjamins Pub. Co., 1991.

Caws, Mary Ann, and Hermine Riffaterre, eds. *The Prose Poem in France. Theory and Practice*. New York: Columbia University Press, 1983.

Ceserani, Remo. "The New System of Literary Modes in the Romantic Age," in *The People's Voice. Essays on European Romanticism*, eds Andrea Ciccarelli, John C. Isbell, and Brian Nelson, *Monash Romance Studies* 4 (1999): 7–25.

Chérel, Albert. *Fénelon au XVIIIᵉ siècle en France (1715–1820). Son prestige, son influence*. 1917. Geneva: Slatkine Reprints, 1970.

———. *La Prose poétique française*. Paris: L'artisan du livre, 1940.

Chinard, Gilbert. *L'Exotisme américain dans l'œuvre de Chateaubriand.* 1918. Geneva: Slatkine Reprints, 1970.

Clayton, Vista. *The Prose Poem in French Literature of the Eighteenth Century.* New York: Institute of French Studies, Columbia University, 1936.

Cohen, Margaret. *The Sentimental Education of the Novel.* Princeton: Princeton University Press, 1999.

Combe, Dominique. *Poésie et récit: une rhétorique des genres.* Paris: Corti, 1989.

———. *Les Genres littéraires.* Paris: Hachette, 1992.

Cronk, Nicholas. *The Classical Sublime. French Neoclassicism and the Language of Literature.* EMF Critiques. Charlottesville: Rookwood Press, 2002.

Cuche, François-Xavier and Jacques Le Brun, eds. *Fénelon. Mystique et Politique (1699–1999).* Paris: Champion, 2004.

Curtius, Ernst Robert. *European Literature and the Latin Middle Ages,* 1948, trans. Willard R. Trask. Princeton: Princeton University Press, 1973.

Declercq, Gilles. "Boileau–Huet: la querelle du Fiat lux," in *Pierre-Daniel Huet (1630–1721): actes du colloque de Caen (12–13 novembre 1993),* ed. Suzanne Guellouz. Paris and Seattle, WA: *Papers on Seventeenth-Century Literature,* 1994, 237–62.

DeJean, Joan. *Ancients against Moderns. Culture Wars and the Making of a Fin de Siècle.* Chicago: University of Chicago Press, 1997.

DeLater, James Albert. "The 1683 *De Optimo Genere Interpretandi (On the Best Kind of Translation)* of Pierre-Daniel Huet: Introduction, English Translation, Notes, and Commentaries." PhD diss., University of Washington, 1997.

Delon, Michel, ed. *Anthologie de la poésie française du XVIIIe siècle.* Paris: Gallimard, 1997.

Delon, Michel, Robert Mauzi, and Sylvain Menant, eds. *Histoire de la littérature française. De l'Encyclopédie aux Méditations.* Paris: Gallimard, 1984, rev. 1998.

———. *Précis de la littérature française du XVIIIe siècle.* Paris: PUF, 1990.

De Man, Paul. "The Rhetoric of Temporality," in *Interpretation: Theory and Practice* , ed. Charles S. Singleton. Baltimore, 1969, 173–209.

Deprun, Jean. *La Philosophie de l'inquiétude en France au XVIIIe siècle.* Paris: Vrin, 1979.

Dictionnaire historique et étymologique de la langue française. Paris: Larousse, 1993.

Duchet, Michèle. *Anthropologie et histoire au siècle des Lumières.* 1971. Paris: Albin Michel, 1995.

Dufresnoy, Marie-Louise. "Les émules de Fénelon," in *L'Orient romanesque en France (1704–1789),* chap. XV. Montreal: Beauchemin, 1946, 253–64.

Dupont, Paul. *Un Poète-philosophe au commencement du dix-huitième siècle. Houdar de La Motte (1672–1731).* 1898. Geneva: Slatkine Reprints, 1971.

Farnham, Fern. *Madame Dacier, Scholar and Humanist.* Monterey, CA: Angel Press, 1976.

Fowler, Elizabeth, and Roland Greene. *The Project of Prose in Early Modern Europe and the New World.* Cambridge: Cambridge University Press, 1997.

Fox, Leonard, ed. and trans. *Hainteny. The Traditional Poetry of Madagascar*. London and Toronto: Associated University Press, 1990.

François Furet, "Terreur," in *Dictionnaire critique de la Révolution française*, eds François Furet and Mona Ozouf. Paris: Flammarion, 1988.

Fumaroli, Marc. *Chateaubriand. Poésie et Terreur*. Paris: Éditions de Fallois, 2003.

Geffriaud Rosso, Jeannette. *Montesquieu et la féminité*. Pise: Libreria Goliardica Editrice, 1977.

Genette, Gérard. *Figures I*. Paris: Seuil, 1966.

———. *Palimpsestes. La littérature au second degré*. Paris: Seuil, 1982.

———. "Introduction à l'architexte," in *Théorie des genres*, eds Gérard Genette and Tzvetan Todorov. Paris: Seuil, 1986, 89–159.

Gillet, Jean. *Le Paradis perdu dans la littérature française de Voltaire à Chateaubriand*. Paris: Klincksieck, 1975.

Gilman, Margaret. *The Idea of Poetry in France from Houdar de la Motte to Baudelaire*. Cambridge, MA: Harvard University Press, 1958.

Goodman, Dena. *Criticism in Action. Enlightenment Experiments in Political Writing*. Ithaca: Cornell University Press, 1989.

Grand dictionnaire universel du XIXème siècle, 1869, ed. Pierre Larousse. Geneva: Slatkine Reprints, 1982.

Granderoute, Robert. *Introduction to* Bélisaire, *by Jean-François Marmontel*. Paris: Société des Textes Français Modernes, 1994, i–lxviii.

Graziani, Françoise. *Introduction to* La Jérusalem délivrée, *by Le Tasse*, trans. Charles-François Lebrun. Paris: Flammarion, 1997, 5–35.

Guitton, Edouard. *Jacques Delille (1738–1813) et le poème de la nature en France de 1750 à 1820*. Paris: Klincksieck, 1974.

Haillant, Marguerite. *Introduction to* Les Aventures de Télémaque, fils d'Ulysse, *by François Salignac de la Mothe Fénelon*. Paris: Nizet, 1993, 9–201.

Hamon, Philippe. *Introduction à l'analyse du descriptif*. Paris: Hachette, 1981.

———. *La Description littéraire. De l'Antiquité à Roland Barthes: une anthologie*. Paris: Macula, 1991.

Hathaway, Baxter. "Are Prose Fictions Poems?" in *The Age of Criticism. The Late Renaissance in Italy*, chap 6. Ithaca, NY: Cornell University Press, 1962.

Haxell, Nichola Anne. "The Name of the Prose: A Semiotic Study of Titling in the Pre-Baudelerian Prose-poem," *French Studies: A Quarterly Review* 44:14 (April, 1990): 156–69.

Heffernan, James A.W. *Museum of Words: The Poetics of Ekphrasis from Homer to Ashbery*. Chicago: University of Chicago Press, 1993.

Hepp, Noémi, *Homère en France au XVIIIe siècle*. Paris: Klincksieck, 1968.

———. "De l'épopée au roman. L'Odyssée et Télémaque," in *Je ne sais quoi de pur et de sublime ... Télémaque*, ed. Alain Lanavère. Orléans: Paradigme, 1994, 223–35.

———. *Deux amis d'Homère au XVIIe siècle*. Paris: Klinsieck, 1970.

Hepworth, Brian. *Robert Lowth*. Boston: Twayne Publishers, 1978.

Herman, Jan. "Le procès Prévost traducteur: traduction et pseudo-traduction au dix-huitième siècle en France," *Arcadia: Zeitschrift fur Vergleichende Literatur Wissenschaft* 25:1 (1990): 1–9.

Hersant, Yves. "Une lyre où il manque des cordes," in *Chateaubriand, Le Tremblement du temps*, ed. Jean-Claude Berchet. Toulouse: Presses universitaires du Mirail, 1994, 279–88.

Hoffmann, Léon-François. *Le Nègre romantique. Personnage littéraire et obsession collective*. Paris: Payot, 1973.

Illouz, Jean-Nicolas and Jacques Neefs, eds. *Crises de prose*. Paris: Presses universitaires de Vincennes, 2002.

Jacques-Chaquin [Lefèvre], Nicole. "Le *Crocodile* de Louis-Claude de Saint-Martin: le Paris fantastique d'une Révolution figurée," in *Studia Latomorum et Historica. Hommages à Daniel Ligou*, ed. Charles Porset. Paris: Champion-Slatkine, 1998, 183–202.

Jacques-Lefèvre, Nicole. *Louis-Claude de Saint-Martin, le philosophe inconnu (1743–1803)*. Paris: Dervy, 2003.

Jechova, Anna, François Mouret, and Jacques Voisine, eds. *La Poésie en prose des Lumières au romantisme, 1760–1820*. Paris: Presses de l'Université de Paris Sorbonne, 1993.

Johnson, Barbara. *Défigurations du langage poétique. La Seconde révolution baudelairienne*. Paris: Flammarion, 1979.

Johnson, Dorothy. *The Farewell of Telemachus and Eucharis*. Los Angeles: Getty Museum Studies on Art, 1997.

Jones, Silas Paul. *A List of French Prose Fiction from 1700 to 1750*. New York: H.W. Wilson Company, 1939.

Juden, Brian. *Traditions orphiques et tendances mystiques dans le romantisme français, 1800–1855*. 1971. Geneva: Slatkine Reprints, 1984.

Kapp, Volker *Télémaque de Fénelon. La signification d'une œuvre littéraire à la fin du siècle classique*. Paris: Laplace, 1982.

Kavanagh, Thomas M. "Rousseau's *Le Lévite d'Ephraïm*: Dream, Text and Synthesis," *Eighteenth-Century Studies* 16:2 (Winter, 1982–83): 141–61.

Kittay, Jeffrey, and Wlad Godzich. *The Emergence of Prose. An Essay in Prosaïcs*. Minneapolis: University of Minnesota Press, 1987.

Kupiec, Anne. *Le Livre-sauveur. La question du livre sous la Révolution française. 1789–1799*. Paris: Editions Kimé, 1998.

Lanson, Gustave. *L'Art de la prose*. 1968. Paris: La Table Ronde, 1996.

Lauret, Jacqueline. "Une épopée en prose au XVIIIe siècle: *Les Incas ou la destruction de l'Empire du Pérou*," in *De l'Encyclopédie à la Contre-Révolution. Jean-François Marmontel (1723–1799)*, ed. Jean Ehrard. Clermont Ferrand: G. de Bussac, 1970, 201–28.

Leroy, Christian. *La Poésie en prose française du XVIIe siècle à nos jours. Histoire d'un genre*. Paris: Champion, 2001.

Litman, Théodore A. *Le Sublime en France (1660–1714)*. Paris: Nizet, 1971.

Little, Roger. "Quelques poèmes en prose de Saint-Lambert," *Revue d'histoire littéraire de la France* 1 (January–February, 1997): 113–18.

Lukács, Georg. *The Theory of the Novel. A Historico-Philosophical Essay on the Forms of Great Epic Literature*, trans. Anna Bostock. Cambridge, MA: MIT Press, 1994.

Manuel, Frank E. *The Eighteenth Century Confronts the Gods*. Cambridge: Harvard University Press, 1959.

Martin, Angus, Vivienne G. Mylne, and Richard Frautschi. *Bibliographie du genre romanesque français 1751–1800*. Paris: France Expansion, 1977.

Masson, Nicole. *La Poésie fugitive au XVIIIe siècle*. Paris: Champion, 2002.

May, Georges. *Le Dilemme du roman au XVIIIe siècle. Étude sur les rapports du roman et de la critique (1715–1761)*. New Haven: Yale University Press, 1963.

McDowell, Paula. "Enlightenment Enthusiasms and the Spectacular Failure of the Philadelphian Society," *Eighteenth Century Studies* 35:4 (Summer, 2002): 515–33.

Mee, Jon. *Dangerous Enthusiasm. William Blake and the Culture of Radicalism in the 1790s*. Oxford: Oxford University Press, 1992.

Menant, Sylvain. *La Chute d'Icare. La Crise de la poésie française dans la première moitié du XVIIIe siècle (1700–1750)*. Geneva: Droz, 1981.

———. *L'Esthétique de Voltaire*. Paris: Sedes, 1995.

———. "Poésie," in *Dictionnaire Voltaire*, ed. Raymond Trousson, Jeroom Vercruysse and Jacques Lemaire. Paris: Hachette, 1994, 168–69.

———. Introduction to *Contes en vers et en prose*, by Voltaire, vol. 1. Paris: Garnier, 1992, vii–xxviii.

Mercier, Roger. "La question du langage poétique au début du XVIIIe siècle. La Bible et la critique," *Revue des sciences humaines* 146 (Avril–Juin, 1972): 255–82.

Meschonnic, Henri. *Pour la poétique* II. Paris: Gallimard, 1973.

———. *Critique du rythme, anthropologie historique du langage*. 1982. Paris: Verdier, 1990.

———. *Les États de la poétique*. Paris: PUF, 1985.

———. *La Rime et la vie*. Paris: Verdier, 1989.

Meschonnic, Henri, and Gérard Dessons *Traité du rythme. Du vers et des proses*. Paris: Dunod, 1998.

Milner, Max. *Le Romantisme, 1820–1843*. Paris: Arthaud, 1973.

Monroe, Jonathan. *A Poverty of Objects: The Prose Poem and the Politics of Genre*. Ithaca: Cornell University Press, 1987.

Monte, Steven. *Invisible Fences. Prose Poetry as a Genre in French and American Literature*. Lincoln and London: University of Nebraska Press, 2000.

Moore, Fabienne. "1711: The Advent of Homer in French Prose. An Anatomy of Madame Dacier's Ground-Breaking Translation," *SVEC* 06 (2008): 193–213.

———. "The Crocodile Strikes Back. Saint-Martin's Interpretation of the French Revolution," *Eighteenth-Century Fiction* 19:1–2 (October, 2006): 71–97.

———. "Baudelaire et les poëmes en prose du dix-huitième siècle. De Fénelon à Chateaubriand," *Bulletin baudelairien* (April–December, 2005): 113–43.

————. "Almanach des Muses vs. Almanach des Prosateurs: The Economics of Poetry and Prose at the Turn of the Nineteenth Century," *Dalhousie French Studies* 67 (Summer, 2004): 17–35.

————. "Homer Revisited: Anne Le Fèvre Dacier's Preface to her Prose Translation of the *Iliad* in Early Eighteenth-Century France," *Studies in the Literary Imagination* 33:2 (Fall, 2000): 87–107.

Moreau, Pierre. *La Tradition française du poème en prose avant Baudelaire*. Paris: Les lettres modernes, 1959.

Mornet, Daniel. *Le Sentiment de la nature en France de Jean-Jacques Rousseau à Bernardin de Saint-Pierre*. Paris: Nizet, 1907.

Mourot, Jean. *Études sur les premières œuvres de Chateaubriand. Tableaux de la nature. Essai sur les Révolutions*. Paris: Nizet, 1962.

————. *Le Génie d'un style. Chateaubriand. Rythme et sonorité dans les* Mémoires d'outre-tombe. Paris: Armand Colin, 1960.

Naves, Raymond. *Le Goût de Voltaire*. Paris: Garnier, 1938.

Paulhan, Jean. *Les Hain-teny merinas*. 1913. Paris: Geuthner, 2007.

Poirier, Roger. *La Bibliothèque universelle des romans. Rédacteurs, textes, public*. Geneva: Droz, 1976.

Ranscelot, Jean. "Les manifestations du déclin poétique au début du XVIIIe siècle," *Revue d'histoire littéraire de la France* (1926): pp 497–520.

Ricard, Jean-Louis. *Étude sur le "Crocodile ou la Guerre du bien et du mal" de Louis-Claude de Saint-Martin*. Maîtrise de Lettres Modernes, Université de Paris VIII, 1994–1995. Paris: Centre international de Recherches et d'Etudes Martinistes, 1996.

Richard, Jean-Pierre. *Paysages de Chateaubriand*. Paris: Seuil, 1967.

Riffaterre, Michel. "La sémiotique d'un genre: le poème en prose," in *Sémiotique de la poésie*. Paris: Seuil, 1983, 148–58.

Roche, Maurice. *Balzac et le Philosophe Inconnu*. Tours: Gibert-Clarey, 1951.

Roger, Philippe. "La trace de Fénelon," in *Sade, écrire la crise*. Paris: Belfond, 1983, 149–73.

————. "L'histoire à toute extrémité," in *Chateaubriand. Le Tremblement du temps*, ed. Jean-Claude Berchet. Toulouse: Presses universitaires du Mirail, 1994, 99–116.

Rosenberg, Aubrey, ed. *L'Histoire des Sévarambes* by Denis Veiras. Paris: Champion, 2001.

————. "Rousseau's *Lévite d'Ephraïm* and the Golden Age," *Australian Journal of French Studies* 15 (1978): 163–72.

————. "Le Lévite d'Ephraïm," in *Dictionnaire de Jean-Jacques Rousseau*, eds Raymond Trousson and Frédéric S. Eigeldinger. Paris: Champion, 1996, 544–7.

Roudaut, Jean. *Poètes et grammairiens au XVIIIe siècle*. Anthologie. Paris: Gallimard, 1971.

Rougemont, Martine de. *Paradrames. Parodies du drame 1775–1777*. Saint-Etienne: Publications de l'Université de Saint-Etienne, 1998.

Roulin, Jean-Marie. *L'Épopée de Voltaire à Chateaubriand. SVEC* 03 (2005).

Russo, Elena. *Styles of Enlightenment. Taste, Politics, and Authorship in Eighteenth-Century France*. Baltimore: The John Hopkins University Press, 2007.

Saint Amand, Pierre. *Séduire ou la passion des Lumières*. Paris: Méridien-Klincksieck, 1987.

Sandras, Michel. *Lire le poème en prose*. Paris: Dunod, 1995.

Santangelo, Giovanni Saverio. *Madame Dacier, una filologa nella "crisi" (1672–1720)*. Rome: Bulzoni, 1984.

Schaeffer, Jean-Marie. *Qu'est-ce qu'un genre littéraire?* Paris: Seuil, 1989.

Scholar, Richard. *The* Je-Ne-Sais-Quoi *in Early Modern Europe. Encounters with a Certain Something*. Oxford, New York: Oxford University Press, 2005.

Sekrecka, Mieczyslawa. *Louis-Claude de Saint-Martin, le philosophe inconnu. L'homme et l'œuvre*. Wroclaw: Acta Universitatis Wratislaviensis 59, 1968.

Seth, Catriona. *Les poètes créoles du XVIIIe siècle: Parny, Bertin, Léonard*. Paris: Presses universitaires de France, 1998.

Sieburth, Richard. "*Gaspard de la Nuit*: Prefacing Genre," *Studies in Romanticism* 24:2 (1985): 239–55.

Spitzer, Leo. *Linguistics and Literary History. Essay in Stylistics*. Princeton: Princeton University Press, 1948.

Stafford, Fiona. Introduction to *The Poems of Ossian and Related Works*, by James Macpherson, ed. Howard Gaskill. Edinburgh: Edinburgh University Press, 1996.

Starobinski, Jean. *Montesquieu par lui-même*. Paris: Seuil, 1971.

———. *Le Remède dans le mal. Critique et légitimation de l'artifice à l'âge des Lumières*. Paris: Gallimard, 1989.

———. "Rousseau's Happy Days," *New Literary History* 11 (1979): 147–66.

Steele, Timothy. *Missing Measures. Modern Poetry and the Revolt against Meter.* Fayetteville and London: University of Arkansas Press, 1990.

Still, Judith. "Rousseau's *Le Lévite d'Ephraïm*: the Imposition of Meaning (on Women)," *French Studies XLIII* 1 (January, 1989): 12–30.

Terdiman, Richard. *Discourses/Counter-discourses: The Theory and Practice of Symbolic Resistance in Nineteenth-Century France*. Ithaca and London: Cornell University Press, 1985.

Thiry, Marcel. "Rousseau et son *Lévite*," *Bulletin de l'Académie royale de langue et de littérature françaises* 41 (1963): 71–80.

Thomas, Downing A. *Music and the Origins of Language: Theories from the French Enlightenment*. Cambridge, New York: Cambridge University Press, 1995.

———. *Aesthetics of Opera in the Ancien Régime, 1647–1785*. Cambridge, New York: Cambridge University Press, 2002.

Todorov, Tzvetan. *Théories du symbole*. Paris: Seuil, 1977.

Tsien, Jennifer. *Voltaire and the Temple of Bad Taste. A Study of* La Pucelle d'Orléans. *SVEC* 05 (2003): 288–422.

Vadé, Yves. *Le Poème en prose et ses territoires.* Paris: Belin, 1996.

Vajda, György, ed. *Le Tournant du siècle des Lumières 1760–1820. Les genres en vers des Lumières au romantisme.* Budapest: Akademiai Kiado, 1982.

Van Laere, François. *Jean-Jacques Rousseau, du phantasme à l'écriture: les révélations du* Lévite d'Ephraïm. Paris: Minard, 1967.

Van Tieghem, Paul. *Ossian en France.* 2 vols. Geneva: Slatkine Reprints, 1967.

———. *Le Préromantisme. Etudes d'histoire littéraire européenne.* 1924. Geneva: Slatkine Reprints, 1973.

Van Tieghem, Philippe. *Les Influences étrangères sur la littérature française.* Paris: PUF, 1967.

Viatte, Maurice. *Les Sources occultes du Romantisme. Illuminisme, théosophie. 1770–1820,* vol. I *Le Préromantisme.* Paris: Champion, 1979.

Viëtor, Karl. "L'histoire des genres littéraires," in *Théorie des genres,* ed. Gérard Genette and Tzvetan Todorov. Paris: Seuil, 1986, 9–35.

Vincent-Munnia, Nathalie. *Les Premiers poèmes en prose: généalogie d'un genre dans la première moitié du dix-neuvième siècle français.* Paris: Champion, 1996.

Vincent-Munnia, Nathalie, Simone Bernard-Griffiths, and Robert Pickering, eds. *Aux origines du poème en prose français (1750–1850).* Paris: Champion, 2003.

Voisine, Jacques. "La contribution du Pygmalion de J.-J. Rousseau à l'autonomie de la prose poétique," in *Voltaire et Rousseau en France et en Pologne.* Varsovie: Editions de l'Université de Varsovie, 1982, 83–91.

Volpihac-Auger, Catherine. *Montesquieu. Mémoire de la critique.* Paris: Presses de l'Université de Paris-Sorbonne, 2003.

Watt, Ian. *The Rise of the Novel. Studies in Defoe, Richardson and Fielding. A Historico-Philosophical Essay on the Forms of Great Epic Literature.* Berkeley: University of California Press, 1974.

Whatley, Janet. "Coherent Worlds: Fénelon's *Télémaque* and Marivaux's *Télémaque Travesty,*" *Studies on Voltaire and the Eighteenth Century* 171 (1977): 85–113.

Zuber, Roger. *Les "Belles Infidèles" et la formation du goût classique,* 1968. Paris: Albin Michel, 1995.

Index

À Rebours (by Joris-Karl Huysman), 155
abbé Faydit
   Les Aventures de Télémaque (by
     Fénelon), 31, 35, 35n21
   telemacomania, 31
absolutism, 182
Académie Royale des Inscriptions et Belles
   Lettres, 76
Achilles' shield, 109
Aeneid (by Virgil), 34, 108
Aeolus, 174
aesthetics
   classical, 85
   non-Western, 216
   post-Romantic, 5n8
   Voltaire and, 87
African culture, 213
Age of Reason, 178, 188, 246
   poets and, 179
Ahasvérus (by Quinet), 7
alexandrine verses, 65, 188, 197
allegory, 103, 110, 120, 128, 139, 175, 195,
   200, 203, 206, 206n65
   in Description de l'Empire de la Poésie
     (by Fontenelle), 67–8
Allgemeine Theorie des schonen Kunste
   und Wissenschaften (by Johann
     Georg Sulzer), 93
Almanach des prosateurs, 68
Amadou, Robert, 203
   preface to *Le Crocodile*, 203n57
America, 199
   North America, 174
   wilderness of, 174
Amiot, Anne-Marie, 186n19
Amours de Carite et Polydore, Les (by
   Jean-Jacques Barthelemy), 120n47
Amours de Cherale (Les), poëme en six chants
   (by Louis-Sébastien Mercier), 238
Anacreon, odes of, 156
Analytical Review (by Johnson), 195n45
ancien régime, end of, 186
anglomania, 59

Annamire, poëme en trois chants (by
   Marie-Uranie Rose Monneron), 7
Apocalypse, 204
Apollo, 68
Apologie for Poetrie (by Philip Sydney),
   81n54
apologues, 151
Apostolidès, Jean-Marie, 63n1
Apuleius, 77
Aragon, Louis, 10, 25, 37–8, 43, 50
   Dadaism and, 38
   Dadaist manifesto of, 51
   Les Aventures de Télémaque (by
     Fénelon) and, 25, 37–8, 40n38, 44,
     49, 53
   prose poems of, 47
Arcadia (by Philip Sydney), 82n58
Aristotle, 64, 81n55, 93, 136, 151, 175
   Poetics, 64
   poetry and, 94
   rhetoric and, 144
Art poétique (by Boileau), 63, 64n2, 68,
   145n3, 155n31
Ashbery, John, 3
Atala (by Chateaubriand), 3, 28, 38, 109,
   140, 144, 176–7, 212, 226n31,
   242–3
   American Indians and, 28, 224, 226, 229
   American wilderness in, 233
   animism and, 234
   Christianity and, 224
   close reading of, 231–3
   descriptive passages in, 233
   Hebrew and, 226
   hybridity of, 229
   language in, 226
   mise en abyme in, 225
   new rhythms and, 223–36
   primitive voice in, 225–31
   prose and, 234
   as prose poem, 223
   realism and, 234
   song of nature, 233–7

"tableaux," 233
warrior's song, 229
Atala, René, Les Natchez, 217n19
Aufhebung, 123
*Aurelia ou Orléans délivrée, poème
    latin traduit en françois* (by Jean
    Roussy), 101n2
    as pseudo-translation, 129
Autels, Guillaume des, 155n31
avant-garde, 85
*Aventures de Néoptoleme (Les), fils
    d'Achille, Propres à former les
    Moeurs d'un jeune Prince*, 57
*Aventures de Periphas (Les), descendant
    de Cecrops* (by Puget de Saint-
    Pierre), 57
Aventures de Télémaque, Les (by Aragon),
    37, 38, 47, 51
    Calypso and, 39, 39n33, 40, 40n35,
        40n36, 41, 41n39
    Calypso's cave, 42
    Dadaist manifesto in, 48
    Eucharis in, 39
    hypertext or imitation of Fénelon's
        popular book, 37
    Mentor in, 39, 40, 41, 48
    Minerva in, 48, 50
    prose and, 50
    sexual symbolism and, 44
    Telemachus in, 39, 40, 40n37, 41
    Ulysses in, 39, 39n33, 40, 41
Aventures de Télémaque, Les (by Fénelon),
    3, 10, 16, 25, 29–62, 35n21, 59, 69,
    77, 84, 87–8, 91, 93, 95, 98, 102,
    107, 109–10, 112, 122, 128, 137,
    165, 175n78, 176, 180, 181
    antithesis, 46–7
    Aragon and, 37–8, 42, 45
    Balzac and, 31
    baroque poetry, 46–7
    Bétique episode, 55
    Bildungsroman, 48, 57
    Calypso in, 38–9, 39n32, 39n34, 40,
        40n36, 40n38, 41–2, 42n44, 47–9,
        61, 114, 127, 171, 174, 245
    Calypso's cave, 35, 35n21, 42–5, 107,
        183, 247
    epic and, 34, 35, 55–62
    Eucharis in, 42

European Enlightenment and, 30
French Revolution and, 33
genres and, 34, 36, 48
hero in, 34
Homeric sources of, 88
indeterminancy and, 35
Le Temple de Gnide (by Montesquieu)
    and, 101
love in, 42
Mentor/Minerva in, 33, 42, 48–50,
    48–9n53, 48n53
novel and, 34, 35, 56
Odyssey (by Homer) and, 53
popularity of, 29
prose and, 175, 182
prose poem (poëme en prose), 80
publication of, 31, 37, 71
Ramsay and, 101n3
seductive power of, 34
sexual symbolism and, 44–8
Telemachus, 41, 42
as translation from the Greek and, 176
Ulysses in, 39n32, 39n34, 42
utopian Counter-reformation and, 34
Virgil and, 88
written for the Duke of Burgundy, 32
Aventures d'Ulysse, dans l'isle d'Aeaea (by
    Simon Mamin), 57

Ballanche, 180, 186
Balzac, Honoré de, 29, 30, 65n7, 186
    Comédie humaine, 30
    Fénelon and, 29–30
Barbéris, Pierre, 33, 38
    Les Aventures de Télémaque (by
        Fénelon), 36
Barquisseau, Raphaël, 216n15
Barthelemy, Jean-Jacques, 120n47
Batteux, Charles, 27, 86n67, 92, 94, 146,
    150–52, 154, 156–7
    Des Beaux Arts, 152
    Des Genres en Prose, 151
    odes and, 155–6
    Principes de la littérature
        (by Batteux), 150
    "Traité de la poésie lyrique," 151
Baudelaire, Charles, 3, 11, 48, 127, 160,
    169, 186, 199n54, 222, 231n47
    Chateaubriand and, 231

Farewell of Telemachus and Eucharis
　　(Adieux de Télémaque et
　　d'Eucharis) painted by David, 247
Franz Liszt and, 247
"Le Tyrse," 247
L'Invitation au voyage, 36
poetry of, 134
prose poems (poëmes en prose) and,
　　2, 4, 9
Petits poëmes en prose (Spleen de
　　Paris), 127, 160, 169, 222
Beattie, James, 141
Beaufort d'Hautpoul, Anne Marie de,
　　120n47
Zilia, roman pastoral (by Anne Marie
　　de Beaufort d'Hautpoul), 120n47
Beauharnais, Fanny de (Mme la comtesse
　　de ***
Mélanges de poésies fugitives et de
　　prose sans conséquence (by Mme
　　la comtesse de*** aka Fanny de
　　Beauharnais), 13
Beaujour, Michel, 10, 11
Beaumarchais, plays in prose and, 15
Beaumont, Pauline de, 172
Beaussol, Peyraud de, 13
Écho à Narcisse, poème en trois chants
　　dans un genre nouveau qui tient de
　　l'héroïde, de l'élégie et de l'idylle, 13
Beaux Arts, Des (by Charles Batteux), 152
Beaux arts réduit à un même principe, Les
　　(by Charles Batteux), 151
Bebee, Thomas, 30
Bélesbat, castle of, 102
Bélisaire (by Auguste-Félix Desaugiers), 61
Bélisaire (by Marmontel), 57, 60
literary descendants of, 60–61
theater and, 61
Bélisaire, comédie heroïque (by Mouslier
　　de Moissy), 61
Bélisaire, drame en 5 ectes et en vers (by
　　Ozincourt), 61
Bélisaire ou les Masques tombés, drame
　　histori-philoso-heroï-comique (by
　　Mondolot), 61
"belles infidèles" translations, 64, 65
Belles-Lettres, 28, 63, 78, 89
Bénichou, Paul, 186n19
Benjamin, tribe of, 162, 168

Benjamin, Walter, 195, 195n45, 207
Benrekassa, Georges, 119n44
Berchet, Jean-Claude, 223n29, 227n37
Berger Extravagant, où parmi les
　　fantaisies amoureuses on void les
　　impertinences des Romans et de la
　　Poësie (by Charles Sorel), 16, 54, 64
Bernabé, Jean, 214
Bernard, Suzanne, 3n5, 5, 7, 10, 28, 159, 213
Poème en prose de Baudelaire à nos
　　jours, 5, 7
Bernis, François-Joachim de Pierre de
pastoral poetry and, 120
Bertrand, Aloysius, 109n22, 214
Gaspard de la Nuit, 214
"Harlem," 109n22
Bible, 3, 9, 27, 120, 132, 136, 146, 150,
　　159, 164–5, 168, 170, 173, 179–80,
　　190, 206, 224–6, 229–30
Adam and Eve, 169
alliance of prose and poetry in, 155
Book of Job, 150
Book of Judges and, 27
Eighteenth Century and, 26
epics in prose in, 169–78
fictions in, 170n69
as historical document, 163
Lamentations of Jeremiah, 150
language in, 167
Le Lévite d'Ephraim (by Rousseau)
　　and, 157–68
literature and, 136, 147–8, 150
lyricism of, 147, 148
odes of David, 150
odes of Moses, 82, 150
Old Testament, 148, 160
original Hebrew, 166
as poetic text, 27, 145, 148–56, 150,
　　155, 163
prose poems (poëmes en prose) and,
　　145–78
prose translations of, 153
Psalms, by David, 150
return to in Eighteenth Century, 148–56
rhetorical categories and, 149
Robert Lowth, 148–56
Rousseau's *Le Lévite d'Ephraïm*: "Une
　　manière de petit poëme en prose,"
　　157–68

Song of Solomon, 150
story of Cain and Abel, 147
Bibliothèque universelle des romans, 53
Bildungsroman, 59, 104
binarism, 48
Bitaubé, Paul-Jérémie, 132, 170, 172,
    207, 240
    "Dialogue entre L'Auteur et un
      Journaliste," 131–3
    *Guillaume de Nassau, ou la fondation
      des Provinces-Unies*, 131, 134,
      259–66
    Joseph, 98, 131, 170–71, 170n71
    prose and, 132
Blair, Hugh, 175n78
Blake, William, 192, 195, 199n54, 201n55,
    204n61
    "bricolage," 195n45
    French Revolution and, 192
    The Marriage of Heaven and Hell, 192,
      199n54, 201n55, 204n61
    Saint-Martin and, 195n45
Blanchot, Maurice, 206
blank verse, 60, 88, 89
Boehme, Jacob, 187, 188, 192, 195n45
Boësnier, 7
    Mexique Conquis, 7
Boileau-Despréaux, Nicolas, 63, 64n2,
    75n42, 80, 86, 98, 135, 141, 145,
    145n3, 175
    Art poétique, 63, 64n2, 68, 145n3,
      155n31
    condemnation of epigrams, 87n71
    Genesis and, 145
    Longinus and, 145
    odes and, 155
    prose poems (poëmes en prose), 80
Boiste, Pierre-Claude-Victor, 99, 180, 207
    L'univers, narration épique, 206
    *L'univers poëme en prose en douze
      chants*, 97, 99, 206
Bonnet, Jean-Claude, 29n1, 237n55
"bons sauvages," 221
Book of Job, 150, 183
    as prose poem, 131
Book of Judges, 160, 166, 166n60
Book of Revelations, 183
Bossuet, Jacques-Bénigne, 33, 87, 131,
    149, 183

Discours sur l'histoire universelle, 33
    prose poems (poëmes en prose), 239
    Quietism and, 181
Bouchaud, 212n3
Boucher, François, 140
Boucher, Gwenaëlle, 84
Bourbon Island, 215
Brémond, Henri, 184, 184n12
Breton, André, 3, 37
bricolage, 195n45
Brunot, Ferdinand, 12n33
Buccolics (by Virgil), 183
Burgundy, Duke of, 32
Bussy-Rabutin, Roger de, 64, 115
    Histoire amoureuse des Gaules, 64
Byron, George Gordon, 218

Cagliostro, Alessandro di, 187, 196, 200
Calprenède, novels of, 227
Calypso's cave, 36, 247
Candler Hayes, Julie, 17n42, 135n21
Cantiques (by Moses), 183
Cassandre (by La Calprenède), 88
Catholic Church, 33, 35n21, 38, 180, 200
    Protestant schism and, 180
Caws, Mary Ann, 6, 10n26
Cazotte, Jacques, 6, 186
    Ollivier, poëme, 6
*Céramiques (Les) ou les Aventures de
    Nicias et d'Antiope* (by Galtier de
    Saint Symphorien), 57
Cervantes, Miguel de, 121n48
Chabanon, Michel Paul Guy de, 11n29, 12n33
Chamoiseau, Patrick, 214
Chansierges, 57
chansons (by Saint-Lambert), 213
Chansons madécasses (by Évariste Parny),
    212–15, 217–18, 218n22, 219, 221,
    222, 229n43
    hainteny and, 216
Chapelan, Maurice, 5
*Charmes de l'enfance (Les), et les plaisirs
    de l'amour maternel* (by Jauffret),
    139n32
Chateaubriand, René de, 7, 9, 27–8, 34,
    38, 69, 109, 127, 134, 138, 144,
    146, 156, 170–78, 180, 185–6, 190,
    211–13, 216, 216n15, 218, 218n22,
    219, 221–2, 247

America and, 212, 223
American Indians and, 221, 223
Atala, 3, 28, 38, 109, 140, 144, 176–7,
    212, 223–36, 226n31, 242–3
classical period of, 141, 230
death of sister Lucile, 172
epic and, 147
Essai sur les révolutions, 140,
    216n15, 223
"Examen des *Martyrs*," 172, 176
Génie du Christianisme, 172, 218n22,
    222–3, 225–6, 231
La Mort d'Abel (by Salomon Gessner)
    and, 147
*Les Martyrs ou le triomphe de la religion
    chrétienne* (by Chateaubriand), 134,
    140, 146, 171–8
Les Natchez, 217n19, 223, 225
the letter A and, 231–3
Mémoires d'outre-tombe (by
    Chateaubriand), 7, 140, 172
musical prose in, 233
New World and, 245
onomatopoeia in, 233n54, 234
Ossian and, 140, 141
Parny and, 214
poetry and, 176, 233
"primitive poetics," 28, 227, 229n43
prose and, 176, 235, 241
René, 223, 227
sound and, 235
style of, 227, 229
Theocritus and, 231
translation of *excerpts from British
    authors*, 140
translation of "Ossianic" poems by
    John Smith, 141
as translator, 141–3
Chenier, André, 12
Chérel, Albert, 30n7, 55, 101n3, 183n8
Chevaliers des îles, Les (by Raphaël
    Barquisseau), 216n15
Christiade, La (by La Baume Desdossats),
    170, 177
Christian authors, 185
    biblical poetry, 170
    prose poems and, 169
    rationality and, 180
Christian mysticism, 180

Christianity, 218n22
    paganism and, 173
Cicero, 77, 92, 131
Clairmont, Mlle de, 103, 129
Clarissa (by Richardson), 226n31
classicism, 2, 64, 137, 145n3, 146, 172, 183
"Claudine" (by Joris-Karl Huysmans),
    109n22
Clayton, Vista, 6, 7
    *Prose Poem in French Literature of the
        Eighteenth Century*, 6
Clélie ou L'Histoire romaine (by
    Madeleine de Scudery), 34, 64
Cléopâtre (by La Calprenède), 64
Clermont, Mlle de, 114
    Montesquieu and, 102
Cohen, Margaret, 59
    *The Sentimental Education of the
        Novel* (by Margaret Cohen), 59
Colardeau, Charles-Pierre, 121
Collin d'Harleville, Jean-François,
    "Dialogue Between Prose and
    Poetry" (1802), 267–72
colonialism, 213
    European, 231
Comédie humaine (by Balzac), 30
comedy, 16, 67
Condillac, Étienne Bonnot de, 189
Condorcet, Nicolas de, 112n29
Confessions (by Jean-Jacques Rousseau),
    146, 159, 160, 163
Confiant, Raphaël, 214
*Considérations sur les causes de la
    grandeur des Romains et de leur
    décadence* (by Montesquieu), 120
Coqueley de Chaussepierre, Charles-
    Georges, 7, 16–17, 16n41
    *Monsieur Cassandre, ou les effets de
        l'amour et du vert-de-gris*, 16n41
    Le Roué vertueux, 7, 16, 17, 25
Corneille, Pierre, 83, 134, 145
Cottin, Sophie, 170n67
    Prise de Jéricho, La (by Sophie
        Cottin), 170n67
Counter-Reformation, 33
*Cours de Belles-Lettres, distribué par
    exercices* (by Charles Batteux), 151
Court de Gébelin, Antoine, 189
court of Chantilly, 102

courtly love (amour courtois), 38
Cousin de Grainville, Jean-Baptiste-
    François-Xavier, 16, 180, 186, 207
Cratylus (by Plato), 232, 232n52
Creole, 214, 221
créolité (Creoleness), 215
Creolization, 214–17, 221
*Crocodile (Le), ou la guerre du bien et du
    mal, arrivée sous le règne de Louis
    XV* (by Saint-Martin), 187, 189,
    192–206, 198n53, 222
    allegory and, 192, 196, 198,
        201–2, 205
    first page, 194
    French revolution and, 192, 203–5
    Marriage of Heaven and Hell (by
        William Blake) and, 192, 204n61
    mock-heroic epic poem in
        prose, 192
    title page, 193
Cronk, Nicholas, 145n4
Curtius, Ernst, 108
Cyclop and Galathea (by Theocritus), 231

d'Ablancourt, Nicolas Perrot, 126, 137
Dacier, Anne Le Fèvre, 125, 136, 145
    Greek language and, 152
    Iliad, 26, 145, 156
    "prose d'art," 137
    prose translation of Homer's *Iliad*,
        74n40, 135, 136, 156
    translations and, 88, 135, 137, 240
Dadaism, 10, 25, 37
d'Alembert, Jean Le Rond, 101, 109–10,
    114, 115, 128, 179, 202n56
    poetics of, 128
Dante (Dante Alighieri), 135
Daphnis (by Salomon Gessner), 137, 146
Daphnis et Chloé (by Longus), 146
    Amyot's translation of, 137
Dargo (by John Smith), 141, 143
David, 152, 157
    harp of, 173, 174
    odes of, 150, 157n36
David, Jacques-Louis, 245, 246, 247
    *Farewell of Telemachus and Eucharis
        (Adieux de Télémaque et
        d'Eucharis) painted by David*, 245,
        245n1, 246

De la Construction Oratoire des mots (by
    Charles Batteux), 151
De la Littérature (by Germaine de Staël),
    239n64
De l'Usage des Romans (by Lenglet-
    Dufresnoy), 81
*De Sacra Poesi Hebraeorum (Lectures on
    the Sacred Poetry of the Hebrews)*
    by Robert Lowth, 148–57
Deborah, triumphal ode of, 157n36
Delacroix, Eugène, 231
Delille, Jacques, 12, 43, 43n45, 141, 239
Deloffre, Frédéric, 53
Delon, Michel, 6n9, 8, 15–16n38–9,
    43n45, 180n2, 189n28, 213
Demosthenes, 50, 131
d'Enghien, Duke of, 172
Denys d'Halicarnasse, 175
Dernier homme, Le (by Grainville), 6, 7,
    207, 208
"Des Estampes et des Poëmes en prose"
    (by Dubos), 91
Desaugiers, Auguste-Félix, 61, 61n93
description, 127
Desdossats, La Baume, 170
Desforges Maillard, Pierre Jean Baptiste, 120
Deshoulières, Mme, 120–21
Deux amis de Bourbonne (by Diderot), 138
"Deux Amis (Les): conte iroquois" (by
    Jean-François de Saint-Lambert),
    212, 213n9
Diabotinus (by Girard), 101n2
"Dialogue Between Prose and Poetry"
    (1802) (by Collin d'Harleville),
    267–72
"Dialogue entre la Prose et la Poésie"
    (1809) Anonymous, 68, 273–94
    in *Almanach des prosateurs*, 131
"Dialogue entre L'Auteur et un Journaliste"
    in *Guillaume de Nassau, ou la
        fondation des Provinces -Unies* (by
        Bitaubé), 131
diction, poetic, 65, 165
    neoclassical, 160
Diderot, Denis, 16, 17n42, 112n30, 140,
    179, 201, 204n62, 238–9n62
    Deux amis de Bourbonne, 138
    Entretien d'un père avec ses enfants, 138
    pastorals and, 138

plays in prose and, 15
rhythmic translation and, 212n3
Salomon Gessner and, 139–40
Supplément au Voyage de Bougainville,
219–20
Dionis, Mlle, 120n47
Origines des graces, 120n47
Discours de l'art poétique (by Tasso), 126
"Discours sur Homère" (by La Motte), 135–6
Discours aux Welches (by Voltaire), 87
Discours sur l'histoire universelle (by
Bossuet), 33
d'Olivet, Fabre, 189
Dornier, Carole, 101n4, 104n13, 106n14,
111n28
drama, 3, 10, 12, 64, 82, 134, 149, 151
biblical topics and, 146–7
juxtaposition of verse and prose in, 15
poetry and, 16
prose and, 15
du Bellay, definition of ode, 155n31
du Mans, Peletier, definition of ode, 155n31
Dubos, Jean-Baptiste, 80, 91, 93, 93n95, 120
Duc de Bourbon, 102
Duchet, Michèle, 213n9
Dufresne, Mme, 7, 120n47
*Idylles et pièces fugitives trouvées dans
un hermitage au pied du mont Ste.
Odile*, 7, 120n47
Dugat, P.-D., 170n67
La mort d'Azaël ou le rapt de Dina,
170n67
Dupont, Paul, 70n26
d'Urfé, Honoré, 64, 118
Duthona (by John Smith), 141, 143

*Écho à Narcisse, poème en trois chants
dans un genre nouveau qui tient de
l'héroïde, d l'elegie et de l'idylle*
(by Peyraud de Beaussol), 13
eclogues, 151
eighteenth century, 13, 93, 127
Bible and, 148
criticism, 60
mythology and, 112, 112n29
Orient and, 80
philosophers, 188
prosateurs, 34
prose poems and, 5

satire and, 103
spiritual and aesthetic "reformation," 27
ekphrasis, 109, 118
elegy, 67, 150
Elegy Written in a Country Church-Yard
(by Thomas Gray), 150
Eliot, T.S., 86
Éloge de la créolité, 214
Émile (by Rousseau)
Calypso in, 52
censorship of, 160
Eucharis in, 51
Les Aventures de Télémaque (by
Fénelon) and, 51, 53
Mentor and, 51, 52
Telemachus in, 51, 52
*Encyclopédie, ou Dictionnaire raisonné
des arts, des sciences et des métiers*
(by Diderot), 26, 63, 84, 91–5, 187,
201, 204n62
entry for "Poëme en Prose" (by
Chevalier de Jaucourt), 91, 97
entry for "Poesie" (by Chevalier de
Jaucourt), 91, 94
entry for "Prose" (unsigned), 92
preface to, 92n93
"Prose" (excerpted and translated from
Johann Georg Sulzer), 93
prose poems (poëmes en prose) and,
91–5
Supplément de, 93, 94, 95
encyclopédisme, 203
Encylopedists, 145, 191
Enlightenment, 2–3, 5, 7–9, 12, 27–8, 60,
63, 84, 99, 102, 122, 125, 147, 179,
185–6, 190, 200, 202–3, 206, 212,
214–15, 245
authors of, 11
Chateaubriand and, 140
episteme of, 25
European, 2, 188
mythology and, 206
novels, 3
pastoral myth and, 123
philosophers, 7
poetry and, 5n8, 151
prose and, 5n8
prose poems and, 3, 10, 11, 65, 155
purity and, 13

rationality and, 27
research about, 146
return to the Bible and, 146
secular, 145
Enlightenment, French, 4, 6, 28, 64, 66, 89, 95
prose poems (poëmes en prose) of, 1–28
Entretien d'un père avec ses enfants (by Diderot), 138
epic, prose, 101n2
epic narratives, 82
epic poetry, 4, 30, 34, 67, 70, 75, 81, 89, 127, 134
German writers, 134n19
Romantic, 192
epic prose, 170
epics, 3, 64, 84, 129, 134, 147, 151, 175
biblical, 169–78
Christian, 171, 172
classical genre, 177
nostalgia for, 55–62
poetic codes of, 56
prose and, 82, 177
Epicurian philosophy, 218
epigrams, 151
epithets, 109, 110
Épopée by Voltaire, 88
Erreurs et de la vérité, Des (by Saint-Martin), 195n45
eschatology, 206
Reformation and, 186–205, 206–10
Escherny, François-Louis, 97–8
Essai sur les révolutions (by Chateaubriand), 140, 216n15, 223
Essai sur les romans (by Marmontel), 56
Essai sur l'étude de la literature (by Edward Gibbon), 202n56
Essai sur l'origine des langues (by Rousseau), 27, 159, 161, 167
"Essai sur l'idylle et le conte pastoral" (by Jauffret), 139n32
Estelle et Némorin (by Jean-Pierre Claris de Florian), 121n48
Études de la nature (by Bernardin de Saint-Pierre), 223
Euphues (by John Lyly), 82n58
Europe, 188
18th century, 3
northern Protestant countries of, 33

"Examen des *Martyrs*" (by Chateaubriand), 172, 176
Examen philosophique de la poésie en général (by Rémond de Saint-Mard), 82–4
exoticism, 214

Farewell of Telemachus and Eucharis (Adieux de Télémaque et d'Eucharis) painted by David, 246
Faydit, abbé, 175, 176
Faye, M. de La
Ode en faveur des vers, 72
Féletz, abbé de, 222
Fénelon, François de Salignac de la Mothe, 3, 7, 10, 16, 25, 27, 29–62, 69, 71, 75, 80, 87, 95, 97, 101, 107, 112, 114–16, 122, 127–8, 132–3, 137, 149, 160, 165, 171, 175, 180, 184–5, 187
Aragon and, 37
Book of Job and, 183
Bossuet and, 183
Calypso's cave, 183
Cambray, Mr. de, 35n21, 52n65
Christian humanism and, 181, 182
classical versification, 246
description of Elysium fields, 183
devout humanism, 33
dogma and tradition, 34
epic poem in prose, 74, 135
French poets and, 92
Greek poets and, 183, 245
hermeticism and, 182
Homer and, 25, 32
humanist utopia, 33
hybrid of polytheism and monotheism, 35
Jansennists and, 183
Latin poets and, 183
Les Aventures de Télémaque, 37–8, 44–7
Maximes des Saints, 35n21
Moses and, 183
nature and, 183
poetic descriptions of, 48
portrayal of love, 38
prose epic of, 79
prose of, 31, 32, 79, 183, 245
prose poems (poëmes en prose) and, 25, 180, 184, 239

Psalms and, 183
Quietism and, 180, 181, 184, 185
Song of Solomon and, 183
sublime and, 183
Traité de l'existence et des atrributs de Dieu, 183
tutor of the Dauphin, 48, 57
views of the poet and, 182
Virgil and, 183
fiction
  biblical, 161
  didactic, 51, 60
  in meter, 81n54
  in prose, 81n54
  romanesque, 60
  sentimental, 226n31
Fielding, Henry, 81n54, 82n58, 131, 237n58
  Joseph Andrews, 81n54, 82n58
Fils naturel, Le (by Diderot), 16
Fleury, Claude, cardinal de, 74n40, 149
  Hebrew sacred poetry, 74
  "Remarques sur Homère à M.
    le Laboureur Bailly de
    Montmorency," 74n40
Florian, Jean-Pierre Claris de, 121n48
  essays about pastoral poetry, 120
  Estelle et Némorin, 121n48
  Galatée, Roman pastoral; imité de Cervantes, 121n48, 169
Fontainebleau, 102
Fontenelle, Bernard Le Bovier de, 81
  allegory of, 69
  Description de l'Empire de la Poésie, 67–8
  distrust of rhyme and, 67
  essays about pastoral poetry, 120
formalism, 8, 145, 247
Fourmont, Etienne, 149
Fowler, Elizabeth, 8
Fraguier, l'abbé, 76, 85, 89, 134
  " A Discourse to shew that there can be no Poems in Prose " (1719), 249–58
  defense of verse, 80
  essays about pastoral poetry, 120
  Fénelon and, 77–8
  Les Aventures de Télémaque (by Fénelon), 79–80
  mémoire of, 78, 79, 87
  myth of Orpheus and, 77

Oriental style, 80
prose poems (poëmes en prose) and, 76–82
"Qu'il ne peut y avoir de poëmes en prose" (mémoire), 76
France, 33
  ancien régime, 179
  eighteenth century, 7, 70, 185
  England and, 58
  epic poetry and, 135
  literary landscape of, 1
  lyrical mode vs. epic, 147
  monarchy of, 80
  political history of, 195
  post-revolutionary society, 11
  post-WWI, 37
Franciade, ou L'Ancienne France. Poëme en seize chants (by François Verne), 7
free verse, 10, 64
French language
  Antoine de Rivarol and, 95–100
  distinction between poetry and prose in, 79
  empire of, 97
  poetry and, 96
  superiority of, 63
French literature, 182
  eighteenth century, 25
  eighteenth-century French poetry, 8
  mysticism and, 185
  prose poems (poëmes en prose), 28
  prose poetry and, 215
  religious sentiment in, 184
  Romantics, 213
French prose and poetry, 69, 95
French Revolution, 33, 202n56
Fréron, Elie, 134
Furet, François, 195
Furetière, Antoine, 66, 69

Gaelic language, 138
Galatée, Roman pastoral; imité de Cervantes (by Jean-Pierre Claris de Florian), 121n48, 169
Gaspard de la Nuit (by Aloysius Bertrand), 214
Gaul (by John Smith), 141, 143
Geffriau Rosso, Jeannette, 117n38

Genesis, 206, 207
    Longinus and, 145
Genette, Gérard, 37n28, 38, 46, 53n68, 56,
    57, 60, 71, 131, 132, 151, 152
Génie du Christianisme (by
    Chateaubriand), 172, 218n22,
    222–3, 225–6, 231
Genlis, Mme de, 180
genres, 34, 99
    boundaries and, 13
    dramatic, 151
    epic, 151
    lyric, 151
    non-lyrical, 64
    poetic, 64
    politics of, 11
Genres en Prose, Des (by Charles
    Batteux), 151
Georgics (by Virgil), 117, 183, 237
Gessner, Salomon, 125, 131, 137, 146,
    148, 150, 158, 160, 170, 237n58
    Bible and, 146–7
    Daphnis, 137, 146
    Diderot and, 139
    Idylles, 121, 137, 158, 160
    La Mort d'Abel (by Salomon Gessner),
        137, 146–8, 150, 158
    lyricism of, 148
    Nouvelles Idylles, 137–9
    Ossian and, 137–44
    poems of, 26, 170
    portraits of, 140
    prose poems (poëmes en prose) and,
        137–44
    rhythmic prose and, 137
    translation and, 137–44, 138n27
Gibbon, Edward, 202n56
    Essai sur l'étude de la littérature, 202n56
Girard, 101n2
    Diabotinus, 101n2
Girondins, 198
Godzich, Wlad, 8
Golden Age myth, 120, 136, 163, 183, 206
    "Peace, Abundance, and Justice," 119,
        119n42
Graffigny, Mme de, 240
Grainville, 6, 208
    apocalyptic vision in prose poem, 7
    eschatological vision, 208

    suicide of, 7, 208
Grand Cyrus, Le (by Madeleine de
    Scudéry), 34, 38, 227
Granderoute, Robert, 60, 60n88, 61n93
Gray, Thomas, 150
    *Elegy Written in a Country Church-
        Yard*, 150
Graziani, Françoise, 126
Greece, Homeric, 134
Greek language, 152
Greek models, 150
Greek poetry
    French poetry and, 96
Greek rhetorical principles, 149
Greene, Roland, 8
Greuze, Jean-Baptiste, 139, 140
Grille, Jacques de, 68, 69
Guérin, 186
Guerre des Dieux anciens et modernes, La
    (by Évariste Parny), 221
    as allegory, 222
Gueudeville, Nicolas, 31, 43, 79, 175, 184
    Les Aventures de Télémaque (by
        Fénelon) and, 32–3
    Louis the Great, 32
Guez de Balzac, Jean-Louis, 65–6, 69, 93
*Guillaume de Nassau, ou la fondation des
    Provinces-Unies* (by Bitaubé), 134
    as pseudo-translation, 131
Guitton, Édouard, 8
Guyon, Mme (Jeanne-Marie), 181, 184

Haillant, Marguerite, 56n75
hainteny, 214, 216
"Hareng saur, Le" (by Karl Joris
    Huysmans), 109n22
"Harlem" (by Aloysius Bertrand),
    109n22
Hebrew language, 150, 154, 226
Hebrew poetry, 27, 74, 152–3n27, 154,
    157n36, 173
    genres of, 149n20
    meter, 149n20
    Robert Lowth and, 152
    translation and, 153
Hebrew prose, 136
Hebrews, 149n19
Heffernan, James, 109n20, 117
Hegel, Georg Wilhelm Friedrich, 123

Hénault, 120
Henriade, La (by Voltaire), 84, 95, 135
  as first French epic poem, 84
Henry IV, 32, 66
Hepp, Noémi, 34–7, 74n40
Herman, Jan, 125
hermeticism, 182
Hervey, James, 150
  Meditations Among the Tombs, 150
Histoire amoureuse des Gaules (by Roger
  de Bussy-Rabutin), 64
Histoire des Sévarambes (by Denis
  Vairasse), 6n12
Holbach, Baron d', 179
Homer, 3, 32, 34, 75, 108, 110, 129, 134–7,
  164–5, 168, 173, 175, 177, 224–6,
  230, 237n58
  Anne Dacier's translation and, 125
  epic poetry and, 25, 74n40, 88, 134
  French educated elite and, 134
  Houdar de La Motte and, 70
  Iliad, 136, 156, 224
  Odyssey, 34, 37, 52–3, 56, 224
  topos, 55
Horace, 89, 94, 108, 152, 155n31, 177
Huber, Michael, 137–8, 158
Huet, Pierre-Daniel, 81n55, 145
  Anne Dacier and, 145
  Traité de l'origine des romans, 81
Hugo, Victor, 145
Huguenotism, 32
humanism, Christian, 184
Huysmans, Joris-Karl, 109n22, 155
  "Claudine," 109n22
  "La Kermesse de Rubens," 109n22
  prose poet and, 169
hybridity ("métissage"), 13, 26, 34
Hymne au soleil (by Reyrac), 6, 98
  as pseudo-translation, 129
hypertextualité, 56

Icarus, 12, 78
idyll, 127, 147
  descriptive, 121
  Greek, 137
  pastoral, 119
Idylles (by Salomon Gessner), 121, 137,
  158, 160
  translated by Turgot, 137

*Idylles et pièces fugitives trouvées dans un
  hermitage au pied du mont Ste. Odile*
  (by Mme Dufresne), 7, 120n47
idylls, 138
*Iles fortunées (Les) ou Les Aventures
  de Bachylle et de Cléobule* (by
  Moutonnet-Clairfons), 57, 60, 185n15
  Bildungsroman and, 59
  England in, 58n84
  Le Temple de Gnide (by Montesquieu), 59
  Les Aventures de Télémaque (by
    Fénelon) and, 59
Iliad (by Anne Dacier), 26, 145, 156
Iliad (by Homer), 136, 156, 224
  prose translation of, 136
  translation by Anne Le Fèvre, 135
Iliade en douze chants (by Houdar de La
  Motte), 70
Illuminations (by Arthur Rimbaud), 47
  Fénelon's Eucharis in, 47
Illuminism, 180, 186–205, 206
  Reformation, 186–205
  Saint-Martin and, 187
  theosophy and, 206
Images ou Tableaux de platte peinture, Les
  (by Philostratus), 30
*Incas, (Les); ou la destruction de l'empire
  de Pérou* (by Marmontel), 6, 212
Indians, American, 174. see also Native
  Americans
  songs of, 212
Inquisition, 199
intentional fallacy, 78
Israel, twelve tribes of, 162, 167, 230

Jabès, tribe of, 162, 168
Jacob, Max, 3
Jacobins, 198
Jacques-Lefèvre, Nicole, 187n20, 192n43
Jakobson, Roman, 133
Jansenists, 38, 181, 183
Jardins, Les (by Jacques Delille), 43n45
Jaucourt, Chevalier de, 1–2, 4–5, 91, 93
Jauffret, 139n32
  "Essai sur l'idylle et le conte pastoral,"
    139n32
  Gessner and, 139n32
Jechova, Hana, 159n40, 185
Jerusalem Delivered (by Tasso), 108, 126

Jesus, 177, 182, 196
jeux de salon, 87
Johnson, Barbara, 9, 36, 133
Johnson, Dorothy, 245, 245n1
Joseph (by Bitaubé), 98, 131, 170–71
   biblical lyre and, 170n71
Joseph Andrews (by Fielding), 82n58
   preface to, 81n54
Joyce, James, 37
   Ulysses, 37
Juden, Brian, 186n19, 188n27, 190n35
Jules César, Tragédie de Shakespeare, 89
Julie, ou la nouvelle Héloïse (by Rousseau),
   53, 82, 146, 159n40, 226n31
   Les Aventures de Télémaque (by
      Fénelon) and, 53
Julius Caesar (by William Shakespeare), 89

Kant, Immanuel, 28, 203
"Kermesse de Rubens, La" (by Karl Joris
   Huysmans), 109n22
Kavanagh, Thomas, 162n52, 168n64
Kittay, Jeffrey, 8
Klopstock, Friedrich Gottlieb, 147,
   147n13, 207
   Bible and, 147–8
   Messiah, The, 147n13
   odes and, 155
   On Sacred Poetry, 147–8, 147n13

La Baume Desdossats, *La Christiade*, 170
La Bruyère, Jean de, 238–9n62
La Calprenède, 64
La Faye, M. de, 71–2
La Fayette, Mme de, *La Princesse de
   Clèves*, 38, 64, 80, 91
*La Franciade, ou L'Ancienne France.
   Poëme en seize chants* (by François
   Verne), 101n2
La Harpe, François de, 89, 175
La Motte, Houdar de, 25, 63–4, 70–75,
   75n42, 77, 81, 85, 86n66, 87, 92,
   122, 131, 157–8
   "Discours sur Homère," 135–6
   Enlightenment and, 75
   Fénelon and, 70
   French theater and, 76n45
   Homer and, 70, 135
   Iliad and, 136

Iliade en douze chants, 70
La Libre Eloquence, 74
   literary experiments and, 70
   as a Modern, 75–6
   ode, 75–6
   Ode en faveur des vers (by M. de La
      Faye) and, 72
   ode in prose, 74, 156
   Œdipe, 71, 85
   Œuvres Complètes, 71
   poetry and, 71, 73, 120
   prose poems (poëmes en prose), 70
   prose vs. poetry, 70–75
   "Réflexions sur la critique," 136
   theories of, 84
Laclos, Pierre Choderlos de, *Liaisons
   dangereuses*, 82
Laforgue, Jules, 169
L'Amante difficile (by Houdar de La
   Motte), 71
Lamartine, Alphonse de, 186, 213
Lamennais, 186
Lamentations of Jeremiah, 150
L'An deux mille quatre cent quarante (by
   Louis-Sébastien Mercier), 238n61
language
   of imagination, 63
   origins of, 27, 189
Languedoc, 121n48
L'Année litteraire, 134
Lanson, Gustave, 69n24
L'Astrée (by Honoré d'Urfé), 34, 38, 64,
   77, 104–5, 119, 122
Latin hymn, 66n13
Latin language, 70–71, 129, 152
Latin models, 150
Lautréamont, Comte de, 38
Le Bossu, 34
Le Clerc, Louis-Claude, 177–8
   Tobie, poëme en quatre chants, 170,
      171, 177
Le Fèvre, Tanneguy, 135
Le Suire, Robert Martin, 120n47
   *Les Noces patriarchales, poëme en
      prose en cinq chants*, 120n47
Le Tasse, 88
Le Tourneur, 141–2
   Mercier and, 240
   translation and, 240

Leclerc, Georges-Louis, Comte de Buffon, 98, 238–9n62
Lenglet-Dufresnoy, Nicolas, 81
  Maximes à observer dans les Romans, 81
Leroy, Christian, 6, 6n11, 7
L'esprit des lois, de (by Montesquieu), 102–3, 118, 120
Lettre à un ami (by Saint-Martin), 187, 198, 200
Lettres persanes (by Montesquieu), 82, 89, 102–4, 114, 122, 126, 180
  Montesquieu's anonymous preface to, 125
  pseudo-translation, 125
  Troglodyte episode, 185n15
Lévite d'Ephraïm, Le (by Jean-Jacques Rousseau), 3, 6, 148, 152, 155, 159n40, 160–61, 163, 166–8, 168n64, 169, 230
  Bible and, 146, 157–68, 162n52
  Book of Judges and, 27
  didactic intentions and, 165
  division into cantos, 163
  La Mort d'Abel (by Salomon Gessner) and, 158
  the language of signs, 167–9
  prose and poetry, 163–6
  as prose poem, 127, 157–68
  Rousseau's prefaces, 160
  staging passions: "Amour de soi" and "Amour propre," 161–3
  suspension of time in, 164n57
Levite story (Bible), 168
  language of gesture in, 167
  prose narrative of, 164–6
L'Homme de désir (by Saint-Martin), 189, 190, 195n45, 205–6, 222
  Le Crocodile, ou la guerre du bien et du mal, arrivée sous le règne de Louis XV (by Saint-Martin) and, 205
  prose poem, 188
"l'homme Dieu," 188
Liaisons dangereuses, Les (by Laclos), 82
Libération (French daily newspaper), 29
Libre Eloquence, La, 74
L'Iliade en douze chants (translation by La Motte), 136
linguistics, prose and poetic styles, 12n33
L'Invitation au voyage (by Baudelaire), 36
Liszt, Franz, 247

literature
  canonization, 13
  European, 213
  generic categorization, 13
  marketplace for, 85
  purity and, 13
Litman, Theodore, 145n3
Little, Roger, 212
Locke, John, 192
Longinus, 145
  Traité du sublime, 145
Longus, 146
  Daphnis et Chloé, 137, 146
Louis XIV, 32, 69, 238–9n62
Louis XV, 84, 102, 140, 201
Lowth, Robert, 27, 146, 148–50, 154–7, 166, 226
  Bible and, 150, 152
  Charles Batteux and, 150–51
  divine inspiration and, 149n21
  Hebrew language and, 152
  Hebrew poetry, 148–56, 149n20
  Hebrew prose, 153
  lectures of, 150n22
  lyric poetry and, 152
  odes and, 155
  prose poems (poëmes en prose), 148–56
Lucian, 77
Lukács, Georg, 82
L'univers, narration épique (by Boiste), 206
L'univers poëme en prose en douze chants (by Boiste), 97, 206
  title changed to *L'Univers, narration épique*, 99
L'Universalité de la langue française (by Rivarol), 95–100
Luther, Martin, 33, 180
Lyly, John, 82n58
  Euphues, 82n58
lyre, 173
  poetry and, 157
lyricism, 12, 64, 125, 146, 147

Macpherson, James, 142–3
  Poems of Ossian, 3, 26, 98, 125–6, 137–44, 140, 215
Madagascar, 214–16, 221
Maillard, 120
Maistre, Joseph de, 186

Malebranche, 83
Malherbe, François de, 65, 65n7, 66, 69, 80, 93
Mallarmé, Stéphane, 3, 169, 222
Malouet, Pierre-Victor, 123n49
    Les quatres parties du jour à la mer, 123
Mamin, Simon, 57
    Aventures d'Ulysse, dans l'isle d'Aeaea, 57
Man, Paul de, 206
Manet, Edouard, 171n73
    "Olympia" (painting), 171n73
Manon Lescaut (by Prévost), 82
Manuel, Frank, 112
Marcillac, Mise de, 101n4
Marie-Antoinette, 68
Marivaux, Pierre de, 16
    Le Télémaque travesti, 3, 16, 53–4, 54n71, 57, 59, 99, 102–5
    Les Aventures de Télémaque (by Fénelon) and, 51, 54
    telemacomania and, 51–4
Marlborough, poëme comique en prose rimée (by Louis Abel Beffroy de Reigny aka Le Cousin Jacques), 13
    frontispiece, 14
Marmontel, Jean-François, 3, 56–7, 98, 212
    Bélisaire, 57, 60, 61
    Encyclopédie, ou Dictionnaire raisonné des arts, des sciences et des métiers, 95
    Essai sur les romans, 56
    Inca characters, 212
    prose and, 60, 241
Marriage of Heaven and Hell, The (by William Blake), 192, 199n54, 201n55, 204n61
    Jacob Boehme and, 192
    Swedenbörg and, 192
Martyrs (Les) ou le triomphe de la religion chrétienne (by Chateaubriand), 134, 140, 171–8
    allegory in, 173
    Bible and, 146, 171
    pagans vs. Christians in, 172
    preface to, 177–8
    as prose epic, 170–72
    prose vs. poetry, 172
Masson, Nicole, 34n13

materialism, 178, 192, 203
Maximes à observer dans les Romans (by Lenglet-Dufresnoy), 81
Maximes des Saints (by Fénelon), 35n21
maxims, 115, 115n34
Meditations Among the Tombs (by James Hervey), 150
Mee, Jon, 195, 195n45
Meister, Henri, 137, 138
mélanges (by Voltaire), 84
Melanges de poésies fugitives et de prose sans conséquence (by Mme la comtesse de*** aka Fanny de Beauharnais), 13
Mémoires d'outre-tombe (by Chateaubriand), 7, 140, 172
Menant, Sylvain, 8, 12, 13n34, 15–16n38–9, 78, 84–5, 120–23, 149n20–21, 180n2, 213
Mentor, 34, 51n58, 245
Mercier, Louis-Sébastien, 3, 7, 28, 30, 98, 186, 211–12, 241
    American Indians and, 240
    Atala (by Chateaubriand) and, 237–43
    Bonnet de nuit, 29n1, 237n58, 238n61, 239n64, 240n66
    connection between reforming language and political reform, 238n61
    drama, 15, 238n61
    English novels and, 240
    French language and literature, 28, 237, 242
    French verse and, 239
    Germaine de Staël and, 240
    "heroïdes" and, 238n61
    Homer and, 240
    L'An deux mille quatre cent quarante, 238n61
    Le Tourneur and, 240
    l'éloquence des choses (eloquence of things), 239–40
    Les Amours de Cherale, poëme en six chants, 238
    Mon Bonnet du matin, 239–40
    neoclassicism and, 238
    Néologie, 241
    new rhythms, 223–36
    poetry and, 237, 237n56, 240
    primitive expression, 240

prose and, 238
prose poems (poëmes en prose), 28,
  237n58, 239, 242–3
Songes et visions philosophiques, 7
Tableau de Paris and, 238n61
visions and, 223–43
Mercier, Roger, 145n2, 149n20
Meschonnic, Henri, 8, 11–12, 153, 179, 211
Messiah, The (by Friedrich Gottlieb
  Klopstock), 147, 147n13
translation into French, 147n13
Messmer, 187
metaphor, 89, 133
meta-poetry, 16
meter, 64, 65, 86n69
Greek verse and, 152, 153
Hebrew sacred poetry, 152, 153n27
revolt against, 3, 64
metermaniacs ("metromanes"), 98
metonymny, 133
Mexique Conquis (by Boësnier), 7
Middle Ages, 66n13
Milner, Max, 227
Milton, John, 135, 147, 170, 207, 208
blank verse and, 88
epic tone of, 206
Paradise Lost, 88n78
prose translation by Dupré de Saint-
  Maur, 141
verse translation by Jacques Delille, 141
verse translation by James Beattie, 141
Minerva, 33
Mirabaud, Jean-Baptiste de, prose
  translation of Tasso's *Jerusalem
  Delivered*, 126
mise en abyme, 109, 172
Mithridate (by Racine)
La Motte's prose rendering of, 85
translation by Houdar de La Motte
  and, 71
Mme la comtesse de*** (aka Fanny de
  Beauharnais), 13
modernism, 3, 9
poets, 65
twentieth century, 64
modernity, 12–13, 214
Moderns, 63, 68, 137, 178
Molière (Jean Baptiste Poquelin), 97
Mon Bonnet du matin (by Mercier), 240

French verse and, 239
monarchy, 32, 69
"Mondain, Le" by Voltaire, 88n75
Monneron, Marie-Uranie Rose, 7
Annamire, poëme en trois chants, 7
Monroe, Jonathan, 11, 15
*Monsieur Cassandre, ou les effets de
  l'amour et du vert-de-gris* (by
  Charles-Georges Coqueley de
  Chaussepierre), 16n41
*Mont Parnasse ou de la Préférence entre la
  Prose et la Poésie, Le* (by Jacques
  de Grille), 68
Montbron, Chérade de, 129
Les Scandinaves, 129
Monte, Steve, 2
Montesquieu, Baron de (Charles de
  Secondat), 3, 6, 6n12, 26, 34, 57,
  69, 82, 98, 101–4, 107, 109–12,
  112n30, 114–19, 122–3, 125–9,
  146, 159, 180, 185n15, 202n56,
  238–9n62
antiquity and, 119
*Considérations sur les causes de la
  grandeur des Romains et de leur
  décadence*, 120
description and, 127
fiction of, 89
gender and, 118
Golden Age myth, 120
idealism and, 103
Le Temple de Gnide, 3, 6, 26–7, 57, 59,
  99, 102–12, 112n29, 113–14, 117–21,
  123, 125–6, 128–9, 131, 146, 159
L'esprit des lois, de, 102–3, 118, 120
Lettres persanes, 82, 89, 102–4, 114,
  122, 125–6, 180, 185n15
mythology and, 103, 112
Pensées, 106, 119
"petit roman," 127
poetics of, 126
pre-Romantic impulse, 106
prose poems and, 113, 119–20, 139–40
pseudo-translation and, 26, 126
as Republican, 119–20
Roman names, 119
moralists, Christian, 171
Moreau, Pierre, 7n15, 68n22, 80n50
Morellet, abbé, 225, 225n31, 226–7

Morelly, Etienne Gabriel, 129
  Naufrage des isles flottantes, ou,
    Basiliade du célèbre Pilpai. Poëme
    héroïque traduit de l'Indien (by
    Morelly) as, 129–31
Mort d'Abel, La (by Salomon Gessner),
    137, 146–8, 150, 158
  translated by Turgot, 137
Mort d'Azaël ou le rapt de Dina, La (by
    P.-D. Dugat), 170n67
Moses, odes of, 150, 157n36, 183
Mount Parnassus, 73
Mouret, François, 159n40, 185
Mourot, Jean, 142n42, 144, 233n53
Moutonnet-Clairfons, 58, 59, 185n15
Musset, Alfred de, 218
mysticism, 180, 185
mythology, 102, 103, 112, 139, 206

Napoleon, 172
narratives
  biblical, 137
  epic poetry and, 127
Natchez, Les (by Chateaubriand), 217n19,
    223, 225
native ("primitive") poetry, 213
Native Americans, 28. *see also* American
    Indians
Naufrage des isles flottantes, ou, Basiliade
    du célèbre Pilpai. Poëme héroïque
    traduit de l'Indien (by Morelly),
    129–31
Naves, Raymond, 73
neoclassicism, 37, 69, 80, 211
Néologie (by Louis-Sébastien Mercier), 241
New Testament, 173
Newton, 192
Nicodeme dans la lune, ou la Révolution
    pacifique, folie en prose et en
    trois actes, mélée d'ariettes et de
    vaudevilles (by Louis Abel Beffroy de
    Reigny, aka Le Cousin Jacques), 14
Night Thoughts (by Arthur Young), 150
nineteenth century, 206
  prose poems and, 97
  women authors of, 104
Noces patriarchales (Les), poëme en prose
    en cinq chants (by Robert Martin
    Le Suire), 120n47

Nodier, Charles, 180, 186, 207
Nouvelle allégorique ou Histoire des
    derniers troubles arrivés au
    Royaume de l'Eloquence (by
    Antoine Furetière), 66–7
Nouvelle revue française, 213
Nouvelles Idylles (by Salomon Gessner),
    137, 139
  translated by Henri Meister, 137–8
novels (romans), 3, 10, 12, 30, 59, 64n2,
    137, 188
  English, 82
  epic literature and, 82
  epistolary, 82, 104, 125
  fictions in prose, 64
  French, 82
  of manners (English), 69
  prose poems (poëmes en prose) and,
    80, 81, 82
  sentimental, 59
Nymphes de Dyctyme ou révolutions de
    l'empire virginal (by Fournier de
    Tony), 7, 120n47

Ode en faveur des vers (by M. de La
    Faye), 72
odes, 70, 74–5, 156
  definition of, 155n31
  history of, 155
  lyric, 156
  sacred content and, 155
  versification and, 71
Odes (by Ronsard), 155
Odyssey (by Homer), 34, 37, 52–3, 56, 224
Œdipe (by Houdar de La Motte), 85
  tragedy in verse and, 71
Œdipe (by Voltaire), 85
  preface to, 85
Old Testament, 10, 148–9, 149n19, 173, 212
  as ancient Hebraic poetry, 149
  parataxis and, 4
Ollivier, poëme by Cazotte, 6
"Olympia" (painting by Edouard Manet),
    171n73
Ommiades, 204n62
On Sacred Poetry (by Friedrich Gottlieb
    Klopstock), 147–8, 147n13
onomastics, 232, 232n51
orality, 211, 213–22, 240

Orient, socio-literary construction of, 80
Origines des graces (by Mlle Dionis), 120n47
Origines du poème en prose français, 7
Orpheus, 77
Ovid, 159, 168

Pan, flute of, 173
Paradise Lost (by Milton), 88n78
paradrame, 16n41
para-prose poetry, self-referential parody, 16
parataxis, 4, 109
Paris, 3, 196
*Pariseide ou les amours d'un jeune patriote
et d'une belle aristocrate, La*, 7
Parny, Évariste, 27–8, 105, 121n48, 186,
190, 211–15, 217–22, 224, 227
anti-slavery literature, 220
Bernardin de Saint-Pierre and, 216n15
Bourbon Island, 212, 216
Chansons madécasses, 212–18,
218n22, 219, 221, 229n43
colonialism and, 214
Creolization and, 214–17
epicurian philosophy and, 218
"exo/poétique," 214, 221
*La Guerre des dieux anciens et
modernes*, 221–2
love songs, 217–20
Maurice Ravel's music and, 213
mock epic genre, 222
new rhythms and, 213–22
orality, 213–22
Poésies érotiques, 215, 221
poetry after the Revolution, 28
poetry of, 240
return to formal conservatism, 221
"succès de scandale," 222
views against slavery, 213n9
war songs, 220–21
Pascal, Blaise, 87, 238–9n62
Pasqually, Martinès de, 187, 196
pastoral, 3, 102, 112, 120, 129, 139, 158
crisis of, 123
critical thought and, 123
eighteenth century, 122
melancholy and, 120–24
myth and, 123
narratives, 104
prose and, 120, 120n47

prose poems, 122
in verse, 120–22
Paul et Virginie (by Bernardin de Saint-
Pierre), 212, 213, 218, 218n22,
219, 223
Paulhan, Jean, 213, 214
Paw, 238–9n62
Pechmeja, Jean, 57
Télèphe, 57
Pensées (by Montesquieu), 106, 119
Père Goriot, Le (by Balzac), 29
periodic order, 94
"petit roman," 127
"petit tableau," 127
*Petites-Maisons du Parnasse (Les),
ouvrage comico-littéraire d'un
genre nouveau, en vers et en prose*
(by Louis Abel Beffroy de Reigny
aka Le Cousin Jacques), 13
Petits poèmes en prose (Spleen de Paris),
(by Baudelaire), 127, 160, 169, 222
Pindar, 152
Piron, 120
plagiarism, 126
Plato, 80, 136, 151, 176–7, 232
Plutarch, 176–7
Poème en prose de Baudelaire à nos jours
(by Suzanne Bernard), 5, 7
poëmes en prose (prose poems), 5–6, 10,
13, 38, 48, 61, 63–5, 78, 80, 82, 85,
91, 94, 98–9, 109, 114, 131, 172;
see also prose poems
aesthetic choices and, 33
Bible and, 4
Bildungsroman and, 57
cantos, 4
description of Calypso's cave in
Fénelon and Aragon, 42
drama and, 16n39
eighteenth century, 2, 15, 25, 28, 82, 109
Enlightenment and, 16, 65
epic and, 57, 82
history and, 4
hybridity and, 15, 25, 60, 92
as impotent, 88
intertextuality, 25
mock-heroic, 16n39
modernity, 8, 25
mythology and, 4

novels and, 57
parody of, 16
post-Baudelairian, 28
pre-Baudelairian, 10, 50
prehistory of, 7, 70
"pseudo-translation," 26
as subgenre, 15
translation of poetry and, 89
twentieth century, 74
by women authors, 7
Poems of Ossian (by Macpherson), 3, 26,
    98, 125–6, 140, 143, 150, 154, 215
characters, 231n49
Gessner and, 137–44
landscape, 141
Le Tourneur and, 140
prose poems (poëmes en prose) and,
    137–44
rhythmic prose and, 138
themes, 144
translation and, 137–44
Poésies érotiques (by Évariste Parny), 215, 221
Poètes et grammairiens au XVIIIᵉ siecle
    (by Jean Roudaut), 5
poetic style, 128
poetic tropes, 65
poetics
    Eighteenth Century, 43
    neoclassical, 154
    "oriental," 154
Poetics (by Aristotle), 64
poetry, 63, 65–6, 68, 77, 82, 127, 177, 246
    17th century definitions of, 63
    ancient (pagan), 173
    ancient Hebrew, 148–56, 149n19,
        149n20
    changes in, 185
    classicism, 151
    constraint of, 78
    crisis of, 120, 155
    defining, 1–2, 9, 92n93
    descriptive, 12, 43
    dramatic, 151
    eighteenth century, 213
    elitism, 78
    epic, 151
    experiments to reform, 3
    fiction and, 63
    French, 148

fugitive, 13n34
"high" poetry, 67–8
Homeric, 152
hybrid, 127
"low," 67
lyricism and, 64
as mirror to monarchy in crisis, 69
modern Christian, 173
music and, 157, 219
mythology about origins of, 26
as object of luxury, 97
painting and, 77
philosophical, 12, 89
post-Romantic definitions of, 5, 28
"primitive" cultures and, 212
in prose, 173
prose and, 9, 89, 95, 153
religion and, 183
royalty and, 68
sacred, 148
spiritualist, 185
translation into prose and, 77
versification and, 2n2, 3, 4, 11, 93, 240
poetry, biblical, 146, 148
poetry, didactic, 151
poetry, lyric, 8, 89, 127, 149, 150–52, 155–7
    music and, 157
poetry, neoclassical, 128, 140, 188
poetry, pastoral, 120, 122
poetry, verse, 65
    crisis of, 3
poetry in prose (*poésie en prose*), 6
poets
    of antiquity, 65n7
    descriptive, 191
    Eighteenth Century, 77
    Latin, 92
    Platonic idea of, 78
    Romantic, 206
Pompadour, marquise de, 140
Pompignan, Lefranc de, 147
    religious message and, 148
Ponge, Francis, 169
Pope, Alexander, 74n40, 88n78
Port Royal, 181
Portraits comtemporains (by Sainte-
    Beuve), 216n15
positivism, 208
post-modernism, 9

post-Romantic period
  authors of, 186
  thought and writing of, 151
Pound, Ezra, 86
Premiers poèmes en prose, Les (by
  Nathalie Vincent-Munnia), 7
Prévost, abbé, 82, 125
  Manon Lescaut, 82
Prie, Mme de la, 102
"primitive" cultures, 212
"primitive language," 227
  warrior's song in Chateaubriand's
    Atala, 228
Princesse de Clèves, La (by Mme de la
  Fayette), 38, 64, 91
  called poëme en prose, 80
Principes de la litterature (by Batteux), 150
Prise de Jéricho, La (by Sophie Cottin),
  170n67
"Projet de poétique" in *Lettre à l'Académie*
  (by Fénelon), 181, 183
Prophets, book of, 136
prose, 63–5, 66n13, 69, 71, 77, 84, 127, 246
  Ciceronian, 77
  egalitarian, 78
  Enlightenment and, 247
  epic and, 122
  freedom of, 78
  French, 68, 141
  history of, 8
  as medium of everyday exchange, 97
  Modern, 175
  noble subject matter and, 82
  pastoral and, 122
  poetry and, 8, 82, 86n69, 92–3, 96–7,
    123, 163, 181, 211
  populace and, 68
  rise of, 3
  traditional poetic traits in, 5
  translations of foreign poetry, 69
  verse and, 95
prose, poetic, 5n8, 98
  Romanticism and, 64
prose, rhythmical ("prose nombreuse"), 60,
  137, 138
prose, Romantic, 175
prose authors
  Eighteenth Century, 69
  French, 82

verse and, 4
"prose d'art" ideal, 65
prose mesurée, 137
prose narratives, 64, 65, 77, 81n54
  qualities of verse poetry and, 3
prose narratives, lyrical, 145
*Prose Poem in French Literature of the
  Eighteenth Century* (by Vista
  Clayton), 6
prose poems (poëmes en prose), 25–8, 138,
  160, 175–8, 180, 240, 245; *see also*
  Poëme en prose
  Ancient Hebrew poetry and, 148–56
  as "bastard style," 76–95
  Bible and, 146, 148–56
  biblical, 170
  biblical epics in prose, 169–78
  birth of, 101–24
  contradictions of, 123
  eighteenth century, 125, 245
  The *Encyclopédie*: ambiguities, 91–5
  Enlightenment, 207, 211, 245, 247
  epic, 56, 129, 131, 169, 192n44
  Fraguier's denunciation of, 76–82
  French Enlightenment, 1–28
  genealogies of, 4–8
  genre and, 9–12, 13–24, 247
  Gessner and, 137–44
  hybridity and, 179
  impossible affiliation of, 76–95
  Le Temple de Gnide (by Montesquieu),
    103–11
  mock epic, 101n2
  modern, 239
  new rhythms and, 211–44
  Ossian and, 137–44
  pastoral, 120–24
  pre-history of, 138, 140
  pseudo-translations and, 124–34
  "Querelle d'Homère" and, 134–6
  Rémond de Saint-Mard on equality, 82–5
  Republican virtues and, 112–19
  spirituality and, 184, 184n12
  Temple de Gnide, Le (by Montesquieu),
    103–11, 131
  translation and, 125–44
  Voltaire and, 85–90
prose poétique (poetical prose), 77
prose poetry, 5n8, 98, 174, 213

definition of, 1–2, 4–5
eighteenth century experiments in, 91
formalist approaches to, 10
French, 5, 213
French academic curriculum and, 5
hybridity and, 69
literary history and, 4
origins of, 5, 9, 69
Romanticism and, 64
sources of, 5
un-Cartesian, 33
prose poets, 169
nineteenth-century French, 27
prose vs. poetry, 63–100, 172
economics of, 85
egality of, 84
Houdar de La Motte (1672–1731) and,
70–75
myth of the French language: Rivarol's
Triumph of Prose, 95–100
prose poem as "bastard style," 76–94
religion and, 181
prosody, 3
Protestants, Bible and, 33
Psalms, by David, 136, 150, 156–7, 183
as prose poem, 131
pseudo-translation
Temple de Gnide, Le (by Montesquieu),
104, 107, 125, 126, 129
pseudo-translations, 114, 129–31, 133,
176, 215
Les Scandinaves (by Montbron), 129
prose poems and, 125–34
Psyche, fable of, 92
Pucelle, La (by Voltaire), 222
Puritanism, 181
Pygmalion (by Jean-Jacques Rousseau),
159, 159n40, 167–9

quarrel between ancients and moderns,
135–6
Quatres parties du jour à la mer, Les (by
Pierre-Victor Malouet), 123
Quietism, 27, 35n21, 180, 187, 206
Fénelon and, 185
prose and, 181
Reformation, 180–85
"Qu'il ne peut y avoir de poëmes en prose"
(mémoire by l'abbé Fraguier), 76

Quinet, Edgar
Ahasvérus, 7

Rabelais, François, 192n44, 202
Racine, Jean, 38, 85, 98, 111, 134, 176–7
Mithridate, 71, 85
poetry of, 86
Ramsay, Andrew Michael, 175
Les Aventures de Télémaque (by
Fénelon) and, 101n3
Les Voyages de Cyrus, 101n3
rationalism, 178
Ravel, Maurice, 213–14, 219–20
Raynal, l'abbé, 238–9n62
realism, 121, 164
novelists and, 59
*Recueil de pièces fugitives en prose et en
vers* (by Voltaire), 13
Reformation, 179–206
Eschatology and, 206–10
Illuminism, 186–205
Quietism, 180–85
Regency, 102, 115, 121
Reigny, Louis Abel Beffroy de (pseudonym
Le Cousin Jacques), 13, 15
*Les Petites-Maisons du Parnasse,
ouvrage comico-littéraire d'un genre
nouveau, en vers et en prose*, 13
*Marlborough, poëme comique en prose
rimée*, 13, 14
*Nicodeme dans la lune, ou la
Révolution pacifique, folie en prose
et en trois actes, mêlée d'ariettes et
de vaudevilles*, 14
*Turlututu, empereur de l'Isle vertu,
folie, bêtise, farce ou parodie
comme on voudra, en prose et en
trois actes*, 15
*Turlututu, ou la Science du bonheur,
poème héroi-comique en huit
chants et en vers*, 13
*Un Rien, ou l'Habit de Noces, folie
épisodique en un acte et en prose,
mêlée de vaudevilles et d'airs
nouveaux*, 15
*Un Rien, ou l'Habit de Noces, folie
épisodique en un acte et en prose,
mêlée de vaudevilles et d'airs
nouveaux*, 15

"Remarques sur Homère à M. le Laboureur Bailly de Montmorency" (by Claude Fleury), 74n40

Rémond de Saint-Mard, Toussaint, 82–4
    essays about pastoral poetry, 120

Renaissance, 69, 82

René (by Chateaubriand), 223, 227

Résurrection d'Atala (anonymous), 225, 229n42, 229n43, 229n44

Rêveries du promeneur solitaire (by Rousseau), 4, 112, 146, 155, 160, 165

Revolution, French, 28, 146, 169, 180, 186–8, 205–7
    Réunion des états généraux 1789, 32

Reyrac, abbé, 95n105, 129, 170
    Hymne au soleil, 6, 129

rhetoric, 66

Rhinocéros, Le (by Guiard de Servigné), 101n2

rhyme, 65, 66n12, 88–9

rhythm, 9, 212, 218, 219, 222, 227, 229, 232n52, 233, 236, 241

Richardson, Samuel, 131, 237n58
    Clarissa, 226n31

Riffaterre, Hermine, 6

Rimbaud, Arthur, 47, 169
    Illuminations, 47
    Les Aventures de Télémaque (by Aragon), 47
    prose poems of, 47

Rivarol, Antoine de, 63, 95–100
    L'Universalité de la langue française, 95–100
    myth of the French language and, 95–100
    triumph of prose and, 95–100
    Voltaire and, 96

Roman comique, Le (by Paul Scarron), 64

"roman noir," 59

romances, 63–4, 64n2. *see also* novels

"romans d'apprentissage," 57

"romans pastorals," 121n48

Romantic authors, 186

Romantic revolution, 85

Romanticism, 1, 2, 8, 26, 64, 84, 146, 151, 172, 245, 247, 247n3
    Chateaubriand and, 223
    poetry of, 206

prose poetry and, 1
    sublime and, 182
    themes of, 176
    views of the poet and, 182

Romantics, 218

Rome, fall of, 120

Ronsard, Pierre de, 155
    Odes, 155

Rosenberg, Aubrey, 6n12, 160, 162n53

Rouchefoucault, François de la, 115

Roudaut, Jean, 5
    Poètes et grammairiens au XVIIIe siecle (by Jean Roudaut), 5

Roué vertueux, Le (by Charles-Georges Coqueley de Chaussepierre), 7, 16–17, 17n42, 25
    "Chant quatre," 19–24
    engravings accompanying the text, 17
    frontispiece, 18
    parody of prose poems, 17
    typography and, 17

Rougemont, Martine de, 16n41

Rousseau, Jean-Baptiste, 98, 147, 190
    pastoral poetry and, 120
    religious odes of, 12
    sacred poetry of, 148

Rousseau, Jean-Jacques, 3, 6, 10, 27, 33–4, 38, 59, 66, 82, 98, 112–14, 120, 127, 146, 152, 155–68, 170, 180, 189–90, 238–9n62, 247
    bon sauvage, 215
    discourses of, 123
    Émile, 50–53, 160
    Essai sur l'origine des langues, 27, 159, 161, 167
    French Parliament's order for arrest of, 160
    invocation to muse and, 163
    Julie, ou la nouvelle Héloïse, 53, 82, 146, 159n40, 226n31
    "l'amour de soi," 161
    language and, 161, 167, 168n64, 189, 232, 240
    L'Astrée (by Honoré d'Urfé) and, 104
    Le Lévite d'Ephraïm, 3, 6, 27, 146, 148, 152, 155, 157–68, 159n40, 160–61, 162n52, 163, 165–8, 168n64, 169, 230

Les Aventures de Télémaque (by
   Fénelon), 51
  linguistic theories of, 170n71
  lyrical prose poetry, 169
  "natural religion," 27
  odes and, 155
  pastorals, 138
  prose poems and, 146, 161, 164, 166, 239
  Pygmalion, 159, 159n40, 167–9
  "religion naturelle," 185
  Rêveries du promeneur solitaire, 4,
    112, 146, 155, 160, 165
  Salomon Gessner and, 138, 140, 158
  social theory of, 161
  telemacomania and, 51–4
  versification and, 158n39
Roussy, Jean, 101n2
  Aurelia ou Orléans délivrée, poème
    latin traduit en françois, 101n2, 129
  "avis du traducteur" *Aurelia, ou*
    Orléans délivrée..., 129
Ruines, Les (by Volney), 6

Sacy, Louis de, 175
Sadi, 89
Saint Amand, Pierre, 102n7, 114
Saint-Amant, Marc-Antoine Girard de, 46
Sainte-Beuve, Charles Augustin, 186,
    192n44, 213, 217n19, 218
  Parny and, 219
  Portraits comtemporains, 216n15
Saint-Lambert, Jean-François de, 191, 212
  abolitionist movement and, 213n9
  Les deux amis: conte iroquois, 212
  Les Saisons, 212
  poetry of, 121, 240
  Zimeo, 213n9
Saint-Mard, Rémond de
  Examen philosophique de la poésie en
    général, 82–4
  prose poems (poëmes en prose) and,
    82–5
Saint-Martin, Louis-Claude de, 180, 186, 189,
    192–206, 199n54, 201n55, 207, 222
  allegory, 206
  Christian beliefs and, 199
  critique of colonialism, 200
  Des Erreurs et de la vérité, 195n45
  desire and, 205

  illuminism and, 27, 180, 185, 187, 203
  language and, 189–90
  mysticism, 186
  "Philosophe inconnu," 187
  revolutionary conflict and, 198
  symbols and, 191
  theosophy and, 188, 206
Saint-Maur, Dupré de, 141
Saint-Pierre, Bernardin de, 121n48, 170,
    180, 191, 2121–3, 215–16, 216n15,
    218n22
  Études de la nature, 223
  pastoralism, 27, 185
  Paul et Virginie, 212–13, 218, 218n22,
    219, 223
Saisons, Les (by Saint-Lambert), 212
Salentum (Fénelon's utopian society), 52
Sandras, Michel, 5n7, 109n22
Sappho, 156
Satan, 177
Saul (King), 173
Scandinaves, Les (by Montbron)
  as pseudo-translation, 129
Scarron, Paul, 64
Scipio, 77
Scipio's dream (by Cicero), 92
Scudéry, Madeleine de, 34, 64, 181
  Clélie ou L'Histoire romaine, 34, 64
  Le Grand Cyrus, 34, 38, 227
  novels of, 32, 64n2, 227
Sénancour, 186
Sentimental Education of the Novel, The
    (by Margaret Cohen), 59
Seth, Catriona, 6n9, 189n28, 213n8,
    215n14
Sevigné, Guiard de, 101n2
Shakespeare, William
  Julius Caesar, 89
Smith, John, 140, 142, 143
  Dargo, 141, 143
  Duthona, 141, 143
  Gaul, 141, 143
  Ossian (by Macpherson) and, 141
  translation of his "Ossianic" poems by
    Chateaubriand, 141
Socrates, 232n52
Song of Solomon, 150, 183, 229
Songes et visions philosophiques (by
    Louis-Sébastien Mercier), 7

Sorel, Charles, 16, 64
Spectateur Français, 97
Spectator, 52
spiritual reformation, 206
Staël, Germaine de, 98, 183, 186, 239n64, 247
Starobinski, Jean, 102–3, 116–17, 119,
    165, 168n64
Steele, Timothy, 2n2, 65, 81n54, 82n57,
    86n69
Still, Judith, 167n62
Strabo, 175
structuralist theorists, 8
Sulzer, Johann Georg, 93–5
Supplément au Voyage de Bougainville (by
    Diderot), 219–20
surrealism, 25, 37
Swedenbörg, Emanuel, 187
Sydney, Philip, 81n54, 82n58
    Apologie for Poetrie, 81n54
    Arcadia, 82n58
symbol, 195
symbolism, 148, 206
*Systeme Dd. (Introduction à une morale
    momentanée* (by Louis Aragon), 51

Tasso, Torquato, 126, 127, 135
    Christian epic poem, 126
    Discours de l'art poétique, 126
    Jerusalem Delivered, 108, 126
Telemachus, 34, 245, 247n2
    in Aragon and Fénelon, 39
telemacomania, 16, 29–62
    epic and, 55–62
    Fénelon's Telemachus, 44–7
    hybridity and, 29–34
    "Je-Ne-Sais-Quoi" hybridity, 29–34
    Minerva as Mentor in, 48–50
    tales from Marivaux and Rousseau, 51–4
    Télémaque, source of inspiration for
        Aragon, 37–8
Télémaque travesti, Le (by Marivaux), 3,
    16, 54n71, 57, 59, 99, 102–5
    Les Aventures de Télémaque (by
        Fénelon) and, 53, 54
Télèphe (by Jean Pechmeja), 57
Temple de Gnide, Le (by Montesquieu), 6,
    26–7, 110, 112, 112n29, 113–14,
    117–21, 123, 125–6, 128, 146, 159
    as first person narrative, 104

motivation of, 114
preface to (1725), 114
prose poems (poëmes en prose) and,
    103–11, 131
pseudo-translation, 104, 107, 125–6, 129
sentimental journey, 103–11
seven cantos of, 107
*Temple du destin (Le), ou l'hommage des
    coeurs françois, à Madame la
    Dauphine. Poëme, en cinq chants, en
    prose* (by Mise de Marcillac), 101n4
Temple du goût, 87
Terence, 126
Terror, the, 188, 192, 195, 204, 206, 207
The Farewell of Telemachus and Eucharus
    (painting by David), 245–8
The Republic, 136
Theocritus, 121, 231, 237n58
    Cyclop and Galathea, 231
    pastoral poems, 108
Theophrastus, 237n58
theory of *imitatio*, 34
theosophy, 188, 206
Thiry, Marcel, 159n42
Thomassin, Louis, 149
Thoughts on Original Composition (by
    Arthur Young), 150
Tobie, poëme en quatre chants (by Le
    Clerc), 170, 171, 177
Todorov, Tzvetan, 195
Tony, Fournier de, 7
    *Les Nymphes de Dyctyme ou révolutions
    de l'empire virginal*, 7, 120n47
    pastoral narratives in prose and, 120n47
tragedies, 67, 84, 89
    prose and, 15n37, 75
    versification and, 71
"Traité de la poésie lyrique" (by Charles
    Batteux), 151
*Traité de l'existence et des attributs de
    Dieu* (by Fénelon), 183
Traité de l'origine des romans (by Huet), 81
Traité du sublime (by Longinus)
    annotation by André Dacier, 145
    translation by Boileau, 145
translation, 65, 136, 137, 152, 240
    French prose and, 137
    prose and, 65
translator's preface, 138

"Tremblement de terre de Lisbonne" (by
        Voltaire), 12
tripartition epic/lyric/dramatic, 151
Troglodyte myth, 122
Turgot, 112n29, 137, 138
*Turlututu, empereur de l'Isle vertu, folie,
        bêtise, farce ou parodie comme on
        voudra, en prose et en trois actes*
        (by Louis Abel Beffroy de Reigny
        aka Le Cousin Jacques), 15
*Turlututu, ou la Science du bonheur, poème
        héroi-comique en huit chants et en
        vers* (by LOuis Abel Beffroy de
        Reigny aka Le Cousin Jacques), 13
"Tyrse, Le" (by Baudelaire), 48, 247
Tzara, Tristan, 37

Ulysses, 245
Ulysses (by James Joyce), 37
*Un Rien, ou l'Habit de Noces, folie
        épisodique en un acte et en prose,
        mêlée de vaudevilles et d'airs
        nouveaux* (by Louis Abel Beffroy de
        Reigny aka Le Cousin Jacques), 15
Uzanne, O., 103

Vadé, Yves, 5n7
Vairasse, Denis, 6n12
        Histoire des Sévarambes, 6n12
Valéry, Paul, 109n22
        "Zurbaran. Sainte Alexandrine,"
        109n22
Valois, Marguerite de, 66
Van Laere, François, 159n42
Van Tieghem, Paul, 137n26, 138, 140–42,
        146n7, 147n13
        literary history of, 140
Van Tieghem, Philippe, 147n13
Vaugelas, Claude Favre de, 68
Venus, 104, 107, 171n73
verisimilitude, 164
Verne, François, 7, 101n2
        *La Franciade, ou L'Ancienne France.
        Poëme en seize chants*, 7
verse, 3, 63, 68, 71, 77, 87, 89; *see also* poetry
        capitalist, 85
        class privilege and, 85
        difficulty of writing in French, 78
        elitist, 85

        market value of, 85
        neoclassic, 33
verse, crisis of, 222
verse poetry, 63
verse writers, 84
versification, 10, 15n35, 64–5, 69–71,
        74–5, 92n93, 94, 97, 106, 128, 136,
        145–6, 175
        classical, 156
        French, 70, 71, 85, 179
        French sacred poetry and, 148
        Hebrew sacred poetry and, 153
        politics and, 179
Viatte, Auguste, 186n19
Vico, 122
Vincent-Munnia, Nathalie, 7, 213
        Les Premiers poèmes en prose, 7
Virgil, 108, 117, 121, 175–7, 183
        Aeneid, 34, 108
        Buccolics, 183
        Dido character in, 38, 171
        Georgics, 117, 183, 237
        pastoral and, 183
        poetry of, 88
Voisine, Jacques, 159n40, 185
Voiture, Vincent, 68, 69
Volney, Constantin
        Les Ruines, 6
Volpihac-Auger, Catherine, 102n6
Voltaire (François-Marie Arouet), 12–13,
        26, 63, 69, 73, 84–5, 86n67, 87,
        95–6, 99, 114, 135, 157–8, 175–6,
        179, 221, 238–9n62
        classical canon, 89
        cynicism and, 103
        defense of verse, 86, 89
        Discours aux Welches, 87
        Épopée, 88
        Fénelon and, 87, 89
        Henriade, 95, 135
        La Pucelle (by Voltaire), 222
        Les Aventures de Télémaque (by
        Fénelon), 87–9
        mélanges, 84
        Montesquieu and, 89
        Œdipe, 85
        Parny and, 221
        pastoral poetry and, 120
        prose of, 89

prose poems (poëmes en prose) and,
    85–90
*Recueil de pièces fugitives en prose et
    en vers*, 13
separation of prose and poetry,
    92, 135
translation of *Julius Caesar* (by
    William Shakespeare), 89
"*Tremblement de terre de
    Lisbonne*," 12
writings in verse, 84
Zadig, 84
Voyage à Paphos, 6n12
Voyages de Cyrus, Les (by Ramsay), 101n3

Wordworth, William, 84, 86, 86n69, 154
    manifesto of, 17

Young, Arthur, 98, 148
    Night Thoughts, 150
    Thoughts on Original Composition, 150

Zadig (by Voltaire), 84
Zilia, roman pastoral (by Anne Marie de
    Beaufort d'Hautpoul), 120n47
Zimeo (by Saint-Lambert), 213n9
Zuber, Roger, 65, 67
"Zurbaran. Sainte Alexandrine" (by Paul
    Valéry), 109n22